BRISTOL: A GATEWAY OF EMPIRE

A GATEWAY OF EMPIRE

C. M. MACINNES

Professor Emeritus Commonwealth History
at the University of Bristol

DAVID & CHARLES (HOLDINGS) LIMITED
NEWTON ABBOT

SBN 7153 42 576

First published 1939 by J. W. Arrowsmith Ltd.

Printed in Great Britain by
Latimer Trend & Company Limited, Whitstable
for David & Charles (Holdings) Limited,
South Devon House Railway Station Newton Abbot Devon

To

THE MASTER, WARDENS AND COMMONALTY

OF

MERCHANT VENTURERS OF BRISTOL

WHOSE FELLOWSHIP HAS PLAYED SO

NOTABLE A PART IN THE

HISTORY OF THE

EMPIRE

" . . . . Yet the thoughts of my heart now are throbbing
To test the high streams, the salt waves in tumultuous play.
Desire in my heart ever urges my spirit to wander
To seek out the home of the stranger in lands afar off.

  There is no one that dwells upon earth, so exalted in mind,
So large in his bounty, nor yet of such vigorous youth,
Nor so daring in deeds, nor to whom his liege lord is so kind,
But that he has always a longing, a sea-faring passion
For what the Lord God shall bestow, be it honour or death.
No heart for the harp has he, nor for acceptance of treasure,
No pleasure has he in a wife, no delight in the world,
Nor in aught save the roll of the billows; but always a longing,
A yearning uneasiness, hastens him on to the sea.

  The woodlands are captured by blossoms, the hamlets grow fair,
Broad meadows are beautiful, earth again bursts into life,
And all stir the heart of the wanderer eager to journey,
So he meditates going afar on the pathway of tides.
The cuckoo, moreover, gives warning with sorrowful note,
Summer's harbinger sings, and forebodes to the heart bitter sorrow.
The nobleman comprehends not, the luxurious man,
What some must endure, who travel the farthest in exile.

  Now my spirit uneasily turns in the heart's narrow chamber,
Now wanders forth over the tide, o'er the home of the whale,
To the ends of the earth—and comes back to me. Eager and greedy,
The lone wanderer screams, and resistlessly drives my soul onward,
Over the whale-path, over the tracts of the sea."

ANONYMOUS, fifth century.

PREFACE

THIS book was first published in 1939, a few months before the outbreak of war. In the following year, when a small number of copies had been disposed of, the whole of the remaining stock was destroyed by enemy action. Thus, the work of several years appeared to have been thrown away. It was, therefore, with considerable pleasure that I accepted the offer of Messrs David and Charles to reprint this volume.

For centuries Bristol has been closely identified with British overseas enterprise. Her geographical position, her wealth, and the energy of her citizens combined to cast her for the role of Empire builder. As the following chapters show, there have been few aspects of British expansion overseas in which she has not shared. Thus, the story of her connections with the Empire is virtually a cross-section of its history.

Throughout, Bristol has been a trading city. Her imperial interests have been mainly commercial. Political theories, constitutional principles, questions of colonial autonomy, have influenced her merchants most when the consequences of their application, amendment or repeal have been reflected in their ledgers. Indeed, it is possible that in the past, this business motive has played a more important part in the Empire's history than historians have been wont to acknowledge. Yet Bristol has been not merely a city of money-grubbers for whom trade was the breath of life. She has given to the Empire in greater measure than most English cities a surprisingly large number of distinguished sailors, soldiers, explorers, administrators, doctors and missionaries. For these, the counting-house had no lure, and they laid up for themselves no treasures on earth, but won immortal fame, and accumulated glory for their native city.

In the course of the past twenty-nine years, vast political, economic and social changes have taken place throughout the world, that will affect the course of history for centuries to come. Great Britain is no longer the dominant power she once was. Her Empire, with whose rise the fortunes of the City of Bristol were so closely linked for so long, has disappeared and with it has gone much that formerly made Britain great. Many of her dependencies in Asia, Africa, the Mediterranean, the Caribbean and elsewhere have become independant nations inspired by a spirit of assertive nationalism which has sometimes been embittered by violent racial hatred. It was natural, of course, that these young nations, after they had gained their independence, should tend to remember the frustrations which their former subordinate status had imposed and to forget the benefits which it conferred. But, in recent years, both at home and abroad the denigration of this country's Imperial past has been overdone. In the course of four hundred years mistakes were undoubtedly made by our forefathers and crimes were committed by ruthless fortune seekers, but similar charges could be levelled at almost every other people on earth. There is, moreover, a credit side to this account which is frequently forgotton, for our record is by no means wholly bad. Indeed, the good that Great Britain has done in the world far outweighs the evils for which it is responsible, and the verdict of history may well be that the two most memorable achievements of the British people are that it produced William Shakespeare and created the British Empire.

ACKNOWLEDGEMENTS

I T is impossible for me to thank everyone who has assisted me in the accumulation of materials for this book, but I hope that those who are not specifically mentioned will take this as an expression of my sincere thanks. In the first place, I have to thank the Colston Research Society, whose grants have rendered much of this work possible. I desire in particular to thank the Master and Society of the Merchant Venturers of Bristol for their readiness in allowing me to examine their records. The Treasurer, Mr. G. H. Beloe, did everything possible to facilitate my work, and his secretary, Miss G. E. Whitaker, has been kindness itself. The officials of the Bristol Chamber of Commerce, the Port of Bristol Authority, Mr. James Ross, F.L.A., the City Librarian, Miss E. Ralph, of the Archives Department, Mr. H. W. Maxwell, Director of the Bristol Museum and Art Gallery, and Mr. W. L. Cooper, Librarian of Bristol University, have generously assisted me in many ways. The Elder Brethren of Trinity House have very kindly allowed me to make transcriptions from their documents. Through the kindness of Miss M. F. Pease I was enabled to use the records at Quakers Friars. I am deeply indebted to Mr. R. W. Pretor Pinney, of Somerton Erleigh, Somerset, for the loan of pictures to illustrate this book, and to Major-General Sir Reginald and Lady Pinney, of Racedown, Dorset, for their special advice on the history of their family. Members of many Bristol firms have also supplied me with information, but considerations of space render it impossible to mention them all here. I should like in particular, however, to thank Mr. G. A. Falk, of the Imperial Tobacco Company, Dr. A. H. R. Fedden, of the Bristol Aeroplane Company, Ltd., Colonel Mark Whitwell and Colonel E. W. Lennard for their helpful suggestions. Dr. J. A. Williamson, Commander J. W. Damer Powell and my colleagues, Mr. R. I. James and Miss E. Birkhead, have each read through various chapters and made useful suggestions. My special thanks are due to my colleague, Lt.-Col. O. D. Kendall, for the great care and labour he has taken in preparing special maps for this volume. I wish also to acknowledge the assistance I have received from my pupils, Miss Elaine Nichols, Mr. J. R. Gauntlett and Mr. F. W. P. Thorne. Miss Doreen Stewart has spent many hours in computations of ships' burdens and in taking down the text of my dictation. Lastly, as on previous occasions, I wish to record my deep and sincere appreciation of the manifold labours of my secretary, Miss P. M. Ridd.

C. M. MAC INNES.

31st December, 1938.

CONTENTS

ILLUSTRATIONS

CHAPTER I

THE PERIOD OF PREPARATION

"In the same valley stands the famous Towne of Bristow, with an Haven belonging thereunto, which is a commodious and safe receptacle for all ships directing their course for the same, from Ireland, Norway, and other outlandish and foren countreys: namely that a region so fortunate and blessed with the riches that nature hath vouchsafed thereupon should not bee destitute of the wealth and commodities of other lands."

WILLIAM OF MALMESBURY (*d.* 1142).

LONG before the days of Cabot, Bristol sailors had been accustomed to look westward, and in the fifteenth century many things combined to prepare that city for the great part she was destined to play in imperial history. Contemporary writers mention that Bristol was not of any great antiquity, but they all declare her to be one of the most beautiful cities of England and very rich.

By the opening of the period of exploration, her fortifications, which in the thirteenth century had been strengthened by the construction of a new wall pierced by three gates, were already accounted of little importance by her citizens, whose chief interest lay in trade. The space enclosed by the wall, with the High Cross as its centre, had grown too constricted for the abounding life of the city. In the later Middle Ages new suburbs appeared. A cloth manufacturing district across Bristol Bridge joined Bristol with Redcliffe which, though a separate village, contained the residences and warehouses of many wealthy merchants. Another grew up in the region between the two rivers, Avon and Frome. At the close of the Middle Ages the city was engirdled by the properties of various religious bodies, and the three thirteenth-century gateways were crowned by churches, St. John's, St. Leonard's and St. Nicholas', from which Broad Street, Corn Street and High Street led to the High Cross.

With the great expansion in English foreign trade which took place in the fourteenth and fifteenth centuries, and the growing predominance of the native trader and sailor as opposed to the alien, the consciousness of the English mercantile group as a distinct entity tended to increase. Thus, in 1445 the Fraternity for Mariners was founded, which required every master mariner on the completion of his voyage to contribute to its funds at the rate of four pence a ton on the cargo of his ship. Like other mediæval gilds the Fraternity had its wardens and other officials. It maintained a priest and twelve poor sailors to pray for all merchants and mariners "passing or labouring" on the sea. St. John the Evangelist on the Welsh Back, a chapel where Masses were said and prayers offered up for sailors at sea, also testified to the importance and piety of the maritime community.

During the later middle ages, in consequence of the growing volume of traffic which passed through the port, a distinctive merchant class arose whose main interest was in foreign trade. Inland commerce and the manufacture of commodities was left to others, who for their part tended to take little interest in over-sea trade. The history of the Canynges is a good example of this development towards specialization. In the time of Richard II, the family was engaged in the manufacture of cloth as well as its export, but half a century later the name of Canynges does not appear in the list of 240 people who accounted to the aulnager. Again, while at the beginning of the century groups of merchants shared the ownership of one vessel among them, before its close a class of men had arisen who were almost solely concerned with the carriage of goods. Some of these owned small fleets and employed hundreds of men, whom they kept continually at work in the fitting, rigging and repairing of ships, or in sailing them to ports at home and abroad. William Canynges the Younger, for example, maintained 800 men in his employ, and his great fortune was built up on the carriage of freight. At his zenith he owned half the shipping of Bristol, but though he was an outstanding figure, he was by no means unique. In 1480 Thomas Strange owned twelve vessels, and another shipper, John Goodman, owned several more. The development of this specialized shipping community, mainly concerned in foreign trade, and rendered familiar through their agents with every new trend in maritime activity from Iceland to Portugal, materially helped to prepare Bristol for the part she was destined to play in the history of exploration and in the foundation of the British Empire.

Though the fifteenth century witnessed some developments in ship construction, the great period of change did not begin until the sixteenth. Then, with continually increasing experience of oceanic conditions, and with a greater knowledge of the influences of climate, currents, tides and winds, a revolution in ship-building began. Compared with the merchantmen of the seventeenth century, those of the later Middle Ages were very large, but they were clumsy and less seaworthy. Still, they served their purpose, for after all, it was in fifteenth-century ships that Cabot, Columbus and others made their great discoveries. In the hundred years immediately preceding the age of Columbus the capacity of merchantmen greatly increased. Thus, at the beginning of the fifteenth century the Bristol Bordeaux wine ships averaged 88 tons, though a few carried as much as 100 tons cargo, and at least one took 179 tons. By the middle of the century the average carrying capacity was 150 tons, but some carried 250 tons, and still the tendency to increase went on. William Canynges the Younger had four of under 200 tons and three ranging between 200 and 250 tons, while the *Mary Canynges* was 400 tons, the *Mary Redcliffe* 500 tons, and the enormous *Mary and John* 900 tons, but she was unique and considered a marvel in her time.

These wealthy merchants, living in their large and comfortable houses in Redcliffe, accustomed to the conduct of trade in a large way, were the very men to take in hand the promotion of voyages of discovery which promised rich returns. As will be seen later, towards the close of the fifteenth century a critical situation developed in an important branch of their commerce, which gave a new significance to the search for fresh markets and sources of raw material. They not only had the desire to explore, but they had the capital to finance such undertakings, and men in their employ, suitably trained by long experience of distant voyages, to carry such explorations through to a successful issue.

Bristol drew on a wide inland area for the commodities which she exported. To her quays came cloth and sculptured alabaster from Coventry; iron, timber and coal from the Forest of Dean; wheat, barley and malt from Worcester, Tewkesbury and Gloucester. Shrewsbury and Ludlow sent their cloth, and, indeed, Bristol was the emporium for all commodities intended for foreign markets which could be brought down the Severn and its tributaries. Besides this, she was a natural exporter for Wiltshire and parts of Somerset, and in her home trade she also had close relations with Chester, Milford Haven, Plymouth and London. Through Bristol passed most of the commodities from

overseas required by the Western Midlands, Wiltshire and a
large area of the south-west. Her home trade was extensive,
but it was to a far-flung foreign trade that she looked for her
chief wealth, and which she regarded as her greatest glory.

Bristol merchants did some trade with the Low Countries
and the Baltic, but this was not of any great importance, for
always their eyes were turned to the West. They considered
their natural trading territory to include Iceland, Ireland,
Gascony, Spain and Portugal, though they entered the Mediterranean and sometimes touched the coast of North Africa. The
Irish trade existed before the Norman Conquest, but by the
fifteenth century the commerce in slaves had long since been
replaced by a more reputable traffic. The merchants of Waterford were free of toll in Bristol, which also traded with Kinsale,
Cork, Limerick, Youghal, Galway, Burrishoole, Sligo and other
Irish ports. This trade had two sides to it: a direct one between
Bristol and Ireland and an indirect one. The former was to a
large extent in the hands of Irish merchants, and the existence
of an Irish community on the outskirts of the city testifies to its
importance. In so far as Bristol merchants were concerned with
Ireland, it was chiefly in bringing peninsular wines and other
products to the Irish markets. Before returning home the ships
were sometimes laden with cargoes of Irish goods for the Low
Countries, where they were exchanged for the manufactured
products of the Flemish towns. On their return they often
called in at London or the channel ports before finally dropping
anchor in Bristol. For the purposes of the present work it is
not the commodities which were handled in this traffic that are
important, but the fact that the Irish trade played its part in
familiarizing Bristol sailors with hazardous voyages and with
oceanic, as opposed to purely coastal, conditions.

Of far greater importance in this direction, however, was the
trade with Gascony. In the fifteenth century it was divided between Gascon and native merchants, and before the accession of
Henry VII, at least half of it was in the hands of the latter.
Though the bulk of the Italian trade was still controlled by the
Italians, Bristol ships challenged that monopoly as well. About
the middle of the century, Robert Sturmy carried cargoes of

wool, cloth, tin and lead to the Levant, where they were exchanged for oriental spices and other luxuries. Though all of these trades were valuable, it was through her close and long association with the Iberian peninsula and Iceland that Bristol became familiar with much legendary information about lands to the westward. This knowledge, before the time of Columbus, induced her citizens to send out a number of exploratory expeditions of which, with one or two exceptions, no records survive.

Spanish wine came to England through Bristol, together with quantities of Spanish fruits, oil, salt, leather, and most important of all, Spanish iron. In return, Bristol ships carried out mixed cargoes of English products and, in particular, lead, tin, corn and broadcloth. Similar cargoes went out to Portugal to be exchanged for wine and Madeira sugar. Thus it came about that Bristol sailors heard the gossip of the Iberian ports, talked with sailors who had returned from the Atlantic islands and in some instances went there themselves. They heard at first-hand from the Portuguese stories of exploration and adventure on the African coast, for long before the opening of the great age of discovery Portugal had been concerned in exploration. The Canaries were discovered in 1341, the Azores in 1431, and under Prince Henry the Navigator and his successors the Portuguese worked their way southward along the African coast until the Cape of Good Hope was discovered, and Vasco da Gama in 1497 made his way by sea to India. From time to time rumours spread through the seaport towns of Spain and Portugal of strange things washed up on the shores of the western islands— logs of unknown woods, wreckage of strange boats, occasionally the bodies of men belonging to a race hitherto unknown in Europe. All this seemed to give substance to the legend of the "Seven Cities," usually located on the Island of Antilia, and to the rumours of the island of Brazil and the Fortunate Islands of St. Brandon. Bristol sailors came home with all this news, and there they encountered other citizens who, returning from still more perilous voyages, brought with them stories of lands and islands to the westward.

Though the Norwegians and later the Danes did their utmost to shut out all foreigners from the Iceland trade, their policy was never wholly successful, for the Iceland fisheries were far too tempting a bait for English merchants, in particular those of Bristol, to resist. The Lancastrian kings were inclined at first to co-operate with the Danish authorities, and caused returned English ships to be set upon; but still the trade continued. William Canynges and others of his contemporaries were deeply concerned in this traffic, and finally, the English Government changed over from a policy of opposition to one of encouragement, and Canynges was supported in his policy of expanding this trade. Bristol ships carried out food, cloth, wine and other luxuries, iron ware, weapons and, indeed, almost everything required by an isolated civilized community. They returned with cargoes of cod, hake, pollack, salmon and herring. It is said that one cargo might range in value from £600 to £1,000 or more, and it was, therefore, natural that this trade should be considered by Bristol merchants one of the most important in which they were concerned. The Iceland market was so good that various attempts were made to establish permanent business settlements in the island, but these were consistently resisted by the Icelanders themselves and prohibited by their Norwegian or Danish masters.

John Wolffe and William Canynges actually received licences from King Christian I of Denmark to trade in Iceland, and Canynges' licence was endorsed by the English King. Nevertheless, the traders of this country were never popular, which, in view of their turbulence and high-handed methods, seems to have been perfectly natural. After the English had slain the governor of the island in a riot, the favour of the Danish King was withdrawn, and the merchants' licences were rescinded. This occurred at the time when the Hansards dominated Danish policy, and were able to secure licences for themselves which excluded the English from any share in the trade of the island. This rivalry of the Germans was so effective that English merchants were driven to conclude that the trade was not worth the labour, cost and danger which it involved. Even though Henry VII, by a treaty with the Danish King, attempted to regulate the connections of his subjects with the island, the English continued to be unpopular there.

The connection of England with Iceland had, however, probably familiarized English sailors with Norse traditions of the discoveries made by the Vikings at the beginning of the eleventh century. The story of Helluland, Markland, Wineland the Good and the other countries discovered by Ericson and his companions was known to every Icelander, and it is possible that there were still actually in existence in Iceland, at that time, maps which indicated the whereabouts of these places. Such stories English sailors brought home with them to the banks of the Avon. Thus it came about that Bristol, which was naturally well suited as a base for oceanic exploration, had these additional reasons for being foremost in the race. The two streams of knowledge relating to the lands or islands which lay to the westward met in this port, and there were probably more people in Bristol familiar with the Iberian and Icelandic sources of information than in any other city in Europe. The decline of the Icelandic trade brought this body of knowledge into the sphere of practical business, for if Iceland was to be lost, why should not Bristol find some new fishing ground for herself to the westward, where there would be no truculent Icelanders, no querulous Danish kings, and where there would be no wicked Hansards to break through and steal?

At first there was some thought of following in the wake of the Portuguese along the west coast of Africa, with a view to the establishment of a new trade in that region, but the Portuguese King soon made it clear that he intended to maintain a close monopoly for his own people over what later came to be known as the Guinea trade. The merchants of Bristol, therefore, impeded by veiled opposition in their former commerce with the Far North, and prevented from expansion in the newly-discovered south, were compelled to concentrate their activities on the exploration of the western ocean. They hoped that, like the Portuguese before them, they would find new islands with which a lucrative traffic might be developed. They failed at first to realize the full implications of the knowledge that they had, and so their early ventures ended in failure. They accepted without question the current geographical theories, so that when they thought of western exploration, they thought in terms of islands which were supposed to be somewhere west of a line running north and south off the coasts of Ireland and Portugal. It was only when, under John Cabot, a ship sailed from Bristol whose commander intended to proceed westward until he reached an island or continent, that substantial progress was recorded.

Eighteen years before that event, however, a ship of 80 tons burden, belonging to John Jay the Younger, a leading citizen of the time and a man deeply interested in western exploration, set out on the quest for the island of Brazil. On 15th July, 1480, his ship left Kingroad, an anchorage later to become famous in the history of English commerce and exploration. Kingroad lies at the mouth of the Avon off Portishead, and was used by ships waiting for the turn of the tide to carry them up to the city's quays, or for favourable conditions of wind and tide to take them out to sea. Hungroad, an almost equally well-known anchorage, lies off the left bank of the Avon between Portishead and Portbury, and there ships were accustomed to make fast to the shore while waiting for favourable conditions of wind or tide, and there also larger ones loaded and discharged. The ship which set out on this perilous adventure on that summer day in 1480 was under the command of a Welshman called Lloyd, reputed to be the most expert mariner in Britain. Lloyd, who hoped to find the island of Brazil somewhere to the westward of Ireland, continued his voyage until he believed himself to be in the region where Brazil was placed on the maps of the time. He then cruised about, south, west, and north, but, as his search took place in that part of the Atlantic which has sometimes been called the Devil's Gap, he found nothing but league upon league of empty and frequently tempestuous ocean. At last, after nine weeks' fruitless cruising, erroneously stated in the manuscript of William of Worcester to be nine months, he returned to an Irish port for the repair of his ship and the refreshment of his men. On 18th September news reached Bristol that the voyage from which so much had been hoped was fruitless. So ended the first known attempt made by the citizens of Bristol to discover new lands to the westward.

The need for a new fishing ground, however, to replace the

uncertain commerce with Iceland was still acute, and in the following year another expedition, of whose organization and subsequent history little is known, was sent out in search of the elusive island. It appears that this venture was financed by a group of Bristol merchants, but were it not for the fact that it led to litigation, there would be no record to prove that it ever took place. On 3rd September, 1481, an inquisition was held at Bristol in which one of the customs officials, Thomas Croft, was accused of engaging in trade during the period of his tenure of office. Croft, however, was pardoned, for the Government had no wish to discourage enterprising citizens who were prepared to risk their fortunes in hazardous expeditions which might turn out to be of great value to the nation as a whole. The evidence suggests that two ships, the *George* and the *Trinite*, were sent from Bristol to search for the legendary island, and that Thomas Croft had an eighth share in each of them. This expedition was definitely utilitarian, for the merchants' concern first, last and always was trade. This is borne out by the fact that Croft placed forty bushels of salt on board one of the ships which was to be used in revictualling for the return voyage, but it also indicates that he hoped a new fishing-ground would be discovered, and that in due course the ships would return with profitable cargoes.

It has been suggested that this second expedition never took place, and that the supposed reference to it is in reality to Lloyd's venture of the previous year. Against this view it can be urged that William of Worcester was a careful observer, and also that among the names of the jurors that sat in Croft's case appears that of John Jay, who would never have been selected as juror in a case in which he was personally concerned. It is clear, however, that if this expedition ever sailed, it was a complete failure.

In addition to the reasons already given for the failure of these two ventures, the time of their sailing was another material consideration. Both of them left Bristol in the summer, that is, at a time when they were likely to encounter adverse winds in the northern Atlantic. Cabot, who took six weeks to reach land, started in May, and the fishermen of the Elizabethan age preferred to set out in March or April, when they were carried by east winds almost the whole way across the ocean. It was only much later that west-bound ships in the summer made southing to pick up the trade winds and then made their way northward along the American coast.

Whatever the truth about the second expedition may be, it is evident that long before Cabot made his successful voyage, the people of Bristol were deeply concerned in the quest for islands or a continent or both to the westward. Pedro de Ayala, for example, in reporting to the King of Spain the news of Cabot's discovery of Newfoundland, states:—

"For the past seven years the people of Bristol have equipped two, three and four caravels to go in search of the island of Brasil and the Seven Cities according to the fancy of this Genoese." [1]

It is possible that these may have been fishing expeditions to the Porcupine Bank, lying out in the Atlantic west of Ireland, for this fishery was probably known in Roman times. But though little is known of these early ventures, quite clearly Bristol was deeply concerned in the western exploration. There is a tradition that as early as 1477, the great Christopher Columbus himself came to Bristol in search of employment, possibly drawn thither by what he had heard of its interest in western discoveries. It seems that he sailed from Bristol to Iceland in one of Canynges' ships, but the merchants of Bristol failed to appreciate the potentialities of their young visitor, and so lost the opportunity of being patrons to one who was destined to change the whole current of human history.

Thus, in the 'eighties and early 'nineties, then, Bristolians were much exercised about western exploration, but it is impossible now to say how many expeditions they sent out before 1497. There is good reason for believing that those referred to by De Ayala were not the only ones sponsored by Bristol. There is, for example, a tradition, based upon a statement made by Robert Thorne the Younger, that his father, Robert Thorne the Elder, and Hugh Elyot discovered Newfoundland in 1494.

[1] Williamson, J. A., *The Voyages of the Cabots*, p. 39.

In the story of Bristol's connection with overseas exploration there are many *lacunae*. Frequently there comes a point at which the documents suddenly fail, and the writer is left with nothing but vague traditions and unsubstantiated statements of daring improvisors. So it is with Cabot. After all the research that has been done on this subject by a distinguished historian, little is known about the whole Cabot episode. Cabot was a Genoese by birth, a naturalized citizen of Venice, who removed from that city to Bristol during the ninth decade of the fifteenth century. He was a man learned in the geography of his time, who is said to have journeyed eastward as far as Mecca, where he saw the caravans coming in from the north-east. If not himself a practical seaman, he understood seamanship, but it is obvious that he must have been a man of unusual qualities. It never has been the custom of Bristol to be over-hasty in taking strangers to her heart, yet in not more than ten years after his arrival, Cabot was accepted as a leading citizen, and in his own name and that of his children was suing for and receiving letters patent from the Crown, which authorized him to make his proposed voyage into the unknown west.

Then there is the mystery surrounding the Thornes, the part they played in the planning and conduct of the voyage, and Elyot and the rest. Rumours, vague traditions, random remarks—that is all that is left to the historian. Even the ship *Matthew* in which Cabot sailed has been, and is still, a subject of debate among those learned in ships and their rigging. There is an unsubstantiated tradition that she was a small two-master of about 80 tons burden, decked in; but as to whether she was clinker or carvel built, or what her internal arrangements were, history is silent. There is evidence to suggest that she was a comparatively new vessel built for general trade, and a ship of her name appears in the customs records of Bristol for several years after 1497.

There is no doubt, however, about the thoroughness with which Cabot prepared for his voyage. The first letters patent were granted to him on 5th March, 1496, well over a year before he sailed. He and his sons and their heirs and deputies were given full and free facility to sail "to all parts, regions and coasts of the eastern, western and northern sea," [1] with five ships and as many men as they thought desirable, but at their own costs. They were to explore the lands of the heathen in those regions, and, provided that these had not been previously explored by a Christian prince, they were to annex them. The patentees were licensed to hoist the English flag in whatever towns they might discover, and they were to hold such towns or other places that they might be able to conquer for the King. The wishes of the inhabitants, apparently, were not to be considered, for, without any further ado, they were to become Henry's vassals. All goods imported from these newly-discovered lands were to be brought to Bristol, and when the costs of the voyage had been defrayed, Cabot was to pay one-fifth of the net profits on every voyage to the King who, as an encouragement, exempted all goods brought back from the payment of customs duties. Cabot was a good business man as well as a bold navigator, who took a long view, and so by the terms of his patent it was enjoined that no one should visit these lands or islands without Cabot's licence, and all subjects were required to assist the venture in every possible way.

In not permitting exploration to the southward, Henry acknowledged the rights of the King of Spain to the regions already claimed by him. The first of the Tudors, however, took the position which was to be maintained by his successors, that any lands not previously claimed by a Christian prince were legitimate fields for English conquest and exploitation. As was usual at the time, it was assumed in this patent that Christendom was perennially at war with the infidels, and provided that the latter could be overcome, they had no rights as against their Christian conqueror. While wishing to encourage Cabot, Henry was not disposed to take any financial risks. He secured himself against loss, but at the same time he provided for possible gain by requiring that he should receive one-fifth of any profit which might arise. An important indication of the influence of the group of Bristol merchants who stood behind Cabot is to be seen in the condition that all goods brought back were to be landed in that port. The promoters hoped that

---

[1] Williamson, *op. cit.*, p. 26.

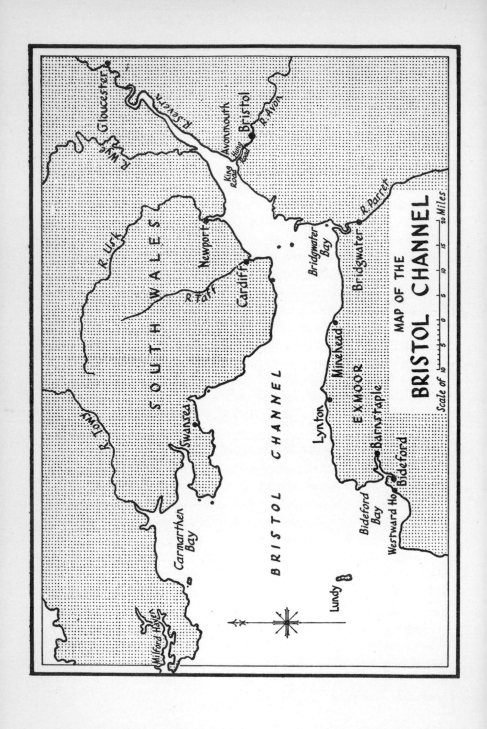

MAP OF THE
BRISTOL CHANNEL

Scale of Miles

their city would thus become the entrepôt for the spice trade which they expected would result from this voyage, and that in this way Bristol in time would take the place of Southampton.

Finally, after all preparations had been made, John Cabot, with one ship and eighteen companions, set sail on 2nd May, 1497. It was a motley company that the little *Matthew* carried down the Bristol Channel on that memorable day of early May —John Cabot, possibly his son Sebastian, that disappointing person who was never destined to arrive at the position for which his abilities seemed to fit him, a Genoese barber, a Burgundian, some unnamed Bristol merchants and under a dozen English sailors. The *Matthew* sailed in a westerly direction for forty-two days, and when 700 leagues lay astern, she sighted land; but it is still a matter of conjecture as to what land it was, Labrador, Newfoundland or Cape Breton. Having hoisted the flags of England and St. Mark on the shore, Cabot sailed along the coast in order to satisfy himself that it trended south and westward and thus to identify it with the Vinland of the sagas. Being assured on this point, and certain that the new land was in truth the north-easterly extremity of Asia, he turned homewards, discovered two more islands, observed that the adjacent seas abounded in fish, and on 6th August dropped anchor once more in Bristol.

Henry VII was satisfied and the merchants of Bristol were jubilant, for the prospect of a rich spice trade was still promising and there was no doubt about fish. Preparations were at once put in hand for another and larger expedition which should sail in the following year. Although it was hoped that the second voyage would start earlier in the year than the first in order to take advantage of more favourable weather conditions, it did not finally leave Bristol until early in May, 1498. Of the five vessels, three or four carried trade goods belonging to the merchants of Bristol and London. Little is known of this expedition except that one ship put into an Irish port. The others probably reached America and returned to England, and it is now believed that he died on this voyage.[1] Otherwise, after this

[1] Hay, D., "The Manuscript of Polydore Vergil's 'Anglica Historia,'" in *English Historical Review*, vol. LIV, pp. 246–7.

short and dramatic appearance in maritime history, this great explorer of whom so little is known, although he did so much, and although his life has attracted the investigations of so many distinguished scholars, vanishes completely from the pages of history. Indeed, his disappearance was so complete that for a long time it was his undeserving son Sebastian who received all the glory. He had done his work, for although Englishmen were slow to follow where he had led, he was the first to show them the path, which, when they followed it, led to imperial greatness.

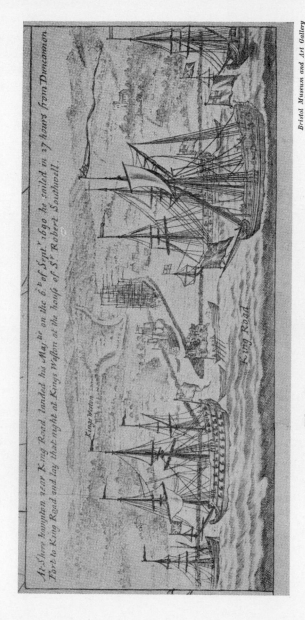

The Severn or Channell of Bristoll

Interior of the Merchants' Hall to-day

CHAPTER II

MARKING TIME

*"Brystowe . . . is a noble towne of grete trate and many shippes belong-
yng to hit.   Hit hath a goodlie haven that cometh thorough the towne and a
sumptuouse bridge over it of lyme and stone after the maner of the bridge of
London.   The shippes and botes comen in to ij partes of the towne, the one is
called the backe the other the keye, and ij leges from the towne is the river
of Severne ther is a goodlie rode called Kyngrode and an other within that
called hungrode, wher ryde the shippes that list not to come before the towne."*

ROGER BARLOW, *A Brief Summe of Geographie* (1540–1).

THOUGH little is known of the actual voyages of John Cabot, and practically nothing but vague traditions remain of the men who accompanied him, it is clear that his exploit deepened the interest of Bristol in western exploration. This interest was still further accentuated through the close commercial connections of the city with the Iberian peninsula. Ship after ship returned home with highly-coloured stories of new islands discovered, new kingdoms overthrown, and of the vast streams of gold, silver, precious metals and spices which were pouring into Spain and Portugal. Though these tales were often preposterous, flavoured with lurid accounts of demons, strange animals and still stranger men, the sober merchants of Bristol were able to penetrate through the rich vegetation of the sailor's imagination to the bedrock of truth which lay beneath. These practical business men had no concern in knight-errantry. Others might squander their substance in the baffling search for the illusive spring of eternal youth ; the only gleam which they pursued was the gleam of gold which came by honest trade.

The Thornes and possibly other Bristol merchants had their agents in Spanish seaport towns, in Portugal and in the Azores. It was natural, therefore, that they should see in the newly-discovered West Indies another market for the disposal of their products. Thus, before 1519, Thomas Tison, believed to have been a factor of Nicholas Thorne, was sent out to the Spanish settlements in the New World with armour, cloth and other products. So the first Englishman appeared in a part of the world which was later to be the scene of so much glory and triumph for England, so much cruelty and despair. Indeed, in those days, before the Reformation split Europe into two irreconcilable camps, Englishmen were numerous in the ports of Spain and Portugal, and some, at least, of them adopted the citizenship of the countries in which they lived without arousing the hostility or disapprobation of their fellow-countrymen at home. It is, in fact, difficult to believe that these hospitable Spaniards, with whom the English of the time were such close friends, could

34

possibly be the fathers or grandfathers of the people whom the Elizabethans so whole-heartedly hated and feared. In consequence of the Reformation and the Counter-Reformation, the change of public opinion in England was so complete that the Spaniards of the later sixteenth century seemed to be a people entirely alien and strange to the kindly folk with whom the Thornes and their contemporaries were on such friendly terms.

On account of the close trading connections between Bristol and the various Iberian ports, her citizens were more closely associated with the overseas developments of the time than were those of any other city in England. Thus, Master Andrew of Bristol was the sole Englishman to sail with Magellan on his famous voyage which was to carry that great captain through the Straits which bear his name, but the Englishman did not survive it. On 9th March, 1520, the day the adventurers left the Ladrones, much refreshed by the fresh fruit and vegetables they obtained there, he died. The succour had come too late. Master Andrew is an example of an Englishman who changed his nationality and settled down in Spain. He had a Spanish wife, and after his death a certain sum of money was paid in his name to the Brotherhood of Senora de la Nuestia.

Of the many names associated with the promotion of early English ventures across the Atlantic there is none more outstanding than that of Thorne. For two generations this one family was closely identified with this movement and with the extension of English trade. In the later decades of the fifteenth century there were three brothers Thorne, Robert, William and Thomas, of whom the first two were merchants. Robert was particularly concerned with the Portugal trade, and was thus familiar with the work of exploration and discovery carried on by the people of that country. He was a prominent citizen of his time, for he was one of the fifteen Bristolians appointed on 13th May, 1510, to act as Commissioners for the office of Admiral of England, and he became Mayor in 1514. He died in 1519, and handed on to his two sons, Robert and Nicholas, his passion for overseas· expansion. As will be seen later, these two worthily carried on their father's work, for they were both members of that small group of Englishmen who, at that early time, foresaw the destiny that awaited their country, provided she had the courage and the vision to turn from the old world to the new.

It is impossible to say exactly what was the extent of the elder Thorne's contributions to late fifteenth - century and early sixteenth-century expeditions from Bristol, and he may well have been concerned with the various abortive attempts which were made in the decade before Cabot set sail in the *Matthew*. Almost certainly he was a staunch supporter of that explorer, and probably sailed with him on his first and second voyages. His son declared that the elder Thorne and Hugh Elyot had discovered Newfoundland, a statement which could not possibly have been made so near to the event unless there was very good justification for it.   For, said Robert Thorne the Younger:—

"there is no doubt (as nowe plainely appeareth) if the mariners would then have bene ruled, and followed their Pilots minde, the lands of the West Indies (from whence all the gold commeth) had bene ours.   For all is one coast, as by the Carde appeareth, and is aforesayd." [1]

But Thorne was not the only man of Bristol concerned in the promotion of overseas exploration.   In 1501 and 1502 groups of Bristol merchants received letters patent which enabled them to carry on the work.   In the former year, three Azoreans, John and Francis Fernandez and John Gonsalvez, together with three Bristol merchants, Richard Warde, Thomas Ashehurst and John Thomas, received letters patent on 19th March.   These enabled the group to go to

"all parts, regions and territories of the eastern, western, southern arctic and northern seas." [2]

The expedition was to be at their costs, and they were to search for and discover islands, countries, regions and provinces inhabited by heathen, wherever they might be, seize them and subdue their people for the King.   All subjects wishing to settle in these newly-discovered lands were to be free to go there, but were to be under the government of Warde and his companions. Thus, at the very beginning of the sixteenth century, the

[1] Hakluyt, R., *The Principal Navigations*, vol. II, p. 178.
[2] Williamson, *op. cit.*, p. 46.

intention of colonization and permanent overseas settlement was definitely placed in the forefront by the Government and the promoters of distant oceanic voyages of discovery. These grantees received full powers of government, and no subject of the King was to go to the new settlements within ten years after their discovery without the permission of the patentees. Even after the expiry of that period, both the royal and the grantees' permission was necessary.

From the context it is not clear and, indeed, in the existing uncertainty which prevailed as to the geography of North America, it was probably not clear, either to the Crown or to the grantees, which lands were referred to in the royal grant. Apparently the area discovered by Cabot was excluded. This left for the patentees either the coast of North America extending south from that region to the Carolinas and Florida, or the coast of Labrador and Davis Straits. The chief modern authority on this subject seems to consider the latter was intended, and that already it was known that the coast was not the seaboard of Asia, and that the promoters were at this early time beginning to think of a possible North-West Passage to the Far East round North America.

The grantees were made free for four years to import any goods in any ships into any ports of England, and to have the special privilege of importing any goods in one ship, which could make any number of voyages in a year, free of all customs subsidies and other dues. Masters of ships were to be allowed the privilege of carrying small quantities of trade goods on their own account, but unprivileged subjects, provided they acted as factors, were to pay the grantees a toll of one-twentieth on all cargoes carried for the first ten years. Unauthorized intruders were to be excluded by force, and the grantees were permitted to appoint officers and deputies who were to exercise their authority in these territories and over the adjacent seas. They were to hold their territory without fee or tribute, though otherwise all sovereign authority was reserved to the Crown. Except in cases of customs and subsidies, in which the limitations of their foreign status was continued, the three Azorean partners and their children were to be treated as naturalized citizens.

From this document it is clear that at the very beginning the Tudor state enunciated the general principles upon which were to be issued, during the sixteenth and seventeenth centuries, all charters of this nature.

On 9th December, 1502, more letters patent were issued to yet another group of Bristol merchants which, however, over-lapped with those of the previous year. It included Hugh Elyot and Thomas Ashehurst, merchants of Bristol, and John Gonsalvez and Francis Fernandez, esquires of the Azores. The adventurers were given privileges similar to but more extended than those granted in 1501, for whereas those of 1501 might go only to lands unknown to Christians, the grantees in 1502 might go to any lands except those first discovered by friendly powers and in their possession. In other words, the patentees of 1501 were obliged to make new discoveries, while those of 1502 could take lands discovered by the Portuguese, provided that they were not in effective occupation. Unprivileged persons were required to have a special licence to proceed to the lands controlled under this patent for a period of forty years after their acquisition. The period of exemption from duty granted to one ship for four years in 1501 was now extended to five, and the patentees were to have the right, for a period of forty years, of levying an import duty of one-twentieth on all goods imported by unprivileged merchants. John Thomas, Richard Warde and John Fernandez were not to be allowed to resort to the territories of the present patentees without their special licence, whatever the terms of the formers' original patent may have been. In special recognition of the heavy charges to which they were put in the furtherance of this enterprise, Elyot, Ashehurst, Gonsalvez and Fernandez were to be exempted for five years from all duties on the cargoes of a second ship, provided she was not of more than 120 tons burden. In this document the two Azoreans were now treated as naturalized English subjects, and were required to pay duties on the same footing as their fellow countrymen. As the patent states that the grantees must

> "in no wise occupy themselves with nor enter the lands, countries, regions or provinces of heathens or infidels first discovered by the subjects of our very dear brother and cousin

the King of Portugal, or by the subjects of any other princes
soever, our friends and confederates, and in the possession of
which these same princes now find themselves," [1]

it appears that Henry VII did not regard mere discovery of
lands by any power as entitling the discoverers to the territory.
A principle was here expressed to which later English rulers
were to adhere. Henry VII and his successors after him recognized that lands belonged to other powers only when they were
effectively occupied, but they repudiated the claim of the Spaniards to the whole of the New World from north to south, based
as it was on accidental visits of Spanish ships, the construction
of a few log cabins, or a Papal decree.

Little is known of the voyages carried out under these patents,
though there is enough evidence to suggest that they did take
place. On 7th January, 1502, a payment of one hundred shillings was made to the "men of Bristoll that found Thisle." On
23rd September a mariner who had brought an eagle from overseas and presented it to the King was given 6s. 8d. Again, on
30th September "the merchants of Bristoll that have been in
the newe founde Launde" received £20.[2] About the same time
references were made to three savages taken in the "New Found
Land," two of whom were at Westminster in the following year
dressed as Englishmen. As their diet consisted of raw fish, it
has been concluded that they were Esquimaux, not Indians, and
that therefore the expeditions of 1502 had been directed to
northern latitudes. It seems, then, that the expedition of 1501–2
was considered important, otherwise the economical Henry VII
would not have parted with £20, nor would the two Azoreans
have been given a pension of £10 each. On 4th May, 1505,
Thomas Thorne received a payment of £20 from the Exchequer,
which may have been in accordance with a warrant issued some
months earlier to Robert Thorne, William Thorne and Hugh
Elyot, allowing them a remission of duties due on a cargo of
a certain ship, provided she was placed at the King's service
when required. The *Gabriel* did not go to Bordeaux for
wine that summer, and it is possible that the two elder Thornes

[1] Williamson, *op. cit.*, p. 57.
[2] *Ibid.*, p. 67.

and Hugh Elyot were absent in her on an Atlantic voyage, but as there are no records of these events all of this is very problematical.

In 1503, 1504 and 1505 the same group of merchants organized, and, in the case of Thorne and Elyot, possibly even went themselves on voyages across the Atlantic. Little is known of any of these expeditions, though there is mention of a priest in one of them, which may indicate an intention of permanent settlement, but this again is highly conjectural. Apparently the company was never very harmonious, and dissensions between its members were common. The year 1505 is the last date of any voyage organized under the patent, which probably means that it was dissolved soon afterwards.

From all this uncertainty and conjecture a few facts emerge. In the opening years of the sixteenth century expeditions bound for the New World were despatched from Bristol, and some leading merchants ventured not only their fortunes but their lives in these undertakings. Though the main motive behind this movement was economic, a few of the promoters were interested in the wider considerations of geographical discovery. As business undertakings these early expeditions were of some importance, for they confirmed an opinion which Cabot formed on his first voyage, that the coast waters off Newfoundland teemed with fish. For over four centuries after the time of these early sixteenth-century adventurers, Bristol was actively concerned in the Newfoundland fisheries. It has already been seen that before Cabot's time conditions in Iceland had become very unsatisfactory, and that Bristol merchants were looking about for new fishing grounds. It is significant, therefore, that in 1503 and 1504, the local records make no mention of the Iceland fishing voyage. So the merchants of Bristol might reasonably have drawn some satisfaction from the first few years of Atlantic voyaging. The development of fishing, however, was not their only concern in these undertakings, for their thoughts were still centred on Asia, and, strengthened by their early successes, they looked for further fields of endeavour. In 1519, when Henry VIII and Wolsey turned their minds to the development of English trade with Asia, they found the London merchants apathetic on the subject, but those of Bristol agreed to fit out and despatch two ships to the East. The royal interest was a mere passing whim, however, and there is nothing to suggest that this expedition was ever organized.

The long life of Sebastian Cabot connects up the early period of English activity in exploration with the great age which began after the turn of the half century. His career is a story of disappointed ambitions and frustrated hopes, for though he was a man of much energy, knowledge and perseverance, whom the great ones of his time were pleased to patronize, his achievements were surprisingly slight. On John Cabot's death Sebastian stepped into his place, did his utmost to carry on his father's work and apparently arrogated to himself much of the glory that was due to that great navigator. At first he was employed by Henry VII, but, with the decline of English interest in exploration which followed on the death of that monarch, he transferred his abilities and his allegiance to the King of Spain, who later became the Emperor Charles V. But even while in Spanish pay and a naturalized subject, he could not forget England, and actually returned there to assist in the promotion of a voyage. Finally, when in old age he became an English subject once more, his life-long enthusiasm for exploration was as keen as ever.

Little is known of Cabot's early voyages, but it is clear that his father had instructed him well and transmitted to him not only his zeal for discovery, but also his wide geographical knowledge and his mastery of the art of navigation. Though still a young man in 1509, probably not more than twenty-five or twenty-six years of age, he was already sufficiently outstanding to be entrusted by Henry VII with the command of another voyage. The motives of this expedition seem to have been mixed. There is reference to the fact that he carried 300 men with him, which would appear to suggest the idea of colonization, but from the course which Cabot followed, it may safely be concluded that already the search for a North-West Passage to the Far East was beginning to influence the minds of Englishmen. Naturally, the geographical knowledge of the New World was vague, and as the expedition set out for the unknown its course was to some extent determined by the actual experience of the explorers.

It seems, then, that early in 1509, Sebastian set sail with two ships and directed his course to Cape Farewell in Greenland. Having, in July, been foiled by ice in his attempt to push north-ward along the west coast of that continent, he turned westward and passed through Hudson Strait to Hudson Bay, which he took to be the Pacific Ocean. As his crew were terrified by the hardships and the prospect of sudden death through floating ice, he was compelled to return to the Atlantic. Thereafter he coasted along the American seaboard, passed Labrador and Newfoundland, and, in general, followed the course which his father had taken some years before. Always he was on the look-out for a passage through to the West, but as he failed to discover this he returned to England, where he found that his patron, Henry VII, had died, and all interest in exploration was at an end. In 1512, therefore, with the full concurrence of the English authorities, he took service with the King of Spain. The young Henry VIII was much too concerned with France, Scotland and the Empire to bother himself about hazardous and costly voyages to distant, unknown regions.

Cabot came back to England in 1520-1 to advocate another voyage, but though Bristol was to co-operate in it, the main authority and responsibility was given to London. Owing, however, to the outbreak of war with France, the ships, which were almost ready to sail, were commandeered for the royal service. He returned to Spain, and in 1526 sailed as commander of an expedition to the estuary of the River Plate. Of this little need be said here, except that it seems to have been badly organ-ized, and Cabot himself was very unfairly treated by his Spanish employers. When he had spent a year off the South American coast, he sent a ship home for supplies and reinforcements, but although Charles V ordered these to be sent, the order was never carried out, and in 1530 Cabot was compelled to return to Spain. His only reward for all this labour and privation was to be tried on several charges and sentenced to banishment. It is pleasant to remember that these charges in no way affected the Emperor's good opinion, and he remained in the Spanish service for another eighteen years. In 1548 he quitted Spain for the last time, and although the Emperor asked for his return he remained in England until his death.

There is a tradition that on his arrival there he at once set about making plans for an expedition to discover the North-West Passage, and the Government gave him a pension of £166 13s. 4d. per annum. This voyage never materialized, and in a short time he was deeply concerned in organizing a joint-stock company, "The Merchants' Adventurers of England for the Discovery of Lands, Territories, Isles, Dominions and Seignories Unknown." · From the outset this new organization directed its energies to the search for a North-East Passage to Cathay. It had 200 members and a capital of £6,000 divided into £25 shares. Sebastian Cabot was Governor, and its charter was issued by the young Edward VI. This was the first company of its kind to be organized in England, and Cabot was largely responsible for the formulation of its ordinances and, in general, acted as expert adviser to his fellow officials. He remained Governor for the rest of his life, and was always anxious to ensure that it should confine itself to the work for which it had been designed. He made his last appearance, as far as history records, when, as a very old man, he attended a farewell party at Gravesend in 1556, to celebrate the departure of an expedition about to sail in search of the North-East Passage.

"The 27 (of April, 1556)," wrote the commander of the ship, "being Munday, the right Worshipfull Sebastian Cabota came aboord our Pinesse at Gravesende, accompanied with divers Gentlemen and Gentlewomen, who after that they had viewed our Pinesse, and tasted of such cheere as we could make them aboord, they went on shore, giving to our mariners right liberall rewards: and the good olde Gentleman Master Cabota gave to the poore most liberall almes, wishing them to pray for the good fortune, and prosperous successe of the Serchthrift, our Pinesse. And then at the signe of the Christopher, he and his friends banketted, and made me, and them that were in the company great cheere: and for very joy that he had to see the towardnes of our intended discovery, he entred into the dance himselfe, amongst the rest of the young and lusty company: which being ended, hee and his

friends departed most gently, commending us to the govern-
ance of almighty God." [1]

His death probably occurred in the following year, but he had
lived long enough to see the realization of some, at least, of the
youthful dreams which he had inherited from his great father.
He saw the apathy to exploration, which had predominated in
England in the early sixteenth century, slowly give place to a
new energy, and he died at the dawn of his country's great age in
maritime enterprise.

It has already been seen that there was at this time a small
but energetic group of merchants in Bristol who were deeply
concerned in trans-oceanic exploration. Of them all there was
none more active than Robert Thorne the Elder and his two
sons, Robert and Nicholas, who carried on their father's work
after his death. In particular, Robert Thorne the Younger was
zealous for the task. He was a man of some learning and cultivation of mind, familiar with seamen and things maritime, but as a
wealthy merchant he was a person of influence and broad outlook, who took a deep interest in the scientific as opposed to the
purely economic side of exploration.

> "As some sickenesses are hereditarious, and come from the
> father to the sonne, so this inclination or desire of this dis-
> coverie I inherited of my father, which with another marchant
> of Bristow named Hugh Eliot, were the discoverers of the
> New found lands." [2]

His childhood and early youth were passed in Bristol, where
his father was the centre of a group whose conversations were
often concerned with speculations as to what lands lay beyond
the western ocean, with discussions about the shortest way to
Cathay, and with the possible outcome of voyages then pending.

He was sent to Seville to represent his father and he became a
citizen of consequence there, well acquainted with sailors and
travellers who came back to Spain from the ends of the earth.
Through the extensive trade which he carried on with the
Canaries, the Azores, the West Indies, and possibly Africa,

---

[1] Williamson, *op. cit.*, p. 22.
[2] Hakluyt, *op. cit.*, p. 178.

his natural inclination to geographical study was still further
stimulated. Though resident in Spain for many years, Thorne
did not forget that he was an Englishman, and he was determined that, in so far as the practical application of such knowledge was concerned, it was his duty to ensure that it should
benefit his native country. Thus, when in 1526 Sebastian Cabot
set sail for La Plata, Thorne invested a considerable sum in
this venture, and in return Cabot agreed that two of his English
friends, Latimer and Roger Barlow, a fellow Bristolian,
should go with him. Both of these men, Thorne confessed,
were somewhat learned in cosmography, and thus he used his
local influence and financial power to enable two skilled English
geographers to go on this expedition to spy out the land for
England.

While the expedition was still away, Thorne, in response to
a request for information from the English ambassador, Dr.
Lee, on the state of the spice trade, produced a memorial on
this subject. At that time there was some talk of the purchase
by England of the Spanish spice trade, and the English authorities were anxious to discover in advance some reliable information about the profits the Emperor derived from it, and about
the prospects of its further development. Thorne summed up
the situation as far as he knew it, but went on to develop his
own thesis that the discovery of a northern passage to the Far
East would prove of far more advantage to England since it
was shorter, 2,480 leagues as opposed to 6,000 leagues by Cape
Horn, or 4,300 leagues by the Cape of Good Hope. If the
English discovered a northern passage, he believed they would
come upon new spice islands in the tropics when they arrived
there from the north-east. He contended that this route would
prove less expensive than those of the south-east and south-west,
as the English would find markets for their cloth in Tartary on
the way to the tropics.

"There is no land unhabitable, nor Sea innavigable," he
declared. "If I had facultie to my will, it should be the first
thing that I woulde understand, even to attempt, if our Seas
Northward be navigable to the Pole or no."[1]

[1] Hakluyt, *op. cit.*, p. 178.

Pending further information, which Thorne hoped to acquire from Barlow and Latimer, he asked Lee to remain silent on this latter part of his memorial until Thorne returned to England. Barlow came back to Spain in October, 1528, in the ship which Cabot had sent home for supplies, and Latimer reached Seville with his commander in July, 1530. Owing to the growing antagonism between England and Spain, resulting from Henry VIII's divorce of Katherine of Aragon, Thorne and Latimer returned to England in 1531. Some time after Barlow's return to Spain, and before their departure for England, they elaborated the now famous *Declaration of the Indies*, which until recently has been regarded as the work of Thorne only. Undoubtedly he provided the main ideas, which are the same as those in the letter to Lee, but the work was written and elaborated by Barlow. This explains the superior literary quality of the second document, and the fact that the latter is identical with a chapter in Barlow's *Brief Summe of Geographie*, which was published in 1540–1, nine years after Thorne's death. In the *Declaration* the writers urge the feasibility of the North-West, or actually the north-polar, approach to the Far East. Looking at the maps of the time, it appeared to Thorne and Barlow that all the region round the Pole was open water, and they both under-estimated the severity of the climate. There might well be, they thought, some peril to be encountered in the shape of drifting ice, some hardship from cold, but neither of them conceived that there was anything like the impassable barrier to be overcome, which later explorers discovered to their cost. If the adventurers chose their time of departure carefully, they would have the inestimable advantage of continuous daylight.

"Thei maie saile with light and day alwais, without darknes or eny night. Wherefore there is diffrence betwene thes perelles and navigatyon, wheras contynuallie thei mai se round about them, and on the contrary when in every 24 hours thei shal saile the most parte in darknes and nyght, and at that tyme thei must saile at aventure for thei shal see no thinge about them. I thinke ther is none so ignorant but this doth perceave." [1]

---

[1] Barlow, R., *A Brief Summe of Geographie*, p. 181.

They reckoned that the only dangerous or difficult part of the passage to Cathay by this route would be for about three hundred leagues before they reached the Pole, and a similar distance beyond. Having passed this, the whole Pacific region would lie open to English exploitation, and they believed that an incalculable store of wealth of all kinds was waiting there for those who had the courage to go by this way, and discover them.

"And for suche an enterprise no man shuld thinke upon the cost in comparison to the grete profyght that maye thereby suceede, nor thinke the labour grete where so moche profyt honor and glory maye folow unto this or naturall realme and King." [1]

Barlow's work was presented to the King when the Privy Council was considering the promotion of an expedition to Tartary by the route which he and Thorne had already advocated. But although nothing came of this scheme, his great work remained to inspire and help later adventurers. Written as it was after the first great series of discoveries had been made, Barlow must rank high not so much as a promoter of, and participator in, the work of exploration, as a moulder of geographical thought in England. In his writings, he drew on his own experience and on the work of the best of his contemporaries, and so his countrymen were furnished with the most up-to-date knowledge of geography then available.

The first fifty years of the sixteenth century thus passed by, and while Spain and Portugal did much to substantiate their claims to the western and eastern worlds respectively, and while France by the successive voyages of Jacques Cartier and others challenged the sovereign rights of Spain to the New World, England did next to nothing to follow up the work of Cabot. Henry VIII did not continue in his father's ways. He turned his back on the New World and all the promise that it held for England, and joined in the old familiar game of European politics. A few natives from the wilds in the royal palace, an "egle," a "brasell bowe and two rede arrowes," "hauks," "wylde catts and popyngays," brought from time to

---

[1] Barlow, *op. cit.*, pp. 180-1.

time from the New World to amuse him, constituted his sole knowledge of the new movement, and these had little significance for the prince who figured so proudly on the Field of the Cloth of Gold, divorced the Emperor's aunt, and broke the bonds of Rome.

The small group of Bristol merchants with their friends in London and Seville thus received no encouragement. Men such as the Thornes, Elyot and Barlow were fully alive to the possibilities of successful exploration, for they knew the weakness of Spain and believed in their country's strength. Denunciations of the old Faith, divorce and the sequestration of church property were more suited to the English palate of that time than voyages through perilous seas, polar exploration and dreams of new worlds to conquer.

John Whitson

Merchant Venturer and Philanthropist

Part of a Map of New England

From Captain John Smith's *Historie of Virginia* in the Lambeth Palace Library (by permission of His Grace the Archbishop of Canterbury)

Reproduced from *Travels and Works of Captain John Smith*, ed. Arber & Bradley (by permission of Messrs. John Grant Ltd.)

CHAPTER III

PIONEERS OF EMPIRE

"Bristow is not so ancient as it is fair, and well featured: The beauty of it being such, as for the bignes thereof it scarce gives place to any City of England, and doth worthily deserve the Saxon name Bright-stad; whose pleasantness is the more, by reason that the River Avon scoures through the midst of it, which together with the benefit of Sewes under all the streets cleers the city of all noisome filth, and uncleannesse."

SPEED, J., *Theatre of the Empire of Great Britain* (1611).

DURING the sixth and seventh decades of the sixteenth century, the profound indifference to exploration and discovery which had prevailed in England during the reign of Henry VIII gave place to an entirely different spirit. Many things combined to produce this revolution in public opinion, not the least of which was economic need. England wanted new markets, for her manufactures were increasing rapidly just at the time when some of her oldest markets were beginning to fail her. The Reformation divided Europe into two hostile camps, and commerce between them became dangerous, if not impossible. Thus, Bristol's well-established trade with Spain was ruined, and the English communities which had flourished for so long in the various Spanish ports ceased to exist. This impelled Englishmen to look elsewhere for new markets, a course to which they had already been inclined in the ordinary way of trade development. Close upon the Reformation came the Counter-Reformation movement, the atrocities of the Inquisition, and Catholic plots against the Queen's life, which hallowed English fear, jealousy and hatred of Spain by making it a national passion. So, England was led along the path of imperial expansion.

In the 'fifties expeditions sailed from London, Bristol and other ports, mainly for the development of some new trade or the prosecution of exploration with a definitely economic end in view, such, for example, as the search for the North-East Passage to Cathay. But in the course of the next twenty years the motive changed. Before 1580 public opinion was beginning to concern itself with the possibilities of the plantation of permanent English colonies in the New World.

In the creation and guidance of this new public opinion the manifold activities and writings of the two Hakluyts exerted a determining influence. In formulating his arguments in favour of English plantations the elder Hakluyt clearly enunciated the mercantile theory. The establishment of English settlements in the New World would confer many benefits upon the Mother Country. They would afford a ready-made market for English manufactures, and in return would supply the Mother Country with those raw materials for the supply of which she was now dependent upon the goodwill of foreign nations. By taking off the surplus of idle people at home, colonies would greatly ease the commonwealth and, moreover, would enable many who otherwise might have been condemned to imprisonment or death to earn an honest living. By helping to expand England's range of manufactured goods for foreign trade, colonies would assist in causing a steady stream of precious metals to flow into the country. Again, the possession and development of colonies would increase England's mercantile marine; they would accustom her sailors to long and arduous voyages and so help to breed up a hardy race of seamen, who would be a source of wealth in times of peace and the chief defence of the nation in times of war. Lastly, English colonies in the New World would assist in the struggle with Spain, and great stores of precious metals might be found there similar to those that had enriched the national enemy. Even if this was not so, colonial ports would be convenient bases from which the Spanish trade could be attacked, and Spain herself cut off from those sources of precious metals upon which her whole power was founded. All of these arguments became familiar to the Elizabethans, and this was the kind of reasoning adopted by the younger Hakluyt when he came, as he so often did, to Bristol, to urge upon her merchants some new maritime undertaking, the foundation of an English colony in Newfoundland or Virginia. His listeners were quick to see the great public good which would come of such proposals, as well as the substantial economic advantages which might accrue therefrom to themselves.

It is no exaggeration to say that Hakluyt's opinions found a more ready acceptance in Bristol than in any other part of England. It has already been seen that long before the sailing of the *Matthew* merchants of that town had turned their minds to western exploration, and, in the closing decades of the sixteenth century, their descendants revered the names of Jay, Cabot, Thorne, Elyot, Barlow and many more. From the fifteenth to the nineteenth centuries, Bristol produced a long line of notable merchants, explorers, captains and colonizers whose names are still honoured in the annals of English maritime enterprise.

On the very threshold of the new age that was to carry the English flag and the English name to the ends of the earth, Bristol put her house in order and prepared herself for the work she was to do. From the days of the old Gild Merchant, the most important traders of the city had co-operated in a loose fellowship under ordinances drawn up from time to time by the City Corporation. But in 1552 the merchants petitioned for, and received, recognition of their separate existence under a charter granted by Edward VI, which incorporated them as "The Master, Wardens and Commonalty of Merchant Venturers of the City of Bristol." The existence of this body meant that capital could easily be mobilized, and plans for proposed developments in trade or for new colonizing activities could be placed before an organized body, whose members commanded great financial resources and had wide and varied commercial experience upon which to draw. Though many of the records of the society have long since vanished, it is plain from those that remain, that for over two centuries and a half this great society exercised an important influence upon the course of English overseas commerce and colonial development. Though always cautious in expenditure and never prepared to gamble, the grave and astute men who met at Spicers' Hall[1] gave serious consideration to any new schemes that might be laid before them, and if they promised well the necessary capital was forthcoming. They dealt with great undertakings in a great way, as merchant princes who resisted the arrogant pretensions of London, and even in their negotiations with the Crown they demanded their *quid pro quo.*

In Bristol, as elsewhere in England, then, the second half of the sixteenth century witnessed the advent of colonial undertakings as an integral part of English maritime enterprise. Bristol was continually bidding farewell to some new expedition bound for parts unknown, whose object might be legitimate trade, piracy, the foundation of a new colony or all three com-

[1] The present Merchants' Hall was not built until early in the eighteenth century.

bined. When it was not wishing God-speed to its adventurous sons, it was welcoming home those who had been absent on some perilous voyage which had been prolonged into months or even years. In 1596, for example, when John Hopkins, twice mayor of the city, returned from his voyage against Cadiz in his own ship, which he had himself equipped, his delighted fellow-citizens met him on Durdham Down to bring him home in triumph. They

"lighted all their tallow candells, and a great bonfire at the High Crosse very beautiful to beholde." [1]

These were the days when all true sailormen looked upon the Spanish Plate Fleet as their rightful prey, and when the talk of the port was all of the Spanish Main, rich Spanish galleons and strange adventures at sea. Sonorous Spanish names of distant places—Rio de la Plata, Terra del Fuego, Tobago, Hispaniola, Eldorado—became household words among the people. The English sea-dog became a popular idol, not only because he preyed upon the national enemy, but because he contrived to clothe his often sordid activities in a shining garment, woven of courage, gaiety and success. Though the men of Bristol took their full share in this great period of English achievement, the practical commercial spirit was never eclipsed among them by pure love of adventure. Indeed, it is doubtful if this was ever anything more than the merest foam on the strong flowing tide of Elizabethan endeavour.

The career of Andrew Barker is an outstanding, though by no means unique, example of the kind of men who harried the Spaniards and were later to defeat the Armada. Like so many others of his time, Barker suffered grievously through the economic upheaval which resulted from the growing antagonism of Spain. When his agent at Teneriffe had been thrown into prison and his goods confiscated, Barker determined to recoup himself at the expense of Spain. With assistance of his friends, two ships, the *Beare* and the *Ragged Staffe*, were got ready, and Barker sailed from Plymouth in 1575. He touched at the Cape Verde Islands where, after some trading, the Portuguese killed

[1] Hunt, W., *Bristol*, p. 136.

an Englishman whose death Barker avenged by the destruction
of two villages. He then proceeded to Trinidad which he
ravaged, and, picking up a Spanish prize on the way, he arrived
at Curaçoa. There, fourteen more of his men were massacred
by the natives, and Barker came into conflict with Roche, the
master of his ship. These difficulties, however, were patched up,
and a Spanish treasure frigate was attacked and captured. Subsequently they were chased by a Spanish man-of-war which
they managed to elude, and they finally reached Nombre de
Dios, where many of his men were struck down with fever and
several died. Undaunted by these misfortunes, they captured
another rich frigate, but by that time the breach between Barker
and Roche had become complete, and finally they fought a duel
on shore. Still the expedition went on. The *Ragged Staffe*,
which had become leaky, was sunk in the Bay of Honduras, and
another Spanish ship was captured. At last, at the Isle of San
Francisco the crew mutinied, and Barker was put on shore,
where he fought with one of the conspirators. It was apparently
the intention of the mutineers to take their commander aboard
again when the ships were about to sail for home, but before
this, he, together with some of his companions, lost his life in a
surprise attack made by the Spaniards. On their way home, the
frigate which was carrying all their treasure was lost at sea, and
the survivors returned to England empty-handed to stand their
trial as mutineers.

Indeed, the Elizabethan freebooter has received more than
his due of praise, for leaving aside the few really great men
among them, they were for the most part rapacious, quarrelsome
and arrogant pirates. The only useful purpose such men served
was to intimidate the Spaniards and enhearten their own countrymen, but fortunately this age produced men of quite a
different calibre. Captain Roger Bodenham, for example, who
trained the future explorer of the North-East Passage, Richard
Chancellor, in his bark *Aucher* on a voyage to the Levant, was a
man of outstanding quality. He lived in Spain for many years,
from whence he made voyages to the West Indies, Mexico and
the Philippines. When Anglo-Spanish relations were becoming
difficult, he acted as an English secret service agent, who not

only collected valuable information for the English Government, but also elaborated a plan for the establishment of an English settlement on the north-west coast of Africa and an alliance with Morocco. Both the Spaniards and the Portuguese on their outward voyages sailed to that latitude in order to pick up the Trades, and Bodenham believed that a strong English establishment there would place the commerce of both countries in English control.

Bodenham's pupil, Richard Chancellor, was also said to be a native of Bristol and, like his master, was clearly a superior type to Barker. He was a man of good family and appears to have been familiar with court life, both in the Empire and in France. He was, moreover, not only a man of culture and refinement but a practical seaman and a mathematician of considerable attainment, who could both make and improve the instruments of his craft. By one of his contemporaries he was described as

"peritissimus et ingeniosissimus Artifex Mathematicus, euis nomen eo libentius publicare decrevi, quod jam e vita discesserit, neque momentum suarum virtutum ullum publicum reliquit, praeter Instrummenta quaedam summa arte fabricata, et dulcissimam suae singularis peritae (in nonullorum Mathematicorum adhuc superstitium amisis) memoriam." [1]

Chancellor was the first of a long line of great English navigators, but death came to him too early in his career, so that he was never able to justify the high hopes of those who knew him as "the incomparable . . . and . . . dearly beloved Richard Chancellor." [2]

After Chancellor's tragic death on his vain search for a North-East Passage to the Far East, the North-West Passage again became popular, and before this was also abandoned many expeditions set sail from England on this hopeless search. Though they all failed of their avowed intention, they resulted in the accumulation of substantial additions to the geographical

---

[1] Digges, Thomas, *Alae Sive Scalae*, 1573, cap. 9, sig. K1 (transcribed by Taylor, E. G. R., *Tudor Geography*, 1485–1583, p. 253).

[2] Taylor, *op. cit.*, p. 91.

knowledge of that part of the world and in the creation of a great tradition of English maritime enterprise, a priceless part of the nation's heritage. Among the best known of these early expeditions were those of Martin Frobisher in 1576, 1577 and 1578. In the promotion of these voyages Bristol merchants were deeply concerned, and the names of Thomas Chester, Thomas Kelke and Thomas Aldworth, all appear in the list of subscribers for the first voyage. Sir William Wynter and his brother George were concerned as well, and were in charge of the fitting out of the second expedition, to which they also subscribed considerable sums of money. It seems, however, that the Wynters were more ready to subscribe than to pay up. Among the disbursements connected with the second and third voyages, the documents contain references to payments made to Christopher Hawlle and Edward Selman, both of Bristol.

On his first voyage in 1576 Frobisher entered the Strait that now bears his name, and he records that he had

> "upon eyther hande a greate mayne or continent; and that land uppon hys right hande, as he sayled westward, he judged to be the continente of Asia, and there to be devided from the firme of America, whiche lieth uppon the lefte hande over against the same."[1]

He took possession of the land in the Queen's name, loaded his ship with a cargo of what he believed to be rich, gold-bearing ore, and returned home. The ore was sent up to London for assay, but the report was unfavourable. In the meantime, Frobisher had set out again for more gold, which he never discovered. Although the dreams of an Eldorado in the north were not at that time realized, the citizens of Bristol at least had the satisfaction of being entertained by two Esquimaux whom Frobisher brought home with him.

> "They brought likewise a man called Calliclio, and a woman called Ignorth: they were savage people and fed only upon raw flesh. the 9th of October he rowed in a little boat made of skin in the water at the Backe, where he killed two ducks

---

[1] *The Three Voyages of Martin Frobisher,* p. 72.

with a dart, and when he had done carried his boat through the marsh upon his back: the like he did at the weir and other places where many beheld him. He would hit a duck a good distance off and not miss. They died here within a month."[1]

Thus, though Frobisher's voyages were failures in so far as their original object was concerned, they extended geographical knowledge and afforded the citizens of Bristol, for a second time, an opportunity of seeing Esquimaux, and provided them with a first-hand demonstration of the management of a kayak. These three successive failures were not enough to cool the ardour of Bristol citizens for Arctic exploration and the search for a North-West Passage.

Drake's circumnavigation of the world has been associated with an incident which has generally been recorded in a manner unfavourable to a distinguished Bristol captain. The Wynters not only helped to support Frobisher's expeditions, but also were deeply concerned in that of Drake. Sir William Wynter invested £750 in the venture, his brother George £500, and a younger member of the family, John, sailed with Drake as one of his captains. According to the original plan, the expedition was intended to be partially exploratory but with a definitely trading end in view, for the merchants of Bristol were anxious to develop a commerce with the South Pacific. Drake was to go and return through the Straits of Magellan, and visit lands heretofore unknown, not in the possession of any Christian prince. If, however, when they reached the Pacific, it seemed advisable to the Admiral, Francis Drake, the voyage was to be extended to 30 degrees south, and it was estimated that the adventurers would be absent from England for about thirteen months. There appears to have been no intention in the minds of the promoters of coasting northward 40 degrees south to 35 degrees north on the Pacific coast of America, a region already claimed and partially occupied by Spain. The avowed object of exploration was Terra Australis as shown on the map of Ortelius of 1570, which was supposed to run north-westward from the Straits of Magellan.

[1] *Adams's Chronicle of Bristol*, p. 115.

It is clear that the original plan was greatly modified by Drake shortly after they set sail from England. This alteration at once led to differences between him and his young Captain, John Wynter, who naturally regarded himself as holding a watching brief for his kinsmen. On the way to the Straits, among other places they touched at Cape Hope, where

". . . the countrey people came . . . shewing themselves very pleasant, insomuch that M. Winter daunced with them." [1]

In spite of this pleasant interlude, however, relations between Wynter and the Admiral continued to be strained, and open disputes occurred. As they proceeded past the Straits and found no Terra Australis, but only adverse winds which drove the ships apart, Wynter put back into the Strait, as being the most likely place for picking up Drake, but whether through design or accident, the latter managed to miss him. Unquestionably, the absence of Wynter gave Drake a much freer hand for raids on the Spanish colonies and a dash across the Pacific. After Wynter entered the Strait the wind never permitted him to issue westwards again; and so it was that he spoke to his men of running for the Moluccas via the Cape of Good Hope, a plan which Drake had considered, and which Cavendish in 1592 spoke of attempting. His crew, however, were on the verge of mutiny, and his master refused to steer the ship as he desired, so he was constrained to return home. Thus, there is no justification for Drake's insinuations as to Wynter's lack of courage. If there had been, certainly young Wynter would have been disgraced when Drake returned three years later, but as there is no record of this, it may be assumed that Wynter's account is perfectly true, a conclusion which is substantiated by the fact that he was never accused by any person of consequence, and that this charge was made only by a mariner, Cliffe by name, some time after the event. Unfortunately, however, the story found its way into Hakluyt's account and was never contradicted until recently. This whole episode illustrates the schism that was almost certain to occur in expeditions which were financed by merchants interested in the promotion of trade and commanded

---

[1] *The World Encompassed*, by Sir Francis Drake (ed. Penzer), p. 194.

by adventurers with an insatiable thirst for loot. The pure explorer, for whom geographical discovery was unassociated with any concrete end in view, was a figure almost unknown among the practical, hard-headed Elizabethans.

With the 'eighties and the growing hostility to Spain came opportunities for open and avowed attempts upon the colonies and shipping of that country. Letters of Marque were issued from time to time to various captains, including some from Bristol. Thus, on 8th January, 1585-6, the High Court of Admiralty authorized John Satchfield, of that city, who was bound in £1,000 to Charles Lord Howard of Effingham, Lord High Admiral of England, to set forth to the seas one ship called the *Seabright* and a pinnace called the *Mariline*, with men, ordinance and victuals sufficient for apprehending ships, goods and merchandise belonging to the King of Spain, and to bring the same to a convenient port of this realm. Satchfield was instructed not to *"breake bulke"* before the Vice-Admiral of the said port was acquainted therewith. He was to cause a just inventory of the said captured goods to be made by six honest men and returned to the Vice-Admiral within six weeks. He was also required to pay the Lord Admiral one-tenth of the value of the goods and ships captured, and not to attack any of Her Majesty's subjects, but only those of the King of Spain.[1] In the same year, Letters of Reprisal were issued to Robert Kitchen of Bristol, and there were others. In these years the Court of Admiralty was busy with the disposal of Spanish prizes containing Brazil sugar and other cargoes brought into the port of Bristol by her privateers.

Even in the tumultuous years before and after the Armada, there was a growing inclination toward the less exciting pursuit of ordinary trade in the New World, and the establishment of English colonies. Thus, on 4th April, 1594, the *Grace* of Bristol, a bark of 35 tons, commanded by Captain Rice Jones, with twelve men, sailed for the Gulf of St. Lawrence. On 19th May they fell in with Cape Spear, then called d'Espère, on the coast of Newfoundland. They then proceeded to the island of San Pedro or St. Peter's, where, laying his vessel under the lee, he

[1] H. C. A., *Letters of Marque, Bonds, etc.*, bundle 1.

caught over 300 cod in less than two hours. In the Bay of St. George he found the wrecks of two Biscayan ships from which he took 700 whale fins. Thereafter, he returned to the Bay of Placentia, where he loaded up with cod and set sail for Bristol, arriving on 24th September.

By the end of the 'seventies, the elder Hakluyt and a few others were turning their minds in earnest to something more lasting than a raid on some outlying Spanish settlement or Spanish ships at sea, or even the development of some new trade. This was the foundation of permanent English colonies in the New World. The principle was by this time generally accepted that such plantations should be established in areas not then effectively occupied by a European power. It was now a century since Lloyd had sailed from Bristol in search of the island of Brazil, and over 75 years since Cabot had first touched land beyond the Atlantic. In the meantime, both Portugal and Spain had staked out claims for themselves in the West and in the East. France had sent Cartier to claim the St. Lawrence region, and, more recently, Coligny had attempted to found an asylum for his fellow Huguenots in Florida.

During the first twenty years of Elizabeth's reign, Englishmen acquired much experience of long ocean voyages, and they had ample opportunity of making a just appraisement of the real power of Spain. Though that country advanced a shadowy claim to the whole of the New World, whether it was occupied by her or not, the Elizabethans knew that there were still great empty lands waiting for settlers, lands well supplied with timber and naval stores which England particularly required, lands whose coastline was indented with harbours and bays and the estuaries of great navigable rivers which flowed from the remote interior. So the elder Hakluyt produced his first pamphlet on colonization, *Notes on Colonisation*, in 1578, a work which he wrote especially for the men whom he knew to be interested in the subject, Sir George Peckham, Richard Wigmore, William Hawkins, Customer Smith, Adrian and Humphrey Gilbert.

From then on he was continually at work producing new pamphlets and giving advice, now to the Muscovy Company, now to the Levant Company, but always with a view to the realization of his Mercantilist principles. His young cousin, Richard, was not so much the promoter of exploration and the advocate of trade expansion as a propagandist of colonization. In the modern age he would have been a famous journalist, for few men have ever shown such inexhaustible energy in collecting news, but with him it was news of a particular sort. He must have been what is known as a good mixer, for he was equally at ease in his conversations with statesmen, rich merchants, tough privateers and illiterate sailors. He was constantly flitting about in the ports of London and Bristol, interrogating, explaining, convincing. In his hatred of Spain and in his determination to see her monopoly destroyed, the younger Hakluyt personified the spirit of Elizabethan England. The union of the Crowns of Spain and Portugal merely added fuel to his burning hate, and after conversations with Wynter and others who had returned with him from the Straits of Magellan, he proposed a scheme of fortifying that waterway. By doing this he believed England would hold the key to the Pacific and dominate an important route between the east and west.

Disappointed at the failure of Gilbert's expedition in 1579, the younger Hakluyt caused translations to be made into English of famous voyages such as those of Cartier, in order that his countrymen should not lose their zest for colonization. In the *Preface to the Reader*, which was probably his contribution to the volume, his zeal for colonies is clearly seen. It was in this that the claim was advanced that England had a legal title to all the temperate parts of North America because of Cabot's discoveries. Generally, he summed up the principles and aims of that able group of men who were already interested in the establishment of an English oversea empire. In *Divers Voyages to America*, which he published in 1582, Hakluyt developed still further his ideas on colonization. The establishment of colonies would provide an outlet for England's surplus population and render more practicable the discovery of a North-West Passage. In his opinion, previous English voyages, such as those of Gilbert in 1578–9, had failed because the motive of greed predominated, and because those in command were inadequately trained in the art of navigation.

This apostle of empire was not merely content with the collection and writing down of facts about English voyages or the advocacy of English settlement in his writings. In 1582 he proceeded to Bristol to urge upon the merchants of that city the advisability of equipping two ships to sail with Sir Humphrey Gilbert on his proposed voyage to Newfoundland. He was apparently already on friendly terms with them, for in November of the same year a favourable reply was sent by Aldworth, the Mayor of Bristol, to Walsingham. On 11th March Walsingham wrote to the Mayor :—

"After my hearty commendations, I have for certaine causes deferred the answere of your letter of Nouember last till now, which I hope commeth all in good time. Your good inclination to the Westerne discouerie I cannot but much commend. And for that sir Humfrey Gilbert, as you have heard long since, hath bene preparing into those parts being readie to imbarke within these 10. dayes, who needeth some further supply of shipping then yet he hath, I am of opinion that you shall do well if the ship or 2 barkes you write of, be put in a readinesse to goe alongst with him, or so soone after as you may. I hope this trauell wil prooue profitable to the Aduenturers and generally beneficiall to the whole realme: herein I pray you confer with these bearers, M. Richard Hackluyt, and M. Thomas Steuenton, to whome I referre you: And so bid you heartily farewell. Richmond the 11 of March 1582

"Your louing Friend

"FRANCIS WALSINGHAM." [1]

But Gilbert was short of funds. He therefore approached the city of Southampton for further financial support, and he promised a monopoly of the trade which would be created by the establishment of his colony. As Southampton had declined mightily since her great days in the fourteenth century, her city fathers were eager to seize an opportunity which promised a speedy return of prosperity and a revival of their decayed fortunes. They agreed to support Gilbert, and pledged themselves to assist him by a modest subscription. But when Bristol heard that her old trade rival was likely to benefit from the proposed

[1] Hakluyt, *op. cit.*, vol. VIII, p. 132.

expedition even more than she would herself, her merchants transferred their support from Sir Humphrey Gilbert to Christopher Carlisle, Walsingham's stepson.

On 27th March, 1583, Aldworth replied to Walsingham telling him this :—

"Right honourable, upon the receit of your letters directed unto me and deliuered by the bearers hereof M. Richard Hakluyt and M. Steuenton, bearing date the 11 of March, I presently conferred with my friends in priuate, whom I know most affectionate to this godly enterprise, especially with M. William Salterne, deputie of our company of merchants: whereupon my selfe being as then sicke, with as conuenient speede as he could, he caused an assembly of the merchants to be gathered: where after dutifull mention of your honourable disposition for the benefite of this citie, he by my appointment caused your letters being directed unto me priuatly, to be read in publike, and after some good light giuen by M. Hakluyt unto them that were ignorant of the Countrey and enterprise, and were desirous to be resolued, the motion grew generally so well to be liked, that there was eftsoones set downe by mens owne hands then present, apparently knowen by their own speach, and very willing offer, the summe of 1000-markes and upward: which summe if it should not suffice, we doubt not but otherwise to furnish out for this Westerne discovery, a ship of threescore, and a barke of 40. tunne, to be left in the countrey under the direction and government of your sonne in law M. Carlile, of whom we have heard much good, if it shall stand with your honors good liking and his acceptation. In one of which barks we are also willing to have M. Steuenton your honours messenger, and one well knowen to us, as captains. And here in humble maner, desiring your honour to vouchsafe us of your further direction by a generall letter to my selfe, my brethren, and the rest of the merchants of this city, at your honors best and most conuenient leisure, because we meane not to deferre the finall proceeding in this voyage, any further then to the end of April next comming, I cease, beseeching God long to blesse and prosper your honourable estate. Bristoll. March 27 1583." [1]

Carlisle's scheme was to establish 100 men at some place other than that chosen by Sir Humphrey Gilbert and to leave them

[1] Hakluyt, *op. cit.*, pp. 133–4.

there for a year, but when he applied to the Muscovy Company for the money he still required, he was informed by the officers of that body that they were prepared to do nothing until he had received a patent which clearly defined his rights of colonization. This he failed to do, and the whole scheme came to nothing. Gilbert sailed in June, asserted the English claim to Newfoundland and perished on the return passage.

In order that the work of colonization should go on apace, Hakluyt believed not only that more training in navigation was necessary, but that England suffered from a lack of ships.

"At this day (1584)" he was assured by his Bristol friends there were "scarce twoo of CC Tonnes belonginge to the whole Citie of Bristowe, and very fewe or none of the like burden alonge the Channell of Severne from Glocestor to the Landes ende on the one side, and Milforde haven on the other."[1]

In 1584 he transferred his allegiance to Sir Humphrey Gilbert's half-brother, Sir Walter Raleigh. In that year he wrote his *Discourse of Western Planting*, which was intended to win over the support of the Queen and Council to the conception of a broad, comprehensive, national policy, more permanent than the quest for gold or the North-West Passage. Although writing in the interests of Raleigh, Hakluyt did not limit himself to arguments in favour of settling Virginia, for he was thinking in terms of the whole coastline of North America, vaguely referred to as Norumbega, with particular reference to that part of it with which Gilbert had been concerned, that is to say from Newfoundland, Cape Breton and Nova Scotia down to Maine.

In 1585 Hakluyt, whose qualities Walsingham had come to appreciate, was granted a prebend in Bristol. From then on to the end of his life he was constantly in that city and always, it would seem, concerned with plans for colonization and the promotion of overseas expeditions. To the day of his death he never ceased in his labours to induce his countrymen to establish permanent colonies, and the disappointing results of the various attempts made during the Elizabethan period served

[1] *The Writings and Correspondence of the Two Richard Hakluyts*, p. 271.

only to strengthen his determination. In his writings he tried to instruct the nation how best this great aim might be achieved.

As yet the times were not propitious, and it was not until the war with Spain ended in 1604 that the necessary combination of merchants, adventurers and skilled navigators could be brought about, which was the essential condition of success. So, the sixteenth century closed with no English colony yet established on a permanent basis. But in the last twenty years a vast quantity of experience had been acquired. Many English captains had become familiar with the eastern coastline of North America, and through the unwearied labours of the Hakluyts, Gilbert, Raleigh, Peckham and many more, the merchants of Bristol and London, Southampton and Plymouth were not only familiar with, but deeply interested in, the conception of permanent English plantations oversea. The new century was ushered in with the successful establishment of the East India Company, a body whose later history was destined to affect every phase of English life and to make her empire unique in world history. In the launching of this great enterprise men from Bristol took an active and leading part, and in the course of the next three hundred years some of the most illustrious names in Anglo-Indian history came from that city.

CHAPTER IV

FROM MASSACHUSETTS TO CATHAY

" *No city in England (London alone excepted) hath, in so short a time, bred more brave and bold seamen, advantaged for western voyages by its situation. They have not only been merchants, but adventurers, possessed with a public spirit for the general good; aiming not so much to return wealthier, as wiser; not always to enrich themselves, as inform posterity by their discoveries. Of these, some have been but merely casual, when going to fish for cod, they have found a country, or some eminent bay, river or haven of importance, unknown before. Others were intentional, wherein they have sown experiments, with great pains, cost, and danger that ensuing ages may freely reap benefit thereof.*"

FULLER, T., *History of the Worthies of England* (1662).

IT has been seen in the last chapter that in the closing decades of the sixteenth century, English maritime enterprise assumed various forms. Explorers set out for the discovery of lands which they hoped would be abundantly supplied with precious metals, or they tried to find new ways to old lands of whose wealth they knew and generally exaggerated. Merchants financed these expeditions, but their chief interest lay in the expansion of old trades or the establishment of new ones, and they tended to judge all this new expansionist movement in the clear, cold light of the counting house. Gradually, the eloquent and persistent exhortations of such men as the Hakluyts, Raleigh and others began to bear fruit. The mind of the nation was won over to the conception of an English overseas empire which, it was now thought, would supply the Mother Country with needful raw materials, and would become an important market for the sale of English manufactured goods in the future. Colonies might even contain great stores of gold and silver similar to those discovered by Spain, for in spite of the peace concluded with that country in 1604, the old Elizabethan argument still carried weight in England, that colonies would be of incalculable strategic importance in the national struggle against the ancient enemy. All of these motives were present in the minds of the Jacobeans, and particular stress was laid on one or other of them from time to time, according as the immediate aim was exploration, trade, disguised piracy or legitimate colonization.

While the expansion of trade and the foundation of plantations became the chief concern of Englishmen in the extra-European sphere, some explorers still set out in the spirit of the Elizabethans for parts unknown, frequently to find lonely graves in the frozen north or in the bright sun-lit waters of the tropic seas, but always to find glory. Bristol traders and merchants took a notable share in the foundation of the English colonies in North America, and they were also well to the fore in the establishment of English commerce with India.

At the beginning of the new century, the younger Hakluyt, after more than twenty years of ceaseless endeavour in the cause of colonization, still preserved his youthful enthusiasm. In 1601 he came down once more to urge the Society of Merchant Venturers to take the great business seriously in hand. London had led the way shortly before by the formation of the East India Company and the despatch of the first English traders to the Far East. In 1602 Bartholomew Gosnold sailed in the *Concord* from Falmouth to explore Virginia, and with him went Robert Salterne of Bristol, who had long been interested in overseas developments. Salterne brought back favourable reports of the country which he had seen, and these, together with the inspired persuasions of Hakluyt, induced a group of Bristol merchants, with John Whitson and Robert Aldworth at their head, to subscribe a thousand marks and organize an expedition to explore North Virginia, now New England, with a view to plantation and trade. Before anything could be done, it was necessary to obtain from Sir Walter Raleigh permission for the expedition to sail, since his patent included the region to be explored. Sir Walter readily agreed to Hakluyt's request, and so two vessels, owned in part or in whole by Whitson, the *Speedwell*, 50 tons, Martin Pring, captain, and the *Discoverer*, 26 tons, William Brown, master, were got ready. Whitson was a leading Bristol merchant of the time, noted as much for his philanthropy as for his interest in colonization, and to-day the names of these two vessels, together with the *Seabrake* and the *Maryflower*, which he also owned, are commemorated in the names of the four houses of the Red Maids' School which he founded.

The expedition set sail from Kingroad on 20th March, 1603, for "the farther discovery of the north part of Virginia." By this time, the advantage of early sailings across the north Atlantic was realized, but even so early in the year, they encountered adverse winds at the outset and were windbound in Milford Haven until 10th April. At last they got under way, and in early June, after a tedious voyage, reached the American coast. The ships were laden with hats, clothes, mirrors, agricultural tools and trinkets, which shows that the intention was not only to trade with the Indians, but also to test the agricultural possibilities of the new country.

They first touched land in the neighbourhood of Fox Island at the mouth of the Penobscot River, and then followed the coastline of New England, entering the mouths of various rivers on the way. They crossed Massachusetts Bay and anchored for some time in a small bay which Pring, in honour of the chief promoter of the voyage, Whitson, named Whitson Bay. This name did not become permanent, however, and the bay later acquired fame as Plymouth Harbour, where the *Mayflower* dropped anchor in December, 1620. While there, Pring conducted some preliminary land explorations and named one of the neighbouring hills Mount Aldworth, after Robert Aldworth, the other chief promoter of the voyage. They planted wheat, rye and various vegetables, all of which Pring reported as doing well. He remained in this bay for about two months and then, having taken a cargo of sassafras aboard, he sailed for home. Robert Salterne, one of the ship's company, brought with him a new kind of fruit tree which he found there. He wrapped it in earth, and he described its fruit as being similar to the peach-plum.

The explorers had carried with them from Bristol two excellent mastiffs. Of these the Indians were much more terrified than of their strange white masters. By the time Pring reached the other side of the Atlantic the crew had had ample time to teach various tricks to the dogs, one of whom, it was said, could carry a half-pike in his mouth, a feat which was much admired by the sailors and made the dogs much dreaded by the Indians.

> "One Master Thomas Bridges a Gentleman of our company accompanied only with one of these Dogs . . . passed six miles alone in the Countrey having lost his fellowes, and returned safly. And when we would be rid of the Savages company wee would let loose the Mastives, and suddenly with out-cryes they would flee away." [1]

Pring and his companions, who reached Bristol after a very successful voyage of exploration on 2nd October, were the first Englishmen who inhabited and grew corn in New England.

[1] Purchas, S., *Purchas his Pilgrimes*, vol. XVIII, p. 325.

In the following year Pring was off again on another voyage, but no longer as commander, nor did he sail from Bristol. He was master in the *Olive Plant*, Captain Leigh, bound for Guiana from Woolwich. The object of this expedition was to make one more attempt to establish a permanent English colony in a region which had already been the scene of disaster to English adventurers. This attempt proved no more successful than its predecessors. The commander quarrelled with Pring, whom he accused of being an "unfaithful servant" and the cause of mutiny among the men. In view of Pring's whole career, these charges seem quite groundless, though it is possible that the less able commander may have resented the superior knowledge and determined character of his subordinate. As the relations between the two became intolerable, Pring finally quitted the ship, and had the good fortune to be taken aboard a Dutchman in which he returned to Europe.

Two years later, in 1606, another ship set sail for New England from Bristol with supplies. This was financed by Sir Ferdinando Gorges and Sir John Popham, Lord Chief Justice of England and formerly Recorder of Bristol. The ship was in nominal command of Captain Thomas Hanham who, in fact, was little more than Popham's representative aboard. The real leader was Martin Pring. On this, his second voyage to New England, Pring took back with him to his native country an Indian chief, Nahanada, who had been seized by Weymouth in the previous year and carried to Europe. The advice and knowledge of this Indian proved to be of great service to the explorers. Little is known of this voyage except that Sir Ferdinando Gorges and Sir John Popham were sufficiently encouraged by it to feel justified in further efforts at colonization. According to Gorges, Pring brought home with him

". . . the most exact discovery of that coast that ever came into my hands, and indeed he was the best able to perform it of any I met withal to the present, which with his relation of the country, wrought such an impression on the Lord Chief Justice and us all that were his associates, that (notwithstanding our first disaster) we set up our resolutions to follow it with effect."[1]

[1] Gorges, F., *Brief Relation.*

Pring, therefore, and through him Bristol, may justly claim an important share in the foundation of New England, which owes its existence, in part at least, to the seamen of that city and the business instincts of her hard-headed merchants, and not merely to religious enthusiasm stimulated by persecution.

For many years after his return from New England Pring turned his attention to other work, for Bristol was not only concerned with the exploration and colonization of the western world. Some of her sons, including Pring, played a conspicuous part in the early history of the East India Company which had come into existence under a charter of Elizabeth in 1600. In 1612 the vessels of the ninth, tenth and eleventh voyages set out together in the same fleet.

The *James*, of the ninth voyage, with Captain Edmund Marlowe of Bristol in command, sailed from the Downs on 10th February, 1612, and arrived back on 3rd August, 1615, but her captain had found an ocean grave in the Far East. While in the Indies, Marlowe showed himself an enterprising and able servant of the Company. On 10th June, 1613, he arrived at Pettapoli, on the east coast of India, in order to re-found an English factory there. Captain Anthony Hippon's post of 1611 had been abandoned in the following year, but the one which Marlowe established endured down to 1687. In 1614 he sailed in the *James* for Siamese Malaya, the name then given to the region around Singapore, in order to develop trade there. At that time, and for many years thereafter, the possession of or access to the Spice Islands was one of the chief aims of European powers in the East. There, Indian cottons and other goods could be exchanged for the much-desired spices for which in those days, when the population was constrained to exist on salt meat throughout the long winter, there was an inexhaustible demand. The Dutch, however, already claimed the Spice Islands, and they were bitterly opposed to the entry of any rival in this trade, as was shown at the cost of many English lives a few years later in the tragic massacre of Amboyna. It can be no matter for surprise, therefore, that Marlowe's venture was not a great success, so he sailed for home from Bantam on 29th January, 1615. When his ship was still within a hundred leagues of the port of departure, he died and was buried at sea. So

"dyed our Captaine Master Edmund Marlow, an excellent man in the Art of Navigation, and all the Mathematicks," [1]

but he was a quarrelsome man and very hard on his crew.

Indeed, the climate of the East seems generally to have been too much for the tempers of many of these early English pioneers. The records abound with references to misunderstandings, disputes and violent quarrels. Naturally, the English were always at variance with the Dutch, the Portuguese, the Persians, the Malays, and the Indians. These varied possibilities of controversies, however, did not satisfy their combative instincts, and so they were always quarrelling among themselves. Insubordination was common, private trading, in spite of the Company's orders to the contrary, the rule, and the merchants in London seem usually to have been ill-informed about the actual state of their affairs. Even among his truculent companions, however, Marlowe was conspicuous for his harshness. He

"governed at sea with much brawling and little justice and ashore with much greatness without skill consuming more money than was necessary . . . he scorns and disdains the name of merchant." [2]

While still in the East Marlowe made his will, a document which refers to his Bristol origin:

" 'I Edmonde Marlowe of the City of Bristowe, gentleman now Captain of the James of London in the East India,' perfectly sound in body and mind, 'yet in regard of the Casuall and uncertayne estate of mans lyfe especially in these dangerous partes of the worlde do make this my last will.' "

In a codicil mention is made of a great variety of trade goods owned by the deceased captain, which was possibly one of the main inducements to such men for undertaking voyages so perilous. In view of the low salaries at that time paid by the

---

[1] Purchas, *op. cit.*, vol. IV, p. 88.
[2] *Letters received by the E.I.C. from its Servants in the East*, vol. II, p. 118.

Company to its principal servants, they can scarcely be blamed for trying to recoup themselves by private trade, for otherwise no gentleman or man of ability would have faced the rigours and risks inseparable from a voyage to the East.

The ships of the tenth voyage were the *Dragon* and the *Hosiander*, and Thomas Best was chief commander. Three Bristolians sailed in the *Hosiander*, Thomas Aldworth, chief merchant, Paul Canning, second merchant, and Lancelot Canning, one of the musicians. Aldworth was a most distinguished citizen of Bristol. He was sheriff in 1609-10, at the same time as his kinsman, Robert Aldworth, was mayor, and he belonged to a family which for a generation before had been deeply interested in colonization and exploration, a family, moreover, which in the future was to be associated with other ventures. On 22nd August, 1611, Aldworth was dismissed from the City Council for reasons which are now unknown, but in view of his immediate appointment to the command of an English ship sailing for the East, and also in view of his career in India and the great respect in which he was apparently held by the Company, it is certain that his dismissal did not imply any personal dishonour. Probably it was due merely to financial embarrassment which afflicted him while he was still a sheriff. Thus he was excused a debt due from him to the Crown, and at any rate, it was through the aid of his Bristol friends and because of his high reputation, that he was able to procure an opportunity of mending his shattered fortunes by a voyage to the East.

From the beginning of the voyage the Admiral, Best, seems to have displayed a lack of cordiality in his relations with Aldworth, of whose social position and superior education he was probably jealous. On their arrival at Surat, these personal antipathies were greatly increased in consequence of a dispute between the two men over a question of policy, a dispute which led to an act of insubordination on the part of Aldworth. The Indian governor received the strangers with great kindness and allowed them to rent a building to be used as their base. In spite of Portuguese hostility, Best contrived to conclude a treaty, subject to confirmation from Agra, and in the meantime, he strengthened the English position by defeating the Portuguese off Swally on 29th November. At the end of the forty days agreed upon no word had yet arrived from the Mogul's court. Best, therefore, proposed to quit Surat altogether, and ordered the merchants to wind up their affairs and come aboard. Aldworth, who seems to have had more imagination and some appreciation of oriental mentality, refused Best's order to abandon the factory. He had heard that the *farmān* was on its way, and he said he would not leave Surat, whether it arrived or not. Finally, however, on 6th January, 1612, the messenger from Agra arrived with the *farmān*, so that Aldworth was able to persuade his superior officer to leave him there, and to sanction the dispatch of Canning with a present for the Emperor. A few days later, on 17th January, the *Dragon* and the *Hosiander* sailed for Java, leaving Aldworth in charge at Surat, which soon became the Company's most important station in the East.

In the past, Best has usually been given the credit for the foundation of Surat, though the men on the spot at the time had no doubt that its establishment was entirely due to the pertinacity of Aldworth. His successor, Kerridge, says it was

"most manifest had not Mr. Aldworth directly refused to follow his (Best's) will, we had left this place and trade." [1]

He also mentions Best's plots against Aldworth which, if success-ful, he considered would have entailed great loss to the Company. He spoke of Aldworth as

"a man of so well government and now experimented in these parts, both which . . . maketh him fitter for that place than any that could be left here." [2]

Another merchant, William Biddulph, speaks in glowing terms of Aldworth's capacity:

"The greatest cause and means of our settling here was Mr. Aldworth, for our General would have been gone three or four times and left this place . . . but Mr. Aldworth stood out with him and would not go aboard."

[1] *Letters received by the E.I.C. from its Servants in the East*, vol. II, p. 169.
[2] *Ibid.*, p. 181.

Bristol was thus associated with the establishment of the Company's headquarters in the East till 1687.

As arranged with Best, Aldworth at once sent Paul Canning with a small party to the Emperor's court to deliver a letter from James I and presents from the Company. Paul Canning came of the ancient and distinguished Bristol family of that name, and seems to have been a person of some considerable importance. Unquestionably that was his own view, but he was a man of hasty temper, which a long voyage and the hot climate of India did nothing to improve. He quarrelled with the two masters of the *Hosiander* and gave Best a great deal of trouble. In India he was constantly in difficulties with his colleagues, and before leaving Surat he quarrelled with the long-suffering and capable Aldworth. By one of his companions, Kerridge, he was described as conceited, jealous and given to drunkenness, but Kerridge was a warm admirer of Aldworth. The surgeon of the *Hosiander*, on the other hand, who does not appear to have shared his companion's aversion to inebriety, says that Canning was generally popular. Of his courage there is no doubt, for when the Portuguese attack on Surat was imminent, while his fellow merchants for the most part remained on shore, Canning went aboard and took his chance with the sailors. He died in Agra on 12th May, 1613, but even in death he was still a storm centre. The Jesuits at first were unwilling to allow a Protestant to be buried in their cemetery there, though under compulsion they subsequently consented. It is from George Canning, the brother of this unfortunate man, that George Canning, the statesman, Lord Stratford de Redcliffe, the famous ambassador to Turkey, and Earl Canning, Viceroy of India, were descended.

With Canning went "2 of the Generalls men and 2 muzisions," one of the latter being his cousin Launcelot, a man of a very different type. His instrument was the virginals, and apparently it was his duty to entertain the ship's company on the tedious outward passage. It was hoped, moreover, that by his art he might win his way and that of his fellow-countrymen into the good graces of the Indian governors, and even the Emperor himself, with whom Best had been commissioned to conclude treaties. On 12th October, 1612, when the party arrived at Amedevar (Ahmedabad), the governor there appears to have enjoyed the music.

"Our Generall caussed a paire of virginalls to be brought ashoare, and upon them one of our musitions plaid: which musick did please them the best of all. Our Generall left thes virginalls with the Governer of Amedevar, and tould him he would present them unto the Kinge, and he likewisse that plaid upon them; and in the meanetyme, so long as he staid ther, he should have both the man and the virginalls att his service." [1]

England was at that time noted for her love of music and she had already made great contributions to the art. To the men of the period it seemed the most natural thing in the world to entertain guests through the medium of harmony. Cheered by this preliminary success, the musicians were full of hope as they went up country to the court of the Mogul. There, however, a different experience awaited them. They were permitted to play before Jahāngīr, and the court player, Trully, who was the other musician, described their sad experiences. Jahāngīr unhappily evinced a profound distaste for the music to which he had consented to listen, and apparently made no attempt to conceal his feelings, whereupon, according to Trully, Canning "dyed with conceiptt." [2] The funeral of the unhappy artist, like that of his cousin, gave rise to difficulties.

"One of the Musicians dyed, and was buried in the Portugalls Churchyard, whom they tooke up, and buried in the high-way: but upon complaint, were compelled by the King to bury him there againe, threatning to turne them all out of his Country, and their buryed bodies out of their Churchyard." [3]

Having despatched the embassy to the Emperor, Aldworth set to work to strengthen the English position in Surat. Fortunately, by capturing one of the Mogul's ships, the Portuguese played into his hands. As some of the Emperor's officials were

---

[1] *The Voyage of Thomas Best to the East Indies*, p. 114.
[2] *Ibid.*, p. 34.
[3] Purchas, *op. cit.*, vol. IV, p. 165.

as much opposed to the English as to their opponents, it is probable that, if it had not been for the tact and persuasive arguments of the English governor, they would have extended the imperial embargo so as to cover English as well as Portuguese goods. Worse still, as many of the Indian officials appear to have been corrupt, they would have been prepared, at a price, to "have again received the Portugalls." But this difficulty was overcome, and by October, 1613, Aldworth felt that it was safe for him to set out with three companions for Ahmedabad to collect goods with which to load the next ship that called at Surat.

Aldworth by this time had formed definite opinions about the situation of the English in India. He believed that if they were ever to be anything more than unprivileged strangers, with no standing in the country, constantly liable to peculation and spoliation, it would be necessary for the relations of the English king and the Mogul to be placed on a more enduring and more respectable footing than had existed heretofore. On 9th November, 1613, therefore, he wrote home to the Company advising his employers to send out to India

> "a suffitient man . . . that may bee Resident in Agra withe the Kinge, and sutch a one whose person may breade regarde, for they here looke mutch after greate men." [1]

It was useless to expect mere traders and ships' captains, however excellent these might be for their proper work, to perform the delicate task of ambassadors. Someone was required who was accustomed to the ways of courts and the arts of diplomacy. There is good reason for believing that the despatch of an embassy under Sir Thomas Roe to Jahāngīr was to some extent consequent upon Aldworth's recommendations. Roe arrived in India in 1615, and it may be gathered from a letter written by Jahāngīr to James I early in 1617, that Aldworth's representations were more than justified.

This missive opened with highflown compliments to the King.

> "When yr Majesty shall open this letter, let yr royal heart be as fresh as a sweet garden, let yr throne be advanced

[1] *Court Minutes of the East India Company*, 9th November, 1613.

highest amidst the greatest of the Kings of the Prophet Jesus, let your Mat be the greatest, and all Monarchies derive their counsel and wisdom from your breast as from a fountain, that the Majesty of Jesus may remain and flourish under your protection." [1]

It goes on to refer to the mission.

"The letter of love and friendship which you sent, and the present tokens of your affection towards me I have received by the hands of your Ambassador Sr. Thomas Roe, who well deserveth to be your trusty servant, delivered to me in an acceptable and happy hour."[1]

In a later letter, having described King James as "a rose in a garden," he announced that:

"I have given my Command to all my Kingdoms and vassals, as well to the greatest as to the least, and to all my seaports, that it is my pleasure and I do command, that to all the English merchants in my Dominions there be given freedom and residence; and I have confirmed by my word that no subject of my Kingdoms shall be so bold (as) to do any injury or molestation to the said English, and that there goods they may sell or traffic with, according to their own will and their own content; and of all things that they do desire in my Kingdoms they may bye carry forth, and trade freely . . .

"And that their ships may come and go to my ports wheresoever they choose at their own will. I have commanded the great Lord Assaph Chan that he take this contract into his care . . . and whatsoever goods shall come from your Kingdom hither unto me of any kind or shall go from my Kingdom unto you shall receive no hindrance or impediment, but shall pass with honour and friendship."[1]

In spite of attacks on his caravans and attempts on his life, Aldworth contrived to maintain the trade at Surat. The Portuguese continued to be a serious cause of trouble, and his policy of neutrality aroused the suspicions and antipathy of the Indians as well. But the arrival of the second joint stock expedition, sent out by the Company in 1614, secured the English position.

[1] 17th-Century Commonplace Book, in the Williamscote Library (Dr. T. Loveday's).

This was under the command of Nicholas Downton, who sailed in the *New Year's Gift*, with Martin Pring as his master. Downton sailed from England on 1st March, 1613-4, and reached Saldanha Bay on 15th June. At Surat, Aldworth received his fellow-townsman, Pring, whom he probably knew when he was a merchant and man of consequence in Bristol. It so happened that another Bristolian, Richard Steel, was in Surat at the same time. Downton put an end to the Portuguese menace by defeating them in 1615, after which he sailed for Bantam on 2nd March, which he reached on 2nd June. He died on 9th August, and was succeeded in his command by Thomas Elkington. Finally, on 22nd December, the *New Year's Gift* set sail for England with a cargo of spice, but Elkington died on the homeward passage, and Martin Pring brought the ship safely to port on 15th June, 1616.

It was intended that William Edwards, Downton's second-in-command, should take over Surat from Aldworth, but, as the latter regarded that place as his own creation, he was strongly opposed to the change. So Aldworth remained at Surat, while Edwards was sent on to Agra as an ambassador to the Mogul. On Downton's arrival at Surat, difficulties again arose with the Mogul's officials, who refused to allow any English goods to be landed unless the English openly sided with them against the Portuguese. After protracted negotiations, in which Aldworth played the leading part, the embargo was lifted and the English cargoes were discharged. While Downton was dealing with the Portuguese, Aldworth was at Ahmedabad collecting trade goods, and he finally left that place with forty cartloads. Although he was provided with an armed guard he had to fight off an attack made by 200 Rajputs, but at last he managed to bring his caravan safely to Swally, where he loaded his Indian merchandise in the *Merchant Royal*. This ship sailed for home on 2nd March, 1613-4, and was the first vessel to bring a cargo direct from India to England. Sir Thomas Roe arrived at Surat in September, 1615, but by that time the climate of India and his untiring efforts had proved too much for Aldworth, who became seriously ill at Ahmedabad, and subsequently died at Nariad, a village nearby. There he was buried in an unknown grave, having in the short time he was in India placed the factory at Surat on a sound basis and done much to consolidate the position of the Company.

Though deeply interested in the Indian trade, and that of the west coast in particular, Aldworth found time to consider and encourage the development of trade with Persia. In the same letter in which he suggested the appointment of an ambassador to the Mogul's court, he drew the Company's attention to the commercial possibilities of that country. In this design he received further information and encouragement from his fellow-citizen, Richard Steel, who arrived at Surat on 16th May, 1614, by the overland route from Persia. Aldworth, in fact, was so taken with the specious Steel and his interesting proposals that he invited him to remain at Surat, in the hope that some opportunity of going further into the Persian business might arise. When Downton arrived he also was interested in the scheme, so much so that he despatched Steel and another merchant, John Crowther, on a journey to the court of Shah Abbas I. They set out from Ahmedabad in January, 1615, and after many adventures and great privations, they reached Isfahan on 15th September. Through the good offices of an Englishman, Sir Robert Shirley, who was resident at the Shah's court and high in that monarch's favour, a *farmān* was granted which permitted the English to trade with Persia. Crowther then returned to India, where he found that although Sir Thomas Roe was in favour of the Persian trade, he did not consider the time to be opportune for any such new development. Moreover, Roe believed that the *farmān* was worthless. In the meantime, Steel started on a long trek to the Mediterranean and England.

"After a tedious passage, partly by the River, partly by Deserts, partly by Sea,"[1]

he came overland from Marseilles and reached Dover on 10th May, 1616, having crossed the Tigris on the previous 16th January.

Meanwhile, Roe wrote to the Company in order to dissuade the governor from listening to Steel, of whose character he

[1] Purchas, *op. cit.*, vol. IV, p. 279.

seems to have formed a truer estimate than did the tolerant Aldworth. Roe said that the Company would

> "fynd a dear reckoning of Master Steeles employment; and, if I durst take such liberty, I could procure you Camells loades of firmaens to no purpose."[1]

It seems probable that Roe was unduly influenced by his unfavourable impression of Steel's character, for Kerridge, Aldworth's successor and friend at Surat, disagreed with the ambassador, and despatched the *James* to Jask where a factory was established.

Steel, however, who seems to have been a man of parts, was well received by the Company and was granted an audience by the King. Whatever his credentials, a man who could make his way overland from India to England was an unusual figure in Jacobean times. As it turned out later, Roe's forebodings were more than justified, for the Company found Steel's expenses "very extraordinary and most distasteful." For the moment, however, Steel was high in favour, and, in spite of Roe's unfavourable letter, he was able to convince the Company that at least one of the five schemes which he submitted to it was sound. This was a plan for the construction of water-works on the Jumna at Agra, a project in which Steel declared himself ready to invest £300, and, moreover, he was willing to superintend the work at a salary of £200 a year.

He left England for India once more on 5th March, 1617, in the *Anne Royal*, one of the five ships commanded by his fellow-citizen, Martin Pring, admiral of the fifth joint stock voyage. After a quick passage, the fleet arrived at Saldanha Bay on 22nd June, 1617. On the way out Steel married at the Cape one of the ladies on board, an alliance which was later to give rise to difficulties. Sir Thomas Roe was violently opposed to the Company's servants in India being encumbered by English women. Already regarding Steel's projects as "idle and vain, smoky, airy imaginations," he was determined that Mrs. Steel should not live or travel on the Company's purse. "I know the charge of women," he wrote, and he told Steel that if he was

---

[1] *The Embassy of Sir Thomas Roe to the Court of the Great Mogul*, vol. i, p. 132.

content to live like a merchant as others did, and send his wife home, he was welcome. Mrs. Steel, however, did not go home and Roe capitulated. Steel became a great favourite with the Mogul, for whom he and some English artisans whom Roe had introduced to him, made "pictures, clocks, coaches and such devices." In flagrant defiance of Roe and the Company, Steel made more money by his private trading than from the hand-some salary he received from the Emperor. After three months he disappeared from Agra, and is next heard of as a fellow passenger with Sir Thomas Roe on his return voyage to England in the *Anne Royal*. So after all, Roe had the additional chagrin of going home in the same ship as the objectionable Mrs. Steel.

On his arrival in England, Steel's reception was somewhat cooler than it had been on the former occasion. At a full court of the Company, held on the 15th of the following September,

> " he was much condempned for his unworthie carriage abroad, having perfourmed nothing that was intended and resolued of at his departure, but hath brought home a great priuate trade, put the Company to an extraordinarye charge by a wife and children, and wronged my Lord Embassador by a false and surmised contestation and arrogating a higher title and place to himself then ever was intended." [1]

Steel's subsequent career was equally unfortunate, for his request for employment by the Company was refused in 1623. Three years later, however, his offer of service was accepted, and he was sent out to Java, but there he was soon up to his old pranks, and in 1627 he was recalled for private trading. So this tumultu-ous person passes ignominiously from the pages of history. In spite of his many defects, Steel at least had the courage of his contemporaries, and it is probable that some of his far-ranging schemes were sound enough. But he was too obviously con-cerned in his own personal advancement to make a good servant of the Company. Nevertheless, he contrived to introduce an element of light comedy into the somewhat arid pages of early Anglo-Indian history, for which he deserves some gratitude from posterity.

Having arrived at Saldanha Bay on 22nd June, 1618, Pring

[1] *Court Minutes of the East India Company*, 17th September, 1619.

spent some time at various places on the coast, and on the following 12th March he continued his voyage to Bantam, where he arrived on 19th June, 1619. He remained for some months in that area, then sailed for Japan on 27th April, 1620, in the *James Royal,* with the *Unicorn* as consort. After a very long and, on the whole, prosperous voyage, Pring arrived once more in England on 18th September, 1621.

In 1622 he became a freeman of the Virginia Company and received a grant of land in that plantation. In the following year he applied to the East India Company for a "gratification," which was refused. But this rebuff was to some extent offset in the same year when he became a member of the Society of Merchant Venturers of Bristol. Pring, however, was more adventurer than merchant, and not at all suited to the prosaic, uneventful life of a Bristol citizen. So, on the outbreak of war with Spain under Charles I, the call of his old life proved too strong to resist, for he wanted a last chance in his old age of having a fling at the ancient enemy. The peaceful life of the Bristol merchant, therefore, was exchanged for his old place on the quarter-deck. On 3rd January, 1626, a letter of marque was issued to him as commander of the *Charles*, and soon prize ships began to arrive in Bristol. A Hamburg ship was captured in July, an English ship was retaken from the Turks in September, and in October, the *Lion* of Calais dropped anchor in Kingroad. A fresh letter of marque was issued to him in November, still as commander of the *Charles*, in which he made his last voyage to Virginia. This must have been completed very quickly, for on 17th February, 1627, this wonderful old sailor died, and was buried in St. Stephen's Church, Bristol. Pring's career was by no means exceptional. Indeed, in many ways he is typical of the explorers and adventurers of his age, whose lives were spent on the sea, who faced danger, privation and triumph with equanimity, and, as Pring, continued their strenuous existence when far advanced in years.

Another Bristolian prominent in Anglo-Indian history at this time was Edward Haynes, whose family lived at Westbury-on-Trym, where he was baptized. Haynes was brought up as a merchant in the Barbary trade, but Sir Thomas Roe induced him to take service with the East India Company. At first he acted as secretary to Sir Thomas, and he sailed with him in the *Lion* on 23rd February, 1615. In 1618, when the ambassador's mission was nearly accomplished, Haynes expressed a desire to enter the Company's service, so Roe gave him his chance by sending him with two merchants in the *Anne Royal* to develop trade with Persia. Writing to Pring on 14th February, 1617–8, the ambassador referred to his action.

"I have sent my servant Haynes for one because by offten discourse hee knowes my entents. I hope hee will proove diligent and honest." [1]

Haynes' departure must have embarrassed his master, for on the same day the latter wrote to the Company saying that he had been unable to send home copies of all letters,

". . . having but one hand to assist mee, and that oftener weake then able." [2]

Haynes, having achieved his wish, rose steadily in the Company's service, and at his death in August, 1632, he was agent in Persia.

The early connections of Bristol with India were thus mainly of a purely personal nature, though they were notable. The East India Company was, after all, a London body, and therefore, in general, closed to men from the Outports. In the middle of the century, when its position in India became very insecure, and it seemed only a matter of time until the Dutch would drive the English out of the peninsula altogether, Bristol had an opportunity of becoming associated with the East India trade. In February, 1650, the Society of Merchant Venturers of Bristol received a communication from the East India Company offering to accept "a sum of money" from the Hall "to put into the joint stock to trade with India." [3] After discussion, the merchants, who were inclined to be suspicious of the offer, since the Company was reputed to be in financial straits, rejected the proposal. This was probably a mistake, for shortly afterwards Blake's

---

[1] *The Embassy of Sir Thomas Roe* . . . vol. II, p. 491.
[2] *Ibid.*, p. 466.
[3] Latimer, J., *History of the Society of Merchant Venturers*, p. 167.

victories at sea, which led to the Treaty of Westminster, redressed the balance in favour of England. A few years later, under a charter from Cromwell, the Company entered upon a new period in its history. The English power quickly revived, and soon the Company was stronger than ever, and never again did it feel constrained to approach Bristol for co-operation. In the sixth decade of the eighteenth century, Bristol, Liverpool and other ports were very anxious to share in the Indian trade, and various schemes and proposals were made. But they never materialized, and Bristol did not share in the Indian trade until that branch of British commerce was thrown open in 1813.

CHAPTER V

NEWFOUNDLAND AND VIRGINIA

"Newfoundland . . . may be called Old-found-land, as senior, in the cognizance of the English, to Virginia and all our other plantations.

"Had this discovery been as fortunate in public encouragement as private industry, probably before this time we had enjoyed the kernel of those countries whose shell only we now possess."

FULLER, T., *History of the Worthies of England* (1622).

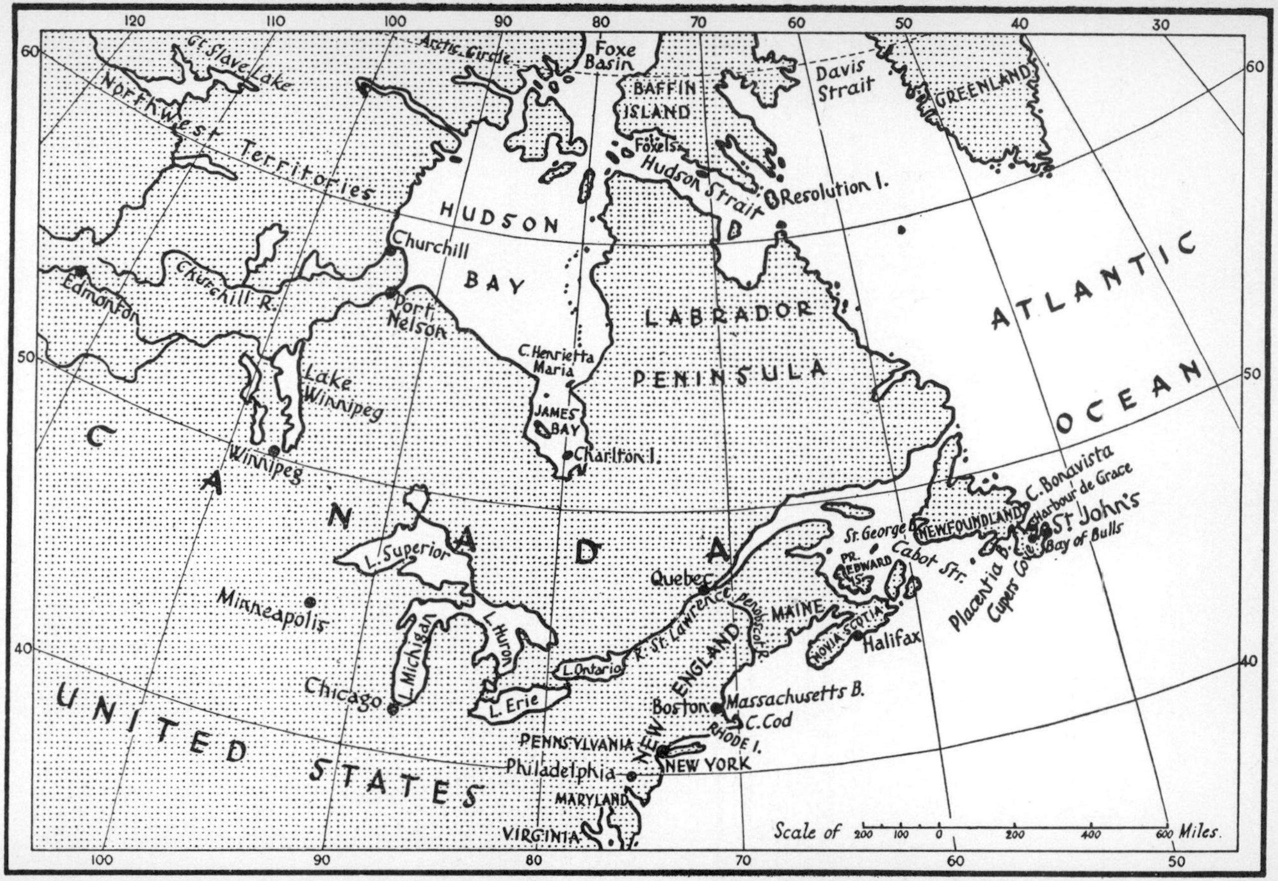

EASTERN SEABOARD OF NORTH AMERICA

PEACE was concluded with Spain in 1604, and three years later, the first permanent English colony in the New World was established at Jamestown, Virginia. These two events were not unconnected, for the men who were foremost in withstanding Spain were also the men who possessed the necessary training and experience for successful colonization.

With Cabot's discoveries, Bristol began a connection with Newfoundland which was destined to last for over four centuries. Raleigh and others refer to the great importance of the fisheries to the west counties, notably Bristol, and Raleigh was especially concerned with the extent to which the Dutch were cutting into this trade. The evidence seems to suggest that Parkhurst, who in 1578 wrote to Hakluyt concerning this area, made his four voyages to the island from the Avon. Bristol gave Gilbert no assistance in 1583, but, as has been seen already, Aldworth and others in the 'eighties were anxious to send out one hundred men who were to remain there for a whole year. Though this plan never materialized, the fisheries grew in importance during the later years of the sixteenth century, and more than one leading Bristol merchant spent a season or more on the Banks. Richard Whitbourne, for example, made the voyage in 1588, and others in the 'nineties followed him in search of new sources of train-oil, which would free England from her continued dependence upon the Spaniards for their olive oil.

"If this train-oil would make good soap," declared the Mayor of Bristol in 1592, in a report on the capture of a French frigate with a cargo of train-oil aboard, "the King of Spain may burn some of his olive trees." The voyage of the *Grace* of Bristol, 1594, already referred to, was undertaken for the same purpose. Her explorations which extended up the Gulf of St. Lawrence as far as the island of Anticosti, and included investigations on the south coast of Newfoundland, convinced the undertakers of the voyage of the great economic importance of the island to England. In consequence of these and other expeditions,

Newfoundland was well-known to early seventeenth - century Bristol. Thus, when the scheme of planting a permanent colony there was mooted, the idea was neither new nor startling. From the first, John Guy was the chief mover in this venture. He was a prominent citizen of the time who became a member of the City Council in 1603, and was appointed one of the Sheriffs in 1605. He was also one of that group of Bristol merchants who subscribed to the Virginia Company, but Newfoundland was his chief concern. He found it very difficult to develop a similar interest among his fellow citizens, and in order to impress upon them the great advantages they would derive from a colony in the island, he wrote a treatise on the subject, which is now lost. The London group interested in the plan included Sir Francis Bacon, Lord Chief Justice Popham, who seems to have been associated with almost every colonial enterprise of the period, and many more.

On 9th February, 1610, John Slany of London and John Guy of Bristol, together with other leading merchants of the two first cities of the kingdom, applied to the Privy Council for leave to establish a plantation in Newfoundland, in a petition which set forth at length various strong arguments in support of their request. From experience many London and Bristol merchants knew that Newfoundland was habitable in the winter, as might be expected, since it lay in latitude 47 degrees north, which was far to the south of England and in about the same position as Bordeaux. It was full of woods, and had fair rivers stored with fish, while fowls, birds, stags and other beasts abounded, all of which made good food as English fishermen knew. With reasonable winds it was only three weeks sail away from England, and the petitioners were anxious to test their impressions of the country by sending out a few men to winter there. They would not be molested by the savages, as none had ever been seen in the part of the island frequented by English fishermen. Already two hundred English ships and six thousand mariners repaired to the Banks each year, which benefited not only private merchants but, by the encouragement which this trade gave to navigation, was of value to the whole commonwealth. As things then were, ships which returned with cargoes of fish went out in ballast, which might just as well be stores for colonists. Moreover, if any foreign power decided to claim the island, great loss would result to England. Indeed, the French in 1580 had already made an attempt to make a permanent footing there, but owing to inefficient organization the settlers had all perished during the winter.

If this proposed venture succeeded, not only would all the existing fishing-grounds be secured for England, but others as yet unvisited might be exploited by the colonists in small boats. Industrious English inhabitants established there would furnish visiting English fishermen with the fresh food they required, and generally, by their knowledge of the country and its coast waters, facilitate their fishing. The woods would become of great importance and the land would be made fruitful. Already the Biscayans had shown the possibilities of whale fishing in that region, and there was no reason why the English in Newfoundland should not do equally well. It was also hoped that the land would produce furs, heath, pitch, turpentine, boards made from pine trees, masts and yards for small ships, soap-ashes, stags' skins, hawks of all sorts, together with seal skins, train-oil made from seals, and possibly copper and iron mines. Again, as Newfoundland was about half-way to Virginia, fortifications there would be of great service to that colony as well. In view of all this, the merchants

"desire to have letters patents for a small parte of the saide Countrie yet never inhabited by any Christian people, with reservation for all the ffishinge and use of the said land, as ever hath bene used heretofore thither by any trading thither eyther of our owne nation or of other Countries, which heretofore have used fishing uppon the said Coasts &ce." [1]

The Privy Council referred this petition for report to the Master, Wardens and Assistants of Trinity House, who on 24th February gave their answer:

"At our meeting about our busines of our Trinity house in Ratcliffe, we have Reade all theise articles touching the foresaid busines of Plantation, and have hadd it debated respectively

---

[1] *Trinity House MSS., Transactions 1609 to 1625*, fol. 1.

and Considered of amongest us And for the saide intended plantation we are of opynion that people may very
well lyve there, and that it may redounde to the greate
Comodity of our Country, aswell in respect of the greate
fishinge used there yeerly by our nation, as other wayes.
Prouided alwaies that thereby the freedome of ffishing w^{ch}
we enioy may not be altered.

HUGH MERRITT M^R.[1]

On the strength of this recommendation, the Privy Council
acceded to the petitioners' request, and on 2nd May letters
patent were issued to Henry Howard, Earl of Northampton, Sir
Francis Bacon and forty-six others. This group included John
Guy of Bristol and his brother Philip, Thomas Aldworth, the
founder of Surat, and eight other Bristol merchants. The new
body then set up was to be styled "The Treasurer and Company
of Adventurers and Planters of the City of London and Bristol
for the Colony or Plantation in Newfoundland." Permanent
settlers were to be established there, who would exchange stock
fish, train-oil and other local products for the stores brought
out in the ships. Food crops were to be planted, domestic animals were to be taken out and reared, and permanent possession
was to be taken of the best fish-curing stations in the bays. The
object of the founders was to make safe for England for ever the
fishing trade in Newfoundland. The grant covered two areas,
the inner one of which consisted of all land in Newfoundland to
the south of a line running westward from Cape Bonavista to
the Meridian of Cape St. Mary. The outer area comprised all
the country between the 46th degree and 52nd degree of north
latitude. It was, of course, intended that the Company should
maintain order in the island, repel foreigners and all unauthorized fishermen, and, in addition, it was to conduct searches for
"mines of gold" and other precious metals.

The Government was empowered to mint money in the colony and to enforce martial law if necessary. Its affairs in England
were to be administered by a council of twelve, of whom Sir
Percival Willoughby was chairman, and John Slany of London
was Treasurer. Guy, who became the first governor, sailed in

[1] *Trinity House MSS., Transactions* 1609 *to* 1625, fol. 1.

June, 1610, carrying in his three ships thirty-nine men and women, together with "hens, ducks, pigeons, cowes, goats, kine and other live creatures." The new Company applied the experience acquired by the Virginia Company, for no men went out with Guy except those "of civil life and of some honest trade or profession." They reached Cupers Cove (now Cupids) after a short voyage of twenty-three days, and established the colony of Sea Forest. Guy at once set his people to work felling trees, building boats and houses and exploring the coast. Except for a man who in December died of remorse for a murder which he had committed in Rochester several months before, and which was the cause of his undertaking the voyage, the colony survived the winter, but with the spring three more died. Others fell ill, but they received little sympathy from Guy, who showed himself to be indeed "a man very industrious and of great experience,"[1] but not over-blessed with the milk of human kindness. If, he wrote, they

"had had as good will to worke, as they had good stomaches to their victuals, (they) would long since have bin recovered."[2]

But in this Guy was less than just, for a Newfoundland winter endured for the first time by a small isolated party of strangers, ignorant of what to expect, was an experience which might well prove trying even to the hardiest. With the spring a Flemish ship arrived from La Rochelle with a cargo of salt, in exchange for which she was laden with masts and spars. On 10th May, 1611, the *Consent* dropped anchor in the cove, to be followed shortly afterwards by the *Vineyard*, which was sent out by the Company to fish. Some of the settlers who had survived the winter returned home in this ship, which also carried a small consignment of charcoal and some fish and skins.

A large house for the Governor was built, and a small vessel of 12 tons burden, which Guy proposed to use in the exploration of the east coast, was also constructed. In pursuance of the Company's plan, he set himself in the summer of 1611 to establish his authority over the fishermen, and on 30th August issued

[1] Stow, J., *Annals*, p. 1019.
[2] Purchas, *op. cit.*, vol. XIX, p. 412.

regulations which imposed severe penalties on those guilty of throwing ballast overboard, setting the woods on fire, and other offences. In the autumn of 1611 he returned home to England, leaving Colston, "a discreet young man," as Deputy Governor. By 7th June of the following year he was back in the colony once more, accompanied by a clergyman, the Rev. Erasmus Stourton.

The dispute which had broken out between Guy and the fishermen in the previous summer became more pronounced. The fishermen resented his interference and denied his authority, an act in which they were supported in England by the merchants of the other Outports. These preferred the old fishing methods and were much opposed to the establishment of any permanent authority in the island, especially as it entailed the recognition of monopolistic rights on the part of London and Bristol. The fishermen, therefore, ignored the Governor's orders, and shortly after his return in 1612 his authority was still further undermined by the arrival at Harbour Grace of the English pirate, Peter Easton. This man remained there for several weeks while he refitted his ships. As Guy was not strong enough to resist him, Easton was able to compel the fishermen to work for him, and impressed many of them for his crews. This open defiance of the Governor's authority, and his obvious failure to withstand the pirates, destroyed completely any possibility that there ever may have been of Guy bringing the truculent fishermen to heel.

Nevertheless, the energetic Governor pursued his plans of exploration. On 7th October he set out in the *Endeavour*, the pinnace which had been built in the previous year, with thirteen men and five others in another small boat. They did not return until 25th November. In the intervening period he explored the coastline of Newfoundland from Cupers Cove by way of Trinity Bay to the head of what is now Bull Arm. From high ground near by he observed, though he did not explore, the Bay of Placentia. On the way he named several bays and islands, and at the head of Bull Arm they encountered Indians with whom they established friendly relations. Guy arranged a time when they should come and trade with him, but when the Indians arrived Guy was not present, and the crew of a fishing boat which happened to be there, terrified at the sight of so many savages, opened fire on them. This unfortunate occurrence at once destroyed any hope of co-operation with the Indians, and proved another cause for the final failure of Guy's colony. Having built a house for future use on McKay Island, Guy started on his return voyage. Heavy storms were encountered which drove the shallop ashore and blew Guy far out of his course. But at last, on 25th November, after a very difficult passage, he reached Cupers Cove.

In the following year the situation of the struggling colony became more precarious. Pirates of many nations descended on the coast, set the Governor's authority at nought, made use of his stores, and mocked his weakness. As the Company was by now much dissatisfied with the small return on the great expense, Guy sailed for England. In 1615 Sir Richard Whitbourne, who had been familiar with Newfoundland since 1583, when he had visited it as a young man, went out at his own charges to establish order in the bays and to protect the fishermen from pirates. But he was no more successful than his predecessor and soon returned home. In the meantime, as the dissensions between the members of the Company were steadily increasing, it was finally decided to divide the land among them into several parts, and so in 1616, what is now the Avalon peninsula was sold to a Welshman, William Vaughan, who named it Cambriola. Two years later, John Barker, the Master, and some members of the Society of Merchant Venturers of Bristol bought some land on the west coast of Conception Bay from the Company, and there founded the colony of Bristol Hope at Harbour Grace. Apparently this new settlement took root, for within four years it was said that the inhabitants had built

"there many faire Houses, done many other good services, who live there very pleasantly." [1]

Its rye was declared to be as good as any in England, and the plantation was

[1] Purchas, *op. cit.*, p. 441.

"well furnished with Swine, and a large breed of Goates, fairer by far then those that were sent over at the first." [1]

Newfoundland, however, was not the only scene of Bristol's early colonizing activities. Indeed, it has already been shown that even before Guy and his friends formed the Newfoundland Company, one group of Bristol merchants had already turned their attention to the exploration of that region now known as New England. Though the colonial efforts of Pring and his companions were failures, they served to increase the geographical knowledge of that part of the North American coast, and in due time others were to follow where these men led. As far as Bristol is concerned, the leading man in the attempt at the colonization of New England was Sir Ferdinando Gorges, who in the cause of plantation is reputed to have spent over £50,000 of his own money. Indeed, the more the beginnings of English expansion are studied, the more evident it becomes how false was the remark of that distinguished nineteenth-century historian that England seems to have peopled half the world in a fit of absence of mind. Colonization in the seventeenth century was the result of no unconscious aberration, but of hard thinking, herculean labour and the expenditure by private adventurers of great sums of money.

Sir Ferdinando Gorges was born in 1565 and he died in 1647. He was thus brought up in the great age of Elizabeth, and as a young man adopted the profession of arms in which he won distinction. He lived through the reigns of James I and Charles I, and died when the long struggle between the Parliament and the King was not yet decided, but when, as a result of a disastrous civil war, the great name of England had temporarily lost most of its Elizabethan splendour. Gorges took no interest in colonization until the close of the Spanish war. There is a tradition that when he was in command at Plymouth his attention was first turned in that direction by some Indians who had been brought back to England by Captain Waymouth and placed in his house to learn English, but of this he makes no mention himself. He explained that the peace with Spain put many men out

---

[1] Purchas, *op. cit.*, p. 445.

of work, some of whom thereupon enlisted as mercenaries in the service of foreign states. But

"some there were who thought it better became them to put in practice the reviving resolution of those free spirits that rather chose to spend themselves in seeking a new world than servilely to be hired out as slaughterers in the quarrels of strangers. This resolution being stronger than the means to put it into execution, they were forced to let it rest as a dream, till God should give the means to stir up the inclination of such a power able to bring it into life. And so it pleased our great God there happened to come into the harbour of Plymouth, (July, 1605), where I then commanded, one Captain Waymouth that had been employed by the Lord Arundel of Wardour for the discóvery of the north-west passage. . . . This accident must be acknowledged the means under God of putting on foot and giving life to all our plantations."

Gorges and Chief Justice Popham were leaders in the formation of the Virginia Company, and were mainly responsible for the second voyage made by Pring to New England. On this occasion, the merchants of Bristol were somewhat tardy in committing themselves to the new undertaking. The Council

"were all of opinion not to adventure anything in that scheme unless the King undertakes to join in the charge and then they will be contributory in some reasonable proportion."[1]

Among the list of subscribers appear the familiar names of Guy and Aldworth. After Pring had returned with what Gorges considered to be the most exact information of that coast that ever came into his possession, the Company determined to go forward. In May of the following year, 1607, two ships, carrying emigrants and supplies, sailed to found the colony of St. George in North Virginia, but the venture was a complete failure.

Though it was many years before Gorges was able to be anything more than an interested spectator of other colonizing activity, owing to the engrossing and turbulent business of the Virginia Company, this first reverse in New England did not turn him permanently from his purpose. At last, in 1620,

[1] Latimer, J., *Annals of Bristol in the Seventeenth Century*, p. 27.

Gorges petitioned for and received a patent which incorporated a new Plymouth Company, commonly called the "Company for New England," under a patent often referred to as "The Great Patent of New England." By this "a body politicque and corporate" was created, called "the Council established at Plymouth, in the County of Devon, for the planting, ruling, ordering, and governing of New England in America." The new Company, which was to consist of not more than forty members, was granted, subject only to the reservation of sovereign rights to the Crown, the whole of that part of North America extending from the Atlantic to the Pacific, and lying between the fortieth and forty-eighth degrees of northern latitude, a region which was thereafter to be known as New England. It at once became evident that the Company was destined to meet with much opposition. For many years before this time, the merchants of Bristol had been accustomed to fish off the New England coast. Under the new patent they were treated to a dose of their own medicine, the taste of which was not at all to their liking. They were now debarred from the New England fisheries by the new Company in the same manner as the fishermen of the lesser Outports had been debarred by them from the Newfoundland fisheries.

The Company at once set itself the task of preventing the infringements of its rights by unauthorized persons who were seeking to trade within its territory or to fish along its coasts. At the request of the promoters, who were anxious to impress upon all possible interlopers the serious nature of their authority, and the fact that they had the support of the Government behind them, the Privy Council, on 18th September, 1621, wrote to the Mayors of Bristol, Exeter, Plymouth and other West Country towns "concerning the restraincte of trade to the Country of New England without the approbacon of the President and Counsell" of New England. This letter states that although membership of the Company was open to all who were interested in the trade or in the development of New England, some persons had refused to co-operate by joining that body, and, against the terms of the Royal Patent, still continued to trade. This the Privy Council was determined to stop, since such practices were

prejudicial to the interests of the adventurers who, it was declared, though without foundation, had risked their money and
the lives of their people in the venture. If continued, such actions would bring the whole scheme into confusion. The
Mayors were, therefore, to understand, and to make it understood by others, that any person who presumed to act contrary
to the royal will in this matter would be punished in such a
manner as

"is fitt to be inflicted uppon those that shall contemme his
Ma^{ts} Royall aucthoritie."[1]

As a final warning to both the Virginia Company and the New
England Company, the Privy Council ordered each of them to
respect the privileges and rights of the other.

This letter was duly transmitted by Sir Ferdinando Gorges to
the Mayor of Bristol, who in turn forwarded it to the Society of
Merchant Venturers as being the body most likely to be concerned. The Mayor also sent on to the Society another document which he received from Sir Ferdinando on the same day.
This was entitled "Articles and orders Concluded on by the
President and Counsell for the affaires of New England for the
better government of the trade and advancement of the Plan-
taĉon in those parts." This is a long and quaint document of
thirty articles which make strange reading at the present time.
It was evidently intended that the Company should act merely
in a supervisory and presumably profit-collecting capacity. The
actual work of colonization and trade was to be conducted by
quasi-subsidiary companies in Bristol, Exeter, Plymouth, Dartmouth, Weymouth and Barnstaple, whose corporate activities
were to be conducted under a highly-complicated and quite
unworkable constitution. Great care was taken to safeguard the
over-riding authority of the President and Council of New
England. Several articles describe the methods by which that
body proposed to maintain a check on the actions of the captains
of ships, the settlers and the merchants of the various towns,
individually and collectively, as well as upon the amorphous
amalgam which they jointly comprised. Intermingled with this

---

[1] *Merchant Venturers' Book of Trade*, fol. 104.

quite impracticable constitution and elaborate system of checks, several other commonplace but more reasonable items appear, which relate to the encouragement of emigrants, the investment of capital and the introduction into the new colony of useful domestic creatures. Article 24, for example, says:—

"... it is further ordered that evy shipp of threescore tons shall carry wth them twoe piggs, twoe calves, twoe couple of tame Rabbetts, twoe Couple of hens, and a cocke wch they shall deliv. at the Island of Menethiggen." [1]

Shortly after the presentation of this remarkable document to the Merchant Venturers, Gorges had a personal conference with some of the members of that body. He informed these men of the terms upon which the President and Council of New England would be willing to grant licences to individual merchants to fish in the coast waters of the territories under their control. The merchants, for their part, undertook to consider this subject, and to communicate their opinions upon it to Gorges. It is apparent, however, that they were in no particular hurry to take further action, for on 12th October Gorges wrote once more to the Mayor of Bristol. He complained somewhat truculently that, in spite of the very great trouble he had taken to ensure that Bristol should share in the great undertaking, the merchants had so far failed to answer his letter or to make any comment on the articles left with some of them. If they thought that he was working in this matter for his own and not the public's good

"I Canne sooner pdon their errors that are guiltye of that Cryme, then tell howe to reforme their natures. In a word I desire of you to give mee acknowledgment under yor hand that you have receyved the letter, & that the marchants have taken notice of the orders thereby expressed the wch I desire you to send mee by this bearer whome I have caused to attend you on purpose for it." [2]

The merchants, however, had no particular wish to share in so cumbrous a scheme, which, as practical men, they believed to

[1] *Merchant Venturers' Book of Trade*, fol. 108.
[2] *Ibid.*, fol. 109.

be unworkable. At the same time, they did not wish to give any affront to Sir Ferdinando, and they wanted to fish in New England waters. The Mayor, therefore, temporized in his reply. The merchants had great difficulty, he said, in coming to any definite conclusion on the subject of the letter and the articles. There were many and great difficulties to be overcome, and those of their number who were most interested in New England and best informed on the subject were absent from home. Moreover, they had understood from Sir Ferdinando's servant that the great man himself was shortly coming to Bristol. Also, since the matter concerned not only that city but several other towns as well, they could not, even if they had been able, give a definite answer before they had consulted with the merchants of those places. Until this subject was thoroughly gone into, they hoped that the New England Company would agree to an arrangement by which individual Bristol merchants might continue their fishing on payment of an agreed percentage on each cargo. [1]

Their real intention was to play for time in order that they might be able to find out what the other towns thought of the proposals, and also what, in fact, were the actual rights of the New England Company. Letters were sent off at once to the City's representatives in Parliament, John Whitson and John Guy, to inform them of Sir Ferdinando Gorges' propositions. Copies of the letters which they had already received, together with other documents, were enclosed, and the two Members were asked to procure a copy of the Company's patent in order to discover if, in truth, its rights and privileges were as wide as Gorges claimed them to be. If this was so, some of the Members were willing to accept the conditions of the licences offered by him, if that was the best that they could expect, for at all costs they did not wish to lose their fishing trade. [2]

This letter came to men who already had a long experience of Sir Ferdinando Gorges, and who were acquainted with the unreasonably monopolistic nature of the Company of New England. The whole question of monopolies, in fact, was at that time a

[1] *Merchant Venturers' Book of Trade*, fol. 110.
[2] *Ibid.*, fols. 111–2.

political issue of the first magnitude. King James I had abused the system, with the result that serious hindrances had been placed upon the development of trade. On the previous 2nd May, a Bill for the *Freer liberty of fishing voyages, to be made and performed in the sea-coast and places of New-found-land, Virginia, New England and other sea-coasts and parts of America* had reached the committee stage.[1] Guy's proposal that the special right of the Newfoundland Company should still be respected, even though that body was by now to all intents and purposes defunct, was rejected. Sir Ferdinando Gorges and Sir John Bourchier,

> "two mercuries . . . who brought incantations in their mouthes by their elegant speeches,"

wished to monopolize the fishing, though they were prepared to allow free fishing to others under licence from them.

> "When also God and nature, by right of creation, had made the sea free," the New England Company had "not one man there, in theis 70 years. They would deny liberty of wood and tymber for stages to dry fish: and to repair or make botses . . . and theis New England men will nether plant themselfes, nor suffer others, neyther eate hay themselfes nor suffer the laborynge oxe: like coles dog: or as bests, like my next neighbors signe of St. George, that is ever redy on horsbacke, but never rydeth forwardes, *nec movet, nec promovet.*"[2]

The Virginia Company, whose representative also spoke, favoured free fishing along the coasts, and this in spite of the fact that his organization had done a great deal more than any other to promote colonization, and therefore might be presumed to have established a right to impose restrictions. In spite of the storm in Parliament, the New England Company maintained its rights and granted licences as it proposed. With all its defects, it did its utmost to encourage investment and emigration. According to its letter to the Mayor of Bristol, which was undated, but which appears to have been written

---

[1] Stock, F., *Proceedings and Debates of the British Parliament respecting North America*, vol. I, p. 30.

[2] *Ibid.*, pp. 37–8.

some time in 1622, the Company did not wish to debar any subjects from fishing, so long as they conformed to the reasonable regulations made by the Company in the common interest, and provided also that they had previously received its licence.

The new Company, in fact, had a bad name, and the consequence was that both investments and emigrants were scarce. Therefore, more propaganda seemed necessary. It was urged that plantations in New England would enlarge the King's dominions, give work to the unemployed, drain the kingdom of its unwanted surplus, increase shipping, train mariners, and in time develop into a new market for English manufactured goods. England would obtain needful raw materials in the new colony and thus terminate her dependence upon foreigners. The economic advantages to emigrants were also stressed, and these might be shared in by both gentle and simple. Lastly, in order that this otherwise very material appeal should demonstrate the great nobility of the promoters, the document closes with the statement that all true subjects should be prepared to dedicate their best service to God.

> "Lastlie and aboue all the rest, by this opertynitye there is noe Countrie wthin this Realme, but by this Course hath a speciall occasion and meanes presented unto them to dedicate their best service to the God of Heaven and earth by endeavouring to advance his glory in seeking howe to settle the Christian ffaith in those hethenishe & Desert places in the world wch whoe shall refuse to further, lett him undergoe the blame thereof himselfe." [1]

This pious and patriotic appeal, however, had little effect upon the merchants of Bristol and the West Country generally. They were too shrewd to be taken in by such high-pressure salesmanship and share pushing, especially when it emanated from such a source as the New England Company. As the difficulties of that body were daily increasing, it was determined to make yet one more appeal to the West Country to encourage the people to help in the plantation of New England. A free gift of two hundred acres of land in fee was offered to everyone who adventured £12 10s., and a further one hundred at a chief

---

[1] *Merchant Venturers' Book of Trade*, fol. 143.

rent of 5s. for each person carried out. But the response from the West was still insufficient, and the Company failed to induce people to settle in New England, and in other respects to carry on its work.

Still, Gorges and his friends did not despair of success, and in 1623 they decided once more to work through the King, hoping that with his royal support the people of Bristol and the West would at last take up the New England plantation with enthusiasm. In compliance with their wishes James sent a letter to the Earl of Pembroke, Lord Lieutenant of Somerset, and his Deputies of Somerset and Bristol, requesting them to urge the people in that part of England to join in the New England undertaking. The royal letter stated that the country was now known to be well-suited for settlement, and its various advantages, both public and private, were enumerated. On account of its geographical position, the West Country was the part of the realm best suited to further this plantation, as also the part which was most likely to benefit therefrom. The Lord Lieutenant and his Deputies, therefore, were required to urge the gentry and others to bestir themselves.

> "Wee hope wee shall not neede to use much pswasion in this pticuler where both publique and private consideracons have soe much force, and yor good affeccons soe ready to farther good workes Nevertheless wee doe expecte to receyve from you an accompte of yor proceedings, and an intimacon thereby whome you finde ready and willing, and whome not, that wee may take such notice of both as there shalbee cause." [1]

On 14th December Pembroke wrote to the Mayor of Bristol enclosing the royal letter, and recommended him to be active in the matter and to report what was being done, in order that, when the King required it, the Lord Lieutenant would have the necessary encouraging information. [2] The King could write and threaten, and the Lord Lieutenant might exhort and order, but neither King nor Lord Lieutenant could compel the independent people of Bristol to venture their persons and fortunes in a cause which they mistrusted. The New England Company's

---

[1] *Merchant Venturers' Book of Trade*, fols. 144–5.
[2] *Ibid.*, fol. 145.

affairs, in fact, were badly managed from the first, and the England of the early sixteen-twenties was an England whose mind was quite clear on the subject of monopolies. Bristol was prepared to be active in colonization when she could conduct the business in her own way, but she had no wish to be a mere puppet, in company with a number of other western towns, to be controlled by a group of powerful people. No matter how patriotic and high-minded the promoters might be, and even though one of them, Sir Ferdinando Gorges, was a distinguished fellow-citizen whom everyone respected, Bristol refused to be coerced.

The Council of New England on 30th December, 1622, issued a patent to Robert, son of Sir Ferdinando Gorges, which granted him a strip of land called "Messachustack," extending along the sea-coast ten miles and inland thirty miles, and including within its terms all islands not previously granted within three miles of the shore. In September, 1623, he went to Weymouth or Wessagusset, a place where Weston had previously attempted to make a plantation. This was the first settlement in Massachusetts Bay and the second in Massachusetts. Other Bristolians also received land from the Company. In 1625 Robert Aldworth and his son-in-law, Giles Elbridge, had an agent in what is now part of the state of Maine. Elbridge had extensive fishing and trading interests on the coasts which were apparently considered to be very valuable, since on 29th February, 1632, the two merchants received a grant of 1,200 acres in the Pemaquid country, and in conformity with the rules of the Company, they were to be allowed an extra hundred acres for every new settler they took there. There is also a tradition that Bristol, Maine, was founded by Gorges' son-in-law.

In spite of the endeavours of Sir Ferdinando Gorges, the Company of New England never prospered, and after an inglorious history the great patent was surrendered in 1635. Gorges wished to retain the land which had originally been apportioned by the Company to him. For many years previously he had been anxious to be appointed Governor of New England, but repeatedly the actual appointment had been postponed. Finally, on 23rd July, 1635, he received his commission, for Charles, apparently, wished to reward the gallant old knight for his long services in the cause of colonization. Moreover, both the King and Laud were somewhat disquieted by the number of Dissenters who had recently settled in New England, and they intended to bring that over-independent part of the Empire under effective control. Even at his advanced age—he was now over 70—Gorges fully intended to take up his governorship. Thus, in his farewell speech to the passengers on board the ill-fated *Angel Gabriel* in Bristol harbour, on the eve of her departure, he said that "if he ever came there he would be a true friend unto them." [1] But he did not go, and in the following year he was conferring once more with the authorities about the turbulent schismatics of Maine, and on the more important subject, as he conceived it, of how best the stiff-necked nonconformists in the new settlements might be brought under one authority. Charles I granted him in 1639 a charter which invested him with almost unlimited powers of jurisdiction, and this may be taken as an illustration of what might have happened if the King had been able to send him out to New England as Governor General.

His cousin, Thomas Gorges, was appointed a Deputy-Governor in 1640, and though he himself was never destined to see the province for which he had worked so much, his last years were filled with labours on its behalf. With all his defects, Gorges deserves to be revered as one of the most notable of early English Empire builders. Long before his death, in spite of his wishes and those of the King to whom he was so devoted, the character of New England was determined by the free immigrants who sought its shores from Bristol and other English ports. Their conception of the new nation that they were founding differed profoundly from the well-disciplined, well-ordered, authoritarian plantation dreamed of and striven for, but never realized, by the master of that "mean old manor house at Wraxall."

[1] Burrage, H. S., *The Beginnings of Colonization in Maine*, p. 281.

CHAPTER VI

THE NORTH-WEST PASSAGE

"And now there came both mist and snow,
And it grew wondrous cold:
And ice, mast-high, came floating by,
As green as emerald.

"And through the drifts the snowy clifts
Did send a dismal sheen:
Nor shapes of men nor beasts we ken—
The ice was all between.

"The ice was here, the ice was there,
The ice was all around:
It cracked and growled, and roared and howled,
Like noises in a swound!"

COLERIDGE.

THOUGH early seventeenth-century navigators had enough geographical knowledge to realize that Thorne's conception of reaching Cathay via the North Pole was quite impossible, the idea of a North-West Passage round the north coast of North America was still attractive, for a short way to the gorgeous East was as seductive as ever. During the reigns of James I and Charles I, much attention was paid to exploration in that direction. Though the avowed goal was never reached, these heroic explorers enriched the national story with a noble list of privations courageously borne, which fill one of the brightest pages in English maritime annals. Hudson, 1610–1; Button, 1612–3; Gibbons, 1614; Bylot and Baffin, 1615 and 1616; Hawkridge, 1617, all in their way achieved fame, and kept the North-West Passage in the public mind.

The merchants of London and Bristol were particularly interested in this search, as they saw in it an opportunity of opening up new trades, in addition to increasing that which already existed with the Far East. If they could reach the Pacific by this backdoor, they hoped that they would come upon hitherto undiscovered spice islands and sources of precious metal, which would free England from dependence upon foreign powers. Thus, when in 1629 it became known in Bristol that an expedition was being prepared in London to make yet another attempt to find the North-West Passage, the Society of Merchant Venturers felt that it also should take action at once. If London was successful by her own unaided effort, the merchants feared that a grant of another royal monopoly would be made, which would for ever shut them out from participation in any new trade that might arise.

In the person of Captain Thomas James they had a man ready to their hand, well-qualified by training and experience to lead any such perilous expedition. Apparently James may have been related in some way to a Bristol family of that name, and thus was well-known to the merchants. He was a barrister-at-law, but a skilled navigator, who in 1628 had been granted Letters of

Marque for the privateer the *Dragon* of Bristol. A group of leading citizens, which included the Mayor, John Tomlinson, together with John Barker, Humphrey Hooke, Richard Longe, John Taylor, Giles Elbridge and other members of the Society of Merchant Venturers, determined to subscribe a sum sufficient to cover the equipment and costs of a ship, which they proposed to place under the command of James. This vessel was to sail in search of the North-West Passage.

Before proceeding with the preparations for the voyage, however, the Society wished to be assured on several important matters. In particular, they wanted to obtain the royal promise that if they should succeed in the venture themselves, or if they should jointly succeed with the ship from London, any trade which might result with newly-discovered lands would be thrown open to them, and not limited to London only. The legal training of James made him an admirable messenger for this purpose, since he could speak for them not only as their chosen navigator, but as an advocate. He was, therefore, sent to London to interview Sir Thomas Roe, who fifteen years before had been sent as the English ambassador to the Court of the Mogul. James was to acquaint Roe with the plan of the Bristol merchants and, if possible, to discover from him how they would stand with the King if they went forward with their expedition. As the preliminaries which preceded the voyage well illustrate the deeply grounded suspicions which were entertained by the merchants of Bristol, in common with those of all the other Outports, for their brethren in London, it may be well to follow the elaborate negotiations at some length. London had been, was then and was destined to be in the future, very avid of privileges, and anxious at all times to keep the Outports, including Bristol, in an inferior and dependent position. She was immeasurably wealthier than her rivals, and in a far better position to influence the Crown and obtain special privileges than any of them. This had caused much heart-burning in the past, and Bristol in the reign of Charles I felt that she had been unfairly treated by the first two Stuart Kings. On this occasion her merchants were determined that they would not spend their time and their money for the benefit merely of their powerful and highly detested rivals.

Sir Thomas Roe, who had close family associations with Bristol, received James cordially, and was greatly pleased by the latter's account of the merchants' intention. On the 25th January, 1630, soon after his interview with James, he wrote to the merchants. He stated that the King had recently given one of his ships to be used by a group of London merchants for purposes of exploration and the search for the North-West Passage to China. Roe had been instructed by the King to take charge of the preparations for the voyage and to ensure that everything possible was done for its success. In the midst of this work, Captain James had arrived with the welcome news that the merchants of Bristol were planning a similar expedition. This information greatly rejoiced the writer on personal grounds, but owing to His Majesty's absence from town, it was impossible for him at that time to give a definite answer to the merchants' request for equal privileges with London. Nevertheless, he hinted that the merchants should have no doubt on this point.

> "His Majesty is so just a Prince, and soe gratious to encourage and reward all vertuous acĉons that I am psuaded he will make noe difference betweene his Subjects, but indifferently proceed to animate you as well as any other. . . . Soe I do promise to the undertakers of yoᵣ Citty, that I will move him as effectually for them as by any one Citty or Societie of men." [1]

Roe knew of no patent which had been granted to the London promoters, though he acknowledged that he had seen a draft in writing which he had no doubt the King would extend to Bristol. But though careful not to commit himself, he wished to be encouraging.

> "This I suppose you shall obtayne at the least, that yf yoᵣ shipp have the fortune to make the passage first you shall have the priviledge wch is due unto you." [1]

---

[1] *Merchant Venturers' Book of Trade*, fol. 185.

Further, even if London made the passage first, Roe believed that Bristol would be given such privileges of trade as her enterprise deserved. Of course, he could not say, and would not presume to promise, that the King would not shut up the whole trade in some new monopoly, a contingency which was not unknown in Stuart times, as Bristol knew to her cost. At any rate, he would do his utmost as soon as the King returned to London to see that, before any patent was granted to anyone, the Bristol merchants would have an answer which would content them. In conclusion, he advised his friends in Bristol to proceed with their arrangements, and to place their trust in the royal justice and the efficacy of his earnest solicitations on their behalf.

Roe was as good as his word, for he took an early opportunity of speaking to the Lord Treasurer, Lord Weston, in the interests of Bristol. Like Roe, that nobleman was disinclined to commit himself to any promise in view of the uncertainty of the royal wishes. As, however, Bristol had done him the honour of making him Steward of the city, he told Roe that he would do all he could to help his friends. Roe suggested, in his first letter to the Bristol merchants, that it would be to the common interest of both the London and Bristol adventurers if those concerned in the two expeditions were to agree upon a common plan as to the manner of the search, and, as far as possible, to pool their knowledge. The letter closes with a private message to the Mayor, with whom Roe was connected by marriage.

". . . ffor yor perticuler I receyved from you a kind letter, wch I have not opportunitie to answere, by reason of my infirmitie but against the next season of venison I will provide you of venison in such measure, as I am able, Soe desiringe you to remember my love to yor wife my sister I will ever rest

"Yo^r very loveing frynd and brother to serve you
"THO: ROE." [1]

The Mayor read this letter to the merchants, who were not wholly convinced by Roe's assurances, so they wrote again to

---

[1] *Merchant Venturers' Book of Trade,* fol. 185.

him to enquire more specifically into the matter of the conditions which the King might require. Throughout this negotiation, in fact, they showed a pronounced tendency to suspect the intentions of Charles. In this second letter to Sir Thomas, which is undated, they expressed their gratitude for his encouragement, but they repeated their request to be informed definitely that they would be allowed to share equally with others in the fruits of the proposed expedition.

> "Wee depend and rely on yor wisdome and goodnesse, to procure such faire conditions for us as others enioy, And as o^r allacritie in undertakinge the voyadge and proporcon of o^r charge merritt." [1]

On 3rd February in order to keep James *au fait* with the course of affairs, the merchants wrote to him enclosing Sir Thomas Roe's letter to them and, presumably, their answer.

> "Hee doth presuppose that wee have already fitted a shipp, But you knowe the Contrary, and that wee have done noe more than to procure adventurers for 800£ or thereabouts." [2]

They intended to defer further arrangements until they knew more accurately what privileges they were likely to enjoy if the expedition proved successful. While anxious to oppose the monopolistic spirit of London, they had no wish merely to share a closed trade with that city. They stated repeatedly in this correspondence that they would prefer any privileges being extended to all his Majesty's subjects. In this Bristol was by no means as generous and broadminded as she seemed. It was not so long since the other Outports had been infuriated by her monopolistic pretensions in connection with the Newfoundland fisheries. Her merchants realized that if they could appear to speak for all the Outports, they were more likely to obtain concessions from the Crown than if they contented themselves with the furtherance of their own narrow interests only. If the King decided to grant a patent, they were prepared to trust to the good

---

[1] *Merchant Venturers' Book of Trade*, fol. 184.
[2] *Ibid.*, fol. 186.

Ætatis suæ 40 ✻ THE TRVE PORTRAICT OF CAP: THOMAS IAMES.

Some hes a time

Admiral Sir William Penn

From the portrait by Lely

offices of Sir Thomas Roe and the "provident circumspection"
of James on their behalf.

They informed James that it would be difficult for them to
procure a suitable vessel at a moment's notice, and that the
White Angel, which belonged to Giles Elbridge, was not available. The *William and John,* another possible ship, was not
expected home for another month, so he was instructed to be
very careful how he committed himself as to the actual time
of departure. Indeed, unless some suitable vessel turned
up in Bristol very soon, it might be necessary for him to
procure one in London. They went on to assure him that they
were giving him this caution not through any sense of dissatisfaction on their part with his proceedings, but merely to
prevent

> "any disreputacon or disparagemt wch may befall both yo[r]
> selfe and us, yf wee should promise and not pforme." [1]

In order to expedite matters and to strengthen the hand of Sir
Thomas Roe, the Society also sent a letter to the Lord Treasurer
which James was instructed to deliver to him in person. In this
it said that the merchants of Bristol were anxious to serve their
King and country, and to enlarge trade for their future benefit,
for which reason it was proposing to send a ship in the following
spring to explore the North-West Passage to the south sea. The
expedition was to be under the command and conduct of the
bearer, Captain Thomas James, a well-deserving gentleman who
was very expert in the art of navigation and a good commander.
He had been sent to London, it continued, to discover the nature
of the patent granted to the London merchants, and whether
similar privileges would be extended to them. The Society
besought his Lordship to use his good offices in order to ensure
that Bristol would be accorded treatment equal with others if
she succeeded in discovering the passage. [2]

Meanwhile, in London, James was fully occupied. Sir John
Wolstenholme, who was associated with Roe in the preparation of
the London expedition, had written to Lord Danby on behalf

---

[1] *Merchant Venturers' Book of Trade,* fol. 186,
[2] *Ibid.,* fol. 187.

of Bristol. In reply, Danby informed Wolstenholme that the King was gratiously pleased

> "to speake wth the man and will then expresse himselfe both thankefull to the towne of Bristoll, for this present enterprize of discoueringe the Northwest passage, as likewise for their good indeavors pformed in this last warr with Spayne, more actiuely and wth better successe, then any other Porte in those parts, where alsoe Captaine James shall receyve grace, and incouragement from his Ma^{ts} owne mouth, for his worthie undertakinge of the voiadge intended, and Sunday next about nyne of the Clocke in the morninge I thinke the fittest tyme, yf you and hee can bee in the presence, or Priyie Chamber, I will not faile to meete either of you there." [1]

Wolstenholme was as good as his word. The King was most gracious to James, from whom he accepted the petition from the merchants of Bristol, which was to the following effect.

> "To the kinges most Excellent Matie the humble peticon of Thomas James, in the behalfe of yor merchants adventurers, citizens of the Citty of Bristoll whereas yor Ma^{ts} most faithfull subjects, the citizens of yor Citty of Bristoll, understandinge that yor Matie hath pleased not onely to desire the discovery of the Northwest passage into the South Sea, but to grace and protect all those that shall indeavor to seeke it, whereby incouraged yor said subjects the merchants of Bristoll have determined to sett out one good shipp well furnished and provided for such a service wch shalbee ready in the beginninge of May next, and in full assurance of yor Ma^{ts} gratious disposition and equall distribucion of yor favors to all your subjects that shal equallie pursue the waies of honor and the benifitt of yor Ma^{ts} kingdomes, they have presumed most humbly to peticon yor Matie that you wilbee pleased to graunt unto them, the adventurers of the Citty of Bristoll, such equall shares and priviledges both of trade and Libertie, as you shall vouchsafe to graunt to others the adventurers of the Citty of London proporconably to their charge and adventures, and they (as in dutie bound) will ever pray for yor Ma^{ts} longe and happie Raigne." [2]

[1] *Merchant Venturers' Book of Trade*, fol. 189.
[2] *Ibid.*, fol. 190.

The King's reply was more definite and favourable to Bristol than the merchants expected.

"His maties answer to his peticon signed by the mr of Requests.

"Att the Court of Whitehall: 3 ffeb: 1630.

"His Matie is gratiously pleased, for the furtherance of the said discouery to graunt to the petitioners such equall Liberties and priviledges of trade as are already graunted to the adventurers of the Citty of London for that purpose, and yf the said discovery bee made by either of them, then the adventurers of both the said Citties are to trade hereafter, and to have advantadge according to the proporcon of their sevall adventures, And his Ma^{ts} Atturney generall is to prepare a graunt accordingly ready for his Ma^{ts} Royall signature. SIDNEY MONTAGUE."[1]

On 10th February Roe wrote to Bristol announcing that the King

"hath gratiously signed the peticon, wch remaynes for a warrant in my hand, and you may confidently rest uppon the justice of his Ma^{tle} wch I will add all my indeavo^r, that you shall have equall rights and priviledges wth those or a parte, that shall take out a Pattent."[2]

The merchants of Bristol, satisfied with the royal promise, wrote to James to express their approval of the manner in which he had managed the presentation of the petition, and also their gratification at its favourable reception by the King. But, still suspicious of London, and anxious to make their own position secure, they intimated that, in their opinion, it would be mutually advantageous both to London and to Bristol if articles were drawn up at once and signed by representatives of both groups, which would provide that, should the passage be found by either, privileges of trade which might arise should be shared equally by both. They informed James that they had not yet found a suitable ship, but that morning Mr. Elbridge had written to a friend in Barnstaple to enquire if there was one in that port. Once more they emphasized their opinion that any new trade

---

[1] *Merchant Venturers' Book of Trade,* fol. 190.
[2] *Ibid.,* fol. 191.

which might result from the discoveries should be thrown open to all subjects, and not limited to one or two ports only. [1]

Preparations for the voyage were now resumed with renewed vigour. On 26th February they reported to Roe the progress so far made, and thanked him for his continued support

"unto this Citty in generall and in pticuler unto the Company of mchants where of wee are all ambitious and will strive to make oᵣselves worthie of it and that posteritie may take notice of yoᵣ noble goodnesse to us in this enterprise." [2]

Now that their own position was somewhat clearer, and they had the royal promise that no special favour would be shown to London, they were inclined to be expansive in their patriotism.

"Yf God shall please soe to Crowne oᵣ indeavors as to make us the instruments there of, wee should accompt the service done thereby to God our Kinge and Countrie, a reward and recompence, all sufficient and abundant, And if others seeke not to appropriate it, wee shalbe willinge to leaue it open to all the kings subjects indefinitely." [2]

They also announced that they had selected a suitable ship for Captain James. She was a vessel of four-score tons burden, and was then in the hands of the carpenter, who was getting her ready for her long voyage. In honour of the Queen, and in order to show their gratitude to the King for the consideration which he had shown them, they proposed to call her the *Henrietta Maria*. So, with all preliminaries settled and the vessel being fitted out, it only remained for the merchants to thank their friends for their help, and, in particular, Lord Danby for acting as their intermediary with the King.

The *Henrietta Maria* was generously equipped with everything which at that time was considered needful for northern exploration. James, to whose mathematical knowledge frequent references are made in these documents, selected a large number of nautical instruments of all sorts to assist him. Indeed, he was so definite and exact about his requirements that he has been traditionally associated with earlier Polar expeditions.

[1] *Merchant Venturers' Book of Trade*, fol. 187.
[2] *Ibid.*, fol. 193.

Though there is little or nothing to substantiate this view, it is certain that he was well-acquainted through study and reading with the experiences and opinions of his predecessors. Thus, for example, he refused to take a large ship, as he considered that past experience had shown that in negotiating ice-floes a small vessel was less likely to be crushed. Again, he thought that one ship was preferable to two for such an expedition as the one he proposed to lead, since storms, ice and fogs were certain to separate the two, and thus lead to much waste of time and energy in mutual searchings for each other.

By 1st April everything was ready, and James proceeded once more on the now familiar road to London to receive his final instructions. These were delivered to him by Sir Thomas Roe, and finally, on 3rd May, 1631, the expedition was ready to sail.

> "One Captaine James, a man of great learning, experience in navigation, and well seen in the mathematical science, set sail from Kingrode, to discover the North-West Passage to the East Indies, which many worthy men formerly desired to find but all failed thereof . . . the ship . . . was well furnished with all necessaries, and victualled for 18 months; having but 20 men and 2 boys." [1]

After a month's sail, the *Henrietta Maria* sighted Greenland on 4th June, and was for the first time damaged by ice-floes. She reached Resolution Island on 17th June, and entered Hudson Strait shortly afterwards. There James encountered very dangerous ice conditions, but after a few anxious days, the ship had clear water ahead of her once more. As she sailed westward she was constantly encountering drifting ice. By 15th July, after weeks of slow progress and constant danger from unending icebergs, the *Henrietta Maria* found herself between Digges and Nottingham Islands. James wanted to continue in a generally north-westerly direction in the hope of finding a passage through to the Pacific, but on account of the ice barriers, it proved quite impossible to adhere to this course. He therefore altered direction and sailed west-south-west to Mansel Island, which they reached soon after. On 18th July he set his course

[1] Adams, *op. cit.*, p. 226.

westward again in the hope of reaching the other side of the Bay, after which he intended to coast northwards. Once more ice blocked his way, but as it was not so dangerous as further north, James continued his course, though progress was very slow, and on 11th August he at last came in sight of the western shore of the Bay at a point 3½ degrees south of the one for which he had been steering.

The triumph of this achievement was somewhat damped two days later when the *Henrietta Maria* ran upon a rock. At first it appeared as if she could never be got off in safety, and that the whole expedition would perish in the inhospitable shoal waters of the Bay. But fortune was with them, and in due course the ship was afloat again, apparently unharmed. Still undaunted, the adventurers pushed on and passed what is now Port Nelson on 17th August, where Foxe, the leader of the London expedition, was fitting out his pinnace. James explored the southern coast of Hudson Bay between Port Nelson and Cape Henrietta Maria, but as Foxe covered the same ground, the honour for this part of the exploration must be shared between them. On 20th August James had his first serious accident. In trying to manœuvre the ship at night eight of the men were injured and

"our Gunner (an honest and a diligent man) had his legge taken betwixt the Cable and the Capstang, which wrung off his foote, and tare all the flesh off his legge, and crushed the bone to pieces, and sorely with all bruised all his whole body; in which miserable manner hee remained crying till we had recovered ourselves, our memory, and strengths to cleere him." [1]

On 29th August Foxe and James met.

"In the morning Captain *Foxe* and his friends came aboord of mee, where I entertained them in the best manner I could, and with such fresh meat as I had gotten from the shoare." [2]

James tried to induce Foxe to winter with him in the Bay, but the London captain was determined to continue the search for the passage and so they parted.

[1] *The Voyages of Captain Luke Foxe and Captain Thomas James*, vol. II, p. 486.
[2] *Ibid.*, p. 489.

"In the euening, after I had giuen his men some necessaries, with Tobacco and other things which they wanted, hee departed aboord his Ship and, the next morning, stood away South-South-west since which time I never saw him." [1]

After this meeting, James continued his explorations of the western and southern shores of the Bay which now bears his name. He spent the greater part of September in cruising about, with no other apparent aim in mind than just cruising. At various times the ship was in great danger through running aground in shallow water. It was not until early in October that he selected his winter quarters on Charlton Island. The origin of this name has sometimes been attributed to Andrew Charlton, one of the owners, but it was more probably given in honour of the Prince of Wales. The ship was anchored in shallow water, stripped of her rigging and sails and, with great difficulty, quantities of provisions were taken ashore. Owing to the intense cold, however, much of their clothing and stores had to be left aboard. In order to save the ship from being carried away by drifting ice or smashed to pieces, she was partially submerged. Some of the men were already on shore when this was done and the remainder supervised the business.

"Our men that were ashoare stood looking upon us, almost dead with cold and sorrowes, to see our misery and their owne. We lookt upon them againe, and both upon each other, with woefull hearts. Darke night drew on, and I bade the Boate to be haled up, and commanded my louing companions to goe all into her, who (in some refusing complements) expressed their faithful affections to mee, as loth to part from me. I told them that my meaning was to goe ashore with them. And thus, lastly, I forsook the ship." [2]

In the meantime huts had been built which, in spite of every precaution, proved to be very cold and dismal abodes.

With this inadequate equipment James and his men faced the rigours of a northern winter. Long before spring their shoes were worn out, and the men went about with their feet wrapped

[1] *The Voyages of Captain Luke Foxe and Captain Thomas James*, vol. ii, p. 489.
[2] *Ibid.*, p. 520.

in rags. Insufficient food supplies was a problem, but the cook contrived so well that

> "all the weeke (except Friday night) we had some warme thing in our bellies euery supper. And (surely) this did us a great deale of good." [1]

Scurvy smote the crew and no one knew the proper methods of combating it, so that, owing to the weakness of the men, it proved difficult to provide an adequate supply of firewood. To these miseries was added the gloomy thought that their ship was now lost and that, even if spring came, they would never be able to return to England. James did his best to keep his men in good cheer, and early in the winter ordered the carpenter to build a pinnace in which they might sail home to England when spring returned, if the ship proved a total loss. The carpenter, who was one of the most gloomy of the ship's company, appears to have been a good craftsman, for before he died in the early spring, most of the work on the pinnace had already been done. They buried the carpenter on a little eminence near the camp, which later on they named Brandon Hill, and before James and his men finally sailed away, other Bristol sailors had been laid beside him.

In May James set to work to free the ship from ice and to patch up the holes which he had made in her hull the previous autumn. This was completely successful, for, after much labour, to their great joy the *Henrietta Maria* was afloat again, apparently little the worse for the unusual dock in which she had lain all the winter. The crew were still further encouraged by the discovery that the beer, wine, provisions and clothing, which had been in ice for six months, were still in good condition. Then followed the long and arduous task of refitting the ship, mending the sails, which had been used as a roof during the winter, and getting the ship ready for sea.

This was an unpleasant time for James and the crew, for several of the men died, the sick men were slow in recovering, various delays occurred, a forest fire was started, and that pest of the wilderness, the mosquito, greatly afflicted these English

---

[1] *The Voyages of Captain Luke Foxe and Captain Thomas James*, vol. II, p. 544.

sojourners in the North. At last, in spite of all, the ship was ready, and they were able to bid farewell to Charlton Island and set out once more on their search. James sailed generally in a northerly direction along the western shores of James Bay and Hudson Bay. His intention was to search north-west of Nottingham Island for a passage out to the westward, which both he and Foxe had failed to find in the previous year. But when he reached 65° 30" north latitude, the *Henrietta Maria* became completely enclosed in ice, and it was quite impossible to proceed further.

"This strooke us all into a dumpe, whereuppon I called a consultation of my Associates . . . requiring them to advise and counsell mee how to prosecute our business to effect."[1]

They gave him seven reasons in writing for returning home; the cold and storms of winter were coming on, and the sea was already covered with "rands and ranges" of ice; if they delayed their return much longer they would never be able to pass Hudson's Strait; the ship was leaking and quite unfit to face another winter.

"Besides all this, our men grow very weak and sickly with extreme labour."

Lastly, the ice ahead of them was so thick that further progress was impossible,

"wherefore we here counsell you to return homeward hoping that God will give us a favourable passage, and returne us home safe into our native countreys, if we take time and not tempt him too farre by our wilfulnesse."

As James himself agreed with these reasons he decided to act on their advice,

"wherefore (with a sorrowfull heart, God knowes) I consented that the helme should be borne up and a course shapte for *England*, well hoping that his Maiestie would graciously censure of my endeauours and pardon my returne."[2]

On 3rd September they passed Resolution Island and on

[1] *The Voyages of Captain Luke Foxe and Captain Thomas James*, vol. II, p. 584.
[2] *Ibid.*, p. 585.

22nd October, 1632, after an absence of over seventeen months, the *Henrietta Maria* dropped anchor in Bristol.

Though this voyage did not add a great deal to existing geographical knowledge, James and his men, nevertheless, performed a very notable feat of seamanship and courage. He must have been not only a remarkable navigator but a leader of conspicuous quality. He and his men were among the first Englishmen ever to winter successfully in the Far North in a region which was subsequently to become familiar to successive generations of their countrymen, and he not only wintered in the North but he brought his ship home again in safety. His account of his voyage has been much criticized for being highly coloured, and undoubtedly he does emphasize the dangers and privations which were encountered, but this is merely another way of saying that James, unlike Foxe and many other Arctic explorers since his time, knew how to write. His story is a vivid record of northern exploration in that age, which cannot fail to stir anyone possessed of imagination. There is a tradition that Coleridge in his *Ancient Mariner* was influenced by James's story. Indeed, Ivor James attempted to prove in his book *The Source of the Ancient Mariner* that this voyage is the chief, if not the only, source of that poem. Though this writer fails completely to establish his case, J. L. Lowes in his work, *The Road to Xanadu*, shows that Coleridge had almost certainly read James's work and that, among other records of travel in the Far North, his imagination had been stimulated by the descriptive writing of this great Bristol captain. Certainly it is known that when Coleridge was a subscriber to the Bristol library, accounts of James's voyage were available there, and the verses quoted at the beginning of this chapter are reminiscent of phrases which occur in *The Strange and Dangerous Voyage* written by James himself.

Because James wintered in the North while Foxe returned home, the latter received much less credit than he deserved from his contemporaries, who were impressed by James's hardihood in facing the rigours of a Polar winter. The editor of the Hakluyt Society's volume containing the voyages of Foxe and James, however, in trying to do justice to Foxe, has erred in the other direction. Supercilious detraction of James, and sneers about the meagreness of his work, do nothing to enhance the reputation of Foxe. The fact is they were both bold and able navigators who, each in his own way, faced unknown problems in the manner which has become traditional with English sailors. Each of them added yet another chapter to the already long record of English tenacity in northern exploration.

On his return James was received at Court, and for a short time was a popular idol. In those troubled times, when Charles I had Parliament by the throat, Englishmen were more concerned with political and religious liberty than with northern travel. Little is known of James's subsequent life except that he joined the Navy. After two years service, in which he earned the approval of the Lord Deputy of Ireland, Lord Strafford, James died in 1635. Henceforward, Bristol merchants confined their attention to more practical activities, and left Polar exploration to men who loved the work for its own sake and not for the economic reward which it might bring. When, after the Restoration, the foundation of the Hudson Bay Company was mooted, Prince Rupert and his friends turned once more to the books of James and Foxe, but as the merchants of Bristol had nothing to do with this venture, it lies outside the scope of the present work.

CHAPTER VII

QUAKERS AND PRIVATEERS

"I make no doubt, it will be to your lasting Honour, that such a Voyage was undertaken from Bristol at your Expence; since it has given the Publick a sufficient Evidence of what may be done in those Parts. . . ."

WOODES ROGERS,

(Dedication to *A Cruising Voyage Round the World*. 1712.)

BEYOND her connection with the foundation of various New England colonies, Bristol took little direct part in the establishment of plantations in the first half of the seventeenth century. Gorges's association with the Virginia and Somers Islands Companies arose directly from his position in London and had nothing to do with Bristol. As will be seen in the next chapter, many people sailed from that port at this time, but they went as individuals without any corporate support from the city, and few of them were leaders.

It is a curious feature of this early history of colonial development that the city took little or no interest in the West Indian islands. All her thoughts and efforts were directed to the North. She concerned herself with the search for the North-East and North-West Passages, with the development of the northern fisheries and the colonization of Newfoundland, Maine and Massachusetts. Yet half a century later, the bulk of her colonial connection was with the South: Maryland, Virginia, the Carolinas and the Sugar Islands. It was as a great tobacco and sugar port that Bristol became famous throughout the world, and it was upon trade in these two commodities in particular that the fortunes of her merchant princes were reared. Yet, as will be seen later, although her northern trade was eclipsed by her prodigious traffic in sugar, tobacco and other semi-tropical commodities, and by the slave-trade, it was always important.

After the events connected with the New England Company and the gallant failure of James to discover a North-West Passage to the Far East, the next association of Bristol with the expansion of the Empire was almost accidental. It served, however, to introduce another Bristol family into imperial history, whose members were destined to play a conspicuous part in the foundation and early history of a famous English colony in the New World. The Penns were a Bristol family, closely connected, as were all important merchants of the time, with the sea. So it was that the future Admiral, William Penn, learned his craft on board his father's ship. During the Civil War he won distinction in the Navy, and later was immortalized in the diary of his young colleague of the Naval Board, Samuel Pepys. The elder Penn was one of the best Admirals of the first Dutch War and was associated with Venables in the capture of Jamaica. This triumph, which was regarded by those responsible as an inadequate substitute for their failure to capture Hispaniola, turned out to be of first-rate importance to England's position in the Caribbean. Jamaica was to become not only the premier English sugar island, but she possessed the safest and most easily defended harbour in the British colonies in that part of the world, and by her geographical situation was well placed for the development of trade, both open and secret, with the Spanish, Dutch, French and other colonies. Moreover, in the eighteenth century, Jamaica became the centre of the English slave trade in the West Indies. Negroes were brought there direct from Africa and from thence distributed to the colonies of many nations. But when Penn and Venables swooped down on the island, its capture meant for them mainly a successful blow struck by the Protestants of England at the ancient enemy. Penn, who was on board the *Naseby* when she brought Charles II back to his people, was knighted by the King. Later, thanks to his friendship with Charles, he became a Commissioner of the Navy. He served in the second Dutch War, but died soon afterwards, and at his own request was buried in St. Mary Redcliffe Church, Bristol. He was one of the most famous seamen born in Bristol and is one of the most neglected.

His eminent son was not by natural inclination drawn to the rôle of Empire builder. Indeed, his first connection with colonial problems was almost accidental. A quarrel broke out between two owners of land in New Jersey, and William Penn was chosen by them to adjudicate in the dispute. A few years later, when it became clear that his experiment in freedom was certain to fail, he decided to make a second trial of his ideas in some new land where ancient tradition, prejudice and intolerance would be unknown, and where, amid new surroundings, men might begin a new way of life. Penn's father was one of many to whom Charles II owed money, a debt which the King never paid. His son offered to accept in lieu of the money a stretch of unoccupied land lying backwards towards the west beyond the Delaware, where he proposed to found a new colony for the people of all nations. In a letter dated 5th March, 1681, Penn reported to a friend how the name had been found for the proposed plantation:—

"5th of 1st mo., 1681.

"Dear Friend,

". . . after many waitings, watchings, solicitings, and disputes in council, this day my country was confirmed to me under the great seal of England, with large powers and privileges, by the name of Pennsylvania; a *name the King would give it* in honour of my father. I chose New Wales, being, as this, a pretty hilly country. . . . I proposed, when the Secretary, a Welshman, refused to have it called New Wales, *Sylvania*, and they added *Penn* to it, and though I was much opposed to it, and went to the King to have it struck out and altered, he said it was past, and would take it upon him; nor could twenty guineas move the under-secretary to vary the name; for I feared lest it should be looked upon as a vanity in me, and not as a respect in the King, as it truly was, to my father, whom he often mentions with praise. . . .

"Thy true friend,

"WM. PENN." [1]

The Quakers of Bristol were deeply interested in Penn's schemes, and a number of them became members of the Free Society of Traders in Pennsylvania, usually referred to at that time as "The Pennsylvania Company." This was a joint stock undertaking, having 200 members drawn from England, Wales and Ireland. The subscribers invested £10,000, and were promised trading facilities in the new province and the allotment of 20,000 acres of land. The objects of this body were to send out servants, build houses, to establish a glass manufactory for the production of bottles, drinking glasses and window glass, to supply America with wheat, meat and other agricultural products from its estate, to manufacture wine, oil, linen and hemp, and to extract from the earth iron, lead and other minerals. This Company, whose offices were established in Philadelphia,

---

[1] Dobreé, B., *William Penn, Quaker and Pioneer*, pp. 147–8.

"*Captain Rogers's People stripping some Ladies of their Jewels in the Neighbourhood of Guayaquil*"

View of Nevis from St. Kitts (N. Pocock)
From a painting in the possession of R. W. Pretor Pinney

had a very chequered career. It suffered from a conspicuous lack of money in the province, its servants were both inefficient and dishonest, and it was violently opposed by many on the grounds of its assumed monopolistic rights. As its trading activities proved a complete failure, the Company devoted its attentions solely to the improvements of its estate. But even in this it failed, and its affairs were finally wound up in 1723.

The new Company started out with great energy and its Bristol members were particularly prominent. Penn and his friends hoped that many woollen-cloth manufacturers of the Bristol and Stroud districts would be encouraged to emigrate to his province. By the autumn of 1681 the expeditious Quakers of Bristol were able to despatch their first ship, the *Bristol Factor*, from the Avon. She arrived in Pennsylvania before the founder himself, and Nicholas Ford, chairman of the Bristol section of the Company, who was a lawyer by profession, was subsequently elected first speaker of the first General Assembly of Pennsylvania. From the beginning, Penn himself took up a determined position on the subject of monopolies, which he repudiated in any form, both as regards his own rights and those of others. In this, as in his relations with the Indians, he showed himself to be a man of wide vision, and his care of the aborigines, in particular, proved that his Christian principles meant something more to him than empty phrases to which lip-homage must be paid. Other Bristolians, who were not members of the Free Society, took land in Pennsylvania. On 27th September, 1681, Penn sold a block of 5,000 acres to a group which included Arnold Browne and William Cole of Bristol, and Ayliff Green of Clifton, for the sum of £100. In addition to the £100 paid down, the purchasers were to pay Penn one shilling per year for each hundred acres as quit rent or £2 10s. for the block. Penn undertook that they would have peaceful and quiet possession of their land, that the Indians would make no claim to it, and that as soon as a public register of lands was settled in the province, all documents relating to this transfer would be placed with him for safe-keeping.

Though Penn might transfer land in Pennsylvania to others and give them every guarantee of security that was in his power, he did not receive the same consideration from the English Government. In post-revolutionary England there was much opposition to the system of proprietary colonies, and Penn, though a Quaker, was suspect by orthodox Parliamentarians because of his known friendship with Charles II and, still worse, with James II. Thus, by Order-in-Council of 1692, it was proposed to take his government away from him and place it in commission, as a preliminary step to joining Pennsylvania with New York. Penn petitioned against this breach of faith. If the Council's decisions were acted upon it would mean for him the loss of all the money which he had personally invested in the province. In order to silence his critics who attacked him because of his pacifist principles, he undertook to provide an adequate defence system for Pennsylvania, and so, for the moment, the proposal was dropped. He still had his opponents in England to contend with, however, and a discontented minority in Pennsylvania, in addition to a fraudulent agent who was shortly to cause him much anxiety and loss. In the 'nineties he busied himself with plans for the development of his colony, and for this purpose returned to England in 1695. In the following year a paper written by him was laid before the House of Lords. This dealt with the economic potentialities of the colonies, and various ways in which their resources might be developed for the good of the Mother Country.

Penn believed that with proper guidance and encouragement the colonies could produce many commodities then imported from foreign countries, and, in particular, he considered this to be true of naval stores. At that time the authorities were gravely concerned with the almost complete dependence of England upon the Baltic for pitch, tar, deals, hemp, masts and other naval stores. Penn contended that New England could produce all these commodities in great quantities and, with proper care, not inferior in quality. Turning to other articles, he pointed out that excellent wine had already been produced by Germans and French as far north as Narragansett County in Rhode Island and Charles II had worn silk produced in Virginia. Oils, fruits, gums, drugs and potashes could be supplied in abundance by the colonies, but if these developments were to take place, more labour was required. Moreover, the Home Government should not cripple these colonial industries by crushing duties. The father of the Quakers believed that more discipline among the people was also necessary, and that the open frauds then general in the tobacco colonies should be sternly suppressed. He supported these suggestions by practical indications as to how they might be carried through. In order that the affairs of the continental colonies should be uniformly dealt with, and so that the problems which were common to them all might be solved for all by a united effort, he ended this remarkable document by making the recommendation that an annual representative meeting of all the colonies should take place, whose purpose would be the adjustment of all matters to a common benefit.

These far-reaching proposals were too broadly conceived for the limited intelligences of the men who, at that time, directed the destinies of England's colonial empire. Many of them were ignored, and some, at least, of the questions to which Penn referred in his memorandum remained unconsidered and unanswered down to the time of the American Revolution. The English Government, however, in the first decades of the eighteenth century, did turn its attention seriously to one question raised by Penn. In spite of the unfavourable attitude of the Navy, which was devoted to Scandinavian and Russian products, strenuous efforts were made to encourage the production of naval stores in the colonies. Several acts of Parliament were passed under which various bounties were offered, but nothing of very great importance was achieved. In time the colonies were conscious only of the various restrictions placed upon their freedom, which were usually a feature of these measures, and so their activities turned more in the direction of building ships for themselves.

It was while he was in England between 1695 and 1699 that Penn paid his longest visit to Bristol, where he married his second wife, Hannah Callowhill, in 1696. He remained in Bristol for over two years, after which he sailed for Pennsylvania. He was soon called home to England, however, on account of trouble which began to threaten him from two quarters. Once more the Government was concerning itself with the rights and privileges of colonial proprietors, and in addition to this public difficulty, his private finances required immediate attention.

The Committee of Trade and Plantations, which had been set up in 1696, still mastered by the spirit of novelty, felt called upon to put the colonial house in order. Among other things it tried to induce all the colonial proprietors to surrender their rights to the Crown, and Penn was asked to state the conditions upon which he would be prepared to relinquish his authority in Pennsylvania. In reply, he demanded that the government and territories of Pennsylvania should, under the Crown, still continue to be administered as a separate province, and that all the laws so far made in Pennsylvania, except those to which he himself had objected, should be confirmed. He demanded also that the patent of the three lower counties of Newcastle, Kent and Sussex, which James II had promised to him, but which had not been completed owing to that King's abdication, should now be confirmed, and that the state should make him a payment of £30,000, together with a duty of one halfpenny per pound upon the tobacco in the country, and in addition, the

"sum or sums the people shall give and grant the governor for the time being for his salary by my assistance." [1]

Penn held that he was justified in making these demands for a number of reasons. The first expedition to Pennsylvania had cost him £10,500 and the subsequent government of the country twice as much. He had purchased the land from the Indians, and the revenue derived from the government of the country was the only substantial recompense he had ever received from the Crown, and

"from henceforward my shop windows will be shut down and my market over." [2]

The required surrender would prevent him from paying back the heavy debts which his connection with Pennsylvania had

[1] Stock, op. cit., vol. III, p. 17.
[2] Ibid., p. 16.

compelled him to incur. His separation from the province would undoubtedly lead to a fall in values in Pennsylvania, just as his last arrival there had caused them to rise by fifty per cent. Since he had been to the province the last time, the revenue to the Queen from customs alone, derived from goods brought into England from Pennsylvania, had risen from £1,500 to £10,000 per annum. The commissioners considered these proposals to be wholly unreasonable; they held that Penn merely proposed to relinquish the shadow while demanding that the substantial advantages should be largely increased, and so the matter ended.

More serious to Penn than the excessive zeal of a new Government committee was the chaotic state of his own private fortunes. For over thirty years he had entrusted the care of his business to a Quaker lawyer, Philip Ford. Penn was careless in financial matters that concerned himself personally, and so Ford was given ample opportunities for fraud, which he used to the full. Being in need of money on the eve of his departure for Pennsylvania in 1699, the Quaker leader borrowed £2,800, and at Ford's request, signed a document which he understood to be a mortgage, but which, in fact, was a deed of sale of his property. Ford died in 1702, but his widow and son, who were well-qualified by nature and training to carry on the practices of the deceased steward, presented Penn with a bill for the staggering sum of £14,000. This was made up of various charges at compound interest, reckoned at short periods, enormous commissions and unreasonable costs. Although Penn had in his possession documents which clearly proved the illegal nature of this transaction, it afterwards transpired that he had not taken the trouble to open the parcel which contained them. In view of this laxity, his Bristol father-in-law's complaint of "his easiness and want of caution" appears to be justified.

Penn at first refused to pay the Fords, and the dispute lingered on for several years. At last, counting on his conspicuous lack of business capacity, they brought the case into court. In this they were aided and abetted by the discontented group who opposed him in Pennsylvania. Penn lost the Chancery suit against him in May, 1707, and the Common Law case in November, but, on the advice of his friends, he still refused to pay, and in consequence found himself in prison in the Old Bailey. Flushed with these successes, the enterprising Fords petitioned the Queen to be recognized as Governor Philip and Governess Bridget of Pennsylvania, but this was too much. The Quaker leader's friends, both in England and America, rallied to his support, and the Fords learned that the Lord Chancellor had made some significant remarks upon their behaviour. This determined them to compromise, and they intimated that they were ready to accept £7,000, a sum which Penn was willing to pay. In a letter from prison written on 28th September, he said:

"I earnestly beseech you to assist James Logan and who else the trustees for the payment of the money advanced here shall nominate, not only to get in, but to turn into money the best you are able, that I may come honourably to you and speedily."

Three months later he was free again, and on 29th December wrote that the Fords were paid and the country redeemed. The necessary sum was raised by a number of London and Bristol Friends, including his father-in-law, Thomas Callowhill, to whom, on 6th October, he had conveyed his lands for the space of one year by a new deed of sale. "I granted my friends a fresh mortgage without naming that base family therein." It appears from a covenant signed on 7th October, 1713, that the total loan amounted to £6,600, of which a number of Bristol Friends, acting through three trustees, contributed £1,500. So that although one Quaker was the villain of the piece, the Bristol Friends played the more gracious rôle of guardian angels.

James Logan, who became Penn's secretary at the time of his second marriage, spent many years in Bristol. While in that city Logan studied foreign languages and mathematics, and assisted his father in teaching. Between 1694 and 1699 he taught in the upper storey of the Friends' Meeting House at Bristol, and there he met Penn, who invited him to go as his secretary to Pennsylvania. In that province Logan, who was one of the few highly-educated men there, at once took a leading part in politics. In the course of his long life he became the trusted secretary and agent of the Penn family, a trust which he never betrayed. Indeed, he was one of the trustees of Penn's will. He was Secretary of the Council, Mayor of Philadelphia, Chief Justice of the Province, and for some time acting Lieutenant-Governor. For over fifty years, in fact, he was a dominating figure in the affairs of the province. His son, William, who was sent to England to be educated, and placed under the care of his uncle, Dr. William Logan of Bristol, Physician at the Infirmary, became in turn member of the Council of Pennsylvania, and succeeded his father as administrator of the Penn estates.

But the Society of Friends in Bristol were not concerned solely with the affairs of the founder of the Quaker province. They were also troubled from time to time by the behaviour of their own members, some of whom went out to Pennsylvania in the course of trade. Once freed from the restrictions of home, and with the Atlantic between them and the old restraints, some young Quakers did not show the kind of conduct which was to be expected from men of their profession. Complaints of their irregularities were sent home to Bristol, where they were considered at the Men's Meeting.

"'Tis desired for the tyme to Come such freinds as goe over on yt. Accot. may be aduized to Carry Certificates of their Conuersations and behauiours, that freinds there May then haue an opertunity to Exhort and Warn them. And that such persons be recomended to Some faithfull freinds in those forreign parts who may admonish and deale with such as shall take any Euill courses wch. brings a reflection on the Metings of freinds there."[1]

Besides disciplinary resolution of this sort, the Society at Bristol made grants from time to time for the clothing of young Friends who were proceeding as apprentices on their first voyage to the West Indies. On 4th September, 1693,

"Margret Harford requested this meeting to assist her to sett out her sonn with som Clothes & Nessesarys she not being able to provide for him. there being now a Master of a shipp yt. Edw. Hacket haue procured to take him with him for one

---

[1] *Minutes of the "Men's Meeting," 11th, 1st month, 1699–1700.*

voiage to the West Indias. Charles Harford & Abr. Lloyd are desired to Inspect the occation & as they shall find meet to suply him with 20 or 30/– wch shalbe reimburst to them out of our publick stock." [1]

Four months later, on 21st January, 1694-5,

"Ch: Jones is ordered by this meeting to dilliuer to Margt. Harford thurty shillings to help cloth & nessesarys for her Son Michael now goeing prentice to Thomas Tandy Mr. of the shipp Warcesters delight." [2]

In that turbulent period, however, a more constant and serious subject of discussion among them was that of the participation of Friends in war. Many members of the Society were concerned in overseas commerce, and in time of war they were liable to and frequently suffered heavy losses. This impelled some of them to arm their vessels, which was bad enough, but in flagrant defiance of the Society's rules a few of them actually equipped ships specifically to prey upon the enemy as privateers. This was a practice which the Friends, under no conditions, would countenance. Thus, for example, in the War of the American Revolution, one Quaker, Christopher Moore of Bristol, was disowned because he

"did . . . take upon him the command of an armed vessel provided with a letter of Marque." [3]

Again, George Champion was disowned because he

"is concerned in ships or vessels, fitted out with Letters of marque in a warlike manner, contrary to the known rules established amongst us." [4]

Privateering was particularly obnoxious to the Friends, for it meant war conducted for private profit. War at any time was abominable, but war carried on as a trade seemed to them to be on a par with the profession of a hired assassin.

Long before the American Revolution, this subject had

[1] *Minutes of the "Men's Meeting,"* 4th of ye 7th mo. 1693.
[2] *Ibid.,* 21st, 11th month, 1694.
[3] *Ibid.,* 1779.
[4] *Ibid.,* 1782.

become a serious matter of consideration among the Bristol
Quakers. At the beginning of the eighteenth century, privateering, which had languished for some time, again became profitable. The outbreak of the Spanish Succession War brought
with it a change in public policy on this subject. In January,
1702, a royal proclamation announced that in future the whole
proceeds of captured prizes, except for Customs House charges
and a quit charge of one-tenth claimed by the Crown, were to
go to the owners and crew of the successful attacker. In spite
of this stimulus, Bristol commerce was seriously impeded by
enemy ships, and some merchants in the Newfoundland and
other colonial trades suffered great losses. It was these two facts
of Government encouragement and substantial loss through
enemy attack, that induced Woodes Rogers to organize and
command what was one of the greatest privateering exploits of
maritime history.

Woodes Rogers's story reads more like the exploit of an
Elizabethan than that of an eighteenth-century mariner. His
character and personal endowments, in fact, were precisely
what are looked for in the contemporaries of Raleigh and Hawkins. Ever since the days of Drake, the South Pacific had been
looked upon by Englishmen as a place of fabulous wealth.
Great, rich and undefended cities were there, beckoning the
enterprising adventurer to come and possess. In addition to
all this, the expedition organized by Woodes Rogers and his
Bristol friends was encouraged by the recent success of two
French ships which made the voyage to the Pacific in 1698. It
would be wrong, however, to think of these Bristolians merely
as pirates. The mind of England's traders was already turning
in the direction of trade with the South Sea before Woodes
Rogers sailed. The South Sea Company, which to-day is chiefly
remembered in connection with one of the greatest periods of
stock gambling in the history of the country, culminating in a
financial disaster of the first magnitude, was in its original design
a genuine, business undertaking.

In Bristol, as elsewhere, the trading possibilities of the South
Sea were much discussed, and in part, at least, the voyage of
Woodes Rogers was the outcome of this newly awakened interest

in a hitherto little known part of the world. In principle, it was the same spirit which had led the Wynter family to invest so much money in Drake's voyage, for the Bristol merchants of the early eighteenth century were as enterprising and keen for the expansion of their trade as their forbears had been a century and a quarter before. A group of the most important merchants of Bristol supported Woodes Rogers's design. Though he was not a native of the city, he was well-established and influential. Even the quiet waters of Quaker life were for some time disturbed by the preparations for this undertaking. It promised well, and at least one member of the Society of Friends was ready to join the group of promoters. Everyone knew that although there was in the mind of Woodes Rogers the idea of establishing new trades with the lands and islands of the South Sea, the expedition was to be mainly a privateering raid carried out on a large scale.

So it came about that at the Men's Meeting on 28th April, 1708, a report was considered which referred to some members of the Society of Friends who were concerned

"as owners of and some as saylers in a Ship or Ships design'd for a voyage into ye South seas and carrying commission to ffight and force." [1]

Two members were appointed to look more closely into this grave matter and

"give such advice as they shall see needfull for ye good of those persons supposed to be concern'd in it, and ye clearing the profession from the Imputation of such practices." [1]

On 26th May the same subject came up again, and once more on 27th October. On this latter occasion, it was reported that on further enquiries which they had made during the summer, the investigators could not find

"that there is any ffriend Concerned in either of ye shipps (nor any son upon said shipps)—saveing T: G (probably Thomas Goldney, grocer) who is now in prison." [2]

---

[1] Minutes of the "Men's Meeting," 28th, 2nd month, 1708.
[2] Ibid., 27th, 8th month, 1708.

In his dedication to his book, *A Cruising Voyage Round the World*, Woodes Rogers refers to those worthy gentlemen "my surviving Owners," and in a list of sixteen Bristol merchants and others, he includes Thomas Goldney. In this list appear Sir John Hawkins, Kt., Mayor of Bristol in 1701; James Hollidge, Mayor in 1709; Christopher Shuter, Mayor in 1711; Captain Freake and Thomas Clements, Sheriffs of Bristol, and John Rumsey, Town Clerk. In spite of this breach of discipline, Thomas Goldney afterwards became a leading Bristol Quaker, and an outstanding figure of his time. A century later, Rogers's original log-book was in the possession of Gabriel Goldney, which seems to 'suggest that Thomas was not merely one, but a leading member, of the group which promoted the exploit.

It was characteristic of the merchants of Bristol that, having taken the organization of a privateering venture in hand, they should see that it was well done. They were determined that if the expedition was to sail, it should only be allowed to do so after everything possible had been done in the equipment and personnel to ensure its success. It was better to make a substantial initial outlay to ensure a reasonable reward than to jeopardize the whole undertaking by cheese-paring economies. Two well-armed ships were, therefore, got ready and furnished with everything necessary for a long and dangerous voyage. Woodes Rogers himself took command of the *Duke*, with Thomas Dover as second captain, and the famous William Dampier, who had already been in the South Pacific, as pilot. The *Duke* was a ship of 320 tons burden, carrying 30 guns and 117 men. Her consort, the *Duchess*, 260 tons, was commanded by Captain Stephen Courtney, and carried 26 guns and 108 men. Both vessels were thus provided with larger crews than was usual for ships of their size. It was hoped that prizes would be captured, which could be manned without materially lessening the fighting efficiency of the *Duke* or the *Duchess*.

Woodes Rogers and his companions set sail from Kingroad on 1st August, 1708. They first touched at Cork, where they remained some time, during which Woodes Rogers complained the crew "were continually marrying." But the captain had no intention of wasting too much time on such frivolities, and the fond husbands were compelled to accept a speedy separation from their lamenting wives. On 1st September they weighed anchor for the Canaries. With all the discomforts of over-crowded ships, the question of discipline was certain to become critical unless the commander showed himself to be a man of firm and determined character. Many of the rank and file among his sailors were not inclined to draw too nice a distinction be-tween privateering and piracy. So when Rogers, having sub-jected a neutral ship to search, allowed her to resume her course unmolested, he was confronted with a mutiny. His companions regarded this observance of the law of nations as mere chicken-hearted squeamishness, which proved to them that their com-mander was unfitted for his post. In this, however, they soon learned their mistake, for Woodes Rogers was not the man to be unnerved by any such spirit of insubordination. The mutiny was crushed, and the ringleaders were placed in irons until they humbly asked to be reinstated, and undertook to behave them-selves for the future. Indeed, though there is only his own story to go upon, it is clear that Woodes Rogers soon won the con-fidence and loyal support of all his men. This seems to be borne out by the astounding success of this long and dangerous voyage.

On their way to Cape Horn, they visited the island of Grande, off the Coast of Brazil, where they were handsomely entertained by the Portuguese and even took part in a religious procession, the ship's band providing the music. Before the Englishmen left, the Portuguese

"propos'd the Pope's Health to us; but we were quits with 'em, by toasting that of the Archbishop of *Canterbury;* to keep up the Humour, we also propos'd *William Pen's* to them; and they lik'd the Liquor so well, that they refus'd neither." [1]

In rounding the Cape, they were driven very far to the south, so that many men fell ill, and it was decided to make for Juan

---

[1] Woodes Rogers, *A Cruising Voyage Round the World*, p. 32.

Fernandez in order that they might go ashore to recover. It was here that Rogers picked up Alexander Selkirk who had been marooned there for four years. There is an unsubstantiated tradition that, on their return to Bristol, Selkirk met Daniel Defoe at the house of Mrs. Daniels in St. James's Square. There he is said to have recounted his story to the "Sunday Gentleman," as Defoe was at one time called in Bristol. He received this appellation because he was pursued by his creditors, and if he was to avoid prison he could only appear on Sundays. While it is doubtful if, in fact, Defoe ever met Selkirk at all, he was unquestionably familiar with his story. Selkirk's adventures caused a sensation in London on Woodes Rogers's return, and Steele, who had interviewed the marooned mariner, wrote an account of his adventures which appeared in *The Englishman*, December, 1713. Defoe was also familiar with Woodes Rogers's book which described the discovery of Selkirk on the island and with Captain Edward Cooke's *Voyage to the South Sea*, published in 1712, as well as with Dampier's *New Voyage Round the World*, a sixth edition of which appeared in 1717. On the basis of this and a vast amount of other reading of accounts of shipwrecks and of books of travel and adventure, Defoe wrote *Robinson Crusoe*, which first appeared in 1719.

Leaving Juan Fernandez, the ships sailed northward, and while waiting for enemy galleons from Manila the shipping of Chile, Peru and Ecuador began to suffer from Roger's attentions. A number of prizes was taken; Spanish settlements were occupied and plundered; wealthy prisoners were held for ransom; and a vast quantity of booty was placed aboard the *Duke* and *Duchess* as well as the two captured ships that now sailed with them. The most important triumph of this expedition, however, was the capture of the rich city of Guayaquil. Rogers and his men held this place for several days. Rogers relates that

"the Houses up the River were full of Women, and particularly at one place there were above a Dozen handsom genteel young Women well dress'd, where our Men got several Gold Chains and Ear-rings, but were otherwise so civil to them, that the Ladies offer'd to dress 'em victuals, and brought 'em a cask of good Liquor. Some of their largest Gold Chains were conceal'd, and wound about their Middles, Legs and Thighs, &c. but the Gentlewomen in these hot countries being very thin clad . . . our Men by pressing felt the Chains, &c. with their Hands on the Out-side of the Lady's Apparel, and by their Linguist modestly desired the Gentlewomen to take 'em off and surrender 'em." [1]

After a long series of successes, much greater than the promoters of the expedition could have expected, even in their most optimistic post-prandial enthusiasm, the four ships, heavily laden with their booty, left the Californian coast for the Island of Guam, one of the Ladrones, on the first section of their return passage to England.

This place was reached on 11th March, and after ten days they left again for the Moluccas, Batavia and the Cape of Good Hope, which they reached on 28th December. On 17th October, 1711, they arrived at the Downs, and on the 14th, finally dropped anchor at Erith. So was brought to a successful end one of the most famous of all the privateering expeditions that ever set sail from England. If the promoters had been able to appropriate the whole of the booty, the venture would have been a splendid investment, as the loot was valued originally at £170,000. Unfortunately for them, the East India Company laid claim to £6,000 for infringement of their monopoly, which led to a long suit in Chancery. At length, the plunder was re-valued at £147,000, but when the crews had been paid and the expenses met, only £40,000 remained for the promoters, and it is said that Woodes Rogers received for his brilliant exploit a paltry £1,500, instead of the £14,000 which he had originally expected.

This exploit of Woodes Rogers forms a fitting finale to the history of Bristol's activity in exploration and privateering. It would, however, be unjust to the memory of that daring leader to think of his voyage merely as one more, and perhaps the greatest, of all the raids carried out by Englishmen against their traditional enemy. It had a serious trading purpose behind it, and the commander himself, when he first proposed the scheme,

[1] Woodes Rogers, *op. cit.*, p. 131.

stressed its mercantile aspect. In the introduction to his book he indicates the nature of the trade with the South Sea which he hoped would result from his voyage. He may justly be regarded, therefore, as an early pioneer of England's commerce in the Pacific, and, in addition, in the course of his published account he strongly advocated the fostering of British trade with the Plate, in which again he was far in advance of his time.

Rogers lived for a short time in Bristol in enjoyment of great credit among his fellow-citizens, but three years of privateering, which had carried him to the end of the earth and back, rendered the peaceful life of an ordinary citizen irksome to him. So he was soon at sea again, and prior to 1717, the best known of his exploits is an expedition to Madagascar, which he undertook in order to collect slaves in that island for sale in Batavia. Finally, in 1717, he became prominent once more. English commerce in the West Indies was at that time suffering grievously from pirates, whose chief base was in the Bahamas. On 30th May, 1717, the Commissioners of Trade and Plantations received a petition from several citizens of Bristol on this subject. The petition was supported by various merchants, who also gave evidence before the Board, and who, on being asked what they might have to propose for the suppression of the pirates, and for the security of the trade of His Majesty's subjects in America, gave their opinions. They believed that though the pirates might easily be suppressed, they would not be effectually prevented for the future unless a permanent settlement was made at Providence. These islands, by their situation, were admirably suited for a base of piratical attack, as they were on the direct trade route between the West Indies and England. They made convenient hiding-places, since the shoal waters which surrounded them made it impossible for men-of-war to be of any use.

In spite of their favourable reception of this petition, the Commissioners appear to have taken no further action but, as the situation was steadily growing more serious, it was decided to approach the King. Woodes Rogers, who was consulted on the subject by some of his Bristol friends, put forward specific proposals which he believed would solve the problem. He contended that as the Lords Proprietors of the Bahamas had not shown themselves able to govern effectively, they should be left in possession of their property-rights, but that the government should be taken over by the Crown. A ship should at once be sent to the Bahamas to re-establish order, and he announced his readiness to accept the position of governor. A petition, signed by George Adams and seventy-eight other merchants of Bristol, was sent to George I. This referred to the "fatal consequences" which would arise

"if either the French, Spaniards or pirates should make a settlement in the Bahamas," [1]

and ended by praying for the acceptance of Woodes Rogers's proposals.

No man in England was better fitted for suppressing the pirates than the most renowned privateer of the age, and so he gladly accepted the post of Governor of the Bahamas, which carried with it full powers to deal with the free-booters who infested these islands and who were causing great dislocation to the commerce of the West Indies. At his new post, in spite of the veiled hostility of the naval officers on the West Indian station and the grudging help which he received from home, Woodes Rogers carried through his work with success. The pirates were scattered, their bases destroyed, and in 1721, now thoroughly identified with the interests of the colony which he governed, he returned to England for more assistance. This was slow in coming, however, and he was kept at home for many years, vainly hoping for the Government to act. Thus, he did not return to his charge until 1728, and he died at Providence four years later.

Woodes Rogers seems to have been a man born out of his time, for he must have had little in common with the placemen and parasites who were already clogging the working of the colonial system. Like the great Elizabethans whom he so much resembled, he was a man of wide capability and of great strength

---

[1] *Calendar of State Papers (America and West Indies)*, 1716–7, p. 347.

of character. Successful merchant, supremely competent commander at sea, efficient and devoted Governor, he might well have been a contemporary of Drake, Hawkins or Raleigh, and not, as he seems to have been, a friend of Defoe and Addison, for he was a strange figure in the eighteenth century among all the artificialities of the Augustan Age.

CHAPTER VIII

EMIGRANTS, FREE AND FORCED

"... rather than fail, they trade in men; as when they sent small rogues taught to pray, and who according received, actual transportation, even before any indictment found amongst them; for which my Lord Jeffries scoured them."

ROGER NORTH, *Lives of the Norths.*

DOWN to the middle of the seventeenth century, public opinion in England was generally favourable to emigration. In the Elizabethan and pre-civil war period, many writers recommended the establishment of colonies as a means whereby the country's problem of over-population might be solved. About the middle of the seventeenth century a complete change of public opinion on this subject occurred. For over one hundred and fifty years after that, emigration was looked upon as a potential source of national weakness. Still, the colonies had somehow to be peopled adequately in order that the Mother Country might benefit to the full from their economic potentialities.

In the later decades of the seventeenth century and throughout the eighteenth, a few free settlers from England continued to find their way to the plantations: Quakers and other Dissenters in the earlier period, distressed Irish and Scottish peasants in the later. In the main, however, the problem of populating the colonies was solved in other ways. Foreign Protestants fleeing from persecution, such as the Huguenots and the Moravians, were encouraged to seek an asylum in the English plantations. Batches of condemned felons were permitted to exchange death on the gallows for life as indentured servants in the colonies. Most important of all, hundreds of thousands of hapless negroes were torn from their homes and carried to a life of slavery in the Caribbean and mainland colonies. In this great movement of people, which was destined so profoundly to affect the fortunes of the whole world, Bristol played a full, though not always an honourable, part.

Very early in the history of Virginia, people from Bristol appear to have settled in that colony. It has already been seen that a group of her merchants were partially responsible for the first attempt to establish a permanent colony in Newfoundland. Before the period of the great migration, which took place between 1620 and 1640, the outward movement of people from Bristol was slight. But in the third and fourth decades of the seventeenth century, many ships set sail from Kingroad with hundreds of colonists who were destined never to see their native land again. Usually they went as members of an organized group, financed and controlled by one or more noblemen, country gentlemen or merchants. These colonists, who included among their number almost every kind of handicraftsman, for the most part went out as indentured servants.

The preparations made by Sir William Throckmorton and his associates for a plantation in Virginia in 1619, illustrates the care that was taken by these Empire-builders. On 3rd August, 1619, Sir Edwin Sandys wrote to Sir George Yardley, the Governor of Virginia, commending these adventurers to him. On the 18th of the same month, the *Margaret*, a Bristol ship, was chartered for the voyage. She was to sail "by the grace of God, from the port of Bristol called Kingrode" on or immediately after the following 15th September, with such men, provisions and goods as the laders should consider desirable. The ship was to proceed to Virginia and to remain there until she had been unladen, after which she was to return to Kingroad. The charge for the use of the ship was to be £33 a month, and she was not to remain in Virginia more than fifty days. Her owners guaranteed that she should be made "stiffe staunche strong well-appareled and victualed" and adequately manned. [1] In the agreement between the captain, Woodleefe, and the promoters, it was stated that the new settlement should be known as Berkeley, and the land round it Berkeley Hundred. The four promoters, Sir William Throckmorton, Richard Berkeley, George Thorpe and John Smyth, were to share all expenses equally among them, and all profits. These articles show that every care was taken beforehand to provide for all possible contingencies, including disputes about the status of the different adventurers, their powers and responsibilities.

In their commission to Woodleefe, Throckmorton and his associates announced that they were about to send the *Margaret* with thirty men to establish a colony in Virginia, and that more would be sent out in later ships. They were making this

[1] Kingsbury, S. M. (ed. by), *Records of the Virginia Company of London*, vol. III, p. 193.

plantation to the honour of Almighty God, for the enlarging of the Christian religion, and to the augmentation and renown of the general plantation in that country, and

"the pticular good and profit of ourselves men and servants as wee hope."[1]

Captain Woodleefe was appointed Governor, with full power and authority to carry on trade with the natives of Virginia and the English settlers there. He was further ordered to see that the day of their arrival in Virginia should annually be observed as a day of thanksgiving. Sundays and holidays were to be observed as ordered by the English Book of Common Prayer. There was to be a general assembly every day before dinner for prayer, and anyone who was absent without the permission of the minister, except the Governor and his assistants,

"shalbee punished with the losse of his supper the same evening."[2]

Special care was to be taken in the selection of the place of settlement, which was to be

"healthy for ayre and accomodate wth fresh water and easy for accesse unto wth shipe pinnace or barge rich alsoe in mould and soyle and of most likelyhoode to bring fourth the best commodities of that country either already knowne or by us hoped for."[2]

Then there followed a long list of the things which it was expected the new colony would produce, and from this it appears that Virginia was looked upon as something more than a garden of Eden, for in addition to the rich and varied crops which were expected, it was assumed to be possessed of great deposits of precious metals.

Minute directions were given as to the powers of the assistants. The chief houses to be erected immediately were to be "built homelike and to be covered wth bordes."[2] The two principal ones were to be a storehouse and another which would serve the dual purposes of prayer and diet. The *Margaret* carried out with

---

[1] Kingsbury, *op. cit.*, p. 200.
[2] *Ibid.*, p. 207.

her a cargo which included household furniture and utensils of almost every kind, tools for carpenters and other craftsmen, agricultural implements, ammunition and, indeed, everything which a party of settlers in a new country might be expected to need. The total cost to the promoters down to the actual departure of the *Margaret* from Kingroad was £733 10s. 5d., a sum which, even when the difference in the value of money between the seventeenth and the twentieth centuries is borne in mind, is surprisingly small.

With the 'twenties, the outward stream of people expanded very rapidly in proportion as popular dissatisfaction with the political and religious policy of the first two Stuarts increased. The *Mayflower*, which sailed from Plymouth in 1620, carried at least one Bristolian and his family. This was Francis Eaton, carpenter, and his wife, Dorothy. Many of the people who went out at this time left the country without the knowledge of the Government, and no record of their departure, therefore, exists. It may be presumed that Bristol sent her fair quota belonging to this group. The records which do remain, however, show that with the full cognizance of the Government, Bristol saw many well-laden ships set sail for the new lands of promise beyond the Atlantic. At this period the majority sailed for New England, but others found their way to Virginia and the West Indies. In 1632 Captain Pierce, in the *Lion*, carried back with him on his return voyage from Bristol 123 passengers to New England. Three years later, Richard Mather, who was to become one of the pillars of New England society and the founder of one of its distinguished families, set sail from Kingroad in the *James*, a vessel of 220 tons. The passengers who were legally taken aboard were first examined by the minister to test their conformity with the discipline of the Church of England. They were also required to take the oaths of allegiance and supremacy. At the time there were many who objected to this, as well as to the payment of a subsidy to the Crown, and these took ship secretly. The *Angel Gabriel*, 240 tons and a strong ship, sailed as consort to the *James* with a full complement of passengers aboard. She reached Pemaquid safely, but later was lost in a storm with all aboard.

In the later 'thirties the Government became suspicious of all this migration to New England. Both Laud and Charles tried to prevent what they considered should have been a controlled stream from developing into a rushing torrent. Regulations were, therefore, made stricter, and before emigrants were suffered to leave the country, they were required to obtain the special permission of the Government. Sometimes petitions for such leave were granted and sometimes refused. Everything depended upon the character and persuasiveness of the chief promoters of the voyage, or the whim of the authorities. On 4th January, 1639, the Privy Council referred a petition of Walter Barret, Walter Sandy, and Company, of Bristol, to its sub-committee for Foreign Plantations for report. From this it appears that the petitioners for several years had been engaged in settling a plantation in New England, an undertaking which they had begun long before the great flood of emigrants had started. All they intended to send out were regular people, "neither factious nor vicious in religion," and their plantation was not associated with any other in the country. They desired to transport 180 persons who would be engaged in producing necessary foodstuffs for the ships employed in the fishing industry on the coast. The petitioners had built and made ready for this purpose two ships. On 21st July of the same year, the Privy Council gave leave to Giles Elbridge of Bristol to carry into New England 80 passengers, together with the usual provisions for the increasing and support of his fishing plantations in that country. He was required to give a bond

"that none of the said persons shall be shipped until publicly before the Mayor of Bristol, they have taken the oaths of allegiance and supremacy." [1]

Similar permission was given in November to John Tyler and others to take out 120 emigrants and a cargo of goods. In the following year the *Charles* was licensed to carry 250 passengers and stores. In January, 1640, Sir Ferdinando Gorges, now in advanced old age, petitioned the Council to be allowed to proceed with more settlers to his plantation in New England. The

[1] *Calendar of State Papers, Colonial (America and West Indies)*, 1574–1660, p. 318.

disorderly condition of affairs there required his attention and more emigrants of the right sort. There were many people conformable to the orders of the church ready to go, who, because of the proclamation of General Restraint recently placed on emigration, were stayed. He, therefore, prayed to be allowed to send forth from Bristol, where he dwelt, shipping necessary for the use of himself and friends willing to join with him for the better plantation of those parts. Laud wrote at the bottom of this petition "Nihil," which may mean that the permission was refused.

During the Civil Wars, many belonging to both sides were driven overseas and, as will be seen later, many more were forcibly ejected. By the time of the Restoration, public opinion had turned definitely against unrestricted emigration from England to the colonies. Indeed, the change had come before the Civil War, for the opposition of Laud and his friends was not based solely on sectarian grounds. Various means were adopted to prevent the emigration of Englishmen, more particularly of handicraftsmen and others trained in some useful avocation. In 1671 strict rules were formulated to govern the departure of fishermen to Newfoundland. No ship was to carry more than 60 passengers for every 100 tons of burden, and before their departure each spring, ship masters were to give bond to the mayor of the port from which they sailed not to violate the provisions relating to the transportation of unauthorized persons. Further, they were to undertake to bring all their men back with them at the close of the fishing season. These rules, however, were not adhered to, for a half-century later immigration into Newfoundland was again considered. In reply to questions on this subject it was stated

"here are brought over by the Bristol Biddiford and Bastable ships great numbers of Irish roman Catholic servants, who all settle to the southward in our plantations, which if a warr with France *etc.* would be a direct means of loosing this country, who would join with any enemy, if some care be not taken to suppress the same, it may not be improbable that these very fellows may turn pyrotts in a little time, especially, after a bad fishing voyage." [1]

[1] *Calendar of State Papers, Colonial (America and West Indies),* 1720–1, pp. 177–8.

Free emigration, however, did not wholly cease in the Restoration period. There was always a slight outward movement of people from England, and in times of religious or political unrest its volume became substantial. The foundation of Pennsylvania led to the emigration of hundreds of Quakers, many of whom sailed from Bristol. It has been seen that the *Bristol Factor* was one of the first three ships to leave with passengers for that colony in the summer of 1681, and was the second to arrive there. She reached Upland on 11th December, where, as the river froze up that night, they remained all winter. The majority of the settlers in Pennsylvania came directly from England, and mainly through the ports of London and Bristol. Bartholomew Penrose, who became a well-known ship-builder in Pennsylvania and the founder of a business which lasted for three generations, was a member of a Bristol family long associated with the Penns. He was a ship-builder in his native city, and went to Pennsylvania with William Penn on his third visit.

Besides an unknown number of free emigrants of lowly status who went out from Bristol during the seventeenth and eighteenth centuries, the colonial records abound with the names of more distinguished people who either were born in that city, or retired to it after many years spent as planters, governors, colonial officials, military and naval officers. Of these, Sir James Russell, one of the earliest settlers in Nevis, was perhaps the most distinguished. Russell was a brother-in-law of Sir Thomas Warner, founder and Governor of St. Kitts. His brother, who became Deputy Governor of Nevis in 1668, settled in St. Kitts in 1637. Russell himself went to Nevis in 1628, and during the absence of the Governor in the following year, took his place. In 1657 he was appointed Governor, and two years later it was reported that he was

"very fit for his present employment and beloved amongst his neighbours."

At the Restoration the planters petitioned that he should be continued in his office, as he was one of the first planters there. He was declared to be a father to the country, and the Government of Charles II wisely decided to retain his services. During the second Dutch War, when all the neighbouring British West Indian Islands were captured by the enemy, Russell gallantly defended Nevis, although supplies were almost exhausted, and although the commonalty would have yielded to the sword rather than face famine, he refused to surrender until relief came.

Henry Morgan, about whom so many stories have been told and who became the subject of innumerable rollicking ballads, was a native of Monmouthshire and apprenticed in Bristol.

> "Henry Morgan of Abergavenney in the county of Monmouth labourer bound to Timothy Tounsend of Bristol Cutler for three yeares to serve in the Barbadoes on the like condicons." [1]

After the expiry of his indentures he made his way to Jamaica, and then began an amazing and varied career. He was in turn privateer, buccaneer, soldier, politician and governor. In 1666 he commanded a ship in an expedition led by the buccaneer, Edward Mansfield, which was sent by the Governor of Jamaica to attack Curaçoa. Later, on account of his activities on the Spanish Main between 1668 and 1670, he was sent home to England to stand his trial as a pirate. Through the influence of powerful friends, however, he was cleared, and in January, 1673–4, he was commissioned by Charles II as Deputy-Governor of Jamaica. His roving disposition and free and easy habits, however, unsuited him for the restraints of a dignified official life, and the Governor complained bitterly that he debased his position by drinking and gambling in taverns with his former associates. At heart Morgan was a freebooter, and the Governor also reported that, contrary to his duty and estate, he endeavoured to set up privateering, which meant at that time piracy. Nevertheless, in the absence of his superior, he waged war on the privateers, and he asked for small "nimble frigates" to hunt them down. Finally, in 1681, as his ill-judged carousals still continued, his commission was withdrawn, though he still remained a member of the Council. Two years later, as there was no change for the better in his social habits, he lost that

---

[1] Bristol Archives, *Servants to Foreign Plantations*, vol. I, fol. 31.

position and all other commands. Finally, in 1688, at the age of 53, he died through over-indulgence in rum, having contrived to crowd into a comparatively short lifetime more adventures, triumphs and misfortunes than might be expected in the combined careers of a dozen men who each lived to the age of ninety.

In the churches of Bristol and its surroundings are to be found tablets, monuments and epitaphs to a surprisingly large number of naval and military officers, government officials of all sorts, travellers, explorers, merchants and planters who, during the seventeenth and eighteenth centuries, served the Empire in various parts of the world. The majority of Bristol's emigrants, however, were poor and undistinguished. They left their native land as bound servants, either voluntary or involuntary, and they included destitute men and women, fugitives from justice, kidnapped children, political and religious offenders, and common convicts.

The system of indenture was usual from the beginning of the colonial era. One of the aims of Elizabeth's great Statute of Artificers, 1563, was to provide for long contracts between masters and servants so as to stabilize the labour market. In so uncertain an undertaking as the foundation of a new colony this was particularly necessary, and when the plantations were established, reliable reserves of labour were essential. The emigrant usually bound himself to serve his master in the plantations for three to five years, in return for which the master undertook to provide him with a free passage, food, clothing and shelter during the period of his indentures, and some adequate recompense at their expiry. At first this usually took the shape of a grant of land, but later it was more common to pay down a lump sum in sterling or in local currency, and in the eighteenth century the alleged equivalent of that sum was paid in sugar, tobacco, or whatever other article happened to be the local staple. The terms of a fairly early indenture were to the following effect:—

"This Indenture . . . Witnesseth that the said Robert doth hereby covenant faythfully to serve the said Sʳ Willm, Richard George and John for three yeares from the daye of his landinge in the land of Virginia, there to bee imployed in lawfull and reasonable workes and labors of them. . . . In consideracon whereof, the said Sʳ Willm Richard George and John doe covenant with the said Robert to transport him (with Gods assistance) with all convenient speed into the said land of Virginia at their costs and charges in all things, and there to maintayne him with convenient diet and apparell meet for such a servant, And in thend of the said terme to make him a free man of the said Cuntry thereby to enioy all the liberties freedomes and priviledges of a freeman there, And to grant to the said Robert thirty acres of land within their Territory or hundred of Barkley in the said land for the terme of his life and of two others then by him to bee named (if hee be then lyvinge) under the yearly rent of twelve pence for each acre, and such other reasonable condicons and services as at or before the salinge thereof shall be agreed betwene the said pties. And to pay each quarter of a yeare ten shillings to the wife of the said Robert at her house in Northnibly aforesaid towards her mayntenance duringe the said terme if hee soe long lyve, Whereof is already payd thirty shillings . . .

"RIC: BERKELEY (seal).

"GEO: THORPE (seal).

"JOHN SMYTH (seal)." [1]

It is stated in this document that by assent he "forsook the voyage," for which he could scarcely be blamed, as in this indenture the masters gave little but expected much.

In 1654 Richard Pell bound himself for three years to work for Robert Read of the city of Bristol, cooper, in Barbados, in return for which Read agreed to provide passage, food, clothing and shelter. At the end of the period of indentures he was to pay him or his assigns

"as much good and merchantable Tobacco Indigo goods or Cotten as shalbee there worth the some of ten pounds Sterling according to the Custome of the country." [2]

When John Morgan, son of Edward Morgan of Bristol, sailor, was apprenticed to Francis Eaton, carpenter on the *Mayflower*,

---

[1] Kingsbury, *op. cit.*, pp. 210–1.
[2] Bristol Archives, *Servants to Foreign Plantations*, 1654–63, fol. 1.

to learn the art, he was to receive at the end of his apprenticeship

> "25 acres of land lyinge in New England in America and alsoe
> to fine oute to him 15 bushells of Wheate." [1]

In Virginia, payment was at first made in money or commodities at the close of the period of service, but by the middle of
the seventeenth century, it became more usual to supply the en-
franchised servant with necessary equipment to enable him to
set up for himself as a small planter. In the records of the
sixties and seventies of the seventeenth century appear many
references to planters who bound themselves to other planters.
This was a symptom of the agricultural revolution that was then
going on in the Islands. The early attempt to develop these on
the basis of small-holdings proved a failure, and many poor
planters gave up the struggle against impossible odds, and accepted defeat. They lost their holdings and became the voluntary bondsmen of others more fortunate than they. Thus, on
6th December, 1656, John Trenchfield of the Island of St.
Christopher's, planter, was bound to Henry Vollens of the
Island of Barbados, planter, for three years to serve in Barbados
and to receive £10. [2]

Sometimes a whole family would emigrate as the bound servants of a particular planter. Their indentures were on the usual
conditions, but in the case of children they tended to be longer,
in order that the planter might have his required amount of
labour out of each. Thus, Richard Drake of Bristol, on 6th
December, 1658, was bound to Andrew Ball for three years,
Thompson Drake for four years, Mary Drake for seven years,
John Drake for ten years, and Thomas Drake, junior, for twelve
years. They were all to receive food, clothing, shelter, and the
usual payment at the expiry of their indentures. [3]

Between 1654 and 1685 ten thousand indentured servants
sailed from the port of Bristol. Their destinations included
almost every English colony which then existed, Antigua,

[1] Bristol Archives, *Apprentices*, 1626—July, 1636, fol. 23.
[2] *Ibid.*, *Servants to Foreign Plantations*, 1654–63, fol. 28.
[3] *Ibid.*, fol. 149.

Montserrat, Virginia, Maryland, Nevis, Jamaica, St. Kitts, New York, Pennsylvania, Caribee Islands in general, Newfoundland, but there are no records of any having gone from Bristol to the Carolinas. To some of the islands the emigration was slight. Thus, for example, Antigua received no immigrants till 1660, when there were 4, none in the following year, 6 in 1662, 10 in 1663, and then none for several years. Very occasionally emigrants proceeded to Montserrat, but in Cromwell's time Barbados received relatively large numbers; in 1654, 59; 1655, 157; 1656, 275; 1657, 508; 1658, 461; 1659, 523; 1660, 348. From then on till 1685, with the exception of the one year 1667, when 152 went out, the number each year was not above 100, and more usually it was less than half that figure. As Jamaica's great period had not yet begun, she received comparatively few servants, but in his observations on the present state of America, M. Cranfield, writing on 7th March, 1675, says:

"some 500 servants have come from Ireland by Bristol ships, these 3 or 4 years." [1]

Again, in January, 1676, he wrote:

"several merchants at Port Royal have correspondents at Bristol, Chester, Plymouth, Southampton, who supply servants, coarse cloths, provisions, iron-work. It is to the interest of the Island that the trade of Ireland and these other places be encouraged, to disappoint those of New England, who never brought any servants or would take off any goods, but in exchange for their fish, peas, and pork carried away our plate and pieces of eight." [2]

Of the mainland plantations, New England, New York, Maryland and Pennsylvania took very few servants, and still fewer went to Newfoundland. These colonies together did not receive as many as went to Barbados in one year during the late 'fifties. Between 1655 and 1678 inclusive, Virginia received no less than 100 a year, and frequently it was 200 or 300. Occasionally it rose to over 500. Of the 10,000 servants who left Bristol between 1654 and 1686, Virginia alone absorbed about 5,000. These

[1] *Calendar of State Papers, Colonial (America and West Indies)*, 1675-6, p. 314.
[2] *Ibid.*, p. 344.

people came from every part of England, Wales, Ireland and one even came from Burgundy.

The supply of indentured servants began to fail before the close of the seventeenth century, though it is true that down to the end of the period which terminated with the American Revolution, a number of emigrants continued to leave Bristol as bound servants. In the eighteenth century, however, Scotland and Ireland were the chief sources of this supply. Still, Bristol newspapers of the period contained from time to time descriptions of emigrants leaving the city, and the advertisements were designed to attract those likely to go. On 14th January, 1726, it was announced:

> "On Sunday Morning 24 Persons were put on Board the Raphannah Frigat (sic) bound for Virginia, who had bound themselves as Servants for 4 Years according to the Custom of that Country: And we are told that, when their Times are expired, each hath a certain number of Acres of Land given them, to manure and plant for themselves. . . . There is another Ship on the River, called the Mercury Galley, bound for Philadelphia in Pennsylvania, on the same Account, and those that bind themselves to go over as Servants are directed to apply to Mr. Henry Allport, at the Globe and Star on the Key (sic). [1]

Again, on 14th January, 1727, the same journal announced:

> "For the City of Philadelphia . . . all Handycraft Trades-Men and Boys, as well as also young Women and Girls, that are willing to go over as Servants to that Pleasant and Flourishing City, in a good Ship, (with a good Commander) now lying at the Key (sic) of Bristol," [2]

should apply to Henry Allport, who would provide them with a suit of clothes and lodging till the ship sailed. Other passengers willing to pay were also to apply there and make their own arrangements.

From time to time, advertisements appeared for servants in Virginia, but Philadelphia seems to have been the most

[1] *Felix Farley's Bristol Newspaper*, 14th January, 1726.
[2] *Ibid.*, 14th January, 1727.

popular destination. These servants went out as the bonds-men of the ship's captain or of a firm of merchants who carried them at their own costs. They were sold in the colonies at a substantial profit. In 1729, for example, one such batch carried from London by the Bristol firm of Hobhouse was sold in Jamaica at prices which ranged between £13 and £30 a head. Though many of these people never returned, the records show that there were some who survived the period of service and came home. But long before the end of the seventeenth century, it was clear that the number of those who would voluntarily bind themselves to serve in the plantations for a period of years was insufficient for the growing necessities of the colonial market. So kidnapping became common, convicts were transported in great numbers and the hapless peoples of Africa were enslaved. Kidnapping and spiriting became the business of some people in Bristol. They kidnapped children at play, decoyed the un-wary into their houses by seductive promises, cropped their hair so as to alter their appearance and sold them into bondage.

In 1645 the Long Parliament required all officers and justices to be diligent in apprehending those who were guilty of kid-napping children and carrying them oversea. The Marshals of the Admiralty and Cinque Ports were ordered to search all vessels carefully for such children. Nine years later, an ordinance was issued by the Common Council of Bristol, from which it appears that these Parliamentary instructions had been disregarded. All servants bound for the plantations were re-quired, before their embarkation, to be articled and enrolled as apprentices, according to the form usual for all apprentices. For thirty years thereafter, the name of every servant legally bound who left Bristol was entered in a book, the *Servants to Foreign Plantations*, which is thus an invaluable record, as it frequently gives the places of origin of the servants, their occupa-tions, age, sex, name, master, and the colony to which they intended to go. It is probable that this enrolment stopped when the negro began to replace the white man as the normal field-worker. Ship masters or others who received unauthorized persons on board their vessels as bound servants were to be fined £20. From time to time the water-bailiff was to search all ships in port, and if any servants were found whose indentures were not enrolled, he was to report to the Mayor or appropriate Alderman.

This ordinance was acceptable both to prospective servants and to ship-masters; but the old abuses still continued. On 16th July, 1662, the Mayor of Bristol petitioned the King to be empowered to examine all ship-owners and servants or passengers going to the colonies, to discover if they went of their own free will, and to keep a register. This power was necessary in order

"to avoid the abuse of husbands or wives running away from each other, children being spirited away, apprentices, rogues, &c: escaping in that way." [1]

For, according to the petition,

"some are husbands that have forsaken their wives, others wives who have abandoned their husbands; some are children and apprentices run away from their parents and masters; oftentimes runaway and credulous persons have been tempted on board by men-stealers, and many that have been pursued by hue and cry for robberies, burglaries, or breaking prison, do hereby escape the prosecution of law and justice." [2]

In spite of all efforts to suppress this abuse it still went on, for complaints against kidnapping and spiriting frequently recur. Some enterprising rogues profited by the honest attempts to enforce the law. They allowed themselves to be kidnapped, received maintenance and clothing, and only complained to the authorities at the last port of call in England. In 1663 occurred one of the strangest cases of all. The Mayor of Bristol that year, John Knight, was a determined persecutor of the Quakers whom he pursued

"with such Eagerness, as if the Persecution of them had been the chief Business of his Office." [3]

---

[1] *Calendar of State Papers, Domestic,* 1661–2, p. 441.
[2] *Calendar of State Papers, Colonial (America and West Indies),* 1661–8, p. 98.
[3] Besse, J., *An Abstract of the Sufferings of the People Called Quakers,* vol. II, pp. 42–3.

Just before the close of his mayoralty, he caused three of them to be put aboard a ship in order that they might be transported to the colonies, but some of the ship's company decided that their victims should be liberated, and they were placed on shore. The sailors drew up and signed a document in which they stated their reasons for this action. This enumerates a medley of arguments, not all of which were to the credit of the signatories. Before the ship sailed, however, the Quakers were put on board again by the water-bailiff, whereupon they were sent ashore and the signatories published their reasons for not receiving them.

"Their Cry and the Cry of their Family and Friends, are entered into the Ears of the Lord, and he hath smitten us even unto the very Heart, saying, *Cursed is he that parteth Man and Wife.*

"And moreover, they that oppress this People, His Plagues shall follow them wheresoever they go, and assuredly we do in part partake of them already for our Consciences will no wise let us rest, nor be quiet, for the Lord hath smitten us with a terrible Fear, so that we can in no wise proceed to carry them."[1]

What seems to have carried even more weight with these tender-hearted sailors was the fear, not only of condign punishment to come, but more of the earthly punishments provided by the laws of England and Barbados for those who transported His Majesty's subjects against their will. They were well aware of the English law on the subject, and they also knew that another in Barbados provided suitable punishments for this offence. Not only would they be punished, but they would be compelled to carry home to England again those whom they had unlawfully carried away. They asserted that they knew these were innocent men who desired to walk in the fear of the Lord, and that they had been put aboard against their will. They were not bound by any indentures and no one had agreed to pay their passage, which possibly was the most convincing reason why they should be put ashore and set at liberty.

[1] Besse, *op. cit.*, pp. 345–6.

Some of the people called Quakers, however, were not so God-fearing and so innocent. Indeed, on at least one occasion some members of the Society, if not guilty of the same crime, were somewhat irregular in their methods of carrying emigrants.

> "A complaint was brought into this meeting that the reputation of truth suffers in this city and elsewhere, by means of John ffallowfield, who at this time follows an employment of transporting persons to Pensilvania which is not as he doth manage it, reputable:
> "This meeting therefore desired Richd. Sneed, Tho. Callowhill, Charles Jones, Tho. Dickson to go and discourage him from this meeting upon this Subject and to advize him as they shall find cause." [1]

Whatever the law might say, the plantations had to be supplied with labour, and in the closing decades of the seventeenth century many Bristol merchants had estates in the sugar and tobacco colonies, and a large proportion of the population of the town was connected with their development. Felons were pardoned on condition that they accepted transportation, and for these there was a ready market. Even in those days of drastic punishments for slight offences the supply of felons fell short of demand. It became customary for justices to terrify "small rogues and pilferers" by condemning them to be hanged, whereupon the court official advised these unfortunates to pray for transportation as the only means of escaping the gallows. The wicked aldermen then shared these prisoners amongst themselves, though it is said that not all the city fathers were thus guilty. The innocent ones, however, did nothing to prevent a practice which they knew to be contrary to the letter and spirit of the law.

When Judge Jeffreys came to Bristol in 1685, he heard of this glaring abuse and dealt sternly with the offenders, "for he delighted in such fair opportunities to rant." He announced that he had come to Bristol with a broom to sweep them.

> "The City of Bristol is a proud body and their head, the mayor, in the assize commission is put before the judge of assize ... when his lordship came upon the bench and

---

[1] *Minutes of the Men's Meeting, 6th of 3rd month,* 1700.

examined this matter, he found all the aldermen and justices concerned in this kidnapping trade, more or less, and the mayor himself as bad as any. He thereupon turns to the mayor, accoutred with his scarlet and furs, and gave him all the ill names that scolding eloquence could supply; and so with rating and staring, as his way was, never left till he made him quit the bench and go down to the criminall's post at the bar; there he pleaded for himself, as a common rogue or thief must have done; and when the mayor hesitated a little or slackened his pace, he bawled at him and stamping called for his guards. . . . Thus the citizens saw their scarlet chief magistrate at the bar, to their infinite terror and amazement."[1]

Jeffreys then proceeded on his way, vowing that the guilty magistrates would hear more on this matter. When Sir Robert Cann, who was personally innocent, applied through his friends in London "to appease him, and to get from under the prosecution," Jeffreys at length consented to see him, and, after much explanation and confession of fault,

"at last he granted it, saying 'Go thy way; sin no more lest a worse thing come into thee.' "[1]

Fortunately for the wrong-doing aldermen, the Revolution occurred before anything further was done. They were thus left in the enjoyment of their blood-money, and the only punishment they ever received was the great fear which the merciless Jeffreys had inspired in them.

Another source of forced labour at this time was afforded by political and religious offenders. After Cromwell's defeat of the Scots in 1649, "the gentlemen of Bristol" applied for permission to transport 500 prisoners to the plantations. This request was granted, and again after the battle of Worcester, 1651, many captured Royalists were brought to Bristol, from whence they were carried into slavery, but owing to delays, many died before they could be placed aboard ship. In the following year, the Council of State instructed the Governor of Waterford to deliver to three Bristol merchants, Robert Cann, Robert Yate and Thomas Speed, as many prisoners as they might wish to carry

[1] Jessop, A. (ed. by), *The Lives of the Norths*, vol. 1, p. 285.

to the West Indies. Many similar grants were made to Bristol merchants at that time, and this practice continued throughout the period of the Commonwealth and Protectorate.

The strict enforcement of the Clarendon Code in the Restoration period produced its crop of labourers for the plantations. In 1665, for example, nine men and three women found guilty for the third time of attending a Nonconformist service, were condemned to transportation for seven years. If they returned before the end of that time, they were to be fined £100 or be hanged and their goods confiscated. The Monmouth Rebellion led to the transportation of hundreds of captured rebels, many of whom passed through Bristol. In a receipt for 100 of these who were to be sent to Barbados on Mr. Nepho's account, under date of 26th September, 1685, appears the name of Azariah Pinney. There are three copies of this list, one of which had a letter preceding it which may be taken as an illustration of the attitude of the owners to their prisoners.

"Sr, where as you have signified to me that you are ordered to give me an exact acc^{tt} of ye hundred Rebells which his Ma^{te} was pleased to grant you, in whome you have transported your Right unto me to be transported according to his Ma^{ts} order to some of his Plantacions in America. . . . I doe assure you that there are in Goale sixty five of them at Dorchester one wounded man . . . now Remaining in Exeter Goale, and three and thirty at Ilchester besides Azarias Pinney who was sent in Custody to Bristoll to be transported who it will be made appeare upon ye Return of my Express sent for that purpose hath been shipd for some one of his Ma^{tes} Plantacons according to his Ma^{tes} order . . ."[1]

Not all the prisoners went as docilely as Jeffreys could have wished. Thus, it is said that 100 prisoners aboard a ship in Bristol harbour mutinied and threatened to knock the captain and crew on the head and go whither they pleased, but the captain was warned in time, and the mutiny was quelled.

Kidnapping, spiriting, and transported political and religious offenders, however, did not suffice, so before the close of the period another source was drawn upon. When the Elizabethan

[1] Hotten, J. C., *The Original Lists of Emigrants* . . . , p. 320.

prophets of empire were putting forward arguments in favour of colonization, they were divided on the advisability of utilizing the prison population of the country. Some considered that the transportation of felons was an undesirable practice, on the general ground that an empire built on such material could not be sound. Others, however, took the contrary view, and, almost from the beginning there was some transportation of convicts. Chief Justice Popham and Sir Ferdinando Gorges were eloquent advocates of this system. Popham, according to one of his contemporaries,

> "provided for malefactors and first set up the discovery of New England to employ those who could not live honestly in the old," [1]

while according to Anthony Wood,

> "Popham was the first person who invented the plan of sending Criminals as founders of colonies, which . . . he stocked out of all the jails in England." [1]

James I, in a commission issued to the various members of the Privy Council, including the Archbishop of Canterbury, stated,

> "Wherein as in all things els binding to punishment it is our desire that Justice be tempered with mercie, Soe likewise it is our care soe to have our Clemency applied as that greate and notorious malefactors may not be encouraged, and yet the lesser offendors adiudged by law to dye may in that manner be corrected, as that in theire punishment Some of them may live and yeild a profitable service to the Common Wealth in parts abroade where it shall be found fitt to imploie them." [2]

Full power was, therefore, given to the members of the Privy Council, of which two always had to be chosen from the Chancellor, the Lord Treasurer, the Lord Chief Justice of England and Sir Ralph Winton, to reprieve from execution convicted

---

[1] Butler, J. D., "British Convicts shipped to American Colonies," in *American Historical Review*, vol. II, pp. 22–3.

[2] Smith, A. E., "Transportation of Convicts to America," in *American Historical Review*, vol. XXXIX, p. 233.

robbers and other felons. Murderers and those found guilty of rape, witchcraft and burglary were specifically excluded from this indulgence. So began a system which was to carry thousands of wrongdoers of all degrees to the plantations in the New World and to the Australian settlements in the Antipodes. It had obvious defects, but it served its purpose, for undoubtedly many, who otherwise would have perished on the scaffold, were given a chance of which not a few profited. At first condemned criminals were permitted to choose between execution or transportation, and many at the time preferred certain death to the unknown terrors which awaited them beyond the sea. In 1718 judges were for the first time authorized to inflict transportation on common felons as a first sentence.

In Bristol many in the eighteenth century were so condemned. The common offences for which transportation was inflicted were grand larceny, breaking and entering houses and shops, receiving stolen goods, assisting prisoners to escape, embezzlement, highway robbery and wilful murder. There was great variation in the sentences given for similar offences, just as there was a great variety in the kind of offence for which the same period of transportation was given. On 27th August, 1750, at the Gaol Delivery in Bristol, Robert Welsh, Elizabeth Watkins and Charity Matthews, who had been convicted of grand larceny, were condemned to transportation

"to some of His Majesty's Collonies or Plantations in America for seven Years." [1]

On the same day, Mary McLane, otherwise McCleane, received the same sentence for

"having feloniously brought into the Gaol of Newgate Two Iron Crows to Assist Anthony Whittle (therein Committed for felony) in making his Escape," [1]

Jonathan Adams received a sentence of fourteen years' transportation in 1759, for

"receiving the Goods of Michael Miller Merchant value ffive pounds which had been feloniously stolen by Landovery

[1] Bristol Archives, *Gaol Deliveries*, 1741–71, fol. 7.

otherwise Dovery well knowing the Same to have been feloniously stolen."[1]

Daniel Bishop, convicted in 1752 and ordered to be hanged, was reprieved, and it was

"his Majesty's pleasure to Extend his Royal Mercy to him on Condition of his being . . . Transported . . . for the Term of his Natural Life."[2]

Another interesting case is that of John Smith, who was capitally convicted of

"ffeloniously stealing the Goods of Sarah Castle Single-woman above the value of ffive Shillings in her shop."[3]

On 23rd August, 1759, this sentence was changed to transportation to America for fourteen years.

The carriage of these prisoners became a regular business, though there was never enough of it for a ship-owner to confine himself to this branch of trade only. Most captains or owners were ready to carry convicts as part of a general cargo, as there was always a ready market for them in the plantations. The transporters signed a bond to land the prisoners in the colonies, and to provide them with food and clothing until they were sold. They were at liberty to sell them as best they could in the over-sea market. An example of such a bond is the following :—

"Know all Men by these presents that we Thomas Kenney Merch^t & Wm Kenney Mariner both of Bideford of the County of Devon are held and firmly bound unto Rowles Scudamore Esquire officiating as Clerk of the Pease for the City and County of Bristol In the Sum of Twelve hundred pounds of lawful Money of Great Britain. . . . To which Payment well and truly to be made we bind our selves."

The document then enumerates eleven persons convicted of felony and ordered to be transported to America for seven years, and continues :—

"Now therefore the Condition of the above Obligation is such that if the above bound Thomas Kenney and William

---

[1] Bristol Archives, *Gaol Deliveries*, 1741–71, fol. 17.
[2] *Ibid.*, fol. 9.
[3] *Ibid.*, fol. 17.

Kenney . . . do within One Month from the Date hereof (if the Wind be fair) or as soon after as conveniently may be (Death and Dangers of the Seas only Excepted) Transport or cause to be transported the said Several Felons to Some or One of His Majesty's Plantations or Collonies in America in order that they may Serve some of His Majesty's Subjects there the Several Forms they are respectively order'd to be transported for as aforesaid. And if they or any of them do in due time deliver or cause to be deliver'd to the Town Clerk of the said City and County for the Time being an authentic Certificate from the Governour or Chief Custom House Officer of the Plantation or Collony where they shall be Landed of their being so Landed then the said Obligation to be Void or Else to remain in full Forse." [1]

Usually it was stipulated that if any of these prisoners returned before the expiry of their sentences they should be hanged, and the records show that such executions took place from time to time. During the period 1741 to 1771, 114 persons were transported from Bristol for various offences and varying periods, [2] while the number in the years 1775 to 1781 was 3. [3] In addition to those who were condemned in the city itself, Bristol was the port of departure for hundreds of convicts in the neighbouring counties. But since the only records of these are stray references which appeared at various times in the Bristol Press, it is impossible to estimate the number of such birds of passage.

Before the American Revolution the outward movement of free emigrants again began to increase. From Scotland and Ireland went thousands of people who hoped to escape from the economic privations which afflicted them. Though convicts were still welcomed in some plantations after the Seven Years' War, there was a growing antipathy to them. In the West Indies even the freed negroes regarded them with contempt, and it is clear that, if the system had ever been of any use in the New World, its justification was now gone. In the meantime, Bristol during a century and three-quarters was a great emigration port, and thousands had passed down the Avon to people the island and

[1] Bristol Archives, *Gaol Deliveries*, 1741–71, fol. 11.
[2] *Ibid.*, fols. 1–28.
[3] Bristol Reference Library, *Jefferies MSS.*, vol. 7, fol. 141.

mainland colonies of the West. Sugar and tobacco, however, had an insatiable need for labour, and so, in spite of all these white emigrants of every kind and degree, the requirements of the plantations were not satisfied. So the hapless peoples of Africa were enslaved to serve the needs of European masters for cheap labour.

CHAPTER IX

GOLD, IVORY AND SLAVES

". . . *the* Bristol *Merchants as they have a very great Trade abroad, so they have always Buyers at Home, for their Returns, and that such Buyers that no Cargo is too big for them. To this Purpose, the Shopkeepers in* Bristol *who in general are all Wholesale Men, have so great an Inland Trade among all the Western Counties, that they maintain Carriers just as the* London *Tradesmen do, to all the Principal Countries and Towns from* Southampton *in the* South, *even to the Banks of the Trent* North; *and tho' they have no Navigable River that way, yet they drive a very great Trade through all those Counties.*"

DANIEL DEFOE, *A Tour Thro' the Whole Island of Great Britain* (1724).

IN modern times the Portuguese were the first to develop a commerce with Africa. It was along the western seaboard of that continent that Prince Henry the Navigator despatched successive expeditions, and many years before Vasca da Gama reached India by sea, the Portuguese had begun to trade with the Africans. At that time the main articles of commerce were gold and ivory.

Through their close commercial associations with Portugal the merchants of Bristol heard of this new trade, and some of them decided to take a share in it. Two ships were prepared for this purpose, but before they were ready the Portuguese heard of the scheme, and, at the request of their King, Edward IV of England forbade the Bristol expedition to sail. Throughout the sixteenth century, the Portuguese continued to guard to themselves the Guinea trade, as it afterwards came to be called, though as the years went by, the peoples of northern Europe showed an increasing inclination to disregard their claim. Thus, in 1552, Captain Thomas Wyndham sailed from Kingroad for the Barbary Coast in command of three well-laden merchant ships, thus beginning the long association of Bristol with the African trade. A few years later Hawkins carried his first cargo of Africans to the New World, but at that time and for many years to come the English decried the system of slavery. They did not, they said, trade in the bodies of men and women, for such a commerce was contrary to Holy Scripture and repugnant to the free spirit of their constitution. Successive groups of English merchants devoted themselves to the Guinea trade, but their main concern was gold and ivory. Indeed, it was not until after the Restoration of Charles II, in 1660, that a company came into existence whose charter specifically mentioned the trade in negroes as one of its objects. When this body, the Company of Royal Adventurers of England trading into Africa, yielded up its charter to the newly-created Royal African Company, slaving had become the chief section of this traffic, while gold and ivory were of secondary importance.

As soon as the possibilities of the Guinea trade were realized, there began a long drawn out quarrel between London and the Outports, which was scarcely terminated when the slave trade itself was abolished. This struggle was merely one phase of a long-contested battle which lasted from the Middle Ages to the nineteenth century. In the Tudor period it became customary for the Crown to grant out monopolistic privileges to groups of merchants or other capitalists as an encouragement to the development of some new industry, or the extension of English commerce in some part of the world hitherto unknown to English traders. Under the early Stuarts this policy was greatly abused, for monopolies were granted not merely as part of a national economie policy of development, but as a fiscal device which enabled the Crown to tap streams of revenue which lay beyond parliamentary control. The merchants of London were rich and close at hand, so it came about that they were able to profit by royal impecuniosity. Ever since the Middle Ages there had been great antagonism between the Outports, who wished to develop direct trade with oversea countries, and London, which wished to become the entrepôt for the whole of England's foreign trade. When the colonial age began, the monopolistic spirit of the metropolis had to be reckoned with, and the Outports had to fight a long battle before their over-mighty sister was vanquished.

In 1619 James I limited the import of tobacco to London, and in 1631 his son granted the monopoly of the Guinea trade to a group of London merchants. This was followed in 1633 by another grant which excluded the Outports from the trade to the Gulf and river of Canada. Such restrictions weighed heavily upon Bristol, whose colonial connections were beginning to develop before 1619, and in view of these repeated indications of royal preference for London, the suspicions and hard bargaining of the Society of Merchant Venturers of Bristol, which preceded the voyages of Captain James, seem amply justified. Bristol merchants had long been aware of the probable advantages arising from a well-established trade with Africa, and ever since the time of Cabot, they had been concerned in the Newfoundland fisheries and vaguely regarded that whole region as their own. It is plain from the records which remain that the repeated monopolies granted to London were a constant source of irritation to Bristol, and as this policy came to be identified with the personal wishes of the King, it was natural that when the Civil War broke out Bristol should lean towards the Parliamentary side.

During that struggle English trade was thoroughly disorganized. The old monopolies of London were disregarded, and the merchants of the Outports became accustomed to almost unrestricted trade with the English colonies. Moreover, in the plantations themselves a revolution in the methods of agriculture occurred. When Englishmen first settled in the West Indies and Virginia it was assumed that, in addition to some large estates, there would be many small farms worked by one man with his family, and perhaps one or two labourers. It soon became clear, however, that the burning tropic sun rendered farming in the Caribbean, as understood in the English shires, quite illusory. Again, the early settlers tried a system of general agriculture and produced a variety of crops, but already by the middle of the seventeenth century, the tendency to specialization was general. In spite of the emphatic expostulation of King James I, Virginia very early in her history turned away from general agriculture, and the cultivation of the crops which the King recommended, to tobacco. In the West Indies there was a general movement toward concentration on the cultivation of sugar. In the existing state of agricultural knowledge, the production of neither of these commodities was suited to smallholder cultivation, so, both in Virginia and in the West Indies, the small holding yielded place to the large plantation which might be the property of an absentee group of capitalists or of an individual planter, living either in the colony or in England. This revolution emphasized the unsuitability of white men for tropical or semi-tropical field-work. In spite of the ship-loads of political prisoners and unfortunates of all kinds who passed from the port of Bristol to a life of slavery in the colonies, it became evident before the close of the seventeenth century that if the plantation system was to endure, some other source of labour supply must be developed. Many of these poor bondspeople were unable to stand the rigours of plantation life. Some returned home, others found a place in the life of the colony, but the vast majority sickened and died long before the period of bondage to which they were condemned was over.

As early as 1619 a cargo of Africans was landed in Virginia, and by the middle of the century negro slaves were to be found in almost all of the southern mainland and island colonies. Their capacity for enduring tropical heat, to which they were accustomed, their docility and great physical strength suited them admirably for the work they were required to perform. Before the Restoration, the Dutch and a few English and colonial ships were engaged in the slave trade, but with the Restoration and the great commercial expansion which marked the closing decades of the seventeenth century, the African trade acquired a wholly new significance.

In 1660 a new African Company was organized. It was mainly designed for the development of the trade in gold and ivory, but when its charter was re-issued in 1663, the traffic in negroes was expressly given as one of its principal objects. This Company was a failure. Mismanagement, war with the Dutch, rivalry with the Outports and efforts to safeguard the Company's monopoly sapped its energies. So, in less than ten years after its charter had been issued in an amended form, its harassed directors were only too glad to relinquish their rights for the sum of £34,000 to a newly-organized joint-stock company. This was the Royal African Company, which at once put a new spirit and energy into the languishing trade with Africa, though already the merchants of London had aroused the determined opposition of the Outports, and, in particular, that of Bristol.

The main lines of the opposition of the Outports had been clearly indicated as early as 1667, when a petition was presented to Parliament by a group of men interested in the colonies, including, among others, Ferdinando Gorges of Barbados, where he was a councillor. This declared that the plantations represented the most considerable section of the nation's trade, and that their rapid development was due to a plentiful supply of negroes. There had always been hitherto, they quite untruly stated, freedom of trade, in consequence of which the plantations had prospered. All of this was now changed since the Company of Adventurers trading into Africa had come into existence, for it obstructed the Free Traders and tried to monopolize the entire traffic of the Coast for itself. Prices had risen, but in addition, as the Company had contracted to supply the Spanish plantations with negroes, the English colonies were compelled to take those that were left over after the best quality negroes had been disposed of, that is to say, the refuse, unsatisfactory for plantation work. In a paper which they sent up with the petition, the signatories pointed out that the colonies employed 400 sail, many of large size, and that they were, therefore, not only the mainstay of English commerce, but one of the chief sources of an assured supply of well-trained and able seamen. Moreover, the ships which went out to Africa and the colonies usually carried English goods of all kinds, cloth, clothing, wrought iron and provisions. They were thus a direct means whereby employment was ensured to many hundreds of work-people at home. These ships brought back to England sugar, indigo, ginger, tobacco and other articles, which not only supplied the needs of the nation, but which, either in a raw or manufactured form, were exported to foreign countries in exchange for other necessities, as well as gold and silver. If the free trade was not restored all of this commerce would languish, for the Company had neither the capacity nor the wisdom to manage the whole trade for the common good.

The petitioners were not concerned with the gold trade, which required the maintenance of forts and a special technique. This could safely be left to the East India Company, but the traffic in negroes required no such outlay of fixed capital. Indeed, it was here that the merchants of Bristol and the Company were to be so often opposed. Bristol held that a skilful captain, who cruised along the Coast and sent his boats up the rivers, could slave as well as or, in fact, better than the Company's ships, which were expected to call at certain emporia where slaves were collected for shipment. In this the Bristol merchants were probably right during the seventeenth and early eighteenth centuries, but when the traffic grew to the enormous proportions which it attained before the American Revolution, casual slaving became difficult and dangerous. By that time slaves were being brought to the Coast from the remote interior, and a regular hierarchy of intermediaries had developed. Such people were more amenable to men who lived on the Coast than to strangers, since the former were well known to them and familiar with the local situation as it changed from week to week.

Some Bristol merchants took stock in the Royal African Company and so merged their interests with those of a body which was mainly metropolitan in composition. William Colston, one of the most notable citizens of Bristol at the end of the seventeenth and beginning of the eighteenth centuries, became a member of the Royal African Company in 1680, and Nathaniel Pinney was also a member. But the majority of their fellow-merchants preferred a free trade, and were loud and continuous in their outcry against the Company and all its works. In spite of the royal prohibition, they not only continued to carry on their trade with the Coast but, in the twenty years after the Company received its charter, they expanded their African connections at a rapid rate. Then came the Revolution, the accession of William and Mary, the Bill of Rights and a breach with the wicked past. Among other things all these changes were interpreted to mean that all monopolies granted by royal dispensing power now became null and void. So the merchants of Bristol were enthusiastic for the Revolutionary Settlement, and directed their energies to the expansion of the African commerce with renewed zest. The Company, however, did not propose to yield up its privileges without a struggle, and so the pamphlet war which had already begun was intensified, while on the Coast the battle between the Outports and London was fought with weapons of a more lethal nature.

In 1696 the Company applied to Parliament for a renewal of its charter. This action at once produced a crop of petitions from the Outports and, in particular, from their boldest representatives, the merchants of Bristol. The plantations, it was urged, now depended almost entirely upon negro labour, and they could only be maintained and developed if a steady flow of

Africans continued. The petitioners, therefore, requested that the whole trade on the coast should be laid open from Accra to Angola. On the 8th of the same month the merchants trading to South Barbary, together with the merchants and tradesmen of Bristol, complained in a petition of the restrictions placed on the African trade, which, they asserted, were ruining them. But the voice of the African interest was strong in London, and everything possible was done to induce Parliament to restore its former monopoly to the Company. Thus, the English legislators were entertained by a spate of petitions from the Outports and counter-petitions from the Company, while in innumerable pamphlets the most opposing views were set forth at great length and with much heat and verbal acrimony.

Everyone now knew that the trade in negroes was a valuable though risky one, and that there were good prospects of substantial developments in the future. The Londoners contended that they were being deprived of a commerce which their energy and capital had called into existence. It was they who had spent money in the erection of forts which they still maintained, while the Outports had spent nothing. In view of these arguments, it was feared in Bristol that Parliament would be convinced by the Company and accede to its demands. If so, the new act would re-impose the old restrictions on the trade, which would be more effectively enforced since Parliament had overhauled the administrative machine and set up the Committee of Trade and Plantations. Again, therefore, in February, 1697–8, the Mayor, Aldermen, Common Council and Merchant Venturers of Bristol sent a joint petition to Parliament. This repeated once more what had already been stated so many times, a story which by now the members of the House of Commons must have known almost by heart. The petition stressed the great value of the plantations to the Mother Country, whose prosperity was due to the labour of Africans. For the good of the state, it prayed that the trade should be laid open from Cape Blanco to Angola. It was supported in the same month by others from the artificers and tradesmen of Bristol and from the dyers of London, asking to be heard on the subject of an open trade with Africa. Still another petition from the Mayor, Aldermen, Common Council and Merchant Venturers of Bristol, together with one from the planters of Barbados, was laid before Parliament. Everyone in the city at that time, in fact, appreciated the rich and growing triangular trade which had developed between Bristol, the West Coast of Africa and the plantations. All were determined that not without the most strenuous struggles on their part would they surrender to the wicked machinations of the well-hated Royal African Company.

In their zeal for Free Trade, Bristolians, however, overreached themselves. The opposition to a·closer trade was reasonable enough, but the.people of Bristol wished to share in the traffic without any special cost to themselves. They refused to be convinced by the Company's arguments that all Free Traders benefited by the forts which it maintained. In the opinion of Bristol and her allies,. it was the duty of the Government to police the Coast effectively by maintaining one or two frigates there, and the upkeep of the forts was a mere waste of money. These white elephants did nothing to expedite the business of slaving, and as military posts they were worthless. The petitioners, therefore, contended that the 10 per cent tax, which it was proposed in the Bill then before Parliament should be placed on all traders to Africa, would be highly detrimental to the plantations as well as to themselves, and they ended their appeal by repeating once more the demand for a completely free trade.

However, the Bill became law. The 10 per cent tax was imposed, but neither the Company nor the Free Traders were satisfied. To the members of the Royal African Company it seemed that they had been deprived of their rights, for the Free Traders were now admitted by law, provided that they paid their 10 per cent. According to them, the consequence was that the trade was now disorganized, and as a direct result of the unreasonable competition of men unacquainted with African conditions, the Company was losing money and the trade was declining, while foreign competitors were increasing in strength. The Company's pamphleteers produced an abundance of evidence to substantiate these statements, while Parliament and the nation were entertained by broadsheets, broadsides and pamphlets which clearly and irrefutably established the most contradictory conclusions. Once more, in 1708–9, the Company renewed its agitation in Parliament with a veiw to a re-issue of its old charter! so the merchants of Bristol began to send up petitions. They were apprehensive that the Company was up to its old tricks and trying to engross the whole trade to itself. As they had much capital invested in the trade, they prayed that the liberty which they then enjoyed should be continued. This would benefit not only themselves, but also the plantations, which now depended mainly on the supplies of negroes which they carried to the New World. They hoped that when the African trade was considered by a committee of the whole House, their petition would receive earnest consideration. Apparently, their continual vigilance was of some effect, for the old monopoly was not restored, and the Company was compelled to negotiate with them on equal terms.

On 26th February, 1712–3, the Company wrote a letter to the Mayor, Aldermen and Common Council of the city of Bristol. The Act by which the trade was thrown open to all on payment of 10 per cent had by that time expired, and the Company was anxious that the merchants of Bristol should join with it in working for the re-establishment of an enclosed trade. According to this letter, the only effect of the Act had been to destroy profits for all except the native entrepreneur on the Coast,

"who took that Advantage to impose what Difficulties they pleased on the Traders, which now we hope will be effectually remedied; especially if we can obtain your Concurrence that we may rest in the quiet undisturb'd Enjoyment of our Properties, by which we shall be enabled to enlarge and ascertain the Profits of this Trade and make it effectually diffusive, to the great benefit of your Corporation. In freighting, buying or building Ships with you, lading them with such Goods and Manufactures as are to be bought in your Country, and vendible in Africa." [1]

Though the letter went on to hint that Bristol could not furnish

[1] Royal African Company, *A Collection of 24 Broadsheets Relating to the Affairs of the Royal African Company*, early eighteenth century. No. 2.

everything required by the trade, the Company magnanimously suggested that it would be willing to supplement Bristol's exiguous supplies from its own stations on the Coast. In the hope, therefore, of benefits certain to accrue from the Company's kind services, it was suggested that Bristol should join with it in seeking for a renewal of its charter on the old conditions. Bristol, however, was not likely to be deceived by any such specious approaches, and so adhered to its old policy of pref-erence for an open trade, free of all restrictions. So the relations between the Outports and London continued to be uneasy, and whenever either of them had an opportunity of outdoing the other, it was seized with avidity.

The outbreak of the War of Jenkins' Ear compelled all British traders to make common cause in face of the enemy. On 7th November, 1739, the London, Liverpool and Bristol merchants trading to Africa petitioned the King for protection. Once more they pointed out how valuable their trade was to the kingdom. It took out great quantities of English manufactured goods, and was the direct means of supplying negroes to the plantations upon whose labours their prosperity was based. Unless British ships of war were maintained on the Coast

"his Catholick Majesty or his subjects or any other persons under Spanish Commissions may send Ships of War, or Privateers"

to prey on British commerce. The petitioners, therefore, requested that a sufficient naval force should be permanently stationed on the Coast, and owing to the nature of the climate, that the ships should be relieved every three or four months. This petition was signed by a large number of people whose names were arranged in three columns, one of which contains many from Bristol and was probably a Bristol list. As the trade continued to flourish, this apprehension appears either to have had no justification or to have been removed by Government action.

But what was of much more consequence to the merchants of the Outports was that the Company was still trying to legalize its monopoly, and Bristol spent large sums of money in opposing this relapse. At last, in 1744, the Board of Trade and Plantations began once more to look into the African trade, and the Merchant Venturers of Bristol were requested to furnish information on the subject. Their standing committee on African affairs was, therefore, directed to forward a reply, making clear the Society's attitude. In the following March, in response to a letter from one of the city's representatives in Parliament, who held a watching brief for the Society, the Master was instructed to say that an engraftment of the Society into the Company would be prejudicial to Bristol, whose traders declined any invitation to join the Company, but as to what the Government should do if that body refused to maintain its forts as at present, the Merchant Venturers had no advice to offer. That was not their business. Nevertheless, their opinion was still that the forts on the African coast were, from the point of view of trade, of no practical value.

The African Committee of the Merchant Venturers again considered this subject on 26th February, 1747–8, and in particular, the Bill then before Parliament. It recommended that a letter should be sent from the Society to the Bristol members of Parliament, to inform them that in the Society's opinion the English forts and settlements on the Coast were at that time of no service except James Fort and Cape Coast Castle. This was a considerable concession in view of the previous repudiation of all forts there. This letter again repeated the opinion which Bristol had held for over seventy years, that the African trade ought to be kept open and that the scheme for a new company was detrimental to her interests. If, however, this new body was to come into existence, the entrance fee for new members should not exceed 40s., and London, Bristol and Liverpool should be equally represented on the Board of Managers. The Merchant Venturers believed that many in the Outports would not choose to become members of the new Company, and that on account of such refusal they should not be debarred from the trade. On 26th March a petition was laid before the House of Commons, in which Bristol again enumerated all the advantages which the kingdom derived from the trade with Africa, and prayed that her opinions should be taken into consideration in any scheme for regulating that branch of commerce which Parliament might consider.

In 1750 an Act was passed for extending and improving the trade to Africa. Article 16 provided that any in Bristol who wished to become members of the new Company should pay 40s. to the clerk of Merchants' Hall. It was also provided by this Act that the affairs of the Company should be managed by a committee of nine, of whom three should be chosen by the Bristol members, three by Liverpool and three by London. This measure thus embodied two of the main points which the Merchant Venturers of Bristol had urged when the Bill was under discussion. But in spite of this success they were never satisfied with anything less than Free Trade. In 1750 the Bristol freemen numbered 156, and 157 two years later, as compared with 135 from London and 101 from Liverpool.

Nothing, apparently, could allay the deep-seated mistrust still held by the Outports for the metropolis. As early as 1753, Bristol was already making complaints. Representatives, chosen by a full assembly of the Company's members in that city, were sent to London to remonstrate about the practice of permitting the Company's officers on the Coast to carry on private trade. In a memorial supported by the merchants of Bristol and Liverpool, addressed to the Commissioners of Trade and Plantations, it was stated that these expostulations were made because the ordinary rank and file members could not otherwise obtain satisfaction. They contended that various clauses of the Act of 1750 had never been carried out, that copies of resolutions, orders and instructions, which should have been sent to Bristol and Liverpool, never left London, and that the members of the Company in these two ports were in consequence ignorant of the Company's affairs. Instead of working for the common interest, the Company's chief officials were concerned only for themselves, for, as soon as they were in power, instead of helping the Free Traders as they were by law bound to do, they had formed themselves into a private joint-stock co-partnership, and were now attempting to establish a monopoly more formidable than any could have been at home. They were actually on the Coast and, therefore, had the whole trade in their power.

All of this could be substantiated by the commanders of Bristol ships. Moreover, the dishonest officials on the Coast, by offering high prices to engross the trade, had raised the price of slaves to a figure higher than ever before known. Outport commanders were denied the use of canoes and canoe-men; they were refused supplies of wood and water, things that even strangers had been allowed before. When these grievances had been laid before the governing committee they were treated as idle and groundless charges, inspired by personal prejudice and party interest.

The new Company, according to the Outports, was guilty of other misdemeanours. Thus it was stated that the nine committee men so managed elections that only three new names had so far been added to the original list. These twelve controlled the elections between them, in order that nine of them should always compose the committee. They had been able to do this by inducing their tradespeople and other obscure friends to pay the required 40s., which they no doubt provided, in order to become members of the Company. In this way their repeated re-election was assured.

> "It is a folly for any person, not being one of the twelve, to attempt getting elected a committee-man for either London, Bristol, or Liverpool; there having been as great interest made against such persons who have offered themselves, as hath happened on some occasions preceding the election of a member of parliament." [1]

So it came about that, as the result of the election was a forgone conclusion, no one in future not a member of the twelve would allow himself to be nominated for a place on the committee.

When Edmund Burke was a Member for Bristol he had to listen to the old, old story of the iniquities of London, the intrigues of the committee and the virtuous forebearance of Bristol. But on this, as on so many other occasions, he was not inclined to be the willing instrument of his constituents. Instead, he treated them to a long homily on the wisdom of the laws of trade in general, and of the African commerce in particular. The Act

---

[1] Donnan, E., *Documents Illustrative of the Slave Trade to America*, vol. II, p. 522.

of 1750, he declared, was formulated by the most experienced men after the most mature deliberation. It contained more checks to prevent abuse than were to be found in the constitution of any existing public establishment, and the Company's affairs were managed more economically than those of any other organization in this or any other country.

"It is not every man who is loud in complaint of grievance, that is equally zealous for redressing it; and nothing is more usual than for men to decry an establishment on account of some lesser Evils, in order to introduce Systems productive of much greater." [1]

In this Burke was scarcely fair to his constituents, for they had a long experience of London methods to go upon, and they knew only too well that the abuses of which they complained were not imaginary. By Burke's time, however, the interest of Bristol in the African trade was beginning to decline, for Liverpool had already surpassed her, and was rapidly establishing a monopoly as against all others.

During the period of the Civil War and Commonwealth, Bristol developed trading connections with various plantations in the Caribbean and on the mainland of North America. The acquaintance which they thus made with colonial needs and the increasing demand for negroes, together with the fact that the Dutch and others were already developing a good trade in slaves, induced them to embark upon that branch of commerce. Thus in the Restoration period Bristol became more and more concerned with the Guinea trade, and the monopolies granted to successive African companies could not deter her venturous sons from exploiting it still further. As, however, prior to 1698, this commerce was illicit, no exact estimate of the extent of this traffic is possible. It is clear from the writings of John Cary, a Bristol merchant and notable publicist, and a determined opponent of the Royal African Company, and also from various references made by several defenders of that body that before the close of the seventeenth century this

[1] Donnan, *op. cit.*, vol. II, p. 552.

branch of the city's commerce was becoming the mainstay of her trade.

Indeed, Bristol was well placed for its development. She was not only a great port, but her citizens were rich, and this enabled them to bear with composure the long interval which usually intervened between the sailing of a ship which they had laden, and whose cargo they had paid for, and the day when she dropped anchor once more in Kingroad with a return cargo of sugar, tobacco, fustic, dye-wood and other colonial products. The great days of Manchester and the North were yet to come, and Bristol was still the natural gateway through which the exports from the south and western Midlands were sent. With slight modifications, the same system of transport prevailed at the beginning of the eighteenth century which was familiar to Canynges and his contemporaries.

With the opening up of the African trade more exact figures become available, and the unwearied efforts of the Royal African Company to have its monopoly re-established proves the enormous importance which that body attached to the growing competition of its chief rival among the Outports. According to a report on the trade to Africa, presented to the House of Commons by the Commissioners of Trade and Plantations in 1707–8, 52 ships cleared from Bristol for the Guinea trade, of which two only belonged to the Company, while the other 50 were owned by separate traders. In the year 1709–10, Bristol paid £1,577 5s. 0½d. to the Royal African Company in duties under the conditions of the Act of 1698. In the eight years 1701-9, according to Gomer Williams, she despatched 57 ships a year to the slave coasts, but this appears to be rather a high estimate.

At first London and Bristol controlled the Guinea trade. In wealth, shipping and experience of foreign trade they surpassed all rivals. For many years Liverpool's participation was of slight importance, as her merchants lacked the capital required to equip ships with suitable cargoes and adequately manned. They had no large accumulations of capital, such as were possessed by the merchants of Bristol, upon which to call, and so they were unable to wait for the slow return on investment which was a feature of this trade. Gradually, with perseverance, they increased their share. At first they confined themselves mainly to the export of provisions, and later coarse checks and silk handkerchiefs of the Manchester make. To begin with, they were not concerned with slaves to any extent, but with the growing knowledge of the economic possibilities of negroes, they entered the lists against London and Bristol. Liverpool's expansion was astounding, it not only challenged, but in time surpassed, both London and Bristol. Various reasons have been given for this victory of the North. Gomer Williams suggests that it was mainly due to the superior business efficiency of Liverpool, whose trade was managed with much greater care than was that of either London or Bristol. According to him, Bristol captains received ample wages, primage, cabin privileges and port charges of from 5s. to 7s. a day, and the Bristol factors received 5 per cent. commission on sales and returns. Liverpool captains received lower wages, no primages and no port charges, and the factors were placed on an annual salary. In Liverpool these men worked their way up from the bottom, and by a long and arduous training became in turn seamen, mates, captains and factors. According to Gomer Williams, the result of these economies was that Liverpool could sell her cargoes for 12 per cent. less than those of Bristol and still show a higher rate of profit.

This writer, however, was a strong champion of Liverpool, and there is good reason for believing that the explanation of that city's triumph is not quite so simple as he makes it appear. If what he says is true, it is difficult to understand why in the closing decade of the eighteenth century, Bristol ship captains engaged in the Guinea trade should demand increases in wages and various privileges which, they declared, would place them on the same footing as their brethren in Liverpool. In the 'eighties and 'nineties are to be found several petitions from these supposedly overpaid mariners, asking that they be given the same wages and other concessions as their fellows in London and Liverpool. They demanded £6 a month sterling for captains the whole year round, for all Bristol sailors objected to the the practice by which half the wages were paid in the Islands in

debased local currencies. This they quite reasonably considered caused them to lose part of their rightful pay. The
captains also demanded £20 cabin money for stores on the outward passage, and £10 on the return. They wanted £14 for
horse hire while they were in the plantations, £6 to be paid the
ship for passengers, an allowance of 5s. a day in the Islands, not
exceeding 90 days, and primage out and home, as was customary
in London and Liverpool. The only result of these demands
was a dry rejoinder on the part of the Society of Merchant
Venturers that they "do not consider the port of London as a
precedent for the allowances to be made to captains here." The
fact seems to be, not that Bristol was less efficient, but that she
quite rightly preferred a well-organized, safe trade to a risky
and uncertain one which sometimes yielded enormous profits
and sometimes a dead loss.

Indeed, the smug assumption of Liverpool's superior economic
efficiency seems to testify more to the local patriotism of
Gomer Williams than to his historical erudition. The facts
would rather appear to be that in the later eighteenth century,
Bristol became very deeply concerned in the actual conduct and
ownership of their many sugar plantations in the Islands. The
West Indian trade was safer, quicker and more certain to produce
regular profits than the Guinea trade, which was always risky
and rendered hateful, not only by the nature of the work involved, but by the high mortality among the sailors engaged and
the violent fluctuation in financial returns. Liverpool was now
supplying an abundance of slaves, so Bristol could confine herself to the cultivation of her tropical estates and the expansion
of her direct commerce with the Caribbean.

The progress of Liverpool was so rapid that by the middle
of the century her two great southern rivals had been outdistanced. Bristol despatched 63 vessels in 1725, capable
of carrying from 150 to 450 slaves each. London at that
time was responsible for the carriage of 26,400 slaves
as compared with 16,950 carried in the Bristol vessels.
In 1749 Bristol had 47 vessels engaged in the Guinea
trade, with carrying capacity for 16,640 negroes, and it was
estimated that the total value of her commitments in the

African trade, ships, general cargoes and slaves, amounted to £260,800. In 1753 the clearings from the African coast were London 13, Liverpool 64, Bristol 27, Lancaster 7, Chester 1, Plymouth 1, Glasgow 4. Eighteen years later 192 British ships in all sailed from Guinea, carrying 47,146 negroes. Of these, 107 ships, carrying 29,250 slaves, were from Liverpool; 58 London ships took 8,136 negroes; 23 from Bristol had 8,810 slaves, and 4 from Lancaster carried 950. Between 1756 and 1786 Bristol sent 588 ships to Africa, while Liverpool sent 1,858.

By that time Liverpool had outdistanced all rivals, and she retained her dominant position until the abolition of the trade. Thus it appears that, except for a few years in the 'fifties and early 'sixties, if even then, Bristol was never the leading slave port of the kingdom. By 1787 London had 26 ships, Bristol 22, and Liverpool 73, which carried a total of 36,000 slaves with an average of 494 per ship. By 1795 the trade had declined all round: London's 14 ships carried 5,149 slaves, Bristol had 6 ships which carried 2,402, Liverpool 59 ships which carried 17,647. Even after the Regulative Laws had been passed, the average carrying capacity of each vessel was 317. In the ten years 1795–1804 inclusive, London sent out 155 ships to Africa, which carried 46,405 slaves to the colonies. Bristol sent 29 ships, which exported 10,718 negroes, while Liverpool despatched 1,099 vessels and carried 332,800 slaves.

Even before the end of the eighteenth century Bristol had begun to become sensitive about her connections with this iniquitous traffic, and to preen herself on the slackening interest of her citizens. Since then this sensitivity has tended to grow, but there is, indeed, little justification for such a feeling. At the time the African trade was an honourable one, and those who took a part in it were no better and no worse than their contemporaries who followed less dangerous callings. To condemn such a commerce from the moral elevation of an age which has seen the spoliation of Ethiopia, the brutal dismemberment of the ancient Empire of China and the rape of Czecho-Slovakia, shows a conspicuous lack of historical perspective. Throughout the greater part of the 18th century the African merchants were highly esteemed by the majority of their fellow countrymen, and when the difference in public opinion between that age and our own is taken into account, they are worthy to compare with the most upright merchants and traders of the present age.

CHAPTER X

THE SLAVE TRADE

"You yourself must be convinced that Negroes are the sinews of a Planta-tion and it is as impossible for a Man to make Sugar without the assistance of Negroes, as to make Bricks without Straw."

JOHN PINNEY (1764).

THE slave trade was always a risky business, for if the profits on an individual voyage were sometimes considerable, they frequently had to be set against previous losses. As England was at war so often in the eighteenth century, her traders were frequently liable to capture by enemy men-of-war or privateers. Both in times of peace and times of war the African coast was infested with pirates, who preyed with equal impartiality upon the peaceful shipping of all nations.

Many examples of the depredations of these freebooters might be given from the maritime records of Bristol, for her ships suffered with the rest. The *Callabar Merchant*, for example, Thomas Kennedy commander, sailed from Bristol in 1719 for the coast of Africa to pick up slaves for Virginia. On 11th September she was attacked by three pirate ships and a brigantine, one of which, carrying 20 guns and 200 men, hoisted a black flag with a death's head in the centre. The *Callabar Merchant* was brought to, after which the pirates boarded her and several of the crew were manhandled. The raiders threatened to destroy the ship and cargo, but later they relented. The unfortunate slaver was compelled to remain in company with the pirates for nine weeks, during which they relieved her of everything she carried which they thought might be of use to them. At last, having re-fitted their ships, they sailed for the island of Anabona, and the *Callabar Merchant* was allowed to proceed on her way with a present of 21 negroes from the pirates. She left the Coast with 160 negroes aboard instead of the 300 which her owners expected her to carry. Of these 160, 36 died at sea, 20 through ill-usage from the pirates and 3 because the crew failed to maintain an effective watch on the cargo. As might have been expected, the negroes who finally reached the Virginian market failed to command good prices. The owners of this vessel, who included the Master of the Society of Merchant Venturers, Abel Grant, and other merchants of Bristol, were given satisfaction by the Commissioners of the Treasury.

Ships were sometimes lost off the American coast in storms. Occasionally trouble broke out with the natives on the slave rivers, which caused catastrophes. In 1759, for example, a sloop commanded by a brother of Captain Ingledieu of the ship *Mercury* of Bristol, when slaving up the Gambia River, was attacked by natives. Finding himself desperately wounded and likely to be overcome by 80 or more negroes who had boarded the ship, rather than surrender to "such merciless wretches" he discharged his pistol into the ship's magazine and blew her up, killing himself and everyone else aboard.

It was a wild life on the Coast, for there was little law and no mercy. Attack and counter-attack, reprisal, betrayal, raids at night and murder were incidental every-day occurrences. The men of the Outports were jealous of the men of London and vice versa. All Englishmen hated foreigners in general, and all foreigners hated Englishmen and each other. Everyone disliked the Free Traders who lived on the Coast, who were friends of no one, but maintained themselves by playing off the native traders against the white men and the white men against the natives.

"The private Traders are about 30 in number, settled on the Starboard side of the River; loose privateering Blades, that if they cannot trade fairly with the Natives, will rob; but they don't do it so much in pursuance of that trading Advice (Amass Riches, my Son) as to put themselves in a Capacity of living well, and treating their Friends, being all well pleased if they can keep their Stock at Par, and with their profits purchase from time to time, Strong beer, Wine, Cyder, and such Necessities, of Bristol Ships, that more frequently than others put in there; of these, John Leadstine, commonly called Old Cracker, is reckoned the most thriving." [1]

There was constant bickering and complaint about traders who gave too high a price for slaves, or were guilty of unfair trading of one sort or another. Sometimes they were in too great a hurry to load and would not wait until some battle between native tribes, which the traders had carefully stimulated,

---

[1] Donnan, *op. cit.*, vol. II, p. 264.

took place: for always after such fights the vanquished were sold and prices usually dropped very considerably. Sometimes, it seems, even officers of the Royal Navy took a hand in the trade on their own account, and upset the plans of the regular merchants. In 1738, for example, Mr. Tibble and Mr. George Tyndall, who were both in the long boat of the man-of-war *Greenwich*, commanded by Captain Cornwall, used the long boat for private trade. They had a storehouse ashore and a canoe to carry goods between the long boat and the ship. These gentlemen, it was stated, through their ignorance advanced the price of slaves and lowered the prices of goods exchanged for gold. They paid £32 per head for negroes at a time when the real price should have been £28, and they sold brandy, perpets and sayes at unreasonably low prices.

Bristol ships and others naturally broke all the Laws of Trade and Navigation. They purchased rum from colonial ships from the colonies direct, which they later exchanged for slaves. From time to time they carried cargoes of brandy from Holland, carefully concealed under the ballast, so as to elude any over-inquisitive visitor. As on the Banks of Newfoundland, so on the Guinea Coast, a flourishing contraband trade went on between British, colonial and foreign ships.

When finally, after a stay on the Coast which sometimes lasted for several months, the ship cleared for the colonies, the possibilities for danger and loss were not yet exhausted. The horrors of the Middle Passage have been so often described that they need not be dealt with at any length here, but in the whole course of human history there can have been few phases of man's activity more filled with cruelty, misery and despair. In spite of all that has been written, the Middle Passage still remains one of the blackest spots on Britain's escutcheon. It is impossible now to picture the terrifying state of mind of helpless savages, torn from their native surroundings, forced by long marches to the coast, along paths strewn with the bones of earlier victims, subjected to all the indecencies of the slave market and the barbarity of the brand, and then, driven like beasts, frequently naked, into horrible ships. To these inland peoples the ocean was a strange forbidding monster, and the vessels in which they were compelled to sail something worse than the blackest hell imagined by man.

"Bristol Ships triple such as are sturdy, with Chains round their Necks; and to keep their own Men sober, and on a barricad'd Quarter-deck: tho' the natural Cowardice of these Creatures, and no other prospect upon rising, but falling into the hands of the same Rogues that sold them, very much lessens the Danger: Nevertheless, it is advisable at all times, to have a diligent Watch on their Actions." [1]

Sometimes the vigilance was not enough, and then a poor tormented creature would make a wild rush to the side of the ship, and end his long agony by a leap from that abode of misery and shame, to find liberty at last in the sparkling tropic sea.

Nor were these poor people always so cowardly as they were said to be, for sometimes, when the brutality was excessive, the vigilance for a moment relaxed, or some native possessing qualities of leadership and courage happened to be aboard, there was mutiny. Usually these risings were easily quelled and fiendish punishments were imposed, but sometimes the white men paid with their lives for the sufferings of which they were the ostensible cause. On 8th May, 1750, the *King David* of Bristol, on her way from the coast of Guinea to the New World, carried a cargo of slaves, none of whom were in chains. This was a fairly common practice, particularly when, as in this instance, several of the crew had died and the negroes were employed to work the ship. On this occasion the captain treated them with great kindness, and according to the contemporary account, with unnecessary leniency. The leader of the slaves, who spoke good English, frequently came into the captain's cabin to speak to the commander. There he had seen where the arms were kept and made his plans accordingly. They raided the armoury about five o'clock in the morning, murdered the captain and five of the crew, and drove the remainder into the hold. The leader told them that if they came up quietly their lives would be spared, but as they emerged they were put in irons, and some of them later were thrown overboard. The chief mate remained below until the last, and only came up when he was informed

---

[1] Donnan, *op. cit.*, vol. II, p. 281.

that unless he did so at once, the negroes would come down and cut him to pieces. When the others were thrown overboard he was brought to the bulwarks in irons with the rest, but one of the leaders stopped this by saying that he would kill the first man who tried to injure the mate, for, if he were slain, he said, who was to look after the ship? At first the vessel was allowed to go with the wind, and then they considered a return to

"the Gold-Coast, or Callabar, or St. Thomas's an Isle near the Coast of Guiney; but the Head Negro being a Fellow of more Sense than common, being persuaded there was no possibility of getting there, it was agreed to go where no white Man liv'd; and Desiada was pitch'd upon; which they made on the 14th of May." [1]

A boat was sent off but did not return, and finally the ship arrived in a French colonial port.

There are other records of a similar nature, but usually, as in this instance, the negroes failed to escape. They were ignorant of navigation, they knew nothing of geography, and frequently the mutineers got drunk on the ship's spirits, and then fell to fighting and murdering each other. Life, indeed, was a very cheap commodity aboard a slaver. An illustration of the attitude of public opinion at this time towards the treatment of slaves was afforded in the trial of Captain William Lugen. Lugen took 200 negroes aboard in Africa and sailed for Carolina. Among others who died on the Middle Passage was the mother of a very young child who was also very ill. The crew tried to induce the other negroes to take care of the infant, but they, fearing infection, refused to do so, and so it was left lying on deck in a dying condition, exposed to the burning sun. As the surgeon declared that it could not live the day through, the captain ordered it to be thrown overboard, and he was acquitted at his trial on the ground that there was no premeditated malice.

Even when, as sometimes happened, a ship made port without any misadventure and with all aboard in good health, the possibilities of trouble for the captain were not yet over. These arose in consequence of the smuggling proclivities of the im-

[1] Donnan, *op. cit.*, vol. II, p. 487.

porter, and intermittently strict enforcement of colonial regulations by the local officials. Thus, in 1687, *The Society* was seized by the Virginia collector for failure to comply with port regulations, including the payment of an import duty on slaves. After vainly trying to obtain justice in Virginia, the owners, in 1690, appealed to the Privy Council, which in turn referred the dispute to the Board of Trade, which referred it back to Virginia again, but what finally came of the matter does not appear. In this case there was a suggestion of smuggling negroes ashore under the pretence that the ship was stranded and that there was a shortage of provisions. A perennial source of dispute was provided by convoys. Ships were often kept for weeks and even months in some colonial or home port before the naval commander decided that it was safe to sail. These prolonged delays entailed great loss to the traders. The colonial authorities co-operated with the naval officers by refusing to allow any goods to be exported in ships which did not sail in the convoy. In general, this rule was sound enough but, as in the case of the *Dolphin and Mermaid* at the beginning of the eighteenth century, it was not always reasonable. In this instance both of these well-manned and strongly armed privateers were all able to take care of themselves. Apparently this was the view taken by the Government, for they were allowed to sail alone.

Throughout the greater part of the eighteenth century, however, special taxes imposed by colonial legislatures on the slave trade were a constant source of irritation to the English trading community. Colonial governments required revenue, and a special tax on slaves was an obvious measure to impose. As negroes were essential for the economic life of the community, their continued importation was certain, and so a reliable revenue would be secured. The importers, however, were violently opposed to these laws, and in numerous petitions to Parliament and to the Commissioners of Trade and Plantations, they prophesied the immediate extinction of their trade unless these measures were disallowed by the Crown. In 1723 the merchants of Bristol trading to Africa petitioned the Commissioners of Trade and Plantations against an Act passed by the Virginian Assembly, by which a duty of 40s. was to be imposed on all negroes imported into that province after the following March. If this measure was allowed to become law, they declared, it would much prejudice the African trade, and consequently the exportation of tobacco and the navigation of the kingdom. It was, in effect, a prohibition of the import of negroes into the province.

> "Yo'r Petitioners therefore humbly pray Yo'r Lordships will Discountenance such proceedings and not suffer a Law so pernicious to the Trade of this Kingdom, to be Confirmed, as likewise to prevent the like Practice in any other of the Colonies abroad." [1]

This was signed by a long list of Bristol merchants, and the Commissioners, having read the petition and considered the Bill, recommended its disallowance.

In the meantime, the Virginian authorities began to collect their duties, as is shown in a petition from a group of Bristol merchants, owners of the ship *Commerce*. This vessel duly landed her cargo of slaves in Virginia, whereupon the owners' agent was compelled by a naval officer, acting under instructions from the local authorities, to pay the duty of 40s. a head, local currency, for each slave. This was apparently done under an earlier Act which had been passed by the Virginian Assembly, but which had been disallowed many years before by the Home Government. Five years later, the Lords Commissioners of Trade and Plantations received a joint petition from London and Bristol against the continued enforcement by Virginia of the duty on imported slaves. The old arguments about the dangers to English trade were once more repeated, and the conclusion was arrived at that

> "it is humbly conceived they have no right thus to tax British trade and for the support of continued revenue charges of that colony or any edifices there." [2]

Bristol accepted without question the current view that colonies existed for the Mother Country's good, and were, in fact, neither

---

[1] Donnan, *op. cit.*, vol. IV, p. 109.
[2] *Ibid.*, vol. IV, p. 120.

more nor less than so many kitchen gardens, a view with which the people of the colonies found it increasingly difficult to concur. In 1731, by imposing an import duty of 15s. and an export duty of 30s. on all negroes brought into or taken out of Jamaica, that colony followed Virginia's example. This gave rise to three petitions, one of which emanated from Bristol.

Shortly afterwards, South Carolina became the centre of another storm. The Provincial Legislature passed two Acts, both of which aroused the hostility of the English traders. One of these related to local currency policy, and by the other an import duty was placed on slaves. This legislation gave rise to a petition signed by over forty men in Bristol, including the Mayor. South Carolina, in reply, however, marshalled its arguments so well that when both sides had been heard, the Commissioners of Trade and Plantations gave their consent to the Bill. At that time this province was suffering from over-importation of slaves. Prices were nevertheless still higher than in other colonies, as the planters, many of whom were little better than small farmers, persisted in buying them on long credits. The result was that many of them were deeply in debt to English merchants in Bristol and other towns. As usual, the petitioners from Bristol stated that unless the tax on slaves was removed they would be compelled to quit the business. Nevertheless, they continued to prosper, although the obnoxious act was enforced. In other instances, as, for example, New York, which passed a similar measure mainly for the purposes of raising revenue, the Commissioners took action in accordance with the protests of the traders of Bristol and other ports.

This problem continued to embitter relations between the English traders and the colonies down to the time of the American Revolution. Thus Burke, in 1774, warned the Master of the Society of Merchant Venturers of a proposed Bill of the Jamaica legislature, which was designed to place special duties on all negroes imported into the island, a measure which the Jamaicans tried to justify because of the excessive importation of recent years. The imposition in South Carolina, in 1740, of the tax on imported negroes is said to have caused the production of Malachy Postlethwayte's treatise, *The African Slave Trade the Great Pillar and Support of the British Plantation Trade in America.* In spite of British prohibitions, the colonies continued to pass similar Acts, for in the plantations everyone required negroes, and a tax on that commodity was a certain source of revenue.

In the last years of the seventeenth century Bristol's colonial trade had grown to what was considered enormous proportions for the shipping of that time. During the twelve months, 25th June, 1699, to 25th June, 1700, 29 ships, with a tonnage of 4,270, arrived from Virginia with tobacco; 28, with a tonnage of 2,435, brought sugar, logwood, cotton, indigo, pimento and dye-woods from Antigua, Nevis, Montserrat and St. Kitts; and 18 ships, with a total tonnage of 2,060, arrived from Jamaica with sugar, cotton, ginger and molasses. Only 9 small vessels, with a total tonnage of 390, reached Bristol from Carolina, New-foundland, New England and Bermuda, with train-oil, fish, rice, skins, furs and timber. Altogether, 172 ships from the colonies entered the port, with a total tonnage of 17,650, and in addition, 68 ships arrived from Ireland, whose total tonnage was 2,228.

Of the 70 vessels registered in Bristol between 1727 and 1769 that carried slaves from Africa to Virginia, 28 were built in that port, 7 in other parts of England, 25 were of colonial make and 10 were prizes. At the time of their departure from Bristol, the average age of these ships was ten years, and one of them, *The Marlborough*, was 29 years old, which appears to suggest that some ships were diverted to the slave trade when their best days were passed. The smallness of these 70 vessels, which may be taken as fairly typical of the slave trade, is surprising. One of them was of 50 tons burden and its average cargo of slaves was 190. Thirteen of this group ranged in size from 51 to 75 tons, with an average slave cargo of 166. The *Bridget*, of 70 tons, however, carried 225. Thirty-eight were in the group 76 to 100 tons, and had an average slave capacity of 233. The *Williamsburg*, of 100 tons, carried 335; the *Tryal*, of 90 tons, took 356 negroes on one voyage and 390 on another; the *Ann*, of 90 tons, carried 310; and the *Bryce*, 100 tons, took 249 on one voyage and 414 on another. In the group of 101 to 150 tons there were 20 vessels, with an average carrying capacity of 250, but the *Greyhound*, of 120 tons burden, carried 410. There were 6 ships of between 151 and 200 tons, whose average slave cargo was 299, though the *Hector*, of 200 tons, had 512. There was one ship of 230 tons which, however, was not really a slaver at all, as she only had 5 negroes aboard.

These figures speak for themselves, and it is not surprising that the loss of life was appalling. References to seventy, eighty, ninety or one hundred deaths in a single voyage recur in the records. Even when the death-rate was comparatively low, the physical condition of the negroes was often so bad that they were scarcely marketable. Good captains tried to keep down their losses, while unfortunate or incompetent ones were full of excuses to their infuriated owners. Captain Japhet Bird wrote home from Montserrat on 24th February, 1722–3, to his Bristol owners :—

"I arriv'd at mounserrat the 22d of January with 239 slaves which Now all sold better then Expectation. . . . Notwithstanding I've had the misfortune of beuring seventy odd slaves . . . but thank god it Can't be said that its owing to Neglect for sr I Can assure you that it have been the Constent care and Indeavour of me for the Interest of those Gentlemen that have Imploy'd me." [1]

On 4th November, 1729, the *John and Betty*, of Bristol, arrived at Jamaica with 150 slaves, having lost 100 on the passage and buried 11 more after her arrival in port and before the sale.

"They are the worst Cargoe of Negroes have been imported for severall Years past. Our day of Sale was the 10th Instant, they were so badd Could not sell Tenn to the planters. We yesterday sold one hundred and five to Messrs. Lamego and Furtado, at eighteen pounds Ten shillings per head, which Considering the Condition the Negroes were in, is the greatest price have been given. The remainder so very bad, Cannot gett £8 per head for them. Wee shall be oblig'd to sell them at Outcry for the most they will yield." [2]

In 1760 Captain Lilly took the *Diamond*, belonging to John King, of Bristol, from Bonny to Maryland. He left the Coast

[1] Donnan, *op. cit.*, vol. II, pp. 297–8.
[2] *Ibid.*, vol. II, p. 382.

with 329 slaves, but lost 99 with the flux, which had somewhat abated when he sighted another ship at sea. To the modern mind it seems fairly evident that the high rate of mortality was directly related to the smallness of the ships, and yet repeatedly reference is made by those engaged in it to the superiority of small to large vessels for this branch of commerce, a view which was shared by the Newfoundland fishermen. Small ships could enter shallow bays and go up shallow rivers without difficulty, while great ships would be compelled to use boats on a large scale, a practice which was tedious, expensive, and often dangerous.

It was the agents' duty to dispose of slaves whom sometimes they described as "low" or "a scabby lot," or again "so reduced that you would not ensure them arriving at their master's plantation alive." The negroes which were carried to Virginia in these 70 Bristol ships came from Calabar, Guinea, Gambia, Madeira, Jamaica, Barbados, St. Kitts, Montserrat, Rhode Island and Antigua. When trade was well-established, cargoes were usually sent direct from the Coast to their final destination, but sometimes market conditions were not favourable, and then the unfortunate slaves were peddled about from island to island and over to the mainland colonies. These were the people who suffered most, for before the whole cargo was finally disposed of, these unfortunates might have passed through several colonial slave markets, and whole families were thus scattered through the plantations from Barbados to Virginia.

The records are full of disputes about insurance rates and whether negroes had died of natural causes or not, also from time to time, altercations arose over the relatively higher rates charged by Bristol firms as compared with those of London. One of these cases came before Lord Mansfield in 1785. Two hundred and twenty-five negroes during the voyage mutinied twice, and 55 died on the Middle Passage. The underwriters contended that the 19 who had been killed in the mutiny or died of wounds should be paid for. The plaintiffs, however, held that all 55 had died as a result of the mutiny, and that the remainder of the cargo had brought a lower price in the colonies because of the outbreaks with which they had been connected.

Lord Mansfield ruled that the negroes who had died from jumping overboard and swallowing salt water had not died from injuries received in the mutiny, and that for these the under-writers were not responsible. They were not to pay any losses which might happen in the boats during the voyage, mortality of negroes by natural causes only excepted. They were not to pay for mortality through mutiny unless the same amount of 10 per cent. to be computed upon first cost of the ship, outfit, and cargo, valuing the negroes so lost as £35 per head.

The ships sailed from Bristol with mixed cargoes for trade in Africa, together with slave provisions, shackles, chains, hand-cuffs, firearms of various sorts, cutlasses and a medicine chest. The following is an estimate for a typical cargo:—

"Estimate for a Cargo wherewith to purchase 250 Negroes at Benny. [1]

	£	s.	£	s.
250 paper brawles at 5/6	68	15		
80 blew Chints of the Smallest Flower and none with Large Spriggs	104			
50 blew Byram pauls	50			
50 Demi long cloaths	60			
100 Large Niccanees fine small stripe	80			
100 Small ditto	60			
100 Cotton Romals with red and blew stripes mixd	60			
30 Photeas blew and white Check'd	20			
			502	15
300 Musquets bright barrels } 100 ditto black }	190			
40 pair common large pistols	28			
40 blunderbusses 18 inches	30			
			248	
2 tonns lead in small barrs abt. 4 lb each			32	
5 cwt. Neptunes 22 in. in the bottom			40	
15 cwt. Monelas			56	5
14 Tonns Iron			230	
1000 Copper Rods			50	
80 wicker bottles brandy			40	
5 cwt. Christial pipe beads			28	
			£1226	

[1] Undoubtedly Bonny.

Provisions and necessaries.

80 cwt. Rice	4 cwt. Tebacco
150 bus. Beans	a Surgery chest and Medicines
30 cwt. wt. bread	14 doz. Candles
10 cwt. wh. Flower	2 bbls. Gunpowder
60 cwt. beeff and Porke	50 Galls. brandy
10 bushells pease	20 dozn. beere
5 bh. Malagetta	10 bushells Grutts
2 Firkins butter	Groceries." [1]
2½ tonns Shipbeere	
12 Groce Tebaccopipes	

In addition to this, there would also be the wages of the crew, insurance and other charges. Some companies sent their buyers ahead to collect the negroes, so that when the ship arrived, she could be loaded at once and despatched for the New World, while the buyer went on to prepare for the next arrival, or carried on a general trade in ivory and other West Coast products. It was more common, however, for the captain to be his own buyer, and for this purpose he was given exact instructions. But the necessities of his calling required that he should also be left with a great deal of discretionary power.

By the middle of the eighteenth century, leading Bristol firms had regular representatives in the chief colonial slave ports. Sometimes these were junior members of the firms who were sent out in order to acquire experience. The letters of these men to their principals make it quite clear that the commerce in slaves was considered a perfectly respectable and everyday business. The colonial correspondents continuously assured their clients in Bristol that everything possible was being done by them to obtain a high price. In order to facilitate the business, they recommended from time to time the kind of slaves who should be sent to particular places, and warned them of negroes taken from certain parts of the African coast. Thus, in 1737

"a Brigantine arrived last Friday called the *Post Boy* of Bristol with 350 Negroes. These are proper for the Havanas and Cuba. As we want Girls we shall take those who are not too much on the Yellow cast, to which these Country Slaves are subject." [2]

[1] Donnan, *op. cit.*, vol. II, pp. 445–6.
[2] *Ibid.*, vol. II, p. 459.

Or again,

"We would you Could be perswaded to Direct your Vessells to the Gold Coast or Widdaw, as Negroes from those places Especially the Latter, are in most Esteem here, and will allways sell at Good prizes, when Bonny Negroes (the men particularly) are held in much Contempt Comparatively wth the Others . . . many of them hanging and Drowning themselves . . . tho it must be allow'd yt the Boys Girls and Women prove good Slaves, but the Men are Wretched bad, and Scarce of any Value, as one of us has Sufficiently Experienc'd and would not Bring them into his Estate on any Consideration." [1]

A list of the charges made by the agents on the sale of a cargo of slaves illustrates the varied activities of the local representatives of Bristol firms. These negroes were sold in Barbados in 1730, for William Freke and Company, Merchants, of Bristol.

	£	s.	d.
"To Cash paid duty of 335 Negroes landed at 5/– per head	83	15	
To ditto paid Jno. Walker for landing 326 and Carr'ng 190 ab. the Ships	4	14	
To ditto paid for 6 pcs Niconees and 3 pcs perpetts for Clouts	5	12	6
To ditto paid for printing notes and for hire of Messingers to give notice round the Island of the Sale	5	11	
To ditto paid for greens and other provisions for the Slaves till Sold	10	17	9½
To ditto paid for Treating Customers during the Sale	25	9	3
To ditto paid for Yardroom and Lodging	12		
To ditto paid the Vendue Master for outcrying	2		
To Commission 5 per Cent	310	7	3
	460	6	9½
To account Currant for Net proceeds hereof being Five thousand Seven hundred and Forty Six pounds Eighteen Shillings and two pence half penny Currant money	5,746	18	2½
	6207	5	

Errors excepted." [2]

---

[1] Bristol Museum and Art Gallery, Jefferies MSS.
[2] Donnan, *op. cit.*, vol. II, p. 383.

The sales were advertised in the colonial papers precisely as if it had been cattle and not human beings that had come to market. "Great regard will be had to ready price as well as to ready money." Indeed, the question of payments continually appears in the letters between the agents and their principals. The planters wanted long credits, five-eighths in cash or at thirty days and the remainder in eighteen months, while the Bristol merchants preferred 75 per cent. of the sale price down and the balance in twelve months. Another difficulty which continually arose was the over-stocking of the markets. This brought the price of good slaves down very low. In the 'thirties of the eighteenth century, for example, great things were expected from the Assiento: so London, Bristol and Liverpool merchants rushed cargoes of negroes to Jamaica, which was to be the entrepôt for the Spanish colonies. Unfortunately, the Spanish inopportunely attacked a British ship, which led to immediate reprisals by a man-of-war, and so the expected boom in the Spanish slave trade did not take place. Like London and other English ports, Bristol suffered from frustrated expectations engendered by that glittering illusion, the Assiento.

A typical advertisement of slaves for sale may be taken from *The Virginia Gazette*, 15th June, 1739:

> "The *Crosse*-Galley, Capt. Joseph Pittman, Master, lately arrived from Africa, with a choice Cargo of Slaves. The sale whereof will begin on Monday the 4 Instant, at West Point, And as soon as discharg'd, will prepare to receive a Freight for Bristol . . . Harmer and King." [1]

Reference has already been made to the complaints of the agents about the quality of the cargoes. Sometimes, when the market was especially good, they grew more insistent on this point:

> "Could your *Fortune* have the good luck to come down here this Summer with a healthy Cargo well assorted we dare say she would find a better Market with us then any where else." [2]

Agents were not always dissatisfied with their cargoes, and

[1] Donnan, *op. cit.*, vol. IV, p. 202, n. 28.
[2] *Ibid.*, vol. IV, p. 324.

Eighteenth-century view of Charleston, the Capital of South Carolina

A view of St. Lucea, 1770

some captains, whose number grew as the eighteenth century advanced, managed to land "choice cargoes" in a good condition. When prices were good the letters home were cheerful and expansive:

"Two days ago . . . we made Sale of the Cargo of the *Pearl*, Jeffries, of Bristol from Angola which avarage £33. 17. Sterling, her Cargo was 250. we had Chaps for more than double the number could we have furnished them. There was in this parcell near 150 Men and large Boys, the Men all to a trifle brought 270 and £280. Five of them sold so high as £290 per head, a very great price we think for Angola Slaves." [1]

These sums were, of course, expressed in colonial currency:

"Our ready money upon the Sale does not exceed a £1000 Stg. but scarcely one sold for longer Credit than January." [1]

The rumour of war naturally affected the slave market. At such times prices fluctuated violently until it was definitely known whether it was, in fact, to be peace or war. As war was almost the normal state, market conditions usually settled down and trade proceeded much as usual, for the British Navy could always be counted upon. In times of peace or war a good cargo of slaves in a reasonable condition usually netted a large sum, which was generally paid to the owners in bills on London in twelve to eighteen months' time. Long before this payment the ship had sailed for the Mother Country with its cargo of sugar, tobacco or mixed colonial products, so that with reasonable fortune, the owners stood to make three profits on the voyage. The trade goods were sold in Africa at a profit, the slaves were sold in the colonies at a profit, and there was money to be made on a cargo of colonial products in England.

The prices of raw negroes varied from plantation to plantation, from season to season, and according to the respective strength of demand and supply. Many other factors also affected the price, such as the place of origin of the slaves, their age, sex and physical condition. Prices ranged from £10 sterling and

---

[1] Donnan, *op. cit.*, vol. IV, p. 322.

sometimes less, to £80 sterling and sometimes more. When the figures were expressed in local currencies they became astronomical. Sometimes a careful agent who considered that the market would probably improve in the near future, or that the value of the negroes would be increased by a short period of seasoning, would send them to the country for a few weeks. By so doing they might be sold at much higher rates. Thus, Henry Laurens of South Carolina, acting in 1769 for Henry Bright and Company of Bristol, by adopting this policy, cleared £400 more for his principals than the negroes would have netted immediately after their importation, even though

> "a third poor pining creature hanged herself with a piece of small Vine which shews that her carcass was not very weighty." [1]

Even with rumours of war in the air, a cargo, with skilful handling, could bring a handsome price. Thus, another cargo of the *Pearl*, of Bristol, in South Carolina in 1755, produced £52,294 17s. 9d. colonial currency or almost £8,000 sterling. Five of these slaves were sold at over £41 sterling apiece, and the remainder ranged between £35 and £40.

The treatment of slaves varied from plantation to plantation, and according to the character of the owner or his staff. Generally speaking, conditions on the continental estates were in some respects better than those on the sugar plantations, where harsher labour conditions tended to prevail. On the other hand, the continental climate was more severe in the winter, and the negroes suffered more from the elements. In addition to trading with the sugar and tobacco colonies, many Bristolians had estates there as well. A fairly complete record of such a connection is preserved in the papers of the Pinney family, and especially in those of John Pinney, who, as will be seen later, was a planter in Nevis for many years in the latter part of the eighteenth and opening years of the nineteenth centuries. When Pinney first arrived in Nevis, he was horrified by the sights and sounds of slavery, but he soon became accustomed to the system, and grew to regard it as the corner-stone of his fortunes.

---

[1] Donnan, *op. cit.*, vol. IV, p. 432, n. 2.

"Since my Arr¹ I've purch^d 9 Negroe Slaves at St. Kitts and can assure you I was shock'd at the first appea^ce of hum^n flesh expos'd for Sale. But surely God ordain'd 'em for ye use and benefit of us: other^se his Divine Will, would have been made manifest by some parti^r Sign or Token." [1]

In another letter, a typical example of the kind of instruction which a planter might be expected to send to his manager is to be seen:

"I desire you wou'd take the first and earliest opportunity of buying me ten new Negroes, I would rather have them of that Age as are called Men-Boys or Women-Girls, never let your Females be more than as four in ten, and never let them be younger than ten years or more than twenty, and be sure never let them be as Old as thirty, if you can help it. . . . And as it seldom happens that Negroes are to be bought in Nevis, get them at St. Kitts or any of the other Islands where they may be had best and Cheapest." [2]

Like many of his contemporaries, Pinney was anxious to be kind to his slaves. As a class the planters did not delight in cruelty, and where the amelioration of the negroes' lot was compatible with what their masters deemed to be their own economic interest, the majority of planters were ready to consider the feelings of their slaves. Pinney, for example, was quite willing that aged slaves, who had passed their time of usefulness, should still continue to receive their usual food allowances and to live on the plantation. He wished to procure for his negroes the clothing that they were accustomed to, rather than new, and to them unpopular, varieties.

"I hope it is unnecessary to recommend to you a mild (not cruel) treatment of my Negroes, and more especially so at the time of their Sickness, a merciful Man is So, even to his Beast: How much more then is it incumbent upon us to exercise it upon those poor Creatures, who only want the light of revelation and Learning to be upon a Level with us." [3]

This was written in 1762, before Pinney went out to Nevis, but after he got accustomed to plantation life and the horrible

---

[1] *Pinney Papers, Business Letter-book,* 1761–75, fol. 67.
[2] *Ibid.,* fols. 1–2.
[3] *Ibid.,* fol. 6.

sufferings of the negroes during their period of seasoning, when so many died under the unaccustomed labour, this point of view tended to alter somewhat.

Negroes were, after all, expensive, and the planter could not afford to waste luxuries on them. Many of Pinney's contemporaries believed that the African was not really human at all, and that too much should not be made of the accidental fact that they *looked* like men.

> "Avoid as much as possible the calling in of a Doctor to the Negroes; they are so exorbitant in their charges, it is impossible for an estate to support it. Simples, good nursing and kitchen physic are the only requisites to recover sick negroes; I was very successful in my practice, and have no doubt but you will be equally so." [1]

This easy complacency, however, was not always justified, for occasionally an epidemic broke out among the slaves. Then the owner was seriously perturbed, for negroes represented hard cash already paid out, as well as essential labour power required to work the estate.

> "I am very Sorry to hear that the small Pox is got into my Plantation, and if you have not already pursued your thoughts of Enoculation, take this as a standing Rule from me for the future: which is, to Enoculate as soon as you shall think proper, always observing that during the Operation you do not keep them to Hot, but in that Habit of Heat which is necessary to encourage the Fever, and to keep the Pox out for by known experience it has been found erroneous and detrimental to the Patients Health and Life, by keeping them to Hot." [2]

When everything was going well, the crops good and the markets promising, the slaves industrious and healthy, Pinney and his like were disposed to be gracious.

> "It affords me great satisfaction to hear that my people behave well—I am happy in rendering them service, and begrudge them nothing the Estate can afford, but we must act with prudence and discretion in all we do; taking care not to

---

[1] *Pinney Papers, Business Letter-book*, 1779–84, fol. 318.
[2] *Ibid., Business Letter-book*, 1761–75, pp. 6–8.

grant particular favours so frequent as to give them an opportunity to look on it as a matter of right—I mean in giving
them *every* Saturday afternoon; you should occasionally vary
the day and when it is dry weather you may defer it several
weeks together; and if any Negroes are so idle and lazy as to
neglect their Provision ground, you should minute down their
names and oblige them to work in the field, while the others
are labouring for themselves. This would prove a material
spur to industry." [1]

The picture which this conjures up is that of a despotism,
and in some respects a despotism not unflavoured by kindness,
in so far as human kindness was possible in a system where one
man owned the bodies of his fellows. When every allowance
has been made, slavery was a detestable state. But in the
English colonies it never became the highly industrialized system
of exploitation which flourished in Cuba in the nineteenth
century. There, it was frankly based on the policy of working
slaves to death. On the English estates of the West Indies and
the mainland, old slaves would be found who lived at ease, and
in what was, for them, comfort. Lastly, the time must be
remembered, and it is doubtful if these hapless Africans suffered
as much or were as brutally regarded by their masters as were
the English people who, in this same period, were driven from
their villages to end their days in the cruel discipline of those
"dark satanic mills" which roused the pity and distress of Blake,
the fury and condemnation of William Cobbett.

[1] *Pinney Papers, Business Letter-book*, 1788–92, fol. 199.

CHAPTER XI

THE SUGAR ISLANDS

"... *all men that are dealers, even in shop trades, launch into adventures by sea, chiefly to the West India plantations. ... A poor shopkeeper that sells candles, will have a bale of stockings, or a piece of stuff, for Nevis, or Virginia, &c.*"

ROGER NORTH, *Lives of the Norths.*

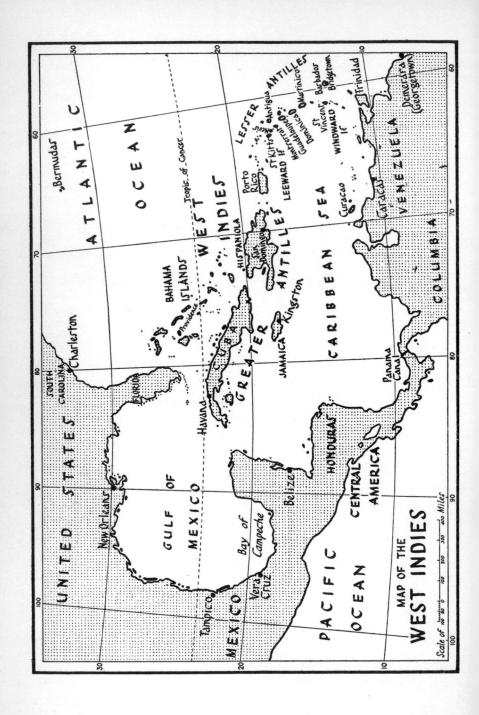

MAP OF THE
WEST INDIES

Scale of Miles
180 160 80 0 100 200 300 400 Miles

EVEN in the heyday of the slave trade, direct traffic between Bristol and the West Indian plantations was also of some importance. As in the closing decades of the eighteenth century the direct interest in the slave trade declined, the West Indian commerce became the most important branch of the city's trade. The close economic connection between Bristol and the colonies, which began in the middle of the seventeenth century and continued down to the final eclipse of the sugar islands two hundred years later, led her citizens to take a close, though sometimes selfish, interest in colonial politics and the vicissitudes of colonial development. Their fortunes waned and waxed with the ebb and flow of colonial prosperity. A great deal of Bristol capital was invested in colonial shipping, the sugar refining industry and tobacco. In addition, tradesmen and artisans of all kinds connected with the repair, equipment, lading and manning of ships, also depended upon the colonial trade. Besides all these, there were woodworkers, cabinet-makers, dyers, timber importers, insurance-brokers and many more who worked in colonial commodities, or in some way were dependent upon their importation and distribution.

In fact, by the beginning of the eighteenth century Bristol had already become a great port, mainly interested in colonial trade. She exported every variety of English and foreign manufacture, and she imported from the colonies a wide variety of products, ranging from codfish and furs to logwood and, in particular, sugar and tobacco. It thus came about that every proposed change in Government policy toward the colonies was carefully considered by the Merchant Venturers and others in Bristol. If, as so often happened, the proposed action was deemed to be in any way adverse to the interests of the city, petitions, letters, memorials and deputations were sent up to the capital, praying that the scheme should be dropped altogether or substantially modified. It was considered to be the duty of the city's representatives in Parliament to hold a watching brief for her trade, and they were kept hard at work by their constituents.   Innumerable petitions were sent up to them on every conceivable subject, which they were expected to lay before Parliament.   They were required to make speeches, to lobby, to interview the Commissioners of Trade and Plantations and to keep the Society of Merchants and the Corporation of Bristol in constant touch with the parliamentary situation. The modern member of Parliament is well paid for the work he does, when his lot is compared with that of the unpaid, constantly harassed, hard-working, genuine representatives who sat for Bristol in the old, unreformed House of Commons. The Society of Merchant Venturers, and sometimes the Corporation, retained permanent legal representatives as well, whose functions varied. Sometimes alone, sometimes in combination with Liverpool or London, Bristol protested against or supported special legislation, and the records mention the payment of various sums which were expended in this work.

When the Commonwealth and Restoration Governments elaborated the Old Colonial System by the passing of the Acts of Trade and Navigation, Bristol, in common with other towns in England and the plantations in general, was at first inclined to be hostile to the new policy. The effect of these laws was to make England the staple for the most important colonial products, and also for all foreign products required by the colonies. Ireland and Scotland tended to be regarded as foreign countries by the English traders at first. Scotland was admitted to the charmed circle in 1707 but Ireland was still excluded. It was contended that this system would benefit the Mother Country in many ways and, in the long run, that it would be in the interest of the whole Empire. Since all imports and exports paid duty, it would benefit the national revenue. By supplying the Mother Country with products which she would otherwise have purchased from foreigners, the colonial trade would help to make England self-sufficient. It would stimulate her manufactures, and since more colonial goods could be imported than were required by the home market, these, in their raw or manufactured state, could be re-exported, and would thus cater to England's favourable balance of trade. Lastly, by confining this commerce to English ships, the Navigation Acts were intended to foster the Mercantile Marine and thus contribute to naval strength.

Bristol quickly adjusted herself to the new situation, and in a few years forgot all her early misgivings about the wisdom of the regulations. Before the close of the seventeenth century, in fact, she became an eloquent advocate of their strenuous enforcement. In 1694 a petition was sent up to Westminster complaining that, in defiance of the law, certain Irish, Scottish and North of England ships were carrying colonial products direct from the plantations to Ireland and Scotland, a practice which the petitioners declared was detrimental to the interests of the Mother Country. They, therefore, prayed that Parliament in its wisdom would take the necessary action to ensure a speedy termination to these practices.

Throughout the eighteenth century Bristol was a determined opponent of Irish participation in the colonial trade, no matter what the inconvience to that country or to the colonies might be. Where possible, in trade matters, Ireland was looked on as a foreign country whose exports and imports must pass through English ports. When, in 1703-4, the Irish Parliament, in an address to Queen Anne, prayed that Irish merchants should be allowed to ship their linens direct to the colonies, the traders of Bristol felt that their interests were threatened. It was agreed that the Master of the Society of Merchant Venturers should instruct the city's representatives in Parliament to oppose this request which, if granted, would be prejudicial to the whole nation and, in particular, to Bristol. This extremely ungenerous and in the long run very unwise policy of the people of Great Britain toward Ireland, continued in force, despite the abortive attempts of Pitt to change it, down to the passing of the Act of Union in 1800. In 1731 the Irish petitioned that sugar should be allowed to enter their ports without previously being carried to England, but the Merchant Venturers saw in this a threat to Bristol shipping and to Bristol refiners, so the petition was finally quashed.

With the outbreak of the American Revolution, Ireland very wisely seized her opportunity. A hostile European alliance was planning the humiliation of England, and the war was going badly in America, so Great Britain could not afford a rebellion in Ireland. Grattan, with 30,000 Irish volunteers at his back, demanded substantial modifications of the Navigation Laws, and resolutions to that effect were accordingly introduced into the British Parliament. In Bristol, however, narrow economic interests on this occasion were placed before imperial requirements, and the inauguration of a more generous Irish policy was bitterly opposed. The leading Bristol representative of the time, Edmund Burke, was enthusiastic for reform, and boldly proclaimed his principles in Parliament and in Bristol, whose narrow selfishness he denounced. This Irish sympathy was a much more potent cause of his rejection by the city in 1780 than was his eloquent advocacy of justice to the American colonies. The opposition was at first successful, and the proposal of 1778 was whittled down to a few minor concessions on the export of Irish linens. Bristol took up the lofty, patriotic attitude which happened at the time to suit her. Such a departure would not only be detrimental to the trade of the port, but injurious to the manufacturers of the whole country. That

"great system of commerce Manufactures and Revenue which ever since the Establishment of the Colonies had been successfully pursued" [1]

for the common good would be ruined. These Irish concessions would injure the landed interest, and they were in every way unjust, for Ireland had no right to such privileges, since her people neither paid the same taxes nor were liable to the same scale of duties as the long-suffering people of England. This opposition to the Irish policy of North's Government in 1778 well illustrates the methods and energy of the Merchant Venturers of that time. A petition was drawn up and sent to Westminster, a circular letter signed by the Master was sent to every city and borough in the kingdom advising it to follow the wise policy of Bristol, a special delegation was sent up to London to manage the anti-Irish campaign, and a special committee of the Society was set up to confer with representatives from other cities and boroughs.

[1] *Merchants' Hall, Index to Proceedings*, 1713-97, 15th April, 1778.

In the following year a Bill was proposed which was designed to enable Ireland to import her sugars direct from the colonies, but once more the Merchant Venturers of Bristol and the vested interests throughout the country were successful. This victory was short-lived, for the Irish were determined, and Great Britain was in no position to be firm. On 21st December, 1779, it was reported in a letter to the Society that it was now proposed to allow Ireland to trade with the colonies, plantations and foreign countries on the same terms as England, and also that Irish glass and woollens were to be freed from certain restrictions. By that time the Society had become more conscious of the perilous state of the country and so, convinced that further opposition to Irish reforms would be fruitless, it resolved that no exception should be taken to these proposals.

This did not mean, however, that Bristol had changed her point of view. With the return of peace, concessions which had been made in a serious national emergency seemed particularly objectionable. In 1785 the Irish colonial trade again came up for consideration, but by that time the harassed North had long since departed, and the young Pitt, disciple and exponent of the theories of Adam Smith, sat in his place. The great economist himself declared that the young prime minister understood the principles of the *Wealth of Nations* even better than its author. But while Pitt agreed in the main with Smith's views on the Old Colonial System, young as he was, he had already learned that in an imperfect world economic truth had frequently to wait on political expediency. The merchants of Bristol, happily ignorant of the Scottish professor and his revolutionary ideas, though still inclined to oppose commercial concessions to Ireland, realized that they must justify their opposition by more convincing arguments than those they had used six or seven years before. They, therefore, concentrated their attention on the fact that Ireland paid a lower scale of taxes and lower duties than were paid by the English. They paid nothing for the upkeep of the Navy and the other public services upon which the existence of the colonies depended.

"The just retribution which our American colonies make for the expense of their establishment for the support they

receive by our exclusive consumption of their produce and
the protection afforded them by our navy will no longer exist
if Liberty is given to import West India productions either in
their raw or manufactured state from Ireland and this country
will be deprived of the advantage arising from the supply of
its own markets. If the import of foreign produce from Ireland
is allowed, similar mischief will accrue to the revenue and
carrying trade." [1]

The petitioners declared that they would welcome any improvement in Irish trade so long as it was not harmful to that of
England, and they felt that an equalization of duties and other
charges should be carried through, so as to place English and
Irish traders on a similar footing.

It was, in fact, along these lines that the mind of that great
statesman, Pitt, was moving. The reforms that he proposed in
1785, however, aroused such a storm in Parliament that he was
compelled first to modify and finally to abandon them altogether.
During the whole of the eighteenth century, in fact, Bristol was
constantly on the alert to oppose any change in public policy
which remotely might interfere with her commerce. When,
therefore, Walpole turned his attention in the 'thirties to the
overhaul of the antiquated fiscal machine, he aroused bitter
opposition, and his great Excise Bill was unpopular in Bristol
as elsewhere. On 25th February, 1735–6, a letter from the
Society's London solicitor was laid before a full meeting of the
Hall. This stated that a petition, signed by West Indian sugar
producers, was about to be laid before Parliament, praying that
they might be permitted to ship direct to European ports south
of Cape Finisterre without first coming to England. As the
sugar refiners and West Indian shippers felt that this would be
contrary to their interests, a committee was appointed to
consider the subject. It was empowered to send a delegation up
to London to co-operate with the Bristol representatives in
Parliament to defeat the plan. The Master was instructed to
approach the Corporation with the request that it should
defray one half of the charges arising from this particular action
and others of a like nature then going on. The petition was

---

[1] *Merchant Venturers' Society, Book of Petitions,* fol. 101.

duly sent up to Westminster and agitation in Parliament was worked up. This activity was at first successful, but although the petition from the West Indies was rejected, the concessions demanded were ultimately made, provided always that the sugars were carried in British ships.

When the Sugar Colony Bill was before the House of Lords, a petition was read from the merchants and traders of the city of Bristol on 30th May, 1739, and ordered to be heard by Council at the second reading. The petitioners stated that if the Bill passed it would be of very considerable ill-consequence to the trade of this city in particular. It would necessarily decrease the number of ships engaged in the West Indian trade, which was upwards of 140. These carried to the colonies and to the West Coast of Africa the produce and manufactures of Great Britain and Ireland. The proposed Bill would ruin the importation of sugar into Bristol and thus destroy the refining industry of the city. It was also prejudicial to the nation at large, since it would throw the plantation trade in great measure into the hands of foreigners. They would replace the English not only as the buyers of colonial sugars, but also as the suppliers of trade goods to Africa and general merchandise to the inhabitants of the British colonies. The price of sugar for the whole nation would rise and refiners throughout the kingdom would suffer.

It was, however, not only the Irish and colonial exporters who had to be watched. There were occasions when the interests of the sugar refiners conflicted with those of the importers and planters. In 1753, for example, the Merchant Venturers heard with dismay that a petition was to be presented to Parliament that when the price of British colonial sugar was unreasonably high, the refiners should be allowed to obtain their sugars from foreign sources. The sponsors of this petition contended that British planters were restricting production in order to raise the price. This was detrimental to the interests of the refiners, who were thus compelled to raise the home price as well as that abroad, and this in turn gave their foreign competitiors a great advantage over them in foreign markets. The Bristol members of Parliament were, therefore, instructed to take immediate action, and to press for the re-imposition of the existing Sugar Act which was shortly to expire.

Another subject which gave rise to continual petitions and perturbation was the imposition of new duties on spirituous liquors. One of the first petitions in the eighteenth century on this subject testified more to the strength of Bristol's fiscal belief than to her aesthetic appreciation. On 18th May, 1713, a petition was laid before the House of Commons from the distillers and sugar-bakers of the city. From this it appears that alleged brandies were manufactured in Bristol which they unblushingly declared to be not much inferior to French brandy, although they were compounded of cider, perry, malt, low-grade sugar and molasses. By the consumption of these healthful beverages, which might more properly have come under the general designation of punch, since they contained at least five ingredients, tillage and husbandry were encouraged, navigation was promoted and many families employed. After a lengthy enumeration of all the advantages which the colonies, the national revenues and the health of the people derived from this manufacture, it was urged that home producers should not be allowed to suffer through competition with French products, now allowed in at unreasonably low rates.

In collaboration with the merchants of London, a series of demands were made on the subject of the sugar trade in 1733. To this the Government replied by placing a further bounty on the export of refined sugar, which enabled it to be sold abroad at a lower rate than in England. The duty on French brandy was raised above that on West Indian rum, while the whole of the duty was remitted to the exporters of raw sugar to the Continent. Another joint protest was made three years later against the imposition of new retail duties on spirituous liquors. Again, in 1742, there was a protest against part of a Bill then before Parliament in which it was proposed to lay a new duty on molasses and spirits. In 1766 the Society was informed by the sugar refiners that if the product of foreigners was admitted for domestic consumption they would be utterly ruined. The Hall, therefore, petitioned Parliament to prohibit such imports and to impose a duty of £12 a ton on foreign sugars brought into

The City of Bristol

Engraved by J. Kip after H. Blundel, 1717

A PLAN of BOSTON, and its ENVIRONS. shewing the true SITUATION of HIS MAJESTY'S ARMY. AND ALSO THOSE OF THE REBELS. Drawn by an Engineer at Boston Octr. 1775.

the country. In 1769 the import duty was still six guineas per ton on raw sugar, while that on the export of refined sugar was £14 10s.

When Pitt was negotiating the commercial treaty with France and it became known that the duties on brandy would probably be lowered, the West Indian interest throughout the kingdom again took the warpath. As at that time those concerned felt that they were labouring under a greater number of disabilities than usual, a long memorial was prepared which, under thirteen separate headings, restated at length the value of the West Indies to the Mother Country, and also asserted that everyone connected with the Islands would be injured by the proposed reductions on French brandies. Already, owing to the competition of smugglers, there had been an alarming contraction in the consumption of West Indian rum, as the people had acquired a taste for the cheaper French commodity. Even if the duty on rum was lowered in proportion to that on French brandy, the retention of a duty of 7s. a gallon on the foreign commodity would still render smuggling profitable. Illicit traders had all the advantages of proximity, low charges on small ships and a free market. The lower the duty on brandy was made the better, because it would lessen the temptation to smuggle. The charges on rum, including freight, insurance, cost of casks and loss by leakage were greater than those incurred by brandy importers. Moreover, the distillation of rum entailed the expenditure of much initial capital. The market was already flooded with cheap spirits, and the new policy, if carried into effect, would increase the quantity of French wines in the country and cause a further depression in the rum market. These difficulties were further exacerbated by the fact that the large quantities of rum which had formerly gone to the American colonies were now, since the Revolution, sent to an uncertain market in England.

The late war had caused an increase in the cost of foodstuffs, cattle, slaves and lumber in the plantations. Though the planters had been led to believe that Nova Scotia and Canada would not only take the surplus of West Indian rum, but would supply the Islands with the lumber, provisions and other things which they had formerly imported from the old mainland colonies, they had been grievously disappointed. None of their hopes had been realized since, for example, both in Canada and Newfoundland, while plantation rum paid sixpence a gallon duty, molasses was allowed in at a penny, and the northern colonies, therefore, distilled for themselves. Moreover, Canada annually imported several thousand puncheons of French and Dutch molasses. All of these misfortunes had occurred at a time when the Windward and Leeward Islands were not yet recovered from the effects of their capture by the enemy, and Jamaica for several years had been impoverished by a series of disastrous hurricanes and unfavourable seasons. This long jeremiad wound up with the familiar assertion that the trade between Great Britain and her sugar plantations was one of the principal sources of national wealth. It brought revenue to the Crown; was a nursery of seamen; provided an extensive market for British commodities, and was the employer of a large part of the national shipping. Lastly, as the planters spent their money in England, they looked for protection and encouragement from the Government, and especially some substantial preference in respect to one of their staple products. They, therefore, prayed for a further reduction of the duty on rum and the prohibition of foreign imports of molasses into Canada. In fact, down to the time when the sugar trade finally succumbed, this kind of complaint continued to be made. After the emancipation of slaves in 1833, the knell of West Indian prosperity was finally sounded. By that time the complaints were not merely that British policy was destroying profits, but that it was destroying the actual property of West Indian planters.

Bristol traders as a body stood to a man behind the rigid enforcement of the Laws of Trade and Navigation so long as this was clearly in their material interests. When, however, it appeared that their modification or suspension would help trade, this whole-hearted admiration of the system was substantially modified. Thus, in the 'sixties of the eighteenth century, it became clear that great advantages would arise from the development of a direct trade between the English West Indian plantations and the Spanish colonies. In exchange for their products, Spanish and other foreign planters would take great quantities of English manufactured goods. Thus, the so-called Free Port System developed. On 19th March, 1766, the Hall declared that Dominica should be made a free port for the importation of foreign sugars, cocoa, coffee, cotton, indigo and cochineal. At the same time, it was held that laws should be strictly enforced against importations of foreign manufactured goods. In due course a Bill before Parliament complied with the wishes of the sugar interests in England and Dominica, and, as it finally passed into law, it applied to Jamaica as well. As the new system proved very satisfactory, both Jamaica and Dominica prayed for extension when the Act of 1766 expired in 1774. The petition on behalf of the Jamaica trade by the Merchant Venturers stated that the Act had promoted the export of English manufactures and the import of needful raw materials such as cotton, indigo and dye woods. In addition, this Act had opened up other important branches of commerce with the Spanish colonies, especially the export from Jamaica of poor quality negroes, for whom there was no demand in the English plantations. On 26th February another petition was sent up to London, this time on behalf of the island of Barbados, which also wished to profit by the Free Port System, and there was another one on behalf of Antigua, which was sent up from the Hall to the Bristol Members in London by express. In all these petitions the new importance attached to the manufacture of cotton in England is evident.

"It was ordered that it should be remarked that it is for the interest of the manufacturers of this kingdom that cotton should be permitted to be imported into those Islands not withstanding any exception to the Petitions from the said Islands. And that the importation and exportation of negroes from the said islands should be put on the same footing as at Dominica."[1]

The petitions for Jamaica and Dominica were successful, and on 18th June, Lord Clare*, one of the city's representatives in

---

[1] *Merchants' Hall, Index to Proceedings,* 1713-97, 26th February, 1774.

* N.B.—Robert Nugent became Lord Clare, Irish Peerage, 1766.

Parliament, wrote to Isaac Elton, Master of the Society of Merchant Venturers:—

"Sir,

"I have the Pleasure of being able to inform you that the Committee upon the Jamaica Freeports met yesterday, and have unanimously agreed upon a Report in Favor of the Proposition for prolonging their Term. . . . A motion has been made for making Barbadoes a Freeport with an exception of certain Articles produced in that Island of which Cotton is one. Let me know the opinion of your Society."[1]

The system was extended again in 1780, and five years later it was regarded as an essential feature of colonial commercial facilities, and so further extensions were demanded. Finally, the Government accepted it as a permanent feature of its fiscal policy, and a limited number of ports, seven of which were in the West Indies, were thrown open. By that time, however, the need for attracting American vessels was even more pressing than the advantages which arose from an extended traffic with the Spanish colonies.

The records show that Bristol was not only interested in the fiscal relations of the Mother Country and her plantations. Owing to her close connections with the Islands, which resulted from the possession by many Bristol families of West Indian estates, the city took a keen interest in almost every phase of colonial life. It was customary for younger sons and junior members of firms to spend some years on the plantations before entering the business at home. Again, when they retired many West Indian planters settled in Bristol and its neighbourhood. They established themselves as merchants or brokers or bought land and set up as country gentlemen. Throughout the eighteenth century there was constant movement to and from the Islands, and the city was much more conscious of the overseas Empire than, with the aid of all the technique of modern propaganda, she was destined to be two centuries later. In consequence of the great earthquake which occurred in Jamaica, it was proposed in 1754 to transfer the seat of Government from

[1] *Society of Merchant Venturers' Letters*, 1754-   , bundle 18.

Spanish Town to Kingston. The Merchant Venturers were requested to support the proposal, and on 2nd September, 1754, a petition was agreed to by the Hall. On 30th December the Committee was requested to present it, and in the following May, Mr. Harris was sent to London to support the arguments of the Society before the Board of Trade and Plantations.

The Merchant Venturers, in fact, had a permanent Standing Committee on West Indian and African affairs to which relevant matters were referred for consideration. If thought desirable, the Committee was empowered to draft petitions which were considered by the whole Society before they were forwarded. A still better example of the intimate concern of Bristol for Jamaica was afforded in 1768. On 18th June of that year, the Master, on behalf of the Society, signified his approval of an Act providing for the division of that island into three counties, and for the appointment of Justices of Assize and Oyer and Terminer. When the enemy was destroying British power in the West Indies and the British Navy seemed powerless to resist, the legislature of Jamaica naturally expected that, in due course, French, Spanish and American ships would attack the island. The authorities, therefore, wrote to the Society of Merchant Venturers of Bristol to say that they feared an attack, and implored assistance from England. The Society was requested to use its powerful voice in stimulating the Government to take speedy action. It, therefore, empowered its West Indian Committee to seal petitions and send representatives to London, while the Master was instructed to write to the city Members in Parliament to enlist their co-operation.

Though Jamaica was the most important English island in the Caribbean, Bristol was also interested in other plantations. In 1709 a group of her merchants complained, through Lord Sunderland, to the Commissioners of Trade and Plantations concerning Colonel Parke's misgovernment of the Leeward Islands. When the Free Port System was established in Dominica, and it seemed that the island was to be of considerable importance to trade in the future, its political dependence on Grenada was regarded by the Bristol traders as a serious handicap. A petition directed to the King-in-Council by the

Society of Merchant Venturers enumerated the various advantages which had resulted from the creation of the free port. The dependence on Grenada for the final determination of lawsuits and all other appeals caused great expense and loss of time, such as no trade could support, and all of this discouraged settlers from establishing themselves in that plantation. The petitioners, therefore, prayed the King to order that a legislature should be established in Dominica independent of any other island. On 21st December it was reported that this petition, together with several memorials of the like nature from the merchants and others of Dominica, London and Liverpool, had been considered. It was recommended that the King should erect Dominica into a separate government, independent of the island of Grenada, having a separate Governor vested with civil and military authority. This was desirable as it would remove the grievances complained of in the memorials and petitions. But there were even more pressing reasons for this departure. As Dominica was situated near to the French islands of Guadaloupe and Martinique, it was exposed in time of war to imminent danger, and in time of peace it was well placed for a contraband trade. It was desirable, therefore, that a competent authority should exist in the island, and that it should not be dependent upon action from a distance.

There are many other illustrations of the close interest taken by Bristol in the Islands at this time. Thus, in October, 1766, the Corporation resolved that one hundred guineas should be contributed

"towards relieving the unhappy sufferers by a dreadful fire which lately happened at Bridgetown, Barbadoes,"

and three years later, a similar sum was subscribed for the relief of the victims of a fire in Antigua. Naturally, the financial condition of the Islands was a constant care of the Society of Merchant Venturers. At one time they agitated for a more efficient method of recovering debts in the West Indies, at another, they were anxious to encourage foreigners to invest money in the British Islands. With the shutting down of food supplies from the American colonies and restrictions on the imports of wheat from Great Britain, which resulted from the change in England's agricultural position, the situation of the West Indies became precarious. Her rapidly increasing population put an end to England's exports of wheat, and so the Islands found themselves in a perilous position. They had long since specialized to such an extent in particular crops that they were almost entirely dependent for their food supplies on the old mainland colonies and the Mother Country. Efforts were made to substitute Canada and Nova Scotia for the revolted colonies, but this was not successful. So the enemies of the disobedient Americans, who happened also to be devoted supporters of the Old Colonial System, were compelled to cast aside their prejudices in order to prevent the West Indies from starving, or from following their continental brethren along the now familiar path of revolution.

It has already been said that the outbreak of war always brought in its train special problems, which those who were concerned in the colonial trade were bound to consider. Disputes over prizes afforded endless material for litigation. Frequently, the point at issue was that the Government imposed such heavy duties and other charges on captured enemy ships and cargoes that the victorious captors were actually in danger of loss. In the course of the Spanish Succession War, for example, the owners of muscovado sugars, captured from the enemy, complained that under a recent Act the customs officers required them to pay £2 10s. 2d. a cwt., which was about double its market value. They also said that the duties on indigo and cotton were unreasonably high. With this view the Parliamentary Committee, to whom the subject was referred, agreed. It was pointed out that, prior to the passing of the Act, muscovado sugar had paid 3s. 4d. a cwt. on importation, and indigo 2d. a pound, while cotton came in free. The Committee considered that the new scale of duties amounted to an entire prohibition of the consumption of sugar in Great Britain. Certain Bristol privateers who captured enemy ships off the coast of Newfoundland were in a still worse situation. Fish could not be stored indefinitely, and if they did not pay the duties, which were so high as to destroy all reasonable profit, they were in danger of losing the whole value of the cargo.

The disposal of prizes, however, could be settled in time, for it was in the interests neither of the Government nor of the traders that duties should be so high as to destroy the incentive for preying on enemy shipping, but the convoy question was never satisfactorily settled. Sometimes, as has already been seen, the naval officer in charge was over-cautious, and delayed the departure of the convoy for weeks and even months. The exports from Bristol consisted chiefly of plantation stores, building materials, hoops, iron work, carpenters' and coopers' tools, mill work, provisions and negro clothing. On the early arrival of these stores depended the "commencement of the crop." On 21st October, 1794, the Bristol West India Society sent a letter to the Admiralty pointing out that early in the previous year the ships for the Islands were detained three months in Cork harbour, which meant that perishable stores were damaged and others were too late for use. Such delays also entailed great expense in wages and food for the crew and, moreover, when they arrived at their destination, it was too late for such vessels to take aboard a return cargo. As the attempts to join the London or Portsmouth convoys were attended with great expense, damage, delay and uncertainty, the writers wished to know definitely when the convoy for that year would sail from Cork, and if a convoy could escort the Bristol ships when they set out to join the others in the Irish harbour.

In spite of all the vicissitudes of war, the capture and recapture of the Islands, hurricanes, slave insurrections, the threat to the whole system of production based upon slavery, consequent upon the persistent attacks of the Abolitionists from the middle of the 'eighties onward, Bristol's imports of sugar, molasses, rum, cotton, dye woods and other West Indian products increased greatly between the close of the Seven Years' War and the abolition of the slave trade. Barbados, Nevis, St. Vincent, St. Kitts, Dominica, Antigua, Tobago, Grenada, Montserrat, Bermuda, Tortola, St. Lucia and the rest sent their quotas, but Jamaica was the queen of them all. In 1770 out of a total of 12,330 hogsheads of sugar, 2,679 tierces and 79 barrels landed in Bristol, Jamaica alone was responsible for 6,268 hogs-heads, 1,829 tierces and 18 barrels; and the relative figures for molasses, rum, and other imports were in similar proportions. Even in the midst of the disastrous war with America, in spite of enemy men-of-war and privateers and the capture of islands, the trade continued to grow. Bristol received 16,139 hogsheads of sugar in 1778, 16,329 in 1779, 16,416 in 1780, while tierces and barrels of sugar, puncheons of rum and molasses show similar increases. With the return of peace trade rapidly re-covered, and even after eight years of war, the returns in 1801 show substantial advances on those for twenty years before. In that year, the total imports of sugar and its bye-products into Bristol were 19,381 hogsheads, 3,735 tierces, 11,081 barrels and 4 boxes of sugar; 2,338 puncheons and 218 hogsheads of rum; and 64 hogsheads of molasses. Of this total, Jamaica was responsible for 10,432 hogsheads, 1,891 tierces and 156 barrels of sugar; 1,819 puncheons and 183 hogsheads of rum; 2 pun-cheons and 144 hogsheads of molasses.[1] There is, therefore, apparently no reason whatever for concluding, as Latimer and others do, that there was an almost complete decline of the West India trade at the end of the eighteenth century. Natur-ally the trade fluctuated a great deal, but the figures here quoted show conclusively that the idea of a permanent and marked decline at that time is absurd.

With their constant market for Bristol goods, their increasing output of commodities for which there was a steady demand in Europe, and their relative nearness, as reckoned in terms of the time taken for a round voyage, the direct West Indian trade, as compared with that with Africa, had obvious advantages over the slave trade. As the change-over took place fewer ships sailed from the Avon to the African coast, but more went direct to the Caribbean. In 1787 there were 30 vessels engaged in the former trade and 72 in the latter. Slave ships at that time averaged 140 tons each, while West Indiamen averaged 241 tons. In addition to the West Indiamen, 7 trading with Hon-duras averaged 224 to 225 tons each. In contrast to this thriving southern trade, that with the old continental colonies never

---

[1] *Bristol Imports and Exports*, 1773–80, and 1801–20.

revived completely. In this same year, only 12 vessels sailed from Bristol to the American states, but the Newfoundland trade still flourished. Thirty-two Bristol ships sailed for the Banks in that year, averaging 93 tons each, as against 191 to 192 tons for the 12 engaged in the American trade. Two ships sailed for Quebec, averaging 180 tons each, and one to St. John, New Brunswick, of the burden of 251 tons.

In addition to the West India trade and the long-established traffic in slaves, a new commerce with Africa developed in the 'eighties of the eighteenth century. Ten vessels were engaged in the business, which mainly consisted of the exchange of English products for African woods. Of the 164 men employed in these ships, 20 lost their lives, many returned home in a sickly condition, and a high percentage went blind. It was, in fact, a dangerous and unpopular trade. Crews were obliged to go far up African rivers, exposed to the risk of massacre by the natives, who regarded all white men as slave traders, and there was the still more unnerving risk of falling a victim to the insidious attack of some strange and deadly tropical disease.

The African trade took a greater toll in human life than the West Indian or any other commerce in which Bristol was engaged. There appears, however, to be good reason for believing that Clarkson's figures did not err on the side of minimizing its bad points. Guinea ships engaged in the slave trade carried 12 men for every 100 tons when the ships were over 300 tons, and in smaller vessels the proportion of men to ships' burden was higher. Two-fifths of the crews in slave ships were able-seamen, while in West Indiamen four-fifths were of this rank. The same wages were paid in both trades, but as the African voyage was always longer, the men were allowed two or three months' pay in advance to cover the cost of equipment. Crews were strictly bound by the terms of the ship's articles to be obedient, to remain with the ship until her return, and not to engage in private trading. Chief mates and carpenters received £4 10s. a month, second mates and boatswains £3 15s. a month. According to Clarkson, the rate of mortality in the slave trade was very much higher than in all others. His conclusions were based on the records of 48 ships in 1784 to 1787, 24 of which were engaged in the African trade and 24 in general commerce. According to him, 216 men were lost in the former and 20 men were lost out of 24 ships engaged in the latter. These figures stand in marked contrast to the figures for 24 ships engaged in the East Indian, the Newfoundland and the West Indian trades, where the mortality in the same year was respectively 2, 2 and 6. These figures, however, bear no relationship to the evidence given in the Muster Rolls for the years 1786–7 and 1787–8, contained in a paper read to the Society of Merchant Venturers in the latter year. According to this, 19 seamen were lost on West Indian voyages in the first period and 17 in the second.

In the eighteenth century Bristol's connection with the West Indies was so close that, in addition to the Society of Merchant Venturers, another body called the West Indian Society came into existence. At some time prior to 1782 this was dissolved, but on 28th February of that year, a New West India Society was formed by a number of gentlemen who met at the Bush Tavern. At its first meeting practically all the members of the old Society joined the new body, and it was agreed that it should be conducted on lines similar to those of its predecessor. Strangers were to be admitted to four meetings of the twelve held in each year, but the remaining eight were to be for members only. This body was concerned with everything which affected the West Indian trade, and it contained among its members retired planters, West Indian merchants, sugar-refiners, insurance brokers and all who had a financial interest in the plantations. John Pinney and his partner, Tobin, became members, and took an active part in the proceedings of the Society.

At the meetings business was combined with pleasure. News from the Islands was circulated from member to member, and pending legislation, either in the West Indies or at Westminster, calculated to affect trade, was earnestly considered. The current price of sugar, food, ships, supplies, slaves and insurance rates all came under consideration. Sometimes the illegal action of shipwrights, who had combined to demand an increase in wages, was the chief topic. At others, it was the scale of freight rates between Bristol and Jamaica, in comparison with those between London and Jamaica. Then again, in order to obtain better wages, the ships' carpenters refused to allow the ships to proceed down the Avon, and this menace had to be countered by an appeal to the magistrates. On this particular occasion, though the authorities soon cleared the river for shipping, the carpenters would not return to work until the highly incensed gentlemen who met at the Bush Tavern conceded their demand, while they moralized on the depravity of the lower orders. But they had their lighter moments. Mr. Thomas Daniel, junior, made a wager with Mr. Maxse for a dozen of claret.

"Mr. Daniel says that the fine of one dozen claret, formerly paid by the Owner of the first ship to arrive either from Jamaica or the Leeward Islands with new Sugars &c is void. Mr. Maxse says not." [1]

And, as there was no mention in the minutes of any such resolution having been passed, Mr. Daniel lost his bet and readily paid. The subsequent minutes contain many references to this amiable practice of celebrating the arrival of the first sugar ship each year by the gift of wine at the expense of the fortunate owner.

So the eighteenth century closed; but already the storm was rising which was destined to terminate the rule of King Sugar, to destroy the planter oligarchies of the West Indies, and to bring to an end yet another phase in Bristol's long commercial history. Yet, though the clouds were gathering when the eighteenth century passed away, all of this disaster was still to come, for the planters as a body did not believe that Emancipation would follow in the wake of Abolition. In the meantime, in spite of all, their prosperity was unimpaired, and they enjoyed the social life of Bristol which had become a resort of fashion. The children of these West India men were already mingling on terms of equality with the elegant throngs that were to be seen at the Assembly Rooms and taking the waters at the Hot Wells.

[1] *The West India New Society*, 1782.

But these butterflies were in Bristol for a season only, and the old city had little in common with the habitués of a spa. She still drew her strength and her prosperity from the men who went down to the sea in ships and did their business in the great waters.

CHAPTER XII

FISH, TOBACCO AND IRON

"It (Bristol) is very populous, but the people give themselves up to trade so entirely that nothing of the politeness and gaiety of Bath is to be seen here; all are in a hurry, running up and down with cloudy looks and busy faces, loading, carrying and unloading goods and merchandizes of all sorts from place to place; for the trade of many nations is drawn hither by the industry and opulency of the people."

THOMAS COX and A. HALL, *Magna Britannia et Hibernia* (1720–31).

FROM the time of their foundation Bristol was concerned in some way or other with almost all of the colonies. Before the Civil Wars her ships were already trading with Virginia, New England and Newfoundland. Sometimes they were absent for a very long time before they saw the Avon again. They left Kingroad with stores and passengers for one of the mainland colonies, whence they carried a cargo to Newfoundland which they exchanged for fish. This was either brought back to the colonial port from which they had come and exchanged for a cargo in that place, or they proceeded direct from the Banks to Spain or Portugal, and finally arrived in Bristol with a cargo of wine, fruits and other Iberian products. In the 'forties the *Deposition Books* of Bristol are full of references to colonial trade, chiefly Virginian, New England and Newfoundland. These proved not only that the commerce was extensive and growing, but that it gave rise to cheating, foreswearing and double-dealing of a high order. Customs officers were continually at issue with dishonest traders, and there were many cases of barefaced theft to be considered. A usual form of dispute arose over the alteration of the trade mark, probably at a price, from the beneficiary. Thus, one deponent stated that he had seen Roger Kemnis take a roll of tobacco

"being a bigg one and weigheing neere about 80 ls weight (as this deponent conceaved), and scrape the said Richard Elsworthies name out of the stick, and in the same stick marked the role with the bunch of grapes being the generall marke for the shipps whole Cargo." [1]

Frequently, the officials were confronted with the problem of deciding between two obvious liars, who on oath made contradictory statements. There is one instance where the statement was made by a man who was known to be a

"periured rogue and rascall, and . . . God had laid his plague

[1] Nott, H. E. (ed. by), *The Deposition Books of Bristol*, vol. I, 1643–7, Bristol Record Society, pp. 191–2.

and iudgement upon him, and . . . he could not live seaven daies at an end."[1]

Nevertheless, this man, whose constitution appears to have been as robust as his disregard for truth, made a complete recovery, and lived to give trouble to other officials at other times. Dishonest traders had recourse to various methods of reconciling the breach of the law with their tender consciences. Sometimes they would allow their finger-nails to grow very long and then swear on the Book a completely false return, after which they would cut their nails and say that, as they had never touched the Book, the oath was invalid. The more cheerful rogues, having sworn to a false entry, were accustomed to drink a bottle of sack which, they said, washed away the effect of the lie.

It has been seen in a previous chapter that at the end of the sixteenth century the Newfoundland fisheries were already becoming the mainstay of the trade of the western counties, and for three hundred years they continued to be an important but declining concern of the Bristol merchants. The seventeenth century opened with the determined attempt on their part to establish permanent settlements in the island. Though Guy failed in his avowed intention, his action served to strengthen the connection which already existed between Bristol and Newfoundland. His hopes were frustrated not only by the interminable personal quarrels of the members of the Company, but also by the bitter hostility of the excluded merchants from the other Outports. If his plans had been carried out, England would have established her control of the fisheries by monopolizing the Beaches almost a hundred years before the Treaty of Utrecht was concluded. This would have saved the country a great deal of diplomatic negotiation and much fighting, and the Bristol merchants endless anxieties and substantial loss. Guy's settlement not only aroused the hostility of other Englishmen; the people of La Rochelle were also disturbed by his arrival and assertion of authority. They complained that he haunted that part of Newfoundland which they had baptized Nova

[1] Nott, *op. cit.*, p. 57.

Francia, and they were very jealous of any Englishman occupy-
ing land there, as they claimed that it had been in their possession
from time immemorial.

While the West Indian and African trades expanded apace,
the Newfoundland fisheries continued to be important, and
year by year a fishing fleet from Kingroad set sail for the Banks.
Like them, too, the fisheries suffered in the early decades of
the seventeenth century from the depredations of pirates. These
were so strong in the Mediterranean that the traders of Bristol
and the Outports were in danger of total annihilation as, unlike
London, they had not the strength to withstand them.

"If once those thieves shall find the way to Bank and New
Found Land, they will undoe the west parts of England." [1]

During the Civil War period the fishing fleets suffered grievously. In 1648 the Merchant Venturers petitioned the Committee for the Navy to send a frigate to protect shipping in the
Bristol Channel. The Royalists had a fleet of twenty ships and
frigates at Wexford, which were intending to cruise off Land's
End and the mouth of the Bristol Channel to cut off homeward
bound Bristol ships returning from Newfoundland and the
Peninsula. In the Dutch Wars the Newfoundland traders
again suffered and repeatedly demanded more effective
convoys.

In a petition to the Privy Council from the merchants and
ship-owners of the city, it was stated in 1667 that French and
Dutch ships of war threatened to destroy their trade unless
more adequate protection was provided. As an indication of the
value of the Newfoundland trade, the petitioners asserted that
the customs duties paid at Bristol on wine, oil and fruit brought
from Spain, Portugal and Italy, in exchange for Newfoundland
fish, amounted in the year to £40,000. They, therefore,
demanded that some competent person should be maintained in
the island for their protection. In the time of William III, the
Mayor of Bristol wrote to the Commissioners of Trade and Plantations enclosing certain proposals which had been drawn up by

·[1] Stock, *op. cit.*, vol. I, p. 101.

the merchants who were interested in Newfoundland. In this, the merchants asked that eight men-of-war and two fire-ships should be sent to the Bay of Bulls in April, or that failing this, Ferryland, Harbour de Grace and St. John's should be effectively fortified.

By the beginning of the eighteenth century a permanent population was established in Newfoundland which, between the departure of the fleet in one year and the arrival of the new one in the following year, lived in a state of lawlessness. As by that time some merchants had permanent establishments in the island, which represented substantial outlays of capital, the home authorities were petitioned that a permanent government should be established there as well as a garrison, and further, that the inhabitants should be exempted from impressment or forcibly being carried away to New England. In order that those engaged in this trade should have an opportunity of expressing their opinion on this, the Board of Trade and Plantations sent these proposals to the western Outports for their consideration. In due course the Mayor of Bristol intimated that Mr. Peter Renew and Mr. William Brown would come up to the Board with a memorial from his city. At that time the merchants appear to have been divided in their opinion. The lawlessness continued, and down to the signing of the treaty of Utrecht, the French menace remained.

Thus, throughout the War of the Spanish Succession, English and French privateers preyed on the shipping of each other. Sometimes Bristol vessels had the good fortune to capture prizes. The case of the *Greyhound*, however, showed that such a victory might be illusory, particularly when the cargo consisted of a perishable commodity such as fish, and when the customs officials were inclined to be exacting. For the 13,000 "couple of fish" in this ship the captors paid £32 4s. to the agent of the Lord High Admiral as his fee. They sold 8,000 "couple of fish" at Bristol, and there being no sale for the remainder, the cargo was taken out to sea and sunk at the petitioners' charge. Nevertheless, the collector of the Customs House demanded 26s. on "every 60 couple of the said fish," including those sunk as well as those which had been sold. In all, this amounted to

£150 more than the petitioners had received for the ship and cargo together.

In spite of such losses some ships sailed for Newfoundland each year. The Mayor stated in a letter to the Commissioners of Trade and Plantations in 1710, that twelve ships were to be sent that year to the Banks for which the merchants requested six men-of-war as a convoy. When it seemed that peace was to be concluded between England and France, Bristol repeatedly petitioned the Government that Great Britain should secure the whole of the Newfoundland fisheries to herself, and at long last put an end to French incursions. They supported this by enumerating at some considerable length the great advantages which Great Britain derived from this commerce, including the commodities which it brought to England and the unsurpassed training which it afforded to English sailors.

The terms of the Treaty of Utrecht were considered satisfactory, for the Government was fully alive to the advantages to the fisheries. The result was that on the whole, fishermen had little to complain of during the first part of the eighteenth century, though always in time of war the demand for protection was made and there were the usual complaints about convoys. By this time the trade was well organized, and with adequate protection, substantial profits might be made. Large sack ships, crowded with men, were sent out each year. These men either paid their own passages or were employees of Bristol merchants for whom they worked during the fishing season. On their arrival, the free passengers took service as bye-boatmen with the fishermen who required additional hands, while the others worked in boats belonging to their masters, which were stored away at the end of each season. The sack ships were partially loaded by these men and partially by the local inhabitants, who exchanged their fish for the miscellaneous cargoes which were carried out by the vessels. As early as possible in the season the sack ships set sail with full cargoes for the ports of Italy, Spain and Portugal, which lesser men avoided because of pirates.

From time to time the merchants were asked to state what difficulties they laboured under, and to indicate in what manner the Government might improve their lot. Though they did not always have anything to complain of or to suggest, they made a reply to such a request during the Seven Years' War which was both lengthy and exhaustive. Newfoundland, they declared, laboured under two inconveniences; fishermen were liable to impressment, and the trade was too exposed to enemy attack. Many English ships had been taken, some English prisoners had died in French prisons, and fishermen and boatmakers had become very scarce. The merchants had sustained great losses, but if proper convoy facilities were provided, all this would be avoided. With greater security insurance rates would drop, and they, therefore, put forward an elaborate scheme for the time of departure of convoys and how the convoys should conduct themselves. It was necessary that the fishermen should be protected by warships stationed in Newfoundland waters. If all of this was done, it would mean that the whole fishery would pass into English hands, and the French would lose employment for at least 200 sail. This document went on to suggest that English fishermen should be encouraged to go into the Straits of Belle Isle and to explore the fisheries on the east coast.

With the outbreak of the Seven Years' War the situation of the fisheries became precarious. As so often before, the Mayor of Bristol petitioned the Government for assistance. He declared that there never could be too many fishermen in Newfoundland, a sentiment with which the Government of the time was in complete accord, as this branch of her commerce was England's greatest nursery of seamen. Owing to the impressment of merchant sailors by the Royal Navy, and the inadequate military protection provided in Newfoundland, all the English who resorted thither were seriously jeopardized. Moreover, in consequence of the insufficient naval escort provided, several English vessels had already been captured by the French, and their crews had been imprisoned in France, where many had died before they could be exchanged. All the merchants engaged in this trade had sustained losses through providing men with clothing and other equipment to be used in Newfoundland, which had been lost when these men were captured by the enemy.

By that time, the supplying of provisions to the fishermen in Newfoundland, including both the permanent settlers and those who came out each year for the fishing season, had become a lucrative trade. It was for this reason that Bristol merchants were divided on the desirability of establishing a permanent government. The coming of a regular governor would also mean the coming of military force. The Island would thus become secure, local merchants could establish themselves, and thus deprive Bristol merchants of their trade. When the Treaty of Paris was under consideration, Bristol once more besought the Government to insist on the complete exclusion of the French from the fisheries. Nugent, one of the Bristol members in the House of Commons, was kept hard at work on this subject by his constituents. While obedient to their requests, he cautioned them to be reasonable in their demands, and not to expect the Government to break treaty engagements for their narrow wishes, even with a beaten foe. It was unwise for the Government to give guarantees which in time might develop into monopolistic claims, adverse to the general interests of the nation.

> "I've been longer upon this subject, than I woud otherwise have been, that such of my Constituents as are concerned in the Newfoundland Fishery may not be transported by their own sanguine Hopes, or by the flattering suggestions of others, into measures which may end in loss and Disappointment, where solid Advantages may be obtained by a just cautious and prudent conduct." [1]

After the conclusion of the treaty of peace, the merchants were still apprehensive about the position of the French in Newfoundland and the want of protection under which the industry laboured. Nugent was, therefore, requested to induce the Government to provide suitable naval forces to ensure the safety of the fishermen. At the end of March he wrote to the Master of the Merchant Venturers to announce that a squadron of six or seven ships, frigates and sloops were to sail early in April for Newfoundland. He also stated that the French fishermen

---

[1] *Society of Merchant Venturers' Letters,* 1754–   , bundle 8.

had been instructed by their Government that they must hence-forward content themselves with a bare participation in the fisheries between Cape Bona Vista and Point Niche. A few years later, it was proposed again that British fishermen should continue their fishery in the Straits of Belle Isle which the French had found so profitable, and that they should explore the virgin fishing-grounds on the east coast. To this a reply was sent from Labrador by twenty-five adventurers there who spoke for themselves and their partners at Bristol, Dartmouth, Exeter, Teignmouth, Poole and London.

The American war caused serious dislocation to the New-foundland trade. Merchants were accustomed to send out a supply of food with their ships in the spring, and later, during the summer, to import more stores from the colonies. At the very time when importation from the colonies became difficult, or was actually prohibited, Great Britain herself, owing to the enormous growth of population which had taken place in the past century, was ceasing to be an exporter of corn. Thus New-foundland was in danger of starvation unless the Government was prepared to make an exception in her case, and permit the export of corn, flour and biscuit. This subject gave rise to a protracted correspondence.

The limitations imposed upon France by the Treaty of Paris were never satisfactory to them, so when trade relations between Great Britain and that country were under discussion in 1786, which culminated in Pitt's commercial treaty, the New-foundland fisheries again came up for consideration. The French were able to convince the British Government that British fishermen had habitually poached in French waters, and a Bill for the more effective regulation of this trade was, there-fore, proposed. Mr. Brickdale, one of the Bristol representatives at that time, kept the Merchant Venturers in touch with the proceedings and sent them a copy of the Bill for their opinion. The Freedom of the City was presented to the Honourable George Berkeley for,

"his great attention to the Act lately passed for regulating the Newfoundland fishery, in which the commercial interest of this city is materially concerned."

Shortly after this, the question of the corn trade again became pressing. Bristol and the Outports favoured the opening of a limited trade in foodstuffs with the American states, as they believed this was the only possible way in which the fishermen and inhabitants of Newfoundland would have the necessary supplies. At home the situation of the corn trade was giving rise to anxiety for, in spite of a great improvement in agriculture, annual consumption was rapidly overtaking annual supply. Less and less corn was available for exportation, and so the idea of a quota was suggested. Bristol considered that the amount provided for her traders was wholly inadequate, as 48 tons of flour a year was less than one ship frequently carried to Newfoundland. The Bristol members were, therefore, supplied with a long dissertation on the nature of the corn trade, with several suggestions as to how, in the general interest, it should be managed. Naturally, what was deemed to be the general interest coincided with the wishes of the Bristol merchants. Throughout the eighteenth century, the Newfoundland trade continued to bulk largely in the minds of Bristolians. Much capital was invested in it, and in a good year as many as thirty ships might go to the Banks, and the fisheries employed many hundreds of the city's population.

Of more recent growth, though of greater significance to the city, was the trade with Virginia. In spite of King James I's denunciation of smoking, and his gloomy forebodings about the future of a province built on smoke, Virginia soon began to specialize in the cultivation of tobacco. Before the end of the century the Home Government changed its policy and did everything possible to encourage this industry. Foreign tobaccos were rigorously prohibited, and, with great difficulty, a flourishing tobacco planting industry in England was finally suppressed. In 1650 the merchants of Bristol and London complained of the evils resulting from the growth of tobacco in the Mother Country. This tobacco, they declared, was less wholesome than that of the plantations, and bad for English agriculture. Thousands of English families living abroad depended upon their tobacco crops, but if English tobacco continued to be grown they would be ruined, the commerce of the nation would suffer and its navigation would decline. They, therefore, prayed that the Government would set about the immediate suppression of this undesirable crop. Again, in 1654, the city's representatives were instructed to do all in their power to prevent the cultivation of tobacco in England, which was to the extraordinary prejudice of local trade, since the constant sale of English crops to a large extent nullified the small advantage such Outports as Bristol gained from the successful prohibition of foreign tobaccos.

At first Bristol was firmly excluded from the Colonial tobacco trade, as both James I and Charles I attempted to make London the tobacco staple for the kingdom. In spite of royal prohibition, however, and the vigilance of the Navy, some tobacco found its way to the city. Finally, in 1639, it was recognized that the exclusive policy was impossible to enforce, and so the trade was thrown open to Bristol and the Outports.

During the Second and Third Dutch Wars the Virginia trade suffered, and Bristol merchants in 1665 complained of the capture by Dutch capers of five "rich and considerable ships" belonging to them and laden with Virginia tobacco. Still, in spite of this, and also of Indian war in Virginia, over-production and the depradations of pirates, the trade continued to expand. As early as 1662, customs duties on tobacco at Bristol totalled £12,000. By April of that year, 8 tobacco ships had already arrived from Virginia and 6 more were expected. On 19th and 20th July, 1666, 18 ships arrived from Virginia, and on 3rd November 30 were at Bristol ready to sail for that plantation. In May, 1666, 18 tobacco ships sailed from Virginia for Bristol, and in the following year 9 Bristol ships were anchored on the same day in the James. With this great expansion of trade there was naturally an increase in bickering among captains and merchants, and between these together and customs officials. The planters felt they were being cheated, and the consumer was certain that he was paying too much for his tobacco. Such a trade seemed designed by Providence to assist the impecunious Stuarts, so heavier duties were imposed. This led not only to smuggling and bribery of officials, but to recrimination of all kinds, more particularly in the gross irregularities in duty imposed in England and Ireland. Still, the trade grew, and the traders' fortunes advanced. Bristol sent to Virginia in exchange for its tobacco household goods of every kind, plantation implements, clothing for the slaves, foodstuffs and luxuries for the planters, but most of all indentured servants and cargoes of slaves. Here, as elsewhere, there was the usual crop of complaints about inadequate convoys, but conscientious officials were thanked, as when, on 10th November, 1700, the Society of Merchant Venturers

"ordered that a gross of sherry be presented Coll: Nicholson Governor of Virginia for his readyness in takeing the Pirats."[1]

In the eighteenth century the same kind of protest against the fiscal policy of the Government continued to be made. Always, according to these, the trade was at the point of extinction unless redress was immediate. In 1713 Bristol went so far as to complain against the practice of planting tobacco on the continent of Europe. This, coupled with a new subsidy, according to the petitioners, would cause certain ruin to their trade. In the following year it was complained that the poor traders of Bristol were being cheated by the wicked planters, who sent inferior tobacco in exchange for the excellent goods of all kinds which were shipped out to them. They were obliged to pay high duties on bad tobacco, which often amounted to more than its market value. Perhaps the greatest uproar of all arose in consequence of Walpole's wise, though ill-judged, Excise Bill. On the ground that less than one seventh of the tobacco duty reached the Exchequer, he proposed to place the tobacco trade under excise supervision. Thereupon, the Society of Merchant Venturers despatched a strong deputation to London to co-operate with similar committees from other cities in the general opposition. Walpole, who wisely preferred to sacrifice his political principle rather than his own career, withdrew the unpopular measure, a decision which Bristol greeted with great rejoicings.

In the Virginian trade, as, indeed, in the trades of most of the colonies, currency disputes constantly arose. Under the

---

[1] *Merchants' Hall, Book of Proceedings*, No. 3, 1694–1708.

policy of the time, none of the colonies were allowed to coin money, for it was intended that they should remit as much bullion as possible to the Mother Country. They were thus driven to subsist for their needs on various makeshift monies, such as tobacco, sugar and paper of doubtful value. As the nature of paper money was at that time imperfectly understood, and as there was no competent banking authority in the colonies, over-issue, with its consequent depreciation, became the order of the day. This being so, Bristol traders were always anxious to ensure that their goods should be paid for in sterling or its equivalent in commodities. At the same time, they were perfectly willing to pay their sailors' wages in depreciated colonial currencies for which purpose they were pleased to consider that these monies stood on a par with sterling. A good example of such disputes occurred in 1751. The Virginia legislature passed a law by which the relative value of sterling was placed at 25 per cent. higher than that of local currency. This meant that if the courts awarded £100 damages in sterling, the officers would levy £125 in provincial money. The Merchant Venturers did not consider this premium sufficient, and so, on the recommendation of a Standing Committee on American Affairs, a memorial was despatched to Westminster.

Even before the Act of Union was passed Scottish interlopers caused Bristol to petition Parliament against them. One such petition was made in 1696, in which it was stated that Scotsmen were unlawfully bringing American products into their country, which later they smuggled into England. The Government was petitioned to suppress this illicit trade on the usual ground that the honest merchants of Bristol would be ruined. Down to the time of the Union between the two kingdoms, the English ports had the law on their side, since under the Navigation Acts Scotland was excluded from the benefits of the colonial trade. With the union, however, the situation was changed. Scotsmen could now compete on equal terms with the English traders, who began to feel the result at once. In this instance Bristol had recourse, as usual, to Government interference. It was afterwards acknowledged that the Glasgow merchants had been charged with various kinds of malpractice of which they were completely innocent. In their petition, the Bristol merchants declared that for some years past, great quantities of tobacco had been brought from Scotland into England and sold there at lower prices than were consistent with the payment of His Majesty's duties, wherefore the honest, fair and long-suffering traders of the second city of the kingdom craved for relief. If this practice, which was contrary to the letter and spirit of the Act of Union, were allowed to continue, it would prove the petitioners' ruin, and compel them to withdraw from these trades. If, on examination, it transpired that the Scotsmen were guilty of these practices, as the petitioners believed them to be, they prayed the Government to devise some method of preventing such enormities in the future. In the furtherance of this anti-Caledonian campaign, the Corporation subscribed £50 to assist the movement for obtaining Parliamentary relief.

The real reason, of course, for the success of the Scottish traders was not their dishonesty but their superior business capacity. They had not behind them the long tradition of maternal government protection which Bristol had, and, moreover, they were prepared to work harder and expect a smaller return on an individual transaction. As they were at the beginning of their trade expansion they had everything to gain, while prosperous Bristol had everything to lose. On this occasion the Government once more listened to the eloquent appeals of the southern ports and raised various actions against the Scottish importer. Though all of these charges were shown to be false, the open hostility of the English Government was for many years a serious handicap to the energetic traders of Glasgow. Once in the trade, however, nothing could permanently hold them back.

It has already been seen that Bristol became the entrepôt of trade between Ireland and the colonies. Sugar, tobacco and other colonial products passed through Bristol to Irish ports, and in return, Irish yarn, linen and foodstuffs were sent to Bristol to be re-exported to New England, New York, Virginia, Maryland and the Caribbean Islands. The Irish trade was to be so regulated as to discourage people from carrying on an illicit trade with foreigners, and certainly, direct trade between Ireland and the colonies was to be prevented at all costs.

At different times Bristol ships accused of piracy or smuggling became involved in the Virginian courts. Sometimes they were discharged, sometimes they were proved guilty. In a letter to Mr. Farrell of Bristol, George Washington, in remitting eight hogsheads of tobacco, said:

> "I have once or twice in my life been very seriously disappointed in the sales of some tobaccos in Bristol. . . ."
> obliges me to add that"

In 1774 another Virginian planter wrote to Messrs Farrell and Jones, of Bristol:

> "I must confess the low price I have got for my tobacco does not afford me great encouragement to try the port of Bristol as a market for that commodity: especially when I consider that part of the same crop, and what was deemed rather inferior in quality netted me £7 12s. 6d. from Liverpool."

He had intended to increase his shipments to Bristol,

> "but I think no man can be expected to run upon ruin with his eyes open." [1]

Bristol also had associations with Pennsylvania, the Carolinas, Maryland, New York and New England, though Virginia and the West Indies together comprised the bulk of the city's trade. When, in the early part of the eighteenth century, the English Government made a determined effort to procure naval stores from the colonies, Bristol traders were active in the design. A body known as the "Naval Store Company of Bristol" for raising hemp in America was formed, which purchased a large area of 3,120 acres from William Penn, and invested £2,000, having raised £5,000 altogether. The results were disappointing, as was shown in a letter written to Joshua Gee on 6th May, 1717. Many years

---

[1] Campbell, C. (ed. by), *The Bland Papers*, vol. i, pp. 33-4.

later, various petitions to Westminster complained at great length of the evils which would result to the colonies, to navigation, to English shipping interests and to the nation at large if the bounty on colonial hemp was withdrawn. From this it appears that Bristol ship-riggers and others depended entirely on colonial tar and similar products, and that the foreigner had been completely driven out of that branch of trade.

When the foundation of Halifax, Nova Scotia, was under consideration, the Merchant Venturers were interested in the project for the settlement of a tract of land in that province. In October, 1748, a request that they should support a petition from London on this subject was referred to a standing committee. In the following year the Hudson Bay trade was considered by the Society. There was great hostility developing against the old monopolistic companies, and Bristol, with her long traditions and associations with the Far North, naturally objected to her exclusion. Liverpool shared this opinion, and as the Hudson Bay Company was then very inactive, it was felt that there was some hope of having this trade thrown open, but after spasmodic efforts the scheme was dropped, and the Company was allowed to return to her long repose, which was only to be broken by the vigorous onslaught of the Scottish traders from Montreal. When Quebec fell in 1759, Bristol received the news with jubilation. The city and the shipping in the port were illuminated, while the Mayor invited influential citizens to the Council House to partake of liquid refreshment, which was drunk to the accompaniment of salvos of artillery. In the following year a similar celebration occurred when it was reported that Montreal had fallen. Ten years later Bristol merchants eagerly looked forward to the development of a valuable trade with the Falkland Islands recently acquired by the Crown.

Some indication of the close connection which existed between Bristol and the North American mainland in the eighteenth century is afforded by the fact that when the Government of Queen Anne decided to establish a regular packet service with the colonies, Bristol was selected as the home port. The packets were to run monthly between England and New York, which was already connected up by overland posts with several provinces, and other services were shortly to be established. The rates for letters between London and New York were to be for every single letter not exceeding one sheet of paper 1s., for every double letter not exceeding two sheets 2s., and in proportion to the same ratio for every packet of letters, and for any packet of any kind of greater weight, for every ounce 4s. The packets, which were to be of the burden of 80 tons, were designed for speed and strength, well-manned and commodiously contrived for entertaining passengers,

"who will be kindly received and entertained on board on easy terms."

These packets were allowed to carry out five tons of freight and to bring home ten tons,

". . . where-by all people may send small parcels to New York or any other place from thence by carriage and be accommodated therein at reasonable rates."

As trade with the colonies developed a regular news service grew up by which those interested were kept in touch with the arrival and departure of ships from day to day. In 1731 the Society of Merchant Venturers was informed that the master of the Jamaica Coffee House, London, proposed to give notice of the arrival of ships and of what intelligence they brought. This letter suggested that similar information should be sent up from Bristol. It was ordered by the Hall that its Standing Committee should appoint some suitable person for that purpose, whose salary should be borne by the Society.

On one occasion Bristol was concerned with the importation of straw hats from Bermuda, which it desired to encourage. But, in fact, it is impossible to enumerate all the ramifications of Bristol's connection with the Empire at that time. The development of a new trade, the grant of a monopoly to the insurance brokers of London, and a dozen and one similar subjects caused agitation in Bristol. The Government was anxious that the city should build larger ships as these would be of more service in time of war. When the length of their voyages is borne in mind, Bristol ships in the seventeenth and early eighteenth centuries were surprisingly small. The *Charming Sally*, for example on her return voyage from Jamaica ran into a whale and almost immediately foundered, a disaster which may help to explain the Government's interest in larger ships. In so far as the direct trade with the mainland and West Indian colonies was concerned, Bristol shippers were perfectly willing to comply with the Government's wishes, but those concerned in the African and Newfoundland trades persisted in declaring that the nature of their commerce necessitated smaller vessels.

Bristol records in those critical days before the collapse of the first Empire reveal the short-sightedness and selfishness which characterized so much of England's policy to her colonies at that time. Always the interest of the Mother Country came first, no matter what the inconveniences to the plantations and Ireland might be. They were to bear these restrictions with fortitude and even thankfulness. One of the clearest manifestations of this unwise spirit is to be seen in the long-continued attempt to limit the American production of iron. This policy was particularly unjustifiable, as England herself was at that time rapidly ceasing to be an iron-producer, and already depended for her import supply on foreign sources. In the colonies were to be found abundant stores of iron ore, and unlimited quantities of wood in the primeval forests, from which charcoal could be made. Yet the iron interests of England, and Bristol with the rest, did their utmost to prevent the development of colonial manufactures. Indeed, they went so far as to prefer the products of foreign producers. This extremely unwise and selfish policy, as the event was to prove, became impossible to enforce. As early as 1695-6 a petition of the ironmongers and others of the city of Bristol was presented to the House of Commons, which opened with a specious observation that the wealth of the nation chiefly arose from the labour of the people, and whatever hindered manufacture "doth put a stop to the trade and profit of this kingdom." This petition prayed for the removal of duties which had recently been placed on foreign iron. The general argument was that this lessened English trade abroad and prevented the Mother Country from supplying her plantations with the iron they required. There was no mention

of the well-known fact that abundance of iron was to be found
in the colonies, for it was felt that developments in that direction would threaten the position of established interests at
home.

By 1717 the situation had become more difficult. English
iron production was continuing to decline, while the Swedish
sources of supply were interrupted by the disturbed state of
Northern Europe. A petition of shipwrights, ironmongers,
smiths and dealers in iron of Bristol, pointed out that there were
in His Majesty's plantations great quantities of iron ore and all
materials needful for the working of iron. If these were
developed it would employ the poor there, who would be able
to pay for manufactured goods from England. The House was
prepared to give encouragement to those who were willing to
engage in this trade by the erection of iron-works.

In February, 1717–8, another petition, sponsored by the
Mayor, Aldermen and principal traders of Bristol, elaborated
the argument of the previous year. The annual consumption of
iron in Great Britain amounted to 40,000 tons, about two-thirds
of which was imported from neighbouring countries. The ex-
haustion of English forests rendered the expansion of the home
industry impossible. Indeed, extinction was certain. Should
anything happen to interrupt importation from abroad, the cost
of iron would rise at once, and those engaged in various
dependent manufactures would lose their livelihood, ship-building, house-building and other necessary services would suffer,
while the colonies would be compelled to depend still more on
illicit supplies from foreigners. All of this could be prevented
if the Government would encourage those who were willing to
develop the manufacture of iron in the colonies, where wood
and iron-ore abounded, where the climate was healthful and
provisions cheap. Colonial manufacturers should be allowed to
make pig-iron only, but in a sufficient quantity to satisfy both
the local and home demand. The petitioners believed that all
the later and more elaborate processes in the manufacture of
iron should be confined to specialists in England. Thus, more
people would be given work, double the quantity of iron could
be produced for the same amount of wood, the price of iron

would fall, the number of manufacturers increase, the poor would be employed, trade supported, navigation encouraged and consumers, both at home and in the plantations, would be supplied with their requirements at cheaper rates than were possible in a clandestine trade.

On 27th May, 1721, John King, Jeremy Innys, John Lewis, Samuel Jacob, Lionel Lyde, Walter King, John Templeman and Samuel Dyke, most or all of whom lived in Bristol, gave power of attorney to three Virginians, John Tayloe, John Lomas and Philip Elway, to manage an iron-works. In the following July a ninety-nine year lease, dated 1670, of an area on the north side of the Rappahannock river was taken over. The Company purchased indentured servants and began mining and continued for about eight years, but probably not much longer. In February, 1721–2, some of the servants appeared in the King George court on charges of unlawful assembly and other crimes. Two of them were sentenced to ten lashes which were to be well laid on their bare backs. Two were fined, and the remainder

"upon their humble submission upon their bare knees before the Court" [1]

were discharged on their payment of fees. Another iron-works in which it appears Bristolians were interested was the Principio works in Maryland. Joshua Gee was a partner in this business in 1728, when the balance of his account was £329. This iron was sent to London and Liverpool as well as to Bristol.

Within a few years the iron-masters of Bristol were beginning to repent the encouragement which they had given to the colonies. Once they had started, the latter were not content to limit themselves to the cruder processes, and so the traders of Bristol again approached the House of Commons. On 14th February, 1737–8, a petition was read from several merchants, iron-masters and ironmongers of the city of Bristol, and on 7th March one from sundry iron-masters and ironmongers, on behalf of themselves and others. The petitioners declared that the people of New England were producing much bar-iron, and

---

[1] Brydon, G. MacL., "The Bristol Iron Works in King George County," in *Virginian Magazine of Biography and History*, vol. XLII, No. 2.

were not only supplying themselves with nails and other iron-ware, but were exporting large quantities to neighbouring colonies, to the great prejudice of the English iron trade. Thus the truth emerged. They had never been so solicitous about the welfare of the colonies as they had stated themselves to be. So long as the interests of the plantations marched with their own, colonial enterprise was to be encouraged, but as soon as any vested interest was touched, the colonies had to be taught who was master in the British Empire. After all, the people of the plantations were to be hewers of wood and drawers of water, and were never to be permitted to do anything which would conflict with an established English trade. A committee was appointed to look into the matter. It was reported from the dockyard that by trial American iron was shown to be equal to the best Swedish, and that if the colonies were encouraged, by the renewal of duties, to import great quantities of pig-iron, they would not be tempted to work up their product to compete with manu-factured goods from England. This gave rise to a dispute between those who favoured strict limitation to pig-iron and those who favoured a freer policy. But the question was un-settled, for as was customary at that time, the matter was shelved since difficulties had arisen.

In March, 1749–50, the Merchant Venturers resolved that support should be given to a Bill then before Parliament pro-viding for the importation of American pig- and bar-iron. But the merchants believed that the erection of slitting and rolling mills in the colonies should be prohibited. As it finally passed, the importation of American iron was limited to London, which at once elicited a petition from Bristol that this trade should be thrown open to the whole kingdom. After some delay and much discussion Parliament gave legislative effect to this request.

Just before the American Revolution the selfish attitude of Bristol was still unchanged. In writing to the Society of Merchant Venturers in February, 1757, to announce the pro-gress of another American iron Bill, Nugent said:

"I was careful to guard it against the Evils which wou'd necessarily arise from a further manufacture of iron in the colonies, by prohibiting the use of slitting mills there, and will venture to say that without this Precaution The Bill, which as it now stands met with great opposition, never wou'd have been suffered to pass." [1]

About the same time Edward Quincey petitioned the House of Commons for a Bill enabling him, and others associated with him, to make steel in America, either with tilt hammers or otherwise, and to import it into Great Britain, in the same way as iron was now imported from America. In their petition the Merchant Venturers declared that if this were allowed, thousands of the industrious poor in the kingdom would be deprived of their living. The free importation of iron was bad enough, but if the same privileges were to be extended to steel, utter disaster would be the result.

There were many complaints and petitions about duties on spirituous liquors. Here again such duties were stated to be a certain cause of the destruction of Bristol's trade, and *ipso facto* of that of the Empire. On 6th March, 1724–5, a petition was sent up to Parliament protesting that the French at Moville were making tar, and the Government was requested to take suitable action. This competition of the foreigner emphasized the unfair disadvantages under which English colonial producers of these commodities laboured. Foreigners did not suffer from the various limitations imposed upon Englishmen by the Act 8 Geo. I, for giving further encouragement for the importation of naval stores. Unless the restrictions contained in that Act were removed, the planters would be obliged to give up the production of naval stores altogether, and England again would be drawn to depend on the goodwill of foreign producers for these very necessary commodities. Indeed, the question of naval stores was constantly cropping up, and although every one was theoretically favourable to the encouragement of colonial production, the necessary co-operation between England and the colonies, which was an essential condition of success, was never achieved. The Americans wanted, and actually made, ships in large numbers, while the English ship-builders and manufacturers of naval stores wished to confine the colonies to the

---

[1] *Society of Merchant Venturers' Letters*, 1754– , bundle 17.

crudest processes in production. In spite of favourable reports, which were made from time to time on American products, naval authorities tended to be conservative, and refused to be changed from their general preference for those of Scandinavia. products.

From the petitions it would seem that Bristol was, throughout this long period of abounding trade, on the verge of utter collapse. Yet, in spite of all the innumerable grievances, restrictions and disabilities, in spite of the dishonesty of the Americans, the wickedness of the Scots and the plots of foreigners and Irish, in spite of the negligence of the Government and the ineptitude and selfishness of every one except themselves, all of which were repeated *ad nauseam* in letters, petitions and memorials, Bristol prospered exceedingly. Her merchants grew rich, her manufactures expanded, and the records contain many references to extension of wharves and other intimations that the capacity of the port was inadequate for the increasing volume of trade, the great bulk of which was with the Empire.

CHAPTER XIII

THE BREAKDOWN OF THE OLD COLONIAL SYSTEM

"... *in the middle of the street, as far as you can see, hundreds of ships, their masts as thick as they can stand by one another, which is the oddest and most surprising sight imaginable. This street is fuller of them than the Thames from London Bridge to Deptford, and at certain times only, the water rises to carry them out; so that, at other times, a long street, full of ships in the middle and houses on both sides, looks like a dream.*"

ALEXANDER POPE, *Letters to Martha Blount* (1732).

THE Peace of Paris was concluded in February, 1763, and with it closed a long period in English history. At last, after many triumphs and reverses, England emerged victorious. Portugal, the once proud mistress of the East, was now a humble ally; the Spanish Empire was moribund; Holland, after her great age in the seventeenth century, was a third-rate power, while the might of France had been broken and her empire destroyed. As far as Britain's colonies were concerned the time had come to talk of many things, for though few at the time realized it, with 1763 a new age began. In the past century and a half the English plantations in America had grown to maturity, and now that the French menace had disappeared from the St. Lawrence, they could reasonably regard the whole continent as theirs to inherit. They were numerous, rich and energetic, and even before the Seven Years' War they had begun to resent the supercilious attitude of the English, and to find such terms as "our colonies" and "the provincials" highly objectionable. They knew that, in spite of their rawness, they had acquitted themselves on the field of battle as well as the best British professional troops. It was an expedition armed and manned by Massachusetts that had captured the great fortress of Louisburg in 1745, and the people of America did not forget how, by the Treaty of Aix-La-Chapelle, without any reference to their wishes, Louisburg had been handed back to France. It was a young Virginian, Colonel George Washington, who had saved Braddock's ill-starred troops from utter annihilation in the narrow defile of Monongahela. Indeed, though vaguely as yet, there was beginning to stir in the minds of some Americans, at least, a spirit which was to grow into a strong national feeling. In 1763 the question yet awaited an answer as to whether this national feeling, when it came, should be based on attachment to or repugnance from the Mother Country.

Unfortunately, no one had succeeded in solving the problem of the relationship which should subsist between a Mother Country and her grown-up children in a manner which was equally acceptable on both sides of the Atlantic. Moreover, as the tragic events which occurred between 1763 and 1783 proved, there was a lamentable lack of comprehension in high places in England about the real character of the Americans, their aspirations, their problems and their strength. English statesmen still persisted in thinking of the colonies as so many kitchen gardens, which existed in order to be exploited for the good of England, and to some, at least, of the aristocratic governors from the old world their leaders were uncultivated provincials.

Down to the close of the Seven Years' War, the Laws of Trade and Navigation were not a very serious hardship to the Americans. The colonies of other countries were even more restricted, and those who administered the laws were generally lenient, so that there was an enormous amount of smuggling. Moreover, the Americans realized that they derived great advantages from the system. Their ships could share in the carrying trade of the whole Empire, they had the protection of the Royal Navy, and so long as Canada was French they depended very largely on the military strength of England. Even with the wider horizon of the post-Seven-Years'-War period, they would probably have remained quiescent, as far as the Old Colonial System was concerned, for many years. But when Grenville began to enforce the laws in a manner which had never before been known, when he intensified their severity and, by direct taxation, tried to compel them without their consent to help England pay for the recent war, the inherent weaknesses of the old Empire were revealed by a flame of discontent which swept the colonies from north to south. The present concern, however, is not with the causes of the American Revolution, nor the apportionment of blame, but to recount its effects upon and the reactions to it of a great commercial city, whose wealth and prosperity were at that time closely bound up with American trade. Bristol was not concerned with discussions about political right, nor did her citizens bother themselves overmuch about finespun theories of imperial relationship based upon established constitutional practice.

Now, as always, Bristol was concerned with trade. Governments which made laws to foster trade were, in the simple computation of the people of Bristol, good Governments which deserved support. Those that passed laws or adopted policies unfavourable to commerce were bad Governments, and deserved to be overthrown. In the main Bristol was right, and certainly, in a dispute such as that which developed between England and her colonies, it was utter pedantry to attach all importance to assertions of narrow, inflexible, legal right. The real issue was a matter of expediency. This, however, was a point of view wholly alien to the narrow minds of George III, Bute, Grenville and the rest of the gang that destroyed the first British Empire. At the same time, it must be remembered that, while the King and his friends were unimaginative and, in some respects, even stupid in their mishandling of the situation, not a few of the Americans were inclined to be truculent, and some from the beginning were determined that there should be no compromise. To use the homely phrase current in the West, some Americans were inclined "to carry a chip on their shoulders," and they hoped that someone would be so unwise as to knock it off. Whoever did must expect trouble, and the English Government fully satisfied this wish.

Briefly, then, such was the condition of affairs when Grenville announced the stiffening of the Navigation Laws. In the preamble to the Sugar Act, it was stated to be the Government's intention to afford the Americans an opportunity of helping to pay for the war and their own military defence by taxing them. At once an outcry arose, which grew still louder when the Government followed up its first mistake with the announcement of its determination to raise still further money by the imposition of stamps on all legal documents in the colonies. The Merchant Venturers of Bristol, many of whose members were deeply concerned in the American trade, and, as the documents proved, were more intimately acquainted with the actual state of American opinion than the majority of the members of the Government, at a very early stage in the dispute became active on the American side. They vigorously objected to a proposal that drawbacks on white calicoes and foreign linens exported to the colonies should be discontinued. On 7th April, 1764, *Felix Farley's Bristol Journal* published a letter from the merchants of New York addressed to the traders of Bristol. In this, the Americans asked their friends in England to oppose the renewal of the Sugar Act with its ominous preamble. According to this letter, the Act which it was proposed to renew had never been enforced until recently, and the immediate effect of this enforcement would be the complete stoppage of colonial trade. As a decline in trade would affect Bristol as well as the colonies, all traders of that city were asked to support their friends in America. For this purpose it was suggested that a meeting of merchants should be called at which this letter might be read and the advantages of opposing the Government's policy be stressed. It should be made perfectly clear that if the Act was passed, it would decrease the trade of the colonies, discourage ship-building, prevent colonial merchants from paying their debts to England, of which large sums were owed in Bristol, and force them to develop their own manufactures.

As the summer of 1764 passed into autumn the resentment and opposition in the colonies grew more intense. Another letter was published in *Felix Farley's* journal in October. This was written by a gentleman in Virginia to his friend in Bristol:

"The Acts of Parliament have made such Impressions upon the Minds of the Northward People and the Men of War so strictly enforce them, that there is an entire Stagnation of Trade. Nothing do they talk of but their own Manufactures; the Downfall of England and the Rise of America is sung by the Common Ballad Singers about the Streets." [1]

By January, 1765, as the Government seemed determined to persist in its ill-advised policy, the Merchant Venturers decided to act. A petition to Parliament was drawn up, and the Master, William Reeve, with Joseph Farrell and Thomas Farr, were instructed to take it up to London. On the same day, the other citizens, led by the Mayor and Aldermen, drew up a similar petition which two of their number, Samuel Sedgley and Henry Cruger, were requested to carry to the metropolis. In February

[1] *Felix Farley's Bristol Journal*, 27th October, 1764.

the news from America continued to be bad. The Americans were much dissatisfied with the duties already imposed upon them and apprehensive of others to come. In retaliation, they were determined to use as little English manufactured goods as possible, and as a step toward the realization of that resolution

"many gentlemen of considerable property there (Virginia) are coming into an Agreement not to use in their Families several of the most staple Articles, the Produce of this Country." [1]

The editor's comment upon this letter was:—

"How far this Scheme may answer their Purpose Time must discover but it consequently will soon be felt here, by its affecting several of our principal Manufactories." [1]

In the meantime, the Society was in communication with the senior Bristol member of Parliament, Robert Nugent, on the desirability of a memorial which it was proposed should be presented on its behalf to the Chancellor of the Exchequer. On 12th March the terms were agreed upon, and the petition was forwarded to London. In it, the Society stressed the fact that a great deal of money was owed by the Americans to the city of Bristol. This indebtedness was still increasing, as their demands for English goods much exceeded the remittances which, in consequence of the Government's policy, they were able to make. As the prosperity of the colonists promoted that of British manufacturers, every encouragement should be given to them. The memorialists, therefore, prayed that since Great Britain and the West Indies took only part of the American exports of timber, lumber, iron, hemp and flax, these commodities should be taken out of the enumerated list, which required them to be shipped first to Great Britain before being sent abroad. If the Americans were allowed to trade directly with the Spanish colonies in these commodities, many valuable things might be obtained in exchange, such as dollars, cocoa, cochineal and indigo. The last two of these could already be imported duty free into Great Britain, so that this concession

---

[1] *Felix Farley's Bristol Journal*, 16th February, 1765.

to the Americans could in no wise injure British traders. With proper encouragement, the memorialists believed that many commodities which at that time were purchased from foreigners for cash could be produced in the colonies, and brought home in English bottoms,

"... than which nothing can be a more nationally usefull application of money, nor more conducive to the national strength by encreasing the number of her Seamen." [1]

The petition also protested against restrictions placed upon inter-colonial trade by recent Acts, and inconveniences caused by the extended powers given to revenue-cutters to stop ships within two leagues of the shore. It also complained of the inconvenient situation of the Vice-Admiralty Court which had been established at Halifax, Nova Scotia, and was inaccessible during several months of the year. In particular, the petition asked that a bounty be granted on timber imported into Great Britain from America, and that free exportation of lumber from America into Ireland, the Western Islands and any part of Europe, south of Cape Finisterre, should be allowed. In spite of this memorial, the expostulations from Bristol and other cities in the kingdom, as well as threats and boycotts in the colonies, the Stamp Act was passed, and zealous officials set to work to see that it was enforced.

The Bristol newspapers of the time contain numerous letters from Virginia, Pennsylvania and elsewhere which describe the anger and hostility to which the Act had given rise, and the resentment which the Americans felt against the system of taxation without representation, and how they protested against the violation of their liberties. Throughout 1765 trade continued to decline, and Bristol merchants were confronted by the gloomy prospect of still further losses to come, and debts in America whose repayment daily became more remote. Another petition was, therefore, prepared by the Society, but it merely repeated what had already been said. Trade between Bristol and America had fallen off lamentably, and unless a speedy

[1] *Merchant Venturers' Book of Petitions*, fol. 1.

remedy was applied, both English manufacturers and the national revenues would be involved in a common calamity. All of these troubles arose through the restrictions laid upon navigation, not only by the commanders of His Majesty's ships on the American coast, but also by the patent officers who exercised their authority with exceeding great rigour.

This gloomy recital was substantiated by a letter which appeared in *Felix Farley's Journal* on 6th November. It was written by a merchant in Maryland to his correspondent in Bristol:

> "Sir,
>
> "We have just received the favour of your letter, requesting us to take a quantity of your goods, to the value of about £1000 and make you speedy remittances for them. You must continue a Stranger to the distresses and embarrassment our mother country has thrown on the trade of N. America and how they have taxed and otherwise incapacitated us to make remittances; to expect that we could be able to comply with your request, or that we could undertake to sell your goods at all and make remittances for them. When the merchants at home feel the weight of our oppressions, perhaps their interest will relieve us; we fear nothing else will . . .
>
> "We are sorry that we can give you no kind of encouragement to send the cargo of slaves here, the people are not able to buy, so that they will bring no price that can answer." [1]

For the moment, however, the Government was adamant, and the best that the Bristol members could obtain was some slight concessions about prosecutions connected with the enforcement of the Stamp Act, and some modifications respecting the export of specie from the colonies.

In the meantime, things in the New World were going from bad to worse, and people in England suffered. Traders as well as manufacturers grew more and more dissatisfied, and there was a growing body of unemployment among men and women. In December a letter from Philadelphia which appeared in *Felix Farley's Bristol Journal* described the situation in that important Bristol market:

---

[1] *Felix Farley's Bristol Journal*, 16th November, 1765.

"At a general meeting of the merchants and traders of this city, it was . . . resolved by them . . . that they would not import any goods from Great Britain until the Stamp Act was repealed.

"I do therefore hereby countermand all the orders which I have heretofore transmitted to you for the shipping of any goods; and I do expect and insist that you pay a strict and literal obedience to this injunction; for, should they arrive and the Stamp Act not be repealed, I shall not dare to dispose of any part of them without a forfeiture of my honour, nor indeed can engage for their, or my own safety.

"I am Sir etc.

"FRANCIS HARRIS." [1]

In every colony there was opposition to this unpopular measure, and even the West Indies, usually concerned only about sugar, slaves and supplies, were deeply disturbed. Writing from Nevis in May, 1766, John Pinney described the reception of the Act by the Islands:

"Soon after the Stamps were landed at St. Kitts, you cannot conceive what a Number of People appeared on the Occasion, the poorer sort were supported & encouraged by the rich; they went to a Gentlemans House in the Country where the Distributor lay Sick, forced him to Town & treated him very Ill, & swore if he did not deliver up the Stamps they woud Hang him which he immediately did to pacify the Mob; they also insisted & forced him to make Oath in several parts of the Town, that he would resign the office of Distributor immediately and never act any more; they then proceeded to burn the Stamps & soon destroyed 5000 £ Sterling in paper; the next Day our little Community follow'd their Steps, at the Bonfire they gave three hurras, Crying out Liberty. No Stamps." [2]

By the beginning of 1766 the English mercantile community was thoroughly roused. London, Birmingham, Liverpool and Bristol co-operated to plead for repeal. Much correspondence went on between the Merchant Venturers of Bristol and the

[1] *Felix Farley's Bristol Journal*, 28th December, 1765.
[2] *Pinney Papers, Business Letter-book*, 1761–75, fol. 97.

city's two members in Parliament. This shows that, although they were unanimously opposed to the Stamp Act, they were not prepared to allow this particular difficulty to absorb their whole thoughts. So, while pleading for greater efforts in the cause of repeal, they did not forget to press their members to work for the establishment of a free port in Dominica. On 17th January two petitions from Bristol were laid before the House of Commons. One of these was from the Merchant Venturers and the other from the tradesmen and manufacturers of the city. On 24th February the House of Commons gave leave for the introduction of a Bill to repeal the Stamp Act, and this news caused great rejoicings throughout the country.

"Never was Joy more general or Citizens' Hearts more sensibly touched than ours Monday last, on hearing the favourable Turn of the American Affairs. The Bells throughout the City rang incessantly the whole Day, and in the Evening were uncommon Bonfires. Several Houses were illuminated, the American Coffee-House in particular, from whose Windows the Merchants trading to that Quarter of the World generously threw Money to the Populace, which, in return, appeared decently grateful. The favourite Toast on this happy Occasion was 'America, and Pitt its kind Protector.'" [1]

The Bill passed its third reading in the House of Commons on 4th March, and on the following day a petition from the Merchant Venturers of Bristol was presented to the House of Lords. Thomas Farr wrote to the Master on 5th March that, on receiving it, he had had the good fortune to be able to place it in the hands of Lord Dartmouth at once, and it was read immediately after the London petition. This document is practically identical in terms with one presented to the House of Commons in January. In both it was stated that the American trade was the most important branch of the nation's commerce. It absorbed large quantities of English staple products and afforded employment to thousands of English working people. Unless the distress under which it now laboured was remedied, the colonies and the Mother Country would be involved in a

---

[1] *Felix Farley's Bristol Journal*, 1st March, 1766.

common disaster. Several millions of pounds were owed by the Americans to England which they could not now pay, and the petitioners were concerned in this debt to the amount of several hundred thousand pounds. The colonials were not only unable to pay, but they had recently refused to order more English goods and had countermanded orders already given. This great commercial crisis was the direct result of the Stamp Act and of the new fiscal policy of England to all her colonies which that measure symbolized. The petitioners also complained that they had several ships now in American ports which, as they could not legally be cleared out during the present confusion, were compelled to remain there at great expense. If they came away without legal clearances they would be liable to seizure, and the petitioners would thus suffer great loss without being guilty of any fraud or fault. The Stamp Act was finally repealed on 18th March, and the victory was duly celebrated in Bristol a few days later.

"A Number of Gentlemen spent the evening at the Nag's-Head Tavern where Samuel Sedgeley and Henry Cruger Esqrs were invited and most heartily thanked for their zeal and Assiduity in their successful Attendance on Parliament to sollicit (sic) the Repeal of the Stamp Act. Many loyal Healths were drunk." [1]

The freedom of the Society of Merchant Venturers was conferred upon the Duke of Grafton, the Marquis of Rockingham, the Right Honourable William Dowdeswell, Chancellor of the Exchequer, and others, for the part they had played in the great victory. In addition, on 3rd September, the Hall resolved that a special letter of thanks should be sent to the Marquis of Rockingham for his services to the trade of England and the colonies during his administration. This is traditionally supposed to have been drafted by Richard Champion, a notable Whig of the time, a famous manufacturer of porcelain and a friend of Burke, for whom he made a celebrated tea-service. After enumerating, in a somewhat flamboyant style, the various services rendered by

[1] *Felix Farley's Bristol Journal*, 29th March, 1766.

the noble Marquis to trade and to the nation at large, the letter concludes:—

"But if your fellow Subjects joining the Testimony of their Approbation of your Conduct will add thereto, our Society desire in the most lively manner, to convey theirs to your Lordship, as to the Friend and Protector of Commerce, the Source of Wealth and Strength of the kingdom." [1]

In the meantime, trade revived. The Americans, though not convinced of England's good intentions, were generally ready to believe the best, and the Merchant Venturers turned once more to the pleasant game of extending British trade by pressing for the extension of the Free Port system in the West Indies. The degree to which the whole country, and Bristol included, still looked backward, showing that it had learnt nothing from the recent dispute, was afforded by the discussions on the Sugar Bill in 1766. Nugent, as well as the Bristol merchants, believed that if foreign sugars were exported from North America, they should be landed in England before being sent abroad. This was to ensure that no stimulus would be given to foreigners to refine sugars for themselves instead of in England. Moreover, colonial vessels which had thus landed their cargoes in England and then proceeded to a foreign port were to be compelled on their return passage to land their goods again in England, pay duty, reload, receive the drawback, if any, and so complete their voyage. In fact, even after all the late agitations, England could not see that the colonies were in a position wholly different from that which they occupied when Charles II returned from his travels.

All these rejoicings and thanksgivings, however, were premature, for George III had not changed, nor had some of his ministers learned anything from the Stamp Act dispute. By the Declaratory Act, the Government reasserted the right of the British Parliament to tax the colonies, and thus did much to nullify the good effect of repeal. Further, as the event was to prove, it was ready to pick up by the Townshend swings what it had lost by the Stamp Act roundabouts. The Stamp Act

---

[1] Owen H., *Two Centuries of Ceramic Art in Bristol*, p. 49.

should have been repealed unconditionally without any accompanying Declaratory Act, or it should have been efficiently enforced. The former course would have conciliated the majority of Americans, and the latter would have convinced them that England was in earnest and that she had the strength to enforce her will. The policy adopted did neither. It gave the Americans an impression of ungenerous weakness and filled their minds with suspicions about the future. These suspicions seemed to be abundantly justified when, on 15th April, 1767, Townshend announced his duties on paper, glass, painters' colours and tea.

Again trade languished, English manufactured goods were boycotted, and the Empire drifted nearer to the abyss. A complete misunderstanding of the problem prevailed in Government circles at home, and in America irreconcilables made converts to their cause. In Bristol and other commercial centres, where the merchants, if nothing else, were realists, there were profound misgivings over this insane pursuit of a shadow by the British Government, while substantial mercantile interests were sacrificed. Writing on 20th August, 1768, in *Felix Farley's Bristol Journal*, "Mercator" defended the colonists and urged a more moderate policy. The importance of the American trade made it imperative that the demands of the Americans should be met as far as possible. To enforce the new objectionable policy would destroy British trade, deny to Americans those liberties that were common to every Briton, and stir up a great struggle in the New World. The argument that the Americans should share with England in contributing to imperial costs by their taxes was false. Englishmen should remember the help which the colonies had given them in the late war, and also that the influx of foreigners there made it necessary to use something other than force if their loyalty was to be retained. For all of these reasons the writer contended that these duties should be abolished.

When, however, repeal became practical politics, the citizens of Bristol were divided over the expediency of this policy. In London, opinion was even more uncertain. For some reason there appears to have been a tendency in the metropolis for many leading merchants to be more susceptible to the blandishments of ministers than they had been during the Stamp Act agitation.

"I like not this cordiality and a good understanding between Great Men and the Merchants, as I think it hath been attended with no good consequences to the colonies. On a former occasion, when the merchants stood upon their own good sense and importance, they procured a repeal of the Stamp Act: but of late the Ministry seem to have cajoled them and laid them asleep; so that the repeal we are to expect next session must flow from the justice and equity of our demand, and leave us no ground to express our gratitude as before to that respectable body of men." [1]

A year later, the *Virginia Gazette* reprinted from a Pennsylvania paper a letter from London.

"That the merchants are encouraged by the Ministers, even to indemnification, is universally believed." [2]

But the second boycott of English goods in America was not nearly so successful as the first.

"I find it has had little effect upon the manufacturers, who like stupid animals must smart before they will move." [2]

English trade with Russia, France and Germany was thriving, and even the Americans themselves no longer co-operated wholeheartedly in the rejection of English goods.

"The stagnation of our trade to the colonies makes no sensible difference to British manufacturers. They either find other markets for their goods, from whence they are transmitted to you, or else they are smuggled in upon you directly from hence." [2]

In Bristol the majority of the Corporation which, however, was considered by its critics to be over-loaded with elderly conservative gentlemen, voted against instructing Lord Clare and

---

[1] Mason, F. N., *John Norton and Sons*. Letter of William Nelson to John Norton, Virginia, 15th August, 1769.

[2] *Virginia Gazette*, 20th September, 1770.

Matthew Brickdale, the city's two representatives in Parliament, to support repeal. A large body of citizens, on the other hand, was strongly opposed to the Corporation's action, and Lord Clare, who was beginning to earn the reputation he afterwards enjoyed of being a party hack, would not give the merchants a clear lead. He was inclined to be a Government man, and he made contemptuous references to the instructions which, he said, had been sent by a number of people unknown to him, although he was well aware that they had been sent to him by an influential section of his own constituents. Indeed, Bristol had been led to take this action in consequence of the acknowledged timidity of the merchants of London.

"Our merchants in London have been extremely shy and very unwilling to take the lead in an affair as interesting to you as America. We have prevailed on the gentlemen of Bristol to begin. They had a meeting and have transmitted to one of their Representatives an account of the CONDI-TIONAL ORDERS for North America to the amount of £200,000. The Londoners have at last followed their example and at a very numerous meeting last week voted unanimously to petition the House of Commons for a repeal of the Act which laid duties on paper, glass, painters' colours and tea."[1]

The Merchant Venturers, therefore, put their trust in Brickdale, who on 17th January, 1770, after announcing that the American question would be considered in Parliament on the following day, asked for an exact statement of the effect which the Townshend measures had had on Bristol trade. Lord Clare asked for similar information on 1st February.

In the meantime, conditions in America were growing steadily worse. By the so-called Boston Massacre of 1770, the opponents of the Government were given splendid anti-British propaganda material, admirably calculated to stiffen resistance and strengthen the patriots. It is not proposed here to recount the serious misunderstandings and misconceptions which followed between 1770 and 1774. Certainly the stars in their courses were fighting

[1] Virginia State Library, *Colonial Papers*, 1759–74, *Committee of Correspondence*.

against the unity of the Empire. The "Boston Tea Party" took place in 1773, and this was followed by punitive action. The Massachusetts legislature was suspended, the port of Boston was closed on 1st June, and the Continental Congress met in Philadelphia on 5th September, 1774. In spite of all that had occurred so far and the growing truculence of American irreconcilables, Bristol as a whole remained faithful to the colonial cause. Though Josiah Tucker, a leading Bristol publicist of the time, was beginning to think that the American colonies were not worth the expense of keeping, and that Great Britain would be well-advised to let them go their way, other leading citizens were resolved that the Americans should receive justice and consideration from the Mother Country.

In this latter group there was none more determined or unwearied than Richard Champion, to whom reference has already been made. He had opposed the Stamp Act, violently attacked the Townshend measures, and described the policy of the Grafton ministry as weak and wicked, because it tried to restrict a people "who are so great a support to our manufactures and commerce." To him, it seemed inexcusable that party-spirit in Bristol should be allowed to interfere in a matter of trade. He believed that if the principal merchants of the kingdom possessed a spirit becoming men who, by their commerce, contributed so much to the power and riches of this kingdom, the trading interest would not have been treated with such contempt. They must now all suffer, the innocent with the guilty, because of their past inaction. While he believed that the Americans had ample cause for dissatisfaction, he nevertheless considered that extreme resistance was hard to be excused, and only to be explained by their accumulated grievances. Down to the actual outbreak of war Champion urged moderation upon his American friends, and advised them not to adopt policies calculated to alienate their sympathizers in England. The Americans, he thought, should have aimed their resentment at successive, inept British administrations, and not at the merchants, who were always America's best friends.

It is plain from Champion's letters that, in spite of the gathering storm, Bristol's trade with the colonies continued to be profitable. Indeed, during the years immediately prior to the Revolution, a new and valuable trade in American corn developed. Champion's chief correspondents were Messrs. Willing and Morris, of Philadelphia, a leading mercantile house in the colonies, the founder of which was a Bristol man. Before the outbreak of war it has been estimated that the annual value of imports from the thirteen American colonies into England amounted to £3,000,000, and that they purchased in return English manufactured goods of an equivalent value. One Bristol firm, for example, employed 400 hands in making serges for America, while another purchased 3,000 pieces of stuff at Wiveliscombe each spring for export to the colonies. Already by 1774 this export had shrunk to 200 pieces, and it ceased altogether during the war. Such shrinkage in trade was a common experience among exporters to America. In the pre-war period Bristol pipe-manufacturers annually exported 600 boxes of pipes to the colonies, but after the outbreak of hostilities this trade vanished. Shipping was in a similar situation. As late as 1775, 529 ships trading with America paid the Mayor's dues at the port of Bristol, but there were only 191 in 1781.

Even after the meeting of the Continental Congress in September Bristol merchants continued to press for reconciliation, and the clearest proof of their support of and sympathy for the American cause was afforded in 1774 by the parliamentary election of that year. Lord Clare, a pro-Government man, was rejected and Edmund Burke was elected. By that time, Clare had become a mere party man, more anxious to convince his constituents of the Government's wisdom than to express to the Government his constituents' will. So it came about that some of his old friends in the city began to think that their once indefatigable member, who on one occasion had vowed that he would work his legs off in their service and still continue to work for them on his stumps, was now more interested in promoting his own advancement by obsequious obedience to his party than championing the interests of his constituents. In 1774, of the two members returned by Bristol, Cruger was an American by birth, who naturally sympathized with his countrymen, and whose father still continued to live in the colonies. The other was Edmund Burke, a life-long defender of the American cause. His maiden speech in the House of Commons was on the state of the American colonies, and he advocated the repeal of the Stamp Act. From then on, he was a stalwart defender of American rights and an implacable enemy of the interfering and coercive policy of the Government. In 1770 his famous pamphlet *Thoughts on the Present Discontents* appeared, and in the following year, in recognition of his known principles and sympathies, New York appointed him as its agent in England. Throughout the early 'seventies he continued his thankless task of defending America. He pleaded for wiser policies, and in 1774 delivered one of the greatest speeches in the history of Parliament on American taxation. The election of such a man as this, in the autumn of 1774, by the second city in the kingdom could only have one meaning. Bristol was staunch for America, for the policy of conciliation and peace.

On 24th November Champion wrote to his friends in Philadelphia to announce the result of the recent election. Lord Clare, after twenty years' representation of Bristol, retired from the contest at the outset, as he found that his popularity was gone and that some of his former friends and supporters were working for Cruger. Brickdale was also very unpopular, so Burke and Cruger were returned. Champion was delighted, and spoke of Burke in his letter as

"a Gentleman whose excellence of private character does not fall short of his very great abilities in publick. Bristol has acquired unusual honour by her choice; the more so as this Gentleman was not personally known to six people in the town, had no previous Canvas made for him, did not arrive till near the week after the poll began, and had the personal weight of Lord Clare with all the Government interest against him. The Election which began without party, men more than measures being the object, did not terminate so."[1]

Brickdale, who was infuriated at the result of the poll, threatened to petition for a new election, and said that he would

---

[1] Guttridge, G. H., *The American Correspondence of a Bristol Merchant, 1766–76*, p. 34.

make this one void. Champion, however, believed that even if he was able to do this, which he much doubted, Burke since his arrival in the city had made so many friends that a second poll would return him by a still greater majority. He, therefore, looked upon the distinguished orator as Bristol's Member for life, which proved that, good as he was as a local politician, he was no prophet. So 1774 ended and the fateful 1775 came in. Even at that late hour there were those, both in America and in England, who still hoped for a peaceful settlement of the dispute. To the majority on both sides of the Atlantic, the disruption of the Empire was regarded as a disaster of the first magnitude, and one which must somehow be averted. In this, as in all revolutions, however, the initiative did not lie with the moderates. They were divided in their beliefs and uncertain as to the policy which should be followed. The fateful decision rested with George III and his minions on the one side and the irreconcilables in America on the other. Between these two groups the only possible arbiter was war. In following the course of this tragic struggle it must always be remembered that this was a civil war, the greatest civil war in British history. There was a large loyalist minority in America and there was a small pro-American minority in Britain. Neither of these considered that the giving of information to their friends, or even the recruiting of armed forces, was treasonable, for in their opinion, the only traitors were those who stood opposed to them. Such men as Champion, who virtually became an American secret service agent, were not traitors to their country, but loyal Englishmen, who thought that the Government of the day had betrayed the Empire. The fact that the majority on one side of the Atlantic took one side and the majority on the other side of the Atlantic took the other, could not alter the fact that this was a civil war, and it was only when the Americans called in France, the traditional enemy of England, that all hope of saving the first British Empire from destruction disappeared.

CHAPTER XIV

THE GREATEST CIVIL WAR IN BRITISH HISTORY

"... this great City, a main pillar in the commercial interest of Great Britain, must totter on its base by the slightest mistake, with regard to our American measures."

EDMUND BURKE, *Letter to the Sheriffs of Bristol* (1777).

THOUGH in the winter of 1774-5, tempers were rising on both sides of the Atlantic, Bristol as a whole was still for peace and conciliation. In January two petitions were sent up to Parliament. One of these was signed by a large number of merchants and others not members of the Society of Merchant Venturers. The other, which covered the same ground, but at greater length, was sent by that body. Already the anti-Americans were beginning to gain strength in the city, however, for when the proposal for a petition was first made in the Hall on 11th January, it was rejected by the casting vote of the Master. A week later, when two of the merchants at large were present to express their opinions, the Society decided to act.

This petition began by stressing once more the great importance of the American trade to Great Britain. It took from Bristol almost every kind of English manufactured goods, East India products and a wide range of other articles of commerce. By the re-exportation of American goods to European countries great profits were derived, and the country received substantial additions to its revenue. Since the West Indian islands depended on lumber, foodstuffs and other stores imported from the Northern Colonies, the rich West Indian trade was also dependent on the American connection. The African trade, upon which the flourishing state of the sugar islands was built, was rendered possible by the American trade. Moreover, this commerce employed many "artists" and manufacturers, gave work to many ships, employed thousands of seamen, and thus materially contributed to the strength of the Royal Navy.

The petitioners then proceeded to give an historical account of the restrictions which had unwisely been placed on their trade since 1763, and they expressed the great apprehension entertained by all merchants about the existing unsettled state of Anglo-American relations. As merchants concerned with trade and Englishmen interested in the welfare of their country, they could not look without emotion on the prospect of widespread unemployment and want among the poor which a continuance of the present policy would involve.   They looked back with regret to the time when trade had been free of all these impediments.   While they did not presume to suggest to Parliament, in whose wisdom they had the most unreserved confidence, what form their relief should take, they trusted that the former commercial policy would be reconsidered.   The destructive breaches made in their trade by the alarms to which it had been for so many years subject might now be closed,

> "the Peace of this great Empire restored—and Commerce once more fixed on the most solid and permanent foundation." [1]

The Government, however, was in no mood to listen to the clamours of a pack of tradesmen who, in the opinion of the remote Olympians of Westminster, were too obsessed by the sordid pursuit of gain to be able to perceive the wider horizons of imperial statesmanship.   Even the great Pitt himself, the friend and eloquent advocate of the Americans, had spoken with scathing contempt of the trading community, as

> "traders and merchants, little paltry peddling fellows, vendors of twopenny wares and falsehoods, who under the idea of trade sell everything in their power—honour, truth and conscience: who, without even regarding consequences and that general ruin might ensue, press forward to the goal of lucre and cut out the shortest passage to their own interests. Men of the most illiberal principles, children of the world, who have no attachment but to the shrine of Mammon."

So the petitions went unheeded, while on both sides of the Atlantic preparations for war went on apace.

Champion and his friends found it increasingly difficult to send letters to America, though in February he was able to inform his Philadelphia correspondents that, in his opinion, Lord North's conciliatory policy was intended merely to divide the Americans.   In March he sent out a full account of the English political situation, and in August detailed information

---

[1] *Merchant Venturers' Book of Petitions*, fol. 65.

about recruiting and the hiring of transports. In the same month he wrote to Messrs. Willing and Morris:

"America is not destitute of friends. She has some in this City, who will exert themselves on her behalf, and who, at the same time that they glory in possessing the name and privileges of Britons, admire those who so nobly protect them."

Champion, however, was disappointed to find that not all those who were connected with the American trade shared his views.

"It is a Truth, though a melancholy one, that the generalty of the American Merchants are not your best friends. . . . God grant us success & put an end to these unhappy Disputes. If we fail, our Inclinations to you will be the same, and we have only to wish our powers were equal." [1]

In December an unsigned statement by him was sent to Philadelphia and was headed: "This news may be depended upon." According to this document, the Government did not intend to establish their chief military base at Boston.

"They will only reinforce the Army there, so as to enable them to maintain their ground, if the Provincials do not carry the place this winter." [2]

Including the three regiments of " Scotch Dutch," Champion estimated that the whole British force in America would not exceed 26,000 men. No other troops were then available, and the Dutch had only been obtained because of the very high price offered for them. Champion intimated that this force was to be divided between New York, Virginia and South Carolina. On 31st of the same month this tireless supporter of the American cause sent a long account of the American attack and capture of Montreal, which he had just received from a captain recently arrived from Quebec, to Lord Rockingham, the Dukes of Portland, Manchester and Richmond, Lords Fitzwilliam and Effingham, Messrs. Edmund Burke, Fox and Montague.

[1] Guttridge, *op. cit.*, pp. 60–1.
[2] *Ibid.*, p. 65.

"I know not, how to thank you sufficiently for the very zealous firm & active part you have taken in endeavouring to rouse this unfortunate country from the Lethargy & supineness which seems so fatally to prevail. You & your friends in the City of Bristol were the first who were bold enough to stem that torrent of Corruption Servility & meanness which but too generally overwhelm the Country. . . To you therefore and your worthy Colleagues are the thanks of every True Citizen & Disinterested Englishman most justly due." [1]

But while the Whigs continued to embarrass the Government and to plead for the Americans, the Empire had drifted into Civil War. On 17th April, 1775, Gage took the fatal road to Concord, and at Lexington the New Englanders proved the excellence of their drilling and the accuracy of their marksmanship. The news of this engagement spread throughout the Empire and filled the West Indian planters with consternation. In a letter to a business friend in Philadelphia, John Pinney spoke with great misgivings of the gloomy news from America:

"I heartily pray that a reconciliation may soon take place between Britain and her Colonies to the satisfaction of all Parties—but I am grieved to hear that a Skirmish has happened between the Troops and Provincials at Boston—I hope to God the report is false, and should be happy to receive a Line from you on the Subject." [2]

His prayer was in vain, for three weeks after he wrote this letter, the more serious battle of Bunker's Hill was fought and the American War had started in earnest.

In the meantime, two parties had definitely appeared in Bristol, whose contribution to the Press grew more acrid as the war advanced. In July *Felix Farley* began to publish a series of letters signed by "The Impartialist of St. Vincent's Rocks." This writer, in spite of his name, was mildly pro-American and anti-war. His general argument was that the exercise of a little more commonsense on both sides would have averted all the trouble, and that British troops were mainly responsible for

---

[1] Guttridge, *op. cit.*, pp. 6–7.
[2] *Pinney Papers, Business Letter-book*, 1761–75, fol. 312.

starting the conflagration as they had been the first to shoot. But since the preliminary skirmish was indecisive, the country must now expect the horrors of a long civil war, a prophecy which proved only too true. He believed that the English who thought that America could be conquered easily were as mistaken as were the Americans who looked for a speedy termination of hostilities and a decisive victory for their arms. Like the Roman Empire before it, the British Empire was divided, and perhaps would "fall an easy prey to the political French and the insulting Spaniards." [1] Although the violence of the Americans was to be deprecated, it should be remembered that they did not dispute the King's right to the throne, nor profess to fight against him, but only against the ministry. As they had only used their arms to defend themselves they did not deserve the name of traitors.

The peace party, however, did not have it all its own way in the Bristol Press during 1775. Government supporters were growing in numbers, and in the summer of that year felt strong enough to take the offensive. On 15th July *Felix Farley* published in the same issue which contained one of the series of letters from the pen of "Political Impartialist of St. Vincent's Rocks" a letter on the other side signed "S.G." This violently attacked the character of the Bostonians. The writer quoted at considerable length and with great relish from the somewhat scurrilous account of them given by Edward Ward in his trip to America in 1699. After a few preliminary abusive remarks upon the character of the men and women of Boston, this letter quotes with great approbation:—

"The buildings, like their women, are very neat and handsome, their streets, like the hearts of their male inhabitants, paved with pebble; more religious zealots than honest men, more parsons than churches, more churches than parishes, for the town, unlike the people, is subject to no division.

"The inhabitants seem very religious, shewing many outward and visible signs of an inward and spiritual grace: But though they wear in their faces the innocence of doves, you

[1] *Felix Farley's Bristol Journal*, 24th June, 1775.

will find them in their dealings as subtile as serpents: Interest is their faith, money their God, and large possessions the only Heaven they court.

"Their industry, like their honesty, deserves observation, for it is common amongst them to go two miles to catch a horse, and run three hours after him, to ride half a mile to work, or quarter of a mile to an ale-house.

"One labourer in England will do more work in a day than a New England planter in a week; for to every hour he spends in his grounds he will be two at an ordinary. They will eat like ploughmen, though they work as lazily as gentlemen, it being no rarity to see them, eat till they sweat and work till they freeze.

"They smoke as they knead their bread, smoke whilst they cook their victuals, smoke at prayers, work and exhortation . . .

"Rum, alias kill-devil, is much adored by the American English: 'Tis held the comforter of their souls, the preserver of their bodies, the remover of their cares, and the prompter of their mirth; and is a sovereign remedy against the grumbling of the guts, a kibe heel, and wounded conscience, three epidemical distempers that affect the country.

"The women are very fruitful, which shews the men are industrious in bed though idle up. Children and servants are in plenty, but honest men and virgins scarce enough. The women have done bearing children by that time they are five and twenty. . . .

"Notwithstanding that seeming sanctity of their people, they are very profane in their common dialects; they can neither drive a bargain or crack a jest without a text of scripture at the end of it. . . .

"Many of the leading Puritans may without injustice be thus characterised. They are saints without religion, traders without honesty, magistrates without mercy, subjects without loyalty . . . faithless friends, implacable enemies, rich men without money." [1]

This polemic was followed on 26th August by an unsigned letter which was much more moderate and reasonable in tone. It begins by dismissing the charges of cruelty made by the Americans against the English soldiers. The writer denies that the British monopoly of American trade was a sufficient

[1] *Felix Farley's Bristol Journal*, 15th July, 1775.

recompense without taxation. Indeed, he argues that the Americans actually derived more advantages from the colonial system than the Mother Country herself,

> "by prohibitory acts of parliament, by drawbacks, by bounties granted to them, and by high duties laid on the goods of other nations. They tell us they do not aim at a *separation*. No, they are satisfied with the union, whilst we do all the drudgery, and find them ships, men, and money to protect and defend them." [1]

In short, according to this writer, they only traded with Britain because it was to their interest to do so, since she was the centre of the Empire, granted them large credits and was actually their best natural market. They had always been inveterate smugglers, a branch of commerce in which the President of their Congress had made his fortune. The trade of England had only been very slightly affected by the American dispute, for, in spite of all that had been said to the contrary, Manchester, Birmingham and Sheffield were now flourishing. He believed, in fact, that as long as there was a stable government in America and the rights of property were respected, it mattered little to the trade of England whether the Americans were governed by Parliament or by Congress.

> "It is not Acts of Parliament, it is neither fleets nor armies but interest alone, that can bind America to Great Britain." [1]

Other letters appeared in the Press which dealt with the disastrous effects of the war. In these, entirely opposed views were set forth at great length. At the end of September one writer, who signed himself "An Englishman," made a spirited attack on the opponents of the administration:

> "I call these friends of American resistance, republicans and enemies to kingly government. They call themselves Whigs and the only real friends of the King and kingdom . . . May God . . . blast their favorite political tenets, and save this

---

[1] *Felix Farley's Bristol Journal*, 26th August, 1775.

kingdom from the worst of slavery, from the slavery of a republican form of government."

As to the alleged attacks made on the character of the Bostonians,

". . . let unprejudiced men stand forth, and say if they have not been a refractory, ill-governable people for some years. . . . Private property they have destroyed and gloried in the deed. King's officers have been tarred and feathered for doing their duty; and this to convince mankind they were an independent state. . . . Such faithful, loyal, liberal subjects, are cruelly used, no doubt, in having their charter taken from them."[1]

In September the Tories felt strong enough to ask the Mayor to call a special meeting of the Council in order to address the King in support of the Government's policy. The meeting was called for the 21st, but as a sufficient number did not turn up to form a quorum, the Tory party asked the Mayor to allow them the use of the Guildhall, so that a public meeting of all citizens might be held. This meeting duly took place on the 28th, and after some opposition, an address was agreed to which expressed abhorsence of the rebellion and a wish for its forcible suppression. At first, in fact, the War tended to draw many recruits to the Government side. Thus, this Tory address was signed by nearly all the clergy and many merchants.

The opponents of the Government, however, were still powerful, and led by John Fisher Weare, Richard Champion and others, a counter-address, praying for conciliatory measures, was drawn up and forwarded to London. Even at the pro-Government meeting, a strong opposition speech was delivered by Mr. Symon, who declared that it was madness for a great commercial city such as Bristol to request His Majesty to continue a bloody civil war with the colonies, which would lay waste some of the fairest countries in the world and destroy the commerce upon which the city lived. Already, in the form of shrinking trade and increasing unemployment and misery among

---

[1] *Felix Farley's Bristol Journal*, 30th September, 1775.

the poor, the citizens had seen enough of the consequences of the Government's unwise policy.

"Will tradesmen and manufacturers, whose very being depends upon commerce, sign an address to effect their own ruin?"

He besought his hearers to combine with their fellow citizens in presenting a united address to the King, praying for a cessation of the present war, and his gracious interposition to put a stop to this ruinous civil strife, so

"that our trade may thereby be restored to its former flourishing state."

Much credit, he declared, was due to the gentlemen who had prepared an address in this spirit yesterday,

"for they have proved themselves the true friends of their country." [1]

He, therefore, exhorted his hearers to support the address of the Whigs.

The Whig address was couched in very humble, loyal language. It expressed the gloomy conviction of honest men who were deeply distressed by the grim spectre of civil war.

"It is with an affliction not to be expressed, and with most anxious apprehensions for ourselves and our posterity, that we behold the growing distractions in America. . . . We are apprehensive, that if the present measures are adhered to, a total alienation of the affections of our fellow subjects in the colonies will ensue; to which affection much more than to a dread of any power, we have been hitherto indebted for the inestimable benefits which we have derived from those establishments. We can forsee no good effects to the commerce or revenues of this kingdom at a future period from any victories which may be obtained by your Majesty's arms over desolated provinces and an exasperated people." [2]

The address went on to say that, in justice to the Americans, it should be remembered that in the midst of so many troubles

---

[1] *Felix Farley's Bristol Journal*, 7th October, 1775.
[2] *Ibid.*, 14th October, 1775.

they had not lost their affection for the Mother Country, nor had they failed to observe the obligations of commercial honour. Although there had been a breakdown of government, American imports still continued as in the most quiet times. The trade of the port of Bristol and the subsistence of a considerable section of the nation depended upon the honourable and amicable behaviour of the Americans. In the single year ending September, 1774, Bristol received no less than one million bushels of wheat, besides great quantities of other commodities essential to navigation and commerce. This all showed that if the royal clemency were manifested to the colonies, they for their part would not be found wanting in a spirit favourable to peace and reconciliation. Though the citizens of Bristol were as anxious as any to preserve the sovereign authority of Parliament, they believed that this could never be done by force and without the affection of the people of America. This petition closes with the gloomy reflection which seems to suggest that its sponsors knew it would be in vain, that having thus placed the issue definitely before the King, they at least would be clear

"from any share whatsoever in producing the calamities which the present proceedings so inauspiciously begun may yet bring upon this nation." [1]

In the same number appeared a letter from Edmund Burke to Mr. Hayes, the chairman of the meeting which framed the petition.

"It gave me as much pleasure as in the present state of things, I am capable of feeling, to be honor'd with such commands from so numerous and so respectable a body of my constituents. I do not yet abandon all hopes, that truth and reason will have their effect; and that the healing endeavor of good and moderate men will triumph over the hasty violence of those deluded people, who, though unable to assist either with counsels or arms, are so forward to give their inconsiderate voices for the continuance of a bloody and expensive civil war, which neither they nor those whom they urge to such desperate course are able to foresee any end of." [1]

[1] *Felix Farley's Bristol Journal*, 14th October, 1775.

Many other letters appeared in the Press at this time which, however, added nothing material to the controversy, though they do illustrate the growing tension in Bristol. In December the Merchant Venturers petitioned the Lords against the Bill prohibiting all trade and intercourse with the Americans. Many Bristolians had large debts owing in the colonies, and they believed that remittances were already on the sea in colonial ships. If the Bill passed in its present form, contrary to the intention of Parliament, the property of many loyal people in Great Britain and the West Indies would be confiscated. Indeed, the Bill was unwisely conceived, badly drafted and calculated only to hinder and harm the people of Great Britain, Ireland and the loyal plantations.

So 1775 passed, and 1776 came in with petitions, counter-petitions and collections for the dependents of those who had been killed or wounded in the American war.

"All the affluent and well-dispos'd Citizens are desired to send in their subscriptions," [1]

and by 20th January the fund amounted to £1,650. By that time the opposition to the Government had greatly weakened. England was at war, and whatever the rights of the Americans might be, the average plain Englishman believed that they were not justified in going to the extremity of taking up arms against the King. Moreover, the horror of civil war was somewhat abated in the breasts of some merchants by the prospect of valuable Government contracts. In February the Merchant Venturers petitioned that the West Indies should be supplied from England with foodstuffs and other commodities which formerly they had imported from the American colonies. The seriousness of this situation is illustrated in a letter written by John Pinney from Nevis about the same time:

"The inhabitants of this Island are greatly distressed for their usual supplies of Provisions and Lumber from America."

[1] *Felix Farley's Bristol Journal*, 23rd December, 1775.

The American War would, he thought, be the ruin of the sugar colonies, and if things did not take a more favourable turn,

"God only knows what will become of us? we must either starve or be ruined." [1]

If the planters turned their cane lands into provision grounds they would not be able to make remittances to Great Britain, but if they did not do that, they must starve.

America declared her independence on 4th July, but Champion still continued to work for the now hopeless cause of peace. He kept the Whig leaders up to date with all news from America, and on the arrival at Bristol in August of Richard Penn with the Olive Branch Petition, he caused it to be printed and published. Copies were sent to all the important Whigs in both Houses of Parliament. In December the Bristol Whigs, led by Champion, feasted at Burke's expense on a day which the King had proclaimed as a fast day. The toast-list sums up the point of view of this group at that time, and Champion wrote to Burke:

". . , we have spent a cheerful, decent day; breaking up before six o'clock; lamenting the hypocrisy of those who have brought the evils upon this country, which now they are wickedly sporting with . . ."

The toasts, "which were cheerfully received" were:—

"1. The King.

2. Recovery from the delusion in which he is held by the enemies of his family, and strength to resist their snares.

3. The Queen and Royal Family.

4. The Hanover succession as by the Law established.

5. The Members for the City of Bristol.

6. May they ever possess virtue and fortitude worthy of their truly independent electors.

7. Lord Rockingham and the Whig opposition in Parliament.

---

[1] *Pinney Papers, Business Letter-book*, 1776–8, fol. 28.

8. Prosperity to the Whig cause, on both sides of the Atlantick, and peace to the British Empire.

9. The glorious and immortal memory of the great King William.

10. Success to the honest endeavours of those who support the liberty and safety of their country.

11. The glorious and immortal memory of the late Duke of Cumberland.

12. May those who resisted the principles of our late excellent Sovereign King George the 2nd be held in detestation; but the supporters of a Whig constitution, be crowned with success.

13. Every opposition to a Ministry whose tyranny has lost an Empire, and obliged a virtuous people to an unwilling separation.

14. A true sense of their condition, to the deluded People of Britain, that they may see the dangerous designs of their arbitrary ministerial leaders." [1]

In spite of these manifestations of Whig opposition, the country, including Bristol, by the end of 1776 supported the war. On 14th January, 1777, an address was agreed to by a general meeting of citizens. After one opponent, who spoke against it, had been turned out, the motion for the address was passed unanimously. This was sent in the name of "the Free-holders, Clergy, Burgesses and Inhabitants of the City of Bristol, at Guildhall assembled," and begged to congratulate the King on the late glorious success of his arms in America, where, in the closing months of 1776, Cornwallis, having captured 100 guns from Greene, had driven Washington before him through New Jersey. Although moved by feelings of humanity to lament the deserved calamities which the defeated colonists had brought upon themselves, they were impelled to state the great blessings they enjoyed under the King's mild and beneficent rule. They looked forward to the re-establishment of peace with America, and they ventured to express the hope that when the war was finally over the Government would adopt a just and wise policy

[1] Owen, *op. cit.*, pp. 178–9.

in relation to the distant parts of the Empire, calculated to establish its future peace, order and government. It is plain from this address that the people of Bristol had still much to learn in relation to the economic policy of the Empire. They trusted as inhabitants of a great commercial city that

"through the wisdom of your Majesty's councils the Trade of America will be made subject to such Regulations and Restrictions, as shall, no less in the Eye of Reason than of Policy, be judged expedient to render it, in its several Branches, most conducive to the Interests of your Majesty's Subjects." [1]

It was said that this document bore the signatures of no less than 1,300 people.

A few days later, even the Merchant Venturers, a body which had been so critical of Government policy at the beginning, also joined in the chorus of congratulation to the King. In this, they spoke as if the war were already over and the Americans defeated.

"The dangerous heighth to which the defection of our misguided Fellow Subjects was risen was truly alarming . . . and sincerely felt and lamented by every man who wished the prosperity of this Nation, as the ruin our Trade must have inevitably followed their success." [2]

The petitioners lamented that the use of force had been necessary, and hoped that, with the return to their allegiance, peace would be restored on terms so tempered with mercy that there would not be again a like revolt so disastrous to trade, which they now hoped would be restored to its former splendour and remain unequalled in the world.

But the jubilation of January, 1777, had little real justification. That year was destined to end in profound gloom, and to usher in another still more depressing. John Pinney came nearer the truth when he wrote on 18th April:

". . . the present gloomy prospect of American affairs, united with our internal deplorable situation causes an apparent dejection in the countenance of every Man, and unless

---

[1] *Felix Farley's Bristol Journal*, 25th January, 1777.
[2] *Merchant Venturers' Book of Petitions*, fol. 82.

some speedy alteration takes place; God only knows, what will
be the event of this fatal War: I tremble for the consequences." [1]

As the months passed the situation in the Islands grew even
worse. In June he wrote: "Our situation here is truly alarming."
Poor crops, the ebb of West Indian credit and the American
war would, he thought, soon ruin the planting community.

"God only knows where it will end! I cannot help thinking,
but our Estates in those Islands are held, at present, on a
very precarious tenure. . . . Enemies all around me! While
at breakfast, a few 'weeks ago, I saw a Brig taken, bound to
St. Christopher, near my own landing. After the sailing of
our last Fleet, we shall be unhappily situated . . . subject to
be pilfered and robed by Pirates in the Night, who may, with
care, carry off our Slaves, to the utter ruin of the Planters." [2]

According to Pinney, West Indian waters swarmed with enemy
privateers. In fact,

"to paint the distress of this little spot in its proper colours,
wou'd require the pen of a Churchill, and the pencil of a
Hogarth." [3]

In that same year, moreover, the menace came nearer home.
Even English coastwise trade began to suffer. American
cruisers and privateers appeared in the English and St. George's
Channels, and the Government was requested by the Merchant
Venturers to rescind certain legislation which prohibited the
carrying of munitions of war and arms by coastal vessels.

So far the war had been a purely domestic quarrel, though
French agents had been busy throughout, and some assistance
had been received by the Americans from France. With the
disaster at Saratoga in October, 1777, the French Government
felt that the issue was sufficiently clear to justify it in openly
espousing the cause of America. The Franco-American treaty
was signed on 6th February, 1778, and France set about
avenging herself on the power which brought so much humiliation to her in 1763. The prospect of England's defeat attracted

[1] *Pinney Papers, Business Letter-book,* 1776-8, fol. 90.
[2] *Ibid.,* fol. 114 ff.
[3] *Ibid.,* fol. 137 ff.

still another old enemy to join in her ruin. Spain declared war
on 1st June, 1779, and the Northern powers drew together in a
hostile alliance. Thus the purely family wrangle of the 'sixties
which, with the exercise of common sense and moderation,
might possibly have been settled amicably, had grown into a
disastrous first-class war.

On 19th January, 1778, a meeting took place at the Guildhall.
Recruits for the army were not coming in fast enough, for though
many believed that the war was unfortunately necessary, it was
not popular with the nation as a whole. Loyal citizens, therefore, were encouraged to offer bounties to young men who came
forward, and the meeting was called to raise a subscription for
this purpose. Before the books closed that evening £14,000
had been promised, and later, according to *Felix Farley*, this
sum was increased to £19,593 19s. The Tories were jubilant,
and proclaimed this offer of money as a testimony to the loyalty
of the people of Bristol, as well as an expression of their con-
fidence in the Government's policy.

The opposition, however, was not yet quite dead, and various
attacks on this subscription appeared in *Bonner and Middleton's
Journal*. To these *Felix Farley* published equally truculent
rejoinders.

"I congratulate my fellow-citizens that, notwithstanding
the snarlings of sedition and the fury of faction, they have
at length shown their loyalty by the liberal subscription at the
Guildhall." [1]

The true designs of the pro-Americans, according to this writer,
were now clear, for the ruin which they had brought on the
Newfoundland and West Indian trades was obvious to all.
Reason and fair argument had been drowned of late, he said,
in the senseless cry of "Wilkes and Liberty," and patriotic
madness. But the scheme of these mock patriots would not do.

"The mask is seen thro'. . . . Regardless of the pretended
charge of the want of humanity and the love of peace of which
the mock patriots so falsely accuse us, let us continue to subscribe . . . and let the patriotic junto know that their father,

[1] *Felix Farley's Bristol Journal*, 24th January, 1778.

Oliver Cromwell . . . put a motto round his money which we shall take a hint from in the present state of our national affairs, Pax quaeritur Bello. 'Peace is to be gained by war.' " [1]

The advertisements and letters which continued to appear in the Press, however, show that, even with the stimulus of bounties, men failed to come forward in sufficient numbers.

The first effect of the accumulated disasters was to increase the support given to the Government. But later the spirit of loyal co-operation was destined to be replaced by one of exasperation and anger. During 1778 the Tories of Bristol subscribed £21,000 to strengthen the hands of the Government, though only £4,500 was actually collected. The decline in the power of the pro-American party was shown shortly after this, however, when a rival meeting, which was called to raise money for the relief of distressed Americans detained as prisoners-of-war, produced a paltry £363. The news of the French declaration of war was heard in the West Indies with dismay. It seemed to the already harassed planters that their precarious position must now be hopeless. Many, like John Pinney, began to think of contracting their commitments and of retiring to England, to which at this time he looked as his only asylum.

It has been seen how, when Great Britain was attacked on all sides, Ireland seized her opportunity. Grattan pressed for a more equitable fiscal policy towards his country than had hitherto been pursued. Whether through conviction or spleen at his recent defeat in Bristol, Lord Clare threw himself into the Irish cause with great energy. In Parliament, he proposed that all Irish goods except woollens should be allowed free import into the colonies, and that all colonial products, except indigo and tobacco, should be imported into Ireland direct. On this occasion Clare was supported by Burke, but while the House of Commons was inclined to consider the proposals favourably, the citizens of Bristol were furious. Lord Clare was accused of diabolical spite against the city which had rejected him, and Burke's action was attributed to his wish for the promotion of the interests of his native country, regardless of those of England.

[1] *Felix Farley's Bristol Journal*, 24th January, 1778.

The Merchant Venturers, merchants at large and the Corporation united in an effort to defeat the ameliorative policy. In spite of his known convictions and theories of Parliamentary representation, Burke was instructed to vote against the Irish proposals. To these orders he was utterly indifferent and continued his efforts for better Anglo-Irish understanding. Although North himself appears to have been sympathetic to the Bristol point of view at first, and actually procured the defeat of a measure in 1779, which was intended to provide for the free importation of sugar into Ireland, he could not disregard unpleasant facts. When Grattan, with an Irish army at his back, threatened to lead Ireland into revolt in the wake of the colonies, North and his Government were constrained to take another line. Bristol was implacable. Though it had to accept the Government's change of front it could avenge itself on Burke. At the election of 1780 both he and the American Cruger were rejected, but this was almost the last time that Bristol was destined to act as a loyal, uncritical supporter of the increasingly unpopular administration of North.

The capture of Charleston on 12th May, 1780, for a moment revived the flagging spirits of the pro-war party. When the news reached Bristol, the city gave itself up to jubilation and, for the last time in that fateful war, the bells of the city churches rang incessantly the whole day. In the evening the Monmouthshire militia were drawn up on College Green and fired a *feu de joie*. Some of the townspeople wished to illuminate the city at night, but as there had recently been some hooliganism and window-smashing, particularly of Quakers' premises, the Corporation refused to grant permission. Also, at that time the alarm caused by the Gordon Riots in London was still fresh in the minds of all, and the city fathers knew that once the Bristol mob was roused, the destruction which it might cause was incalculable.

Even before the capture of Charleston, however, the unpopularity of the Government had already been growing, and that event could do no more than exercise a temporary check to the receding tide of public goodwill. In January, 1780, a meeting of the Corporation was held to consider another petition to the

Government. The Mayor stated that he had called this meeting at the earnest request of several members of the Corporation who, he supposed, would now explain their intention. It subsequently came out that he was himself much opposed both to the meeting and to the petition. Nevertheless, it was moved that the Corporation of Bristol should present a petition to Parliament similar to that already sent up from York and other cities. After some amendment had been made it was finally passed, according to *Felix Farley*, unanimously. A correspondent writing in that paper on 12th February, however, asserted that it had been passed by a majority vote only, that the Mayor had declared his opposition to it, and that in its final form, it was innocuous. As given in *Felix Farley's Bristol Journal*, the petition stated:

> "The unhappy and destructive contest so long subsisting between this country and the American colonies, having first annihilated a large proportion of the national commerce, has at last plunged this kingdom into a most expensive war with the powers of France, and Spain; by which means, while it hath been the occasion of increasing the public burthens to a degree beyond example, it has greatly diminished the ability of supporting them; and the great increase of Taxes is so heavily felt that many of the manufactures and branches of Commerce which are still retained, must sink under the pressure of any additional weight.
>
> "In order to prevent such extensive ruin, your petitioners humbly submit to this honourable House, the necessity there is, that no part of the public revenue drained from the industrious and laborious be diverted from the purposes for which it was granted, and that public ecomomy (sic) supply the place of new taxes; the abolition of pensions unmerited by public services and of places which are sinecures; the reduction of the exorbitant emoluments of office and a strict attention to economy in making public contracts would furnish, on occasion, in the present emergency, some of the most safe and reasonable resources, would induce a spirit of frugality, the want of which has been long lamented and reduce the influence of the Crown within those bounds to which our wise ancestors deemed it expedient for the safety of the constitution that it should be limited."

By such a zeal for the public good, renewed confidence in

public measures would be restored, and the inhabitants of these kingdoms would again become a great, happy and united people.

"Your petitioners, therefore, humbly pray that this just and necessary reformation in the public expenditure may be adopted; and the savings accruing therefrom be faithfully applied to the national service in such manner as in the wisdom of Parliament shall seem meet." [1]

In September John Pinney reported that a large part of the West Indian supply fleet had been captured by the enemy. A year later Cornwallis surrendered at Yorktown, a surrender which Pinney described with pardonable anger, which, however, was unjust to the unfortunate commander. He regarded it as

"A Capitulation . . . that ever must disgrace the annals of Great Britain,"

and he expressed the widespread feeling in the West Indies when he wrote:

"When I reflect on the impending ruin that seems quivering over old England, I am lost in thought. Alas! I am afraid her Sun is set, to rise no more." [2]

On 23rd January, 1782, the Corporation of Bristol petitioned the House of Commons against a further continuance of the war. They prayed that the King should be advised to make a total change in the policy "which has involved the Nation in such complicated misfortunes." [3] On the following day another general meeting of citizens was held for the same purpose, at which Joseph Harford twitted the pro-war party for its silence. It had, he said, been given ample opportunity of trying its experiment and it must now be convinced that the subjugation of America by force was impossible. He had some harsh things to say also about the misconduct of the war and the incapacity

[1] *Felix Farley's Bristol Journal*, 5th February, 1780.
[2] *Pinney Papers, Business Letter-book*, 1779-84, fols. 144–5.
[3] *Felix Farley's Bristol Journal*, 26th January, 1782.

of ministers. Even the West Indian planters, in their petition to Parliament, had made charges of gross negligence and inattention to business as violent as any made by the most irreconcilable Whigs. On the motion being made that a petition be presented to the King against the present war, heated discussion arose. The general opinion seemed to be that it was quite useless again to approach the Throne, where experience had shown

"Petitions would only be received, as they have been . . . for years past . . . with studied contempt." [1]

It was unanimously agreed, therefore, that this petition should be sent not to the King, but to the House of Commons.

After going over again all the misfortunes which the war had brought on the country, and stating that its prolongation would bring utter ruin to the West Indian trade, the only important branch of commerce still left to England, the petition closes:

"Your Petitioners, therefore, humbly request this Honourable House would adopt some measures as its wisdom may suggest for enabling his Majesty to put an end to the unnatural, unfortunate and expensive war in America, and for producing a radical alteration in the management of the public affairs, by which alone the evils impending over us and our posterity can be averted." [2]

Brickdale presented this petition, but Daubeny, an inveterate enemy of the Americans throughout, opposed it because, he declared, it did not represent the wishes of the majority of his constituents, and further, the charges made against the Government and the conduct of the war were ill-founded.

Lord North fell in March and, greatly to the satisfaction of Bristol, Lord Rockingham assumed office. General Conway, who had played some part in the overthrow of the late Government, received the Freedom of the City as his reward. The Corporation

[1] *Felix Farley's Bristol Journal*, 26th January, 1782.
[2] *Ibid.*, 2nd February, 1782.

sent its congratulations to the new Government, and also to the King, who at last had got rid of his inefficient, incapable ministers, and who had appointed in their places men of high rank and proved ability. The Government was thanked for accepting, at this alarming crisis in the nation's history, the heavy task of office, and it was agreed that every member of the Government who was not already enrolled should be given the Freedom of the City. In particular, the thanks of Bristol were extended to its late member, Edmund Burke, who had taken office at a reduced salary, and was introducing a Bill proposing drastic economies. The other rejected pro-American member, Henry Cruger, was Mayor of Bristol in 1782, which shows the change which had come over public opinion in the past two years. He also was publicly thanked by the meeting at which he presided in January for the countenance he had afforded the meeting and for the candour and impartiality with which he had presided. Rodney, who became a public hero after his victory of the Saints in 1782, landed in Bristol and spent the night at the Royal Fort. A few months later he returned to receive the Freedom of the City, and that was the last incident which connected Bristol with this long and unhappy episode in British history.

After the peace the traders of Bristol returned to their old policy. To them it seemed absurd that, because the American colonies had thrown off their political allegiance, Great Britain should put handicaps on her own trade in a way which served merely to bring greater commercial depression. In spite of the Revolution, the West Indies still depended on the exchange of their rum and sugar for American lumber, foodstuffs and other stores. The prohibition of trade between the colonies and the United States injured the West Indies far more than the rebel plantations, but there were many in high places in England who could not see this obvious fact. For these, vengeance was to be the keynote of British American policy, a determination which was destined to bring unnumbered misfortunes in its train. The story of that unhappy trade dispute to which this very unwise attitude inevitably led is outside the scope of the present work, but Bristol may console herself with the thought that in this particular madness she had no share. Indeed, by repeated petitions and other expressions of public opinion, she did her utmost to convince the Government that common sense and the true economic interest of the Empire lay in the direction of an expanded and unrestricted trade with America.

CHAPTER XV

JOHN PINNEY, PLANTER AND MERCHANT

"*The merchants of this City have the greatest Trade, but they Trade with a more entire Independency upon* London, *than any other Town in* Britain. *And 'tis evident in this particular, (viz) That whatsoever Exportations they make to any part of the World, they are able to bring the full returns back to their own Port, and can dispose of it there.*"

DANIEL DEFOE, *A Tour Thro' the Whole Island of Great Britain* (1724).

FOR almost a century and a half the Pinneys were connected with the West Indian trade, and though the fortunes of no particular family can be taken as typical, the various phases of the Pinney interest in Nevis and the West India trade may reasonably be regarded as a sample. There were many Bristol families whose association with the Islands extended through several generations, but for the most part their records have partially or wholly perished. The Pinney family have preserved a fairly complete set of business papers, and one of them, John Pinney, planter and merchant, was, fortunately for the historian, an inveterate letter writer whose views could always be counted upon to be vigorous. In previous chapters the official connection of the city with the West Indies has been traced, and in the present one it is proposed to follow the story of this particular family in order to express that relationship in terms of men and women, as contrasted with tierces and puncheons. In the *Pinney Papers* it is possible to discover how closely the merchants of the city were concerned with the plantations, and to follow the ups and downs of the Anglo-West Indian interest, its hopes and fears, its enormous success and its utter collapse.

The Pinney family were concerned during the reign of Charles II with the export trade to the West Indies. Nathaniel Pinney, a member of the Royal African Company, exported lace and other textiles to the Islands. His brother, Azariah Pinney, was involved in the Monmouth Rebellion, and was condemned by Judge Jeffreys to transportation to the West Indies. Fortunately, Nathaniel was able to buy him, and so, theoretically, Azariah went out as his brother's bondsman. He was one of the fortunate transportees, for his exile was not of the ordinary kind and his transportation was a costly affair. The equipment of this victim for political and religious liberty on the ship which carried him to his alleged bondage was of a highly consoling nature. Among other things, it included 6 gallons of sack, 4 gallons of brandy, 2 cheeses, 3 pairs of hose, 4 pairs of worsted,

2 pairs of shoes, a hat, shifts and handkerchiefs, tobacco and pipes, bed, bolster and rug, trunks, a Bible and other books, sugar, spice and so on, which totalled £9 17s. 6d. He travelled as a gentleman, wearing his sword and attended by his private servant. His outward passage cost his brother £5, in addition to 6s. 6d. for the boat hire to carry him from the city quay down to Kingroad where the ship was lying at anchor. There were many other charges as well, including £15 given to him, and his ransom came to £65, so that before he finally left the country his family had been put to some considerable expense on his behalf.

With the arrival of Azariah in the Caribbean the family business expanded in all directions. Within a year of his landing there his brother began to consign to him various parcels of lace, cotton and lutestrings. At first these remittances were very small in value: £81 10s. 6d., £21, £50 14s. 3½d., but the business grew rapidly, particularly in the export of West Indian sugar to England. As early as 1687, one consignment sent by Azariah to his brother in Bristol totalled £6,226.[1] In the following year, an invoice of sugar was for £1,681,[2] and still another invoice signed by him in 1689 came to £19,790,[3] while another, under date of 29th October of the same year, was for £17,386.[3] The man who had been prepared to risk all in the cause of religion under the worthless Monmouth possessed the qualities of sobriety and serious-mindedness which were calculated to make him a successful West India planter and merchant. Monmouth's support came partially from the solid Protestant middle class as well as from the deluded peasantry of the West Counties, and it was this middle class Protestant group that was to be mainly responsible for carrying through a revolution in English industry and commerce in the following century. Azariah Pinney was, in fact, a great business success in Nevis. By the middle of Queen Anne's reign he had already returned to England and established himself as a merchant in London. When the French invaded the island of Nevis in

[1] *Pinney Papers, The Private Account Book of Nathaniel Pinney*, fol. 3.
[2] *Ibid.*, fol. 9.
[3] *Ibid.*, fol. 10.

1705–6, his losses were considerable, and from statements made at the time it is clear that he was still not only an exporter of sugars to England, but an importer into the Islands of miscellaneous cargoes of trade goods, plantation equipment and other things required by the planters.   In spite of the setbacks of war his business flourished, and his son became a leading man in the island. Although a merchant of London in 1707, he was still consigning sugars from Nevis to Bristol, and goods were also received on his behalf from that port in the island.

His son, John Pinney, carried on the business with success, and in the course of his residence in the West Indies became Chief Justice. From invoices and letters of 1719, it appears that although part of his trade was with London, part was also with Bristol. In the meantime, the firm of Nathaniel Pinney had disappeared, and for the next sixty years or so the Pinneys were mainly West Indian planters, officials and exporters of sugar to England who had no commercial representative of their family resident in Bristol. John Pinney, after an active life in the island of Nevis, died there, and his son, J. F. Pinney, of Bettiscombe, Dorset, inherited the West Indian estates, which he placed in the charge of an agent, William Coker. It was the duty of this man to keep his employer informed about the state of his property and generally to superintend his estates.

"Dear Sir,

". . . Your Houses in Town are in bad Repair, that in Bristol Street has been partly repaired. . . . Mr. Oliver . . . advised me by all means to ship to Bristol . . . and assured me that Mr. Laroche was a Gentleman of much Consequence. Upon this I engaged 15 Casks on the Britania Wm Olive, which were all he could take and consigned them to the above Gentleman." [1]

J. F. Pinney died soon after this communication was received, and his property in the West Indies was bequeathed to his cousin, John Pretor, who duly announced his succession in a letter to Messrs. Shaw and Coker, of London, on 30th November, 1762.

[1] *Pinney Papers*, box 14.

"My Cousin Jn° Fre^k. Pinney died the 11th Instant and has by his Will left me Devisee and sole Executor. . .

"P.S. My Cousins Will directs for me to use the Name of Pinney only, which name I have assumed ever since his Burial. . . My former Name was Pretor." [1]

So John Pinney, planter, merchant and man of affairs, makes his appearance, and so began his connection with the island of Nevis which was destined to continue to the end of his life. As his career covers so long a period and illustrates the various vicissitudes of fortune to which the West Indian planters were liable, and the varied experiences through which so many of them passed, it may be dealt with at some considerable length. He was a constant letter writer who kept exact records of his various transactions. Through his writings it is thus possible to learn at first hand what kind of men the planters were, the problems with which they were confronted, and the methods they adopted for their solution.

Pinney decided to go out to Nevis himself as soon as the Seven Years' War was over and arrangements could conveniently be made for his departure. At five o'clock on the morning of 13th October, 1764, he sent his last letter ashore from the *London Merchant*, then in the Downs. This announced his departure, and in it he lamented that, as they were then weighing anchor, he would have no opportunity after all of receiving

"my Bristol Water, wh^h I am not a little Sorry for, as I know the Distress I shall be in, for want of it." [2]

His estates in Nevis had been left in a sorry condition, and he was determined to remain there until he had placed them once more on a satisfactory basis. Under date of 6th February, 1765, he wrote from Nevis that he had arrived in that island on the 22nd of the previous December, after a good passage. Had it not been for a stop at Madeira they would have made Nevis in 29 days. Pinney, however, was very content that his voyage was extended in this way,

"as I had the misfortune to have my Gum Cut & torn in a

[1] *Pinney Papers, Business Letter-book*, 1761–75, fol. 13.
[2] *Ibid.*, fol. 61.

shocking manner by our D^{rs} attempting to draw one of my teeth. I never met with one of the Faculty so ignorant, for he coud not devise one method (neither did he offer to apply any thing to ye wound) to stop ye bleeding, tho it was so violent, that many thought I could not exist long, in ye situation I was in. At last with much diff^y I stopd it, & had the good luck next day to make Madeira, where I immediately applied to a Surgeon and by his assistence found great relief." [1]

In the course of the next fifty years he was destined to make this passage on many occasions. He returned to England for the first time in 1773, and set sail for the island again on 26th December, 1774, which he reached on 11th February, 1775. On 31st August, 1783, he landed once more in England after what he describes as a pleasant voyage of 41 days. On this occasion he hurried on to London to procure lodgings for his wife and family who followed him by slow stages. He was very angry with Mr. Weeks, his father-in-law, who, without his permission, brought his sons up from Salisbury to London on the night of his wife's arrival.

"Contrary to my desire and direction between ten and eleven o'clock at night he reached our lodgings—was imprudent enough to send up my boys without any previous notice or appearing himself. As we had not the least idea of their being in town, and not conceiving it possible for him to act so opposite to my wishes, after receiving my letter, we received them as strangers—we did not know them nor they us; until Mrs. Josiah Nisbet, who was present, exclaimed, 'Good God! Don't you know them?—They are your Children.' Upon hearing that exclamation I was stupified, and should have remained so for some time, had I not been roused by the situation of Mrs. P—— it affected her so much, that she knew not what she did—she set her head-dress in a blaze by the candle—happily the boys perceived it and cryed out, which enabled me to extinguish it, before it had done any material injury—such a scene of distress and joy I never before experienced—we did not recover ourselves for the whole night." [2]

---

[1] *Pinney Papers, Business Letter-book,* 1761–75, fol. 64.
[2] *Ibid., Business Letter-book,* 1783–7, fol. 3.

In 1790 Pinney went out to Nevis and again in 1793. At 4 a.m. on 24th December, 1793, he wrote a letter to his old friend, James Tobin, when off Lundy Island, and it was to be taken ashore by the pilot. At that highly unsuitable hour for correspondence he was naturally full of gloomy forebodings about the economic future of the West Indies, and the large commitments of the house of Tobin and Pinney, which he feared might bring it down, so he was unable to sleep. His gloom was probably accentuated to some extent by his sorry physical condition.

"Being now very Sea sick . . . had I not written to Mrs. P—— yesterday, I could not now have done it; for I can scarcely see." [1]

England was once more at war with France, and so Pinney was obliged to sail in a convoy.

On 1st February, 1794, he wrote from Cork Cove to Tobin, complaining about the meat which had been supplied. This illustrates the possibilities of a ship's cuisine in those days before the steamer and the refrigerator:

"The Beef bought of Mr. Bonbonous for the Ships Stores Maies tells me is in a decayed and rotten state unfit for use . . . the ships company . . . brought him up a Piece which had been boiled for their Dinner, which was very bad. . . ." [2]

On examination, all that was visible appeared to be in a decayed condition, and it was therefore to be thrown away. The tierces of beef were to be surveyed in the West Indies,

"as the decayed beef here would not sell for sixpence, but in the West Indies it may fetch a triffle, as Negroes don't regard it much, if it can be used at all so as they buy a good pennyworth." [2]

Pinney added that he had not himself seen the beef, for when the survey was made he wisely went ashore. A month later he was still in Cork Cove, waiting on the Commodore and writing to

[1] *Pinney Papers, Business Letter-book*, 1792–5, fol. 86.
[2] *Ibid.*, fol. 97.

Tobin about his investments in the Bristol and Cirencester Canal. Like all other merchants, he was furious with the Government for its inadequate convoy arrangements. At last, owing to the repeated remonstrances made by the merchants of Bristol to the Government, the Commodore decided that it was time to set sail, but not until trade had suffered grievously. According to Pinney, who was scarcely an impartial observer, inefficiency was the chief characteristic of the naval authorities, for if his original plan had been carried out whereby the Bristol ships were to join with the main convoy at an agreed place,

> "we should . . . have been at our several destined Ports, instead of which, we have been lying here (Cork Cove) ever since Christmas, at an enormous expense, and the Planters in the West Indies are in the utmost distress for the want of their Plantation Stores." [1]

But at long last the signal to set sail was given, and they duly arrived at Nevis in safety.

When Pinney first went out as a young man to that island he was determined not to succumb to the usual seductions of a planter's life. He was fully resolved to rebuild the fortunes of his family which had languished somewhat during the tumultuous 'fifties and 'sixties, when England was usually at war, and when his kinsmen were so often absent from their estates.

> "I am determined not to follow the Vices of yᵉ Country, but to live the Life of an Honest, Sober, and Diligent Planter, for yt was my only Motive of coming here, and it is the only step I can take to ease myself of my present incumbrances. As it was my late Kinsman's pleasure to leave his Estates involved, I shall think it incumbent upon me to clear them as soon as possible; therefore with the blessing of God I intend to reside here till I have paid off yᵉ last Shilling." [2]

As soon as he arrived he threw himself with great energy into his work. In the course of the next nineteen years, thanks to his unremitting assiduity, the Pinney plantations were more thriving than they had ever been. As he felt he could not afford

---

[1] *Pinney Papers, Business Letter-book,* 1792–5, fol. 105.
[2] *Ibid., Business Letter-book,* 1761–75, fols. 64–5.

the luxury of a manager, he dismissed Coker and took charge himself. Immediately his letters describe a new dwelling-house which he had built, a new sugar mill, and how he had cleared a previously uncultivated estate, planted sugar, purchased mules, negroes and provisions, all of which cost him over £2,000. Within a few years he was an established planter, who exported large quantities of sugar and bought supplies, of the quality of which he continually complained. Indeed, John Pinney was somewhat exacting in his standards, and his correspondence affords a good illustration of the difficulties which beset those who carried on a business which entailed communication with merchants and agents three thousand miles away and several months in terms of time.

"I have inclosed a Protest ag^t. the Shippers of the Pickles which were entirely spoil'd by being ill-pack'd & having no Stoppers nor Covers save a little Brown paper." [1]

Again, in another letter he complained bitterly of a cargo which he received. Bristol mahogany furniture was much dearer than that of London and inferior, and London captains were more obliging than those of Bristol. On another occasion during the American War he never received supplies which were sent out to him, and the consequence was that the negroes were in dire need of clothing, foodstuffs and implements. But even in war-time he expected his provisions to be up to standard when they managed to elude enemy capture. In June, 1777, Pinney ordered "2 Glocester and 1 Cheddar cheeses" to be sent out to him, but in the following year he was complaining as usual.

"The cheese was not so good as I could have wished, pray send always the best than can be procured, it being for my own table and what I am fond of." [2]

Even before he set out to his estates for the first time, the manager, William Coker, discovered that the new master was a man of affairs. Pinney took the trouble to discover the best consignee in Bristol, and he recommended Mr. Laroche of that

---

[1] *Pinney Papers, Business Letter-book,* 1761–75, fol. 137.
[2] *Ibid., Business Letter-book,* 1776–8, fol. 183.

city, whose reputation stood very high. Later on he appears to have preferred another Bristol merchant, William Reeves, but he could not increase his consignments of sugar to him, though anxious to do so, as "Laroche has behaved to me in every respect genteel and becoming the gentleman." For the future, therefore, Pinney decided to reduce his consignments to London and increase those to Bristol. But shortly after this he had an opportunity of letting two of his plantations at a good figure and of selling all his available sugar on the spot, so Reeves had to do without any remittances from him that season.

It has already been seen that the sugar islands depended on the outside world for almost everything they consumed. Their chief sources of supply were the northern continental colonies and England. Freed from the necessity of producing general food crops, they were able to confine their attention almost solely to the production of sugar and its bye-products, rum and molasses. A typical order included building lime, iron, food-stuffs for the negroes, textiles, slaves' clothing, clothing for the family, and household effects. The ships in the spring brought out besides these articles, tools and materials for building, bolts, locks, fishing lines, equipment for boiling sugar, hogs-heads, "half a bushel of gruts in a jug," soap, candles, hair cloths, bushel-bags and an enormous list of other things.[1] As London was not very satisfactory, Pinney showed a marked preference for Bristol.

"The Hoes which I received from London last Year, are so exceedingly bad, that my Negroes are continually com-plaining, they bend at every stroke and will not enter the ground."

If the Bristol products turned out to be better, he intimated that he would give larger orders in the future, and to obtain what he required he was ready to pay a good price,

"for Negroes with bad Hoes, labour twice as much as they do with good ones."[2]

---

[1] *Pinney Papers, Business Letter-book*, 1776–8, fol. 127.

[2] *Ibid.*, fol. 20.

Apparently Bristol merchants satisfied his needs, for in later letters appear orders for large consignments made up of every variety of plantation equipment, household effects and personal necessities.

In the course of his trade he established close connections with several leading Bristol merchants. The outbreak of the American War dislocated the sugar trade. American and later French privateers swarmed in the adjacent seas, and before peace came Nevis, together with other British islands, passed into French hands. Still, though with difficulty, Pinney carried on his business, and in spite of the constantly recurring lugubrious reflections upon the state of the world of which his letters are full, his fortunes continued to increase. Years before 1780, he had already carried out his intention of restoring his plantations to their former prosperous state. As early as 1778, he announced that he was going home in order to supervise the education of his growing family. He determined to contract his business in the West Indies in so far as this was possible, because from experience he knew too much about the dangers of the sugar trade, and the risk of being too dependent upon remittances from the Islands. In the course of the previous fifteen years or so he had been able to form an accurate conception of the profits to be made in England by a sugar broker and West Indian exporter. But though he was determined to leave Nevis, he still intended to keep his estates, and when he finally sailed for home in 1783, he left them in charge of his kinsman, Gill.

In England, he decided to establish a partnership with one of his planter friends from Nevis. This man, James Tobin, considered that London was the most suitable place for this purpose. After a short experience of the climate of the metropolis, however, Pinney decided that if the firm was to be established it must be in Bristol, otherwise he would not proceed further with the scheme. Indeed, he developed a violent distaste for London, and in this respect, at least, would have applauded the denunciations of Cobbett.

"I have experienced extreme ill-health from the heaviness of the atmosphere—I have been obliged to take frequent excursions into the country to make my life supportable: The thick air of the city causes so great a pressure on my brain as to give me the most violent head-aches, accompanied with such a dejection of spirits as to render me unfit for business." [1]

He, therefore, felt compelled to take up his residence in some airy part of Bristol, a place to which he seems always to have been attached. There, he believed, he would not feel the ill-effects of the heavy atmosphere as "I can so easily take an airing on the Downs." [2] Nor was he disappointed, for shortly after his coming to Bristol, he announced:

"The Bristol waters, under the blessing of God, have restored my health, and I believe this part of the kingdom will agree with my constitution—the country and rides about this city are delightfull." [3]

After some correspondence Tobin at last consented which, indeed, was natural as Pinney loaned him sufficient money to enter into the partnership. When other planters in the Islands heard of the scheme, many of them, and, it would seem, some of the less sound financially, were eager to become clients. The astute Pinney, however, managed to evade these unwished for advances without giving offence. So the house of Pinney and Tobin came into existence, which, again in spite of continual forebodings, prospered exceedingly under the constant care and vigilance of the senior partner. Pinney wrote letters to all his friends whose financial standing was good, to solicit their custom. He developed the export side of the business, and in a few years the firm had wide connections which extended as far as Glasgow. In time it had its own ships, which were built in Bristol under the vigilant eye of the indefatigable Pinney. In his letters he continually reminded his correspondents in the West Indies of the necessity of remitting full cargoes. Bristol firms owned their own ships, whereas those of London had little or no concern with the shipping. In 1789 he transferred his interest to his son, Azariah, but as the boy was only fourteen

[1] *Pinney Papers, Business Letter-book,* 1783–7, fol. 7.
[2] *Ibid.,* fol. 11.
[3] *Ibid.,* fol. 77.

years old, the transfer was merely nominal, and John continued to take a close interest in the business and, as he said himself, to act as its attorney.

While establishing himself as a successful West Indian merchant in Bristol, Pinney continued to direct his plantations in the West Indies. Their superintendence from a distance caused him a great deal of vexation and trouble. His appointment of his kinsman, Gill, showed that this keen business man at times allowed his heart to dictate to his head. In spite of many amiable characteristics, Gill lacked those qualities of perseverance, methodical mindedness, business acumen and sobriety which Pinney himself possessed in a high degree. In one of his early letters to Gill he expressed the hope that his new manager would write regularly, but only when business required.

"Unless your letter is of material consequence I never wish to receive a copy by itself, for the expense of postage in this country, is a considerable article." [1]

He went on to instruct his kinsman as to the size of paper which was to be used, for at that time the outlook was obscure and the expenses of his family were increasing very much too rapidly to suit him. What with no rain in Nevis, the low price of sugar in England, and the great charge to which he had been put in connection with the establishment of the new firm, he had enough financial burdens on his hands already without unnecessary losses, which were due to the defects of his manager. To begin with, Gill did not take sufficient care in the oversight of the sugars which were sent home. In consequence, Pinney paid much higher duties than were necessary. He instructed Gill, therefore, at some considerable length, to take greater care with the packing, in order that each hogshead should contain the maximum amount of sugar, as free as possible from moisture for which the owner naturally disliked to pay.

But this was merely the beginning of Gill's incapacity and misdemeanours. He was a bad correspondent and did not answer half the letters which Pinney sent him, for which, in view of Pinney's incessant writing, he may be partially, at least,

---

[1] *Pinney Papers, Business Letter-book*, 1779–84, fol. 318.

forgiven. Pinney was sure that he must have received one of these letters, as the sweetmeats, turtle and Madeira which he had ordered in it duly arrived. There was no reply to his request for information, however, and though he had sent out corks for the wine these had not been used, with the result that a dozen of the bottles had leaked out on the homeward voyage. Again, although he gave Gill exact instructions as to the form of the report he should send home, and the methods he should use in keeping the accounts, these were entirely ignored.

> "I have forebore to make any remarks on the contents of your several letters: which I am truly and very sincerely sorry to say, do not correspond with the ideas I have entertained of you, as a man of business." [1]

Again,

> "if you will take the trouble to peruse my letters, and read over yours; I am sure you will be surprised at your own negligence in the conduction of my affairs, and at your not writing in a more explanatory manner." [1]

He then referred to four separate requests and orders which Gill had entirely neglected to acknowledge or answer. In one letter the remiss manager promised to send information which he completely forgot to do. The result was that Pinney was kept in ignorance about the state of his plantations. After a further catalogue of Gill's own omissions and blunders, while still expressing the utmost personal regard for his worthless kinsman, Pinney wrote: "I am fearful your present line of life doth not suit your disposition," and he indicated that when Gill returned home, he would still be willing to assist him in any other career which he might wish to choose. Even this intimation of impending dismissal, however, did not perturb the incorrigible manager. He still continued in his evil practices, and utterly disregarded the explicit instructions about the methods of bookkeeping and general business technique which he received from his employer.

Business letters remained unanswered, plantation equipment

---

[1] *Pinney Family Letter-books*, D. 1, fol. 48.

John Pinney

From a portrait in the possession of R. W. Pretor Pinney

Looking up the River from below the Rope Walk, Wapping

By Rowbotham, 1825

was allowed to deteriorate without any thought of replacement, while the sugars which were shipped home declined both in quantity and quality.

> "Not a line have I received from Mr. Gill by any of the late opportunities, notwithstanding that there has been a hurricane, and every gentleman, but myself, has received particular advices of their several losses."[1]

The truth was that Gill could not resist the temptation of dipping too freely into the stores of rum kept on the premises. So, while the plantations went to rack and ruin, he passed his time in a prolonged orgy. The situation became so unsatisfactory that one of Pinney's old neighbours in the island intervened on behalf of the absent planter. The sybaritic Gill was replaced by a more reliable man until Pinney could send out a new manager. In spite of all, however, the long-suffering, kindly Pinney was still disposed to help his disappointing kinsman. If he reached England alive, Pinney wrote, he hoped that he would soon recover by the aid of his friends from the result of his prolonged debauch. Gill, apparently, was not unique in falling a victim to the charms of rum, but Pinney was ready to excuse him, on the ground that his responsibilities had proved too heavy for him, and so he had been driven to put additional quantities of spirits into his already too-strong grog.

He soon had another manager appointed and on his way to Nevis, his old friend, William Coker. This man was never wholly satisfactory, though he was a great improvement on the unfortunate Gill. Coker's chief fault at first arose from over-eagerness to show himself a good business man. This took the form of cutting down the special allowances made to captains, crews and others concerned in the transport of sugar. This was a form of economy of which Pinney strongly disapproved. He was always anxious to ensure that captains were well-paid, and thus was much opposed to Coker's economies. This opposition arose not only from consideration to humanity, but because he knew that as these men had to be trusted, they were more likely to be

---

[1] *Pinney Family Letter-books*, D. 1, fol. 147.

honest and diligent when they felt that they had been fairly and
generously treated. When war broke out again in 1793, Coker
received strict instructions about the various ways in which he
was to hide the business papers and valuable stores of rum. He
was to keep a watch on the bay at nights, and brick up part of
the cellar containing the valuables in such a way that it would
be completely concealed if any invaders happened to land in
the island. No manager, however, was completely satisfactory,
so, war or no war, Pinney decided to forego the pleasures of
Bristol society and the delights of his new house, No. 7, Great
George Street, which, after so much difficulty and anxiety, was
completed in 1790, and to sail for Nevis to superintend his
affairs in person.

From Nevis he wrote to his partner and his son, warning
them of the dangers of taking orders from firms which were
unsound. The price of sugar was so uncertain at the best of
times that great forethought was necessary, but the war had
reduced the business to a gamble. Then, also, there was the
threat from the East which became more menacing as the
campaign against slavery developed. "Our present situation is
truly alarming," for though war had not yet actually broken
out, it was expected, and

> "should Mr. Pitt suffer Sugars from the East into this country
> at the same Duties as from the West, our property, in a very
> few years, will be of little or no value, we shall be obliged to
> give up the cultivation of the Sugar-cane and turn our
> thoughts to something else.
>
> "This possibly may be too strong a picture written in a
> gloomy mood, but cannot divest myself of the idea—it appears
> to one self evident, as the East India Company can import
> Sugars considerably superior to ours in colour at a less price." [1]

The Government, he wrote in 1795, was doing everything to
ruin the West Indian planters, and the buyers, in expectation of
still further governmental interference, were standing off, hoping
that prices would fall still further. In this Pinney believed they
would be disappointed. The fall had already taken place in

---

[1] *Pinney Papers, Business Letter-book*, 1788–92, fol. 319.

consequence of the pessimistic outlook of the planters, who had reduced their crops, and this in turn would raise the price.

Pinney, in fact, had long since seen the writing on the wall, and he had no belief in the perpetuity of West Indian prosperity. He did all he could to contract his West Indian commitments in order to secure himself and family before the disaster came, and this suspicion about the future of the West Indies was deepened as the Anti-Slavery campaign developed.

"Anxious to have it in my power to spend my later days in this country peacably and quietly, as independent of the Islands as the nature of my affairs will admit, I have made up my mind respecting my own private concerns in the West Indies that is, never to advance or lend another shilling in that part of the world on any security there, be it what it will." [1]

He found the continual disputes over insurance, the quality of goods which his firm sent out, and the innumerable other worries inseparable from his business, increasingly hard to bear as he grew older. Whenever possible, like so many other planters of his time, his money was invested in canals, East India stock, American funds, and anything, in fact, but the sugar islands.

Though a patriotic Englishman, he very much regretted the rupture with the old continental colonies which destroyed so many of his former business associations. He was foremost among his fellows in pressing for reasonable trade concessions to the Americans after the war was over, for he fully grasped the obvious fact, which so many in authority in England failed to understand, that the prohibition of American ships in West Indian ports was more disastrous to the West Indians than to the Americans. It was from the latter that the plantations had been supplied with a large proportion of their foodstuffs, timber, barrel-staves and fish. It was his contention that permission should be given to small American ships to trade with West Indian ports, which would benefit rather than injure the Mother Country. Though the Government finally made substantial concessions, Pinney was not very optimistic about

---

[1] *Pinney Papers, Business Letter-book*, 1788–92, fols. 89–90.

the future of Great Britain, of whose political situation he took a most gloomy view. But

> "what will be done, God only knows. This devoted Country is torn to pieces by parties—I should not wonder to see a Fox with a fire-brand at his tail, set this kingdom in flames. My Nevis property I look up to, as an asylum, when this Country is drowned in blood—the day I do not think far distant: some serious convulsion in the state there must be." [1]

It was only a few years before this that, when still in Nevis, he had spoken of his little property in England as his only asylum in a distressed world. The English political situation in the 'eighties and 'nineties filled him with the most depressing forebodings.

> "Our Parliament is dissolved and the election of this Place comes on next Saturday—I hope to God a decided majority will be returned in favour of the present Ministers: for I verily believe F—— (Fox) wants to be a second Oliver Cromwell, to set this Country in flames."

He closed this letter with a more optimistic hope that the Government would "grant the Americans liberty to trade in their own bottoms to our Islands." [2]

Whatever the Government decided to do, however, it appears from his letters that Pinney developed a very strong dislike for the West Indies. As, in spite of all, the island of Nevis had brought him fortune, this attitude was scarcely gracious.

> "If you should ever hear an observation that my Son was born in the West-indies, you will in reply notice, that myself and all my Progenitors were born in the West of England, and have been there settled for ages past." [3]

In those days of waning West Indian popularity, he wanted to make it quite certain that the opprobrious suggestion of a dash of the tar brush could not with any justification be made of his family.

[1] *Pinney Papers, Business Letter-book*, 1783–7, fol. 47.
[2] *Ibid.*, fol. 55.
[3] *Ibid., Business Letter-book*, 1781–4, fol. 279.

"My greatest pride is to be considered as a private Country Gentⁿ. therefore, am resolved to content myself with a little and shall avoid even the name of a West Indian." [1]

When Pinney returned to England at the close of the American War and decided to live in Bristol, he had great difficulty in finding a suitable house. After much negotiation and repeated declarations on his part that he wanted a house in the airy part of the city, he announced:

"I find houses in Bristol sell so extremely high, in proportion to their annual value, I shall content myself in being a renter—not a purchaser." [2]

But a rented house did not suit him very long. He found one, No. 5, Park Street, which pleased him well enough except that he objected to some of its furniture. Nevertheless, he decided to take it, at what he considered the monstrous figure of 100 guineas a year, the landlord to pay all taxes,

"which I preferred to £90 and for me to pay the taxes— My rent commences on the 5th of April, but I have liberty to enter when I please—I shall endeavour to get into it next Saturday fortnight." [3]

It was then 25th February, 1784.

This house soon wearied him, and he decided to build one for himself. For several years thereafter his letters are full of references to it. At one time he was complaining of the slowness of the workmen, at another the stone which he had ordered was not delivered when promised. Now it was the misdemeanours of the work-people, now the shortcomings of the furnishers. But at last, after scoldings, expostulations and vituperative letters to all and sundry, it was completed. When he finally took possession of the house he was very proud of it, and although he was but newly arrived in the city, it became in a mild way the rendezvous of Bristol's intelligentsia. Here, among others, he entertained Southey, Wordsworth and Coleridge, three of the most striking young men of their age. Pinney's

---

[1] *Pinney Papers, Business Letter-book*, 1776–8, fol. 219.
[2] *Ibid., Business Letter-book*, 1781–4, fol. 265.
[3] *Ibid.*, fol. 293.

children became close friends of Wordsworth, who later, together with his sister Dorothy, lived for some time in the family house at Racedown, in Dorset. At No. 7, Great George Street, the imaginative Coleridge was inspired by the stories which he heard of Nevis to dream of emigrating there himself with his two friends, Southey and Wordsworth, and of making the name of that distant island "more illustrious than Cos or Lesbos." But the somewhat cantankerous and reactionary old planter must have had little in common with young men who greeted the outbreak of the French Revolution with such lyrical raptures.

More to his taste were his associations with such men as Nelson, whom he first met in the West Indies, and with whom he appears to have maintained some acquaintance after he finally settled in England. When Nelson returned home, flushed with the victory of Cape St. Vincent, Pinney joined in the national chorus of praise of the heroic admiral. On 11th March, 1798, he wrote:

"Dear Sir,

"Having by me a few dozen of fine Nevis old Rum, and as Mr. H. H. Tobin is about sending you some Articles you desired him to get, I have packed in a box two dozen of it, addressed to you at Portsmouth, which I request you will do me the honor to accept of.

"Our earnest prayers and wishes are for your success and happiness, and that you may meet and live to enjoy every honor and reward a grateful Country can bestow on a Man who has rendered it such essential service; and notwithstanding the severity of the wounds you have received in your Country's cause, you still persevere in being her Champion, at a juncture the most critical, when its salvation depends on the exertion of such Men as You.

"My Wife and Daughter send their love to Lady Nelson, and hope, in your absence, she will allot a large portion of her time to spend with them—to whom I beg my best respects and am with the highest consideration

Dear Sir!

Your sincere and most Obed Ser^{t.}

JNO. PINNEY." [1]

---

[1] Add. MSS., 34,906, fol. 334.

When he was not writing about business affairs or his new house or the gloomy state of the country, he was concerned with the education of his own or his friends' children. One headmaster, Mr. Williams, suffered from the gout, and his indifferent assistant was left to do all his work for weeks at a time, so there had to be a change of schools. The Stoke Bishop School was not satisfactory as the writing-master was not up to his work, and so on. Pinney was determined that his sons should have a good education, and two of them were packed off to the continent to study the language and peoples of France and Germany. This old planter was not the man to be put out of his stride by any such occurrence as the world-shaking French Revolution. So the sons were bidden to continue their studies and travels while Europe moved rapidly on to war, and France passed from mild constitutional reform to the atrocities of the Terror. Like his predecessors, his eldest son was required to spend a few years in the island of Nevis before settling down as a Bristol merchant. Part of Pinney's estates were, therefore, transferred to the young man, and a hundred new negroes purchased to enable him to begin with good prospects.

These letters, in fact, are full of everyday human affairs which reveal the kind of men the planters were, and the kind of things in which they were interested. The man who dealt in large investments was equally careful about small wastes.

"I am sorry to acquaint you that Kate (a negress belonging to his manager, Coker,) has behaved very ill, by leaving several small accounts unsatisfied—and notwithstanding Mrs. P—— gave her 1 P^r of shoes and 6 y^{ds} of Muslinett for a Gown. she had the impudence to go to Messrs Whitty and North-cote's and take up another 6 y^{ds} to make herself a petticoat, which they have charged to me, 16/6. Some altercations arose in consequence of it, and I have refused to pay it; but, at the same time, I think it incumbent upon me to make Kate pay the money: I therefore earnestly request you will compel Kate to pay me the money she owes me, and the above 16/6, so as I may receive it in a bill of exchange by our first ship to this Port—She deserves no indulgence or favour from me." [1]

---

[1] *Pinney Papers, Business Letter-book,* 1783–7, fols. 136–7.

At other times he was deeply engaged in helping his friends to avoid~paying duties on small luxuries which they tried to smuggle into England.

"You will receive a Barrel of Sugar directed for you, and marked FH in the middle of which you will find two Potts of preserved Tamarinds, the difficulty of getting Sweetmeats landed, and conveyed Safe has induced me to take this Method." [1]

Again,

"Dear Madam!

"Capt Clarke being fearful that your madeira would be seized, he sent it with your chocolate, in small quantities, to my house.—I sent the chocolate with your turtle last Saturday, and you will now receive 3 doz. & 9 bottles of madeira wine . . .

"Mrs. P—— as well as myself, lament that it will not be in our power to accept of your kind invitation to partake of the turtle." [2]

And, on another occasion,

". . . they are so strict at the custom house here that the Captains cannot venture to take above 3 or 4 doz. of wine— about which quantity you may send by every convenient opportunity." [3]

Apparently it was the custom to take the Madeira from that island out to Nevis, from whence it was later smuggled in small quantities into England.

"I have received the several articles you sent by the Nevis after vast deal of trouble from the Revenue officer—they obliged me to pay dutys for the *whole*—My Children, therefore, must go without their Sweetmeats in future, for they are not worth the duty done in brown sugar." [4]

[1] *Pinney Papers, Business Letter-book*, 1761–74, fol. 181.
[2] *Pinney Family Letter-books*, D. 1, fol. 42.
[3] *Pinney Papers, Business Letter-book*, 1783–7, fol. 242.
[4] *Ibid., Business Letter-book*, 1788–92. fols. 36–7.

This decision evidently caused a domestic revolution in the Pinney ménage, and at last the indulgent father was compelled to forego his economic intentions.

> "My children having been accustomed to take Sweetmeats &c with them to School, I take the Liberty to countermand the Direction given in my Letter No. 57—You will therefore please to send the following,"

for once the children had won their battle, he was surrendering completely.

> "Put up with brown Sugar as usual—viz—1 large Pot of green Sweetmeats, of Lemons and Citrons, without Pappaws or Limes—2 kegs of Tamarinds—Guava Marmalet and Jelly, which you will pack in the middle of a Barrell of Cassandra Bread.—The large Pot of Sweetmeats only mark with the letter S.—The following Articles get Mrs Clarke to put up with white Sugar in the best Manner for our own Use—to make a Present to some Friends that have Hot Houses—And I request you will send by the first Ship a Pot of Cow-Iteh prepared in Syrup, and a Bundle of Worm Grass dried in the Shade, as I want it to take myself for Worms.
>
> "By the Nevis you will please to send three or four Barrels of my best Sugar for Family Use, also a Cask of 60 Gallons, at least, as I cannot enter less, of my oldest and best Rum, and as many dozens of Madeira and Malmsey Wine by each Ship as the Captains think they can bring with Safety—As I expect to see you at Xmas I shall defer having Home my Butt of Madeira Wine until next year—I shall order out two more Butts, that my new Cellar here may be properly supplied." [1]

The man who emerges from these letters was in no respect remarkable, but he may be taken as a very good sample of the group to which he belonged and of which he was so ashamed. He was a keen man of business, a true agriculturist in his constant pessimism which was never dissipated, even when fortune smiled most brightly upon him. He was exacting in business, stern and explicit with his servants, sometimes

---

[1] *Pinney Papers, Business Letter-book*, 1788–92, fols. 65–6.

interfering and fault-finding. But at the same time, as was shown in his treatment of Gill, he could be generous to wrong-doers, even to a fault. He was, in fact, a Bristol merchant in the good old tradition, not afraid to concern himself with little things, but equally unabashed by large undertakings.

CHAPTER XVI

THE END OF BRITISH PLANTATION SLAVERY

"The trade to the West Indies and North America is the most considerable of any part of the kingdom, except London. The Guinea trade has also been very flourishing, but inferior to that of Liverpool."

GOUGH. Additions to Camden, *Britannia* (1806).

IN the years succeeding the American Revolution the West Indian trade once more became prosperous. Slaves poured into the Islands from Africa, and the output of sugar and other products increased rapidly. Though such men as John Pinney, who lived perpetually in expectation of disaster, warned their friends of the doom that lay over them, few, even of the pessimists, believed that it was so near. At the close of the 'eighties the plantation colonies were prosperous and influential, and were still considered the brightest gems in the imperial diadem. Yet in a little over half a century from that time their prosperity was already gone, they had lost their political influence in England, and the British people were beginning to look on them as troublesome liabilities.

This complete reversal of fortunes was accomplished in successive stages. First there was the long campaign for the abolition of the slave trade, followed, after a respite of a few years, by the agitation for Emancipation. Then, in 1838, the apprentices were freed earlier than the planters expected, but still the Islands prospered. In 1846 came the triumph of Free Trade and the disappearance of all those special privileges in the British market which they had hitherto enjoyed under the Old Colonial System. The Navigation Acts were repealed in 1849, and irretrievable ruin came with the passing of the Sugar Equalization Duties Act in 1851. This measure placed their products on the same footing in the English market as beet sugar from Europe, East India sugar and, worst of all, sugars produced by slave labour in Cuba, Brazil and other foreign plantations.

Taken as a whole, the British Anti-Slavery movement fills one of the noblest pages in the nation's history. It made a direct appeal to the Englishman's love of liberty and to all that was generous and kindly in the ordinary man. It attracted to its banners many illustrious names, among whom were to be found some of the greatest parliamentarians who have ever lived. When Wilberforce rose in his place in the House of Commons on 12th May, 1789, to plead the cause that was destined to be his life's work, he was supported by Pitt, Burke and Fox. Later debates on this subject produced some of the most splendid oratory to which the British House of Commons has listened in its long history. In that Golden Age of English parliamentary eloquence, the debates on the slave trade stand out for the splendour of diction with which the champions of the Africans placed their case before their fellow countrymen.

In those years, when the whole world was ringing with the clarion call of freedom which pealed forth from France, and to which Wordsworth and many more listened with such rapture, these champions of liberty in England did scant justice to their opponents. Slave ship captains, planters and merchants were accused of the blackest crimes of which man was capable. They were denounced as merciless monsters, in whom the lust for gain had destroyed every finer feeling. Such criminals were deemed to have no right to consideration, and so, led by the orators, with Wilberforce and Pitt at their head, the whole nation rose to pour contumely on these fiends in human shape. Mastered by the zeal of the proselyte, the nation forgot the immediate past, and how, only a few years before, it had proclaimed the prosperity of the West Indies to be the cornerstone of imperial power.

Thus it came about that a movement which, in the main, was so generous, was unjust to slavers, planters and to all concerned with the Guinea and West Indian trades. The conviction of the diabolical wickedness of those concerned in the slave trade became so deeply rooted in the public opinion that even to-day, many descendants of West Indian planters and merchants are frequently quite unjustifiably ashamed of the commerce of their ancestors. In sober fact, however, there is no justification for these misgivings. The slave system for over a century and a half was fostered and encouraged by the whole nation, and proclaimed to be an essential feature of British greatness. If the burden of guilt for this system is to be placed anywhere, it must rest not on the shoulders of a handful of merchants and planters, but on the broad back of the British people.

The present chapter is concerned with the Anti-Slavery movement only in so far as it affected the fortunes of one city, a city, however, which was more identified with West Indian commerce than any other in Great Britain, and, thus, it may be taken as an epitome of the whole movement. As far back as 1740, a writer in the *Gentleman's Magazine* had denounced the evils of the slave trade and slave owning. He requested the merchants of Bristol and Liverpool, in particular, to show what arguments they could urge in its favour. But it was not until the close of the American War that the Anti-Slavery forces began to gather in strength. In a letter to his friend James Tobin, then in Nevis, John Pinney refers to this subject as early as 1783.

"The people here seem devoted to our destruction—they entertain the most horrid ideas of our cruelties—it now pervades all ranks of people—they think Slavery ought not to be permitted in any part of the British dominions; it is incompatible with their constitution. I assure you, I expect to see all our Sugar Colonies under the dominion of some wiser European power." [1]

Thus it would seem that when Clarkson began his agitation the nation in some respects was ready to receive his message. In 1787 he visited Bristol, and with his arrival there the Anti-Slave Trade movement started in earnest. Clarkson describes how in the evening he first came in sight of the city that he knew he was about to injure so seriously. The church bells were ringing loudly, and a feeling of melancholy overcame him when he thought of the work which lay before him. But once in the city which was one of the chief strongholds of the system that he was determined to destroy, he found a number of people ready and anxious to assist him. Some of these were members of the Society of Friends, a body which had long since set its face against slavery, but there were others, including the great Dean Tucker himself, and several members of the Free Churches. The Merchant Venturers, it should be remembered to their credit, readily gave permission for him to examine their documents, and make such transcriptions from them as

[1] *Pinney Papers, Business Letter-book,* 1783–7, fol. 20.

he chose. Nevertheless, evidence was hard to obtain. Many were ready enough to help Clarkson, but were afraid to do so because of local public opinion, while others naturally declined to denounce a commerce upon which their livelihood depended. Through the kindly offices of a friendly publican, Clarkson was enabled to visit the most notorious taverns in Marsh Street, where the slave captains recruited their crews. The pious reformer was horrified by the scenes of debauchery and vice which he there beheld. Apparently he had had little experience of such places and no basis for comparison, since from his descriptions these nautical hostelries do not appear to have been very much worse than similar taverns of that kind to be found in every seaport town.

Early in 1788 the Anti-Slavery group in Bristol took the field.

"Yesterday a meeting was held in this City to petition parliament to annihilate the African trade, and carried without a division." [1]

Thus Clarkson's efforts in Bristol soon resulted in action. In that same year Parliament turned its attention to the regulation of the slave trade. It prescribed the number of negroes who henceforward might be carried from Africa in one ship by laying down the proportions of negroes to tons. The Merchant Venturers made counter representations and supplied Mr. Brickdale, who seconded the motion for the rejection of the measure, with relevant facts and figures. During this long campaign Bristol collaborated with Liverpool and London, and the records of the Merchant Venturers mention various sums paid from time to time to cover the cost of representatives sent to London, or the fees of experts who had to be retained to fight the reformers.

Early in 1789 it became known that a determined attack was to be made on the slave trade, and those likely to be affected in Bristol were directed to be ready. The Merchant Venturers called a meeting which took place in their Hall on 13th April.

---

[1] *Pinney Papers, Business Letter-book,* 1788–92, fol. 17.

Several resolutions were passed, and a committee was appointed to conduct the defence. Among the members who were elected to serve were nine merchants who were at some time mayors of Bristol, five who were sheriffs, seven who had been or were to become Masters of the Merchant Venturers and many other distinguished citizens, which illustrates the enormous influence of the Guinea and West Indian trades at that time. When, therefore, Wilberforce opened his campaign on 12th May, his opponents were ready. Although he had all the eloquence and heavy guns on his side, his adversaries were able to produce such a convincing array of sound arguments, based mainly on the sacred rights of property, that the project was defeated. The West Indian champions were supported by several petitions from Bristol and its vicinity.

There was one from the Mayor, Commonalty and Burgesses of Bristol, and another from the Master, Wardens and Commonalty of the Merchant Venturers. There was a petition from the West Indian planters, West Indian Merchants and others residing in the city of Bristol and its vicinity. The principal manufacturers, ship-builders and traders of the city sent yet another, and there was also one from the Merchant Traders to the Island of Newfoundland. The petitioners united in expressing their serious apprehension for the future well-being of their own and the nation's commerce, on hearing that the House of Commons was about to consider a motion for the abolition of the slave trade. The African trade, they declared, represented a considerable section of British commerce, and upon its continuance the West Indian plantations depended for their existence. If it was abolished these colonies must decline, and so a definite superiority in trade and naval strength would be given to foreign nations. The African trade was far too important to be jeopardized by an experiment, which, unless concurred in by the co-operation of all Powers, could be of little service to the Africans themselves, but if the proposal of Mr. Wilberforce was carried, all these petitioners felt that they had a first claim to compensation from the state. This would mean that Great Britain would be required to pay out a large sum of money at the very time when, by the passing of this measure, its resources had been

Early " Bristol " box-kite type of aeroplane, 1910–11

" Bristol " Blenheim Bomber

The New Zealand emigrant ship, " Charlotte Jane "

reduced. The opulence of Bristol depended largely upon the West Indian commerce, and the petitioners prayed that only such measures as were deemed necessary in the interests of humanity should be imposed. Three-fifths of the commerce of the port was represented by the African and West Indian trades. If the slave trade was abolished the whole trade of the city must decline, and thus cause great loss to the planters and utter ruin to thousands of individuals whom this commerce maintained. Without a constant supply of negroes from Africa the cultivation of sugar could not be continued. Again, as the West Indies were the chief market of the English herring trade, their decline would entail disaster to the English fisheries, the great nursery of English seamen. Moreover, as the trade of the French, the Spanish, the Dutch and the Danes would still continue, the passing of this measure would place the English planters in a very unfavourable position.

All improvements or plans for the establishment of new plantations in the sugar colonies would at once be frustrated, and even the old well-established estates would be compelled to diminish their production. Some of the petitioners had advanced large sums for the establishment of new plantations which, when the trade was abolished, must be written off as dead losses. The prosperous sugar refining industry which had grown up in Bristol would be utterly ruined by the inevitable decline in the import of sugar from the Islands, which in turn would throw many hundreds of common work-people wholly out of employment. The petitioners had heard with great satisfaction how already, in anticipation of the wishes of Parliament, certain colonial legislatures had passed various humane laws designed to protect the rights of their slaves, and they did not doubt that other colonies would soon follow this example. They trusted that the Bill would not be passed, but if Parliament proved so unwise as to allow it to become law, they hoped that it would see the necessity of postponing its action to some remote and distant period, and in that unfortunate eventuality it looked to the justice of the British legislature for suitable compensation.

The ship-builders, shipowners and others declared that they had invested large sums of capital in docks, ships, warehouses and other buildings, that they employed large numbers of people, and that they chiefly depended on the African and West Indian trades. Any measure calculated to diminish either of these branches of commerce would annihilate the trade of Bristol and injure that of the neighbouring country towns. With the abolition of the slave trade would go not only the ruin of the West Indies, but of all those merchants and others who were in any way connected with the plantations. They drew the attention of Parliament to the fact that since the passing of the new regulation in the previous year, New England alone, in anticipation of a boom, had fitted out no less than forty sail for that branch of commerce, and that the French trade was also increasing. The Newfoundland traders joined in the general outcry by declaring that they were much alarmed by the proposed abolition of the slave trade. Among the many other injuries which this unwise measure would inflict, not the least would be its disastrous effects upon that most valuable industry and great nursery of seamen, the fisheries of Newfoundland. The annual export of dried fish sent thence to the West Indies was very considerable, and if stopped would prove fatal to the industry. They, therefore, prayed that the House would not agree to any proposal for the total abolition of the slave trade, but would impose only such regulations as it might think necessary in the interests of humanity.

Various letters also appeared in the Bristol papers dealing with the Bill, all of which were strongly on the side of the planters. One writer pointed out that there were many grave abuses among the English working classes which the reformers would do well to remove before they set out to ameliorate the lot of the negroes in the plantations. The negroes were, in fact, in some respects more fortunate than the slaves in English prisons and many toilers in factory and mine. Another letter referred to the slave insurrection which had already started in Martinique. The negroes there had heard that the English Parliament had freed the slaves in the English plantations, whereupon those on several of the most considerable of the estates in Martinique had assembled together, to the number of 4,000, retired to the mountains and declared that they would no longer be slaves. The English planters warned the British Government to beware of similar manifestations in their own colonies, and later events were to prove that there was some justification for their fear.

Wilberforce was defeated in 1789, but in the following year he induced Parliament to allow the evidence which he and his friends had collected to be heard by a committee. In this same session, 1790, the Guinea trade was threatened from another quarter. The reformers introduced a Bill to promote the establishment of a new joint stock company, which was to have privileges and a constitution similar to those of existing bodies of the kind. The object of the new company was to carry on a direct commerce between England and Africa, including both the West Coast and the hinterland not hitherto explored by Europeans. It was to receive a grant of land on the peninsula of Sierra Leone, and its promoters hoped that the new settlement would become an asylum for liberated slaves, and mark the beginning of a new and better period in Anglo-African relations.

This apparently praiseworthy venture roused the fury of the vested interests. Among many others, the Merchant Venturers petitioned against the measure. The Society was determined to take all necessary steps calculated to ensure its rejection, and it authorized its Treasurer to defray any expenses incurred thereby. The Hall declared that past experience had taught the absolute necessity of viewing with a jealous eye the creation of such a body, liable only in its corporate capacity and not individually. The argument that such fears were groundless, since the proposed body would be directed by distinguished and reputable people, had no weight, as in time the administration of the company might well pass into the hands of designing individuals. Its establishment could only be justified when the conduct of the trade concerned was too onerous for private people. That, however, did not apply in this instance. Sierra Leone had always been a free port, and, indeed, the right of the French to trade there was specifically recognized by the Treaty of Versailles, 1783, and it was thus unwise to assert a right to land on that part of the coast. The creation of this company would adversely affect the rights of British subjects and infringe the Act 25 Geo. II, c. 31. Under that statute, Free Trade on the West Coast of Africa between Sallee and the Cape of Good Hope had been guaranteed to all His Majesty's subjects. The Sierra Leone river afforded the only safe achorage to be found there the whole year round. Ships in need of food, wood, water or repairs were accustomed to proceed there. By limiting the use of this river to the ships of one company, great injury would thus result to a trade of the utmost national importance. In spite of all, the Sierra Leone Company received its charter, and with several leading Abolitionists as its directors, began its somewhat checkered career.

Meanwhile, in his letters, John Pinney was lamenting the disastrous effects produced on West Indian securities by the Anti-Slave Trade campaign. Negro risings had spread desolation through San Domingo and other French sugar colonies, and he believed the time was not far distant when a similar fate would afflict the British West Indies as well. The price of sugar was high and likely, he thought, to remain so, which, taken with the growing abstention of its use encouraged by the enemies of the trade, would soon render valueless all sugar estates in the West Indies. One gleam of hope lessened the gloom, for in 1791 Wilberforce was defeated in the House of Commons. This respite, however, was short, for in the following year the Anti-Slave Trade party carried their measure through the Commons. When it reached the Lords it was decided that the evidence should be heard all through from the beginning again; but by 1793 England had other things to think about, and so the decision arrived at by the House of Commons in 1792, that the trade should be abolished gradually, beginning from 1st January, 1796, was never carried into effect. That clarion call to freedom which had so enheartened the lovers of liberty in 1789, by 1793 had become the death-rattle of the French monarchy. For years to come, reforms had to yield place to the problem of withstanding the French menace. Year after year Wilberforce, still faithful to his crusade, though many fell away or deserted, brought in his motion for the abolition of the slave trade, but with the thunder of French victories in their ears and the shadow of Napoleon growing till it appeared to cover the earth, his countrymen were no longer responsive to the far-off cry of afflicted Africans.

So the eighteenth century passed out and the slave trade still continued. The West Indian planters were confident, proud and prosperous, flushed by successive victories, but with a new century the tide turned rapidly. On 26th June, 1802, *Felix Farley* published a letter in which the writer exhorted his readers to support that candidate in the forthcoming parliamentary elections who stood for the rights of the Africans. He had been convinced by irresistible proof of the enormous barbarism and inconceivable injustice inseparable from the trade in slaves. It had depopulated great tracks on the coast of Africa, and brutalized, to a degree scarcely conceivable, those Englishmen who were engaged in it. The civilization of Africa, the establishment of a peaceful trade with that continent and the introduction of the light of Christianity among its peoples were all rendered impossible by its existence. By now the whole nation was convinced that the trade must be abolished, and even the planters were more reconciled since there was no word of emancipating the slaves. So far Parliament had merely mitigated some of the evils of the Middle Passage and passed a resolution for the abolition of the trade which, however, remained a dead letter. John Pinney, like others interested in the West Indies, was now prepared to view Abolition with equanimity.

"As to the Abolition of the Slave Trade, so far from its being injurious to well settled Estates in the old Islands, it will have a contrary effect, it will increase their value and be a check to new Settlements—Not a negro has been purchased for my Son's Estate a great many years and the number, I believe is increased." [1]

In 1806 even Liverpool capitulated. That central stronghold of the trade returned at the head of the poll at the elections in that year a man whom *Felix Farley* described as

"the justly celebrated Mr. Roscoe . . . notwithstanding

---

[1] *Pinney Papers, Business Letter-book,* 1805–7, fol. 273.

every effort was made by the slave merchants and their friends to oppose him; because during his life (which had been spent in Liverpool) he has never ceased to express his abhorrence of their traffic in human blood." [1]

The ownership of slaves now became an important source of income to the planters. At last they had come to realize that kindness was good business, for by humane treatment their natural increase could be made sufficient to render additional supplies from Africa unnecessary. Still, slavery was a degrading institution, and it is apparent that the most kindly planter could not rid his mind of the belief that the negroes were beasts and not men. In a letter to his old friend, James Tobin, then in Nevis, Pinney wrote in 1806,

". . . if those Negroes were advertized there can be no doubt of their selling at £70 Stlg P head round, if not more, as the Slave trade will be completely abolished the 1st of January next." [2]

Other letters written about the same time refer to the apprenticing of negro boys to useful trades and the hiring out of negroes for profit. Others speak of sales and still others of the correction to be administered. Pinney wrote to his manager in Nevis on 22nd October, 1804:

"By my Son's letter . . . you will see that . . . he will embark with his Wife and one female Servant (her maid) on board the Pilgrim. . . . Keep the sick people away from being seen by Mrs. F. Pinney & suffer no correction to be within her hearing." [3]

From such letters as these it is abundantly plain that even when a kindly master was concerned, the slaves were always liable to vindictive treatment and uncertainty. Thus,

"I desire you to inform Billey Jones that his late conduct in beating Wm Fisher appears to me in so reprehensible a

[1] Felix Farley's Bristol Journal, 15th November, 1806.
[2] Pinney Papers, Business Letter-book, 1805–7, fol. 286.
[3] Ibid., Business Letter-book, 1804, fol. 34.

light that I am only sorry he was not severely corrected if I had been on the spot he should not have escaped with impunity: and if he ever presumes to lift his hand against him again or attempts to do him any other injury, it is my request that he might be publickly corrected—In future, when he is not employed in his trade on the Estate, let him work out, but not on his former terms—let him pay what other Negroes of his trade do and which I shall insist upon until he is brought to a due sense of his duty." [1]

In other letters Pinney refers to a female slave who had caused trouble.

"The proper place for Jeannetta is the field to which she was brought up, as a punishment for her atrocious conduct but under no pretence suffer her to go off the island." [2]

References recur to runaway slaves and their apprehension, but the arbitrary nature of the system is best illustrated by another reference to the redoubtable Jeannetta.

"It is my Son's Wish to sell Jennetta's Children, not herself, as she has done him so much injury, & begs you will let him know their value & what you think you shall be able to get for them." [3]

Thus, even kindly slave owners failed to recognize that their slaves had the most elementary human rights, and whole families, at the whim of their master, might be torn asunder and scattered over many estates.

In the years after the abolition of the slave trade public opinion in Bristol, as throughout the country generally, slowly turned against the whole system of slavery. In 1813 a branch of the Church of England Missionary Society for Africa and the East was established in the city, and at a great public meeting enormous enthusiasm was shown when the speakers referred to the responsibilities of England to Africa. Bristol was much exercised at the close of the Napoleonic wars over the possibility

[1] *Pinney Papers, Business Letter-book*, 1805–7, fols. 81–2.
[2] *Ibid.*, fols. 81–2.
[3] *Ibid.*, fol. 321.

that the clause providing for the abolition of the slave trade would be omitted in the peace treaty. It is significant of the change which had come over public opinion in the preceding quarter of a century that the Mayor of Bristol presided at the large public meeting which was called to consider the subject. All the speakers combined in unmeasured condemnation of the slave trade, and several resolutions were passed. "Perish commerce rather than live the slave trade," and "a negro is a man!"[1] fairly accurately sum up the attitude of Bristol as expressed at this meeting. The audience wept at the tales of horror which were recounted.

> "Weep on my generous countrymen . . . you may exult, you may even luxuriate in the thought that all the chords of your heart are vibrating in perfect unison with the sympathies of a whole nation. . . . Sir this traffic in human flesh is an infernal traffic and could have no other origin than the malignancy of fiends and furies of hell.[1]

Already, indeed, that distressing note of self-righteous and unctuous piety, which became so lamentable a feature of the Anti-Slavery party's propaganda, was making itself heard.

The attempt first made by Wilberforce after the close of the Napoleonic War to establish a compulsory register of slaves in the colonies, so as to prevent illicit slave trading, found a mixed reception in Bristol. Several letters on this subject appeared in *Felix Farley's Bristol Journal* on this subject whose writers generally concurred in condemning the scheme as unwise. Finally on 10th February, 1816, that journal announced

> "a petition from this city to the House of Commons against the Slave Registry Bill most respectfully signed was this week forwarded to London to be presented to our members."[2]

The general feeling was that such a measure, if passed, would constitute an unwarrantable interference in the internal affairs of the colonies, and when, therefore, Parliament rejected it,

[1] *Felix Farley's Bristol Journal*, 9th July, 1814.
[2] *Ibid.*, 10th January, 1816.

partly for this reason and partly because of its veiled and insulting suggestion that the colonies were breaking the law; Bristol was satisfied.

In the Press of this period frequent mention is made of the reforms which the colonies had already carried through, and which were conceived in the interests of their slaves, but the fact is that very little was done. Indeed, the West Indian colonies did practically nothing to put their houses in order during the years of respite from serious attack which they enjoyed between 1807 and 1822. They seem to have been quite incapable of learning anything from the hard won experience of the recent past. They could not comprehend that with the advent of the steam engine, and the rise of the new industrial system, a new age had dawned in which they were anachronisms. To the great majority of them, scientific agriculture was a closed book which none of them had the wisdom to open. So they cropped and re-cropped their land by means of most inefficient forced labour. They were not farmers but gamblers, migratory exploiters, not genuine colonists who made a permanent home in the Islands. For more than a hundred and fifty years they had been the spoilt children of the British commercial system, and they failed to adjust themselves to the new condition. Until well into the nineteenth century they still continued to believe that they were the most valuable overseas possessions of England. The slave trade had been abolished, it is true, but what of it? For they believed that British imperial might was bound up with their well-being, and England would never allow the sacred rights of private property to be infringed. At the first whisper of criticism they began to talk of their rights, and to remind the Mother Country that she should not forget what had happened in 1776. Unless the West Indian colonies received from Great Britain the consideration to which they were entitled as her most valuable overseas possessions, they, like the old continental colonies before them, would be compelled to secede. The planters were so certain that the sugar islands were the cornerstone of imperial prosperity and power that they were satisfied that these grave warnings would be sufficient. They failed utterly to grasp the obvious fact that since 1789 the whole position was changed, and that the sugar islands were no longer the priceless imperial gems they had once been.

Thus, though Wilberforce had never concealed his intention of carrying on his great crusade until the whole system of colonial slavery in the British Empire was utterly destroyed, the West Indian planters continued in their old ways. The customary wasteful agriculture still went on, slaves continued to be flogged as of old, negro families were torn asunder, and the slaves were treated as domestic animals, while the planters with their heads sunk over their ledgers, like the ostrich which puts its head in the sand, continued to believe that they were safe because they could see no danger. Instead of appreciating the obvious fact of their very privileged position in the English commercial system, they grumbled loudly about the injustices from which they suffered. Foreign planters were being plentifully supplied with cheap negroes from Africa, while they were compelled to manage as best they could on the natural increase of the slaves they already possessed. It is clear that Emancipation was inevitable, but if the planters had been wise in their generation, it might have been postponed for many years, and when it came they might have obtained better terms.

The Anti-Slavery Party was aided in its work by the growing feeling against the old out-worn limitations imposed upon trade by the Mercantilist system. Nowhere were these more obvious than in the privileged position held by the West Indies. In the long run it was not merely Emancipation which killed them, but the triumph of Free Trade. The apostles of the new economic gospel were prepared to impose their principles on all British dependencies, and to sweep away at a stroke every vestige of imperial preference. But this was all in the future, and in the years after the Battle of Waterloo the planters were lulled in a false security, until, in the early 'twenties, the Anti-Slavery forces took the field again with the avowed intention of uprooting the whole system of colonial slavery.

The now ageing Wilberforce retired from the leadership of the movement in favour of the young and enthusiastic Fowell Buxton. Once more the Bristol papers began to publish editorials, letters and notices which related to this subject.

Although many wealthy people were still deeply concerned in the Islands, and were zealous defenders of their rights, the majority of their fellow citizens had gone over to the camp of the enemy. Still, as the columns of *Felix Farley* show, there were some who were prepared to defend the rights of the planters. "A Colonist," writing on 10th May, 1823, declared that while he had no wish to defend cruelty, he believed that the negro was happier than many labourers in many parts of the world, and he felt justified in protesting against the operation of an *ex post facto* law. The Mother Country had encouraged his ancestors to invest their money in slaves, and he derived his living from that source. Compensation, he thought, was impossible, and Emancipation, without conferring any benefit on anyone, would merely destroy the British West Indian colonies.

A fairly reasonable attitude was manifested at the public meeting held in the following week, as was shown by a petition sent up to Parliament. In this, the signatories prayed that Parliament would make an enquiry into the state of colonial slavery with a view to its abolition

"by means consistent with the safety of the colonies and justice to all his Majesty's subjects." [1]

The chairman, James George, Mayor of Bristol, while convinced that slavery was inconsistent with justice and Christianity, would only agree to the proposal for its abolition provided adequate compensation were given to the proprietors.

"Your Petitioners having considered the inconsistency of the system of Colonial Slavery with the Christian Religion as well as the danger to which that system exposed the White Inhabitants of the Colonies and the Property of the Planters generally; and being satisfied that the cause of Religion, the interests of the State and the well-being and prosperity of the Colonies, require that means should be taken, without delay, gradually, cautiously and with just regard to the Rights and Property of the Colonists, as well as to their claims for Compensation . . . to remove from our Country that heavy responsibility, which the sanction given by the Government

[1] *Felix Farley's Bristol Journal*, 17th May, 1823.

and the People to the System of Slavery in the Colonies, has brought upon this enlightened Nation; and to relieve a vast multitude of our suffering fellow-creatures from a lamentable state of degradation and oppression." [1]

An opposition meeting was held by the West India group, which declared that the Government could be trusted to safeguard the interest of the negroes, and that a petition should be sent to Parliament pointing out that resolutions passed at the Guildhall meeting did not express the unanimous opinion of Bristol.

A somewhat protracted correspondence ensued in the Press. In this, the opposing views were set forth at great length and were stated and restated *ad nauseam*. "A Lover of Liberty" was astonished to hear that certain speakers at the public meeting had declared themselves ready to admit the principle that slave owners had a claim to compensation for the loss of their slaves. This letter is a fair example of the extremes to which many of the reformers were now prepared to go. Indeed, the very virulence with which they stated their arguments must have done much harm to their cause, and certainly, it justified the contemptuous references which were frequently made to them by their opponents. It was against morals and religion, declared this champion of liberty, to give compensation to those who had acquired their property

"by flagrant and encouraged rapine and afterwards purchased and enjoyed in the teeth of every dictate of justice and humanity."

If the nation paid this compensation it would be one of the most scandalous impositions to which any people had ever submitted.

"How shall we atone for the injuries which we have suffered the negro to endure for so many years." [2]

"Moderator" favoured slow Emancipation, which would enable the negro to adjust himself to his new position and alleviate the difficulties which Emancipation would bring on the proprietors. To this moderate letter "A British Planter" replied

[1] *Felix Farley's Bristol Journal*, 17th May, 1823.
[2] *Ibid.*, 24th May, 1823.

that the planters had absolute property in their slaves, and he contended that "Moderator's" proposals, though calculated to help the negroes and save the public from expense, would press very heavily on the planters. Although, as "Moderator" stated, slavery might be opposed to English law, "British Planter" insisted that it was recognized by the laws of the colonies. This was the relevant consideration, and they were in this respect in a position similar to that of the continental colonies before the Revolution. It was British interference with their laws and with their domestic institutions which they feared and hated most. "Moderator" wished to safeguard the interests of the planters, but "A British Planter" pointed out that the majority of the Anti-Slavery Society slurred over the question of any compensation. The allegation that the decline in West Indian prosperity was due to slave labour he considered to be erroneous, as the obvious reason was that the price of sugar in the English market had fallen from £25 per hogshead to £15. Slaves could not, as "Moderator" suggested, acquire land, except at the expense of their masters, and, moreover, this experiment of transferring land had already been tried in Barbados with most disastrous results for all concerned. He wound up by suggesting that the funds of all Anti-Slavery societies should be used to buy all slaves offered under a writ of *venditioni exponas*. Each negro should have a certain small valuation placed upon him, and when he had earned enough to pay off this sum, he should be set free by the society. This would avoid injury to the planter, and would test the practicability of the system of hiring labour and also, the society would be performing a useful task instead of causing irritation and discontent.

The correspondence between "A British Planter" and "Moderator" continued in 1824, and the discussion was enlivened by contributions from J. S. Fry. Some of the Anti-Slavery party now denied that, in fact, the planter had any property rights in his slaves. In a letter published by *Felix Farley* on 17th January, 1824, J. S. Fry put this point of view in its most uncompromising form. If, he argued, the principle was true that no man could give a better title to property than he

himself possessed, then the planters had no property rights
whatever, and, therefore, had no claim to compensation of any
kind. "A British Planter's" claim to an absolute right in his
slaves was untenable, since the British legislature itself never
had any property rights in Africans to confer. It was true that
Great Britain had allowed her subjects to carry slaves from
Africa, but those who did so did it of their own free will.
According to Fry, the planter was in the same position as a man
who had received from another a score of Frenchmen whom the
latter had seized and carried away as slaves. The receiver could
have no property rights in these Frenchmen, because the man
from whom he had purchased them had no rights to transfer.
In the same manner, the planter could derive no title from the
legislature since the legislature had none to give.

> "It is really wonderful to hear a Briton stand forward in
> these days, as the advocate of such a horrible doctrine as the
> absolute property of men in the persons of his fellow-
> creatures." [1]

From 1824 onward, Bristol had its branch of the Anti-
Slavery Society. Many of its members were merciless in their
attacks, and according to them, the planters were pictured as
something worse than pirates, who not only battened on the
blood of their helpless victims, but actually practised gross
cruelty because it afforded them pleasure. To these champions
of the African all thought of compensation was preposterous.
To give such men money for their emancipated slaves would
be on a par with giving the highwayman compensation for the
surrender of his booty. In the welter of the mutual vituperation
and bitter recrimination, "Moderator," in a series of letters,
continued to elaborate his scheme of Emancipation, which, in
principle, was similar to that actually adopted by the British
Government in 1833.

The mind of Bristol, in fact, was divided between reforming
zeal and self-interest. The enemies of slavery contended that
under no condition could man be the property of man. Whatever concessions they may have entertained with respect to the

---

[1] *Felix Farley's Bristol Journal*, 17th January, 1824.

speed of Emancipation, they did not attempt to conceal their real intention of destroying the whole system of slavery at whatever cost this might be to those whose fortunes were invested in the West Indies. The planters were driven to take the offensive, and in their extremity, they went so far as to justify the slave trade itself. So the correspondence went merrily on, punctuated by appeals to conscience, humanity, British law and Holy Scripture. While one side drew lurid pictures of the fiendish cruelties practised on the sugar estates, the other described the idyllic Garden-of-Eden condition in which the negroes lived.

In this flood of conflicting argument, spiced by zeal, self-interest and dialectical display, the feeling on both sides became more and more bitter, and certainly in Bristol the slave question was well to the fore. It is difficult for the impartial historian not to feel that, in its enthusiasm, the popular side was not only deplorably self-righteous about its cause, but grossly unfair to its opponents. In the minds of these zealots the principles of Christian justice were apparently to be applied only to the negroes, but under no circumstances to their owners, whom the smug Anti-Slavery group were now branding as criminals. *Felix Farley*, which tried to be fair to both sides, was driven to declare:

"We cannot help thinking that the man, who, surrounded by slaves, maintains as pure a morality as he does who breathes the untainted air of liberty, is worthy of honour as a moral miracle." [1]

In April of that year, 1824, a petition was sent up to Parliament on this subject, sponsored by the Anti-Slavery Society, and signed by gentlemen, clergy, bankers, merchants and other inhabitants of the city of Bristol. The signatories expressed their great satisfaction at the ameliorative policy enunciated in the resolutions passed by Parliament in the previous year. They trusted that the Government would do its utmost to ensure that these resolutions would be carried into effect in spirit and in letter, and that they would be extended to all British sugar

[1] *Felix Farley's Bristol Journal*, 20th March, 1824.

islands. They rejoiced to learn that Parliament had now placed the slave trade on the footing of piracy, and that the Imperial Government was trying to induce the Government of the United States to follow its example. Good as all of this was, the petitioners could never be satisfied until Parliament had declared itself in favour of sweeping away the whole system of colonial slavery.

The British Government found it difficult to enforce its ameliorative policy. Some of the colonial legislatures neglected to carry out the instructions sent out to them, while others were in open opposition to the whole system. As a natural consequence of this, feeling in England against them steadily hardened. This was shown in the resolutions of a public meeting held in Bristol on 2nd February, 1826. Having expressed the usual abhorrence of slavery, the meeting went on to deplore the fact that the Government's policy had so far met with such little success. It was persuaded that

"it is only by authoritative interference of Parliament, that this cruel and pernicious state of society will be effectually ameliorated and safely terminated." [1]

By this time reform was in the air, and it is significant of the new age that this attack became part of the general onslaught which was then developing against the Old Colonial System in general. This meeting was satisfied that the system of slavery derived great support from those commercial regulations which, by means of bounties and protective duties, not only enhanced the price of slave labour to British consumers, and imposed on them the necessity of contributing to uphold a system which they reprobated as impolitic and unjust, but also tended to aggravate the misery of the slaves and to render their liberation more difficult. At this meeting, the citizens declared that they were ready to bear their fair share in repaying the slave owners for any pecuniary losses which Emancipation might bring upon them.

[1] *Proceedings of the Anti-Slavery Meeting* . . . 2nd February, 1826.

In the following November a meeting of planters and others interested in Demerara and Berbice took place in Bristol to protest against the recent despatches on compulsory manumission sent out to those colonies by Lord Bathurst. Such a policy was opposed to the true interests of the negroes, dangerous to the safety of the colonies and an unjust violation of the sacred rights of property. After some discussion it was decided to petition the King-in-Council against any order requiring compulsory manumission. This petition was duly drawn up, but it was never presented, as it was felt that a similar memorial prepared in London covered the ground so completely as to render it unnecessary. In February the West India Society voted £150 as its share in the cost of conducting this campaign. Liverpool voted £200 and the total bill came to £500.

Once more, in 1828, the Anti-Slavery Society in Bristol organized a great public meeting to protest against the continuance of the evils which it had so often denounced, and the attack on slavery was combined with a general denunciation of the system of bounties. The resolutions passed at this meeting led to more letters in the Press which, with a few unimportant variations, traversed the old familiar ground. *Felix Farley* now became querulous in his lament that

"despite the spate of pamphlets and replies the minds of many are not yet clear, indeed they have been clouded by the virulent outpourings." [1]

This journal, in fact, apparently disgusted by the violence of the Anti-Slavery Party, was becoming the staunch defender of the rights of slave owners, though it still continued to abhor the system of slavery. In an editorial on a petition of the West India merchants presented to Parliament in 1830, the editor stated:

"Most sincerely do we congratulate the West India Merchants that through the influence of the noble Chairman of this Committee and the inherent strengths of their case, they

[1] *Felix Farley's Bristol Journal*, 21st June, 1828.

have at length a prospect of that relief which has so long and so cruelly been denied them by the government of the Mother Country." [1]

It advised the West Indians not to be so submissive and to use every constitutional method to obtain their rights, notwithstanding the unfair attacks that were made upon them. A stormy meeting took place in the autumn at the Great Room in Prince Street. Speakers were shouted down and the chairman was forced to leave the meeting, but the extremists triumphantly carried several resolutions against slavery. Bristol was thus full of reforming zeal, and was shortly to win notoriety throughout the kingdom by its Reform Bill riots. So, amid the noisy and tumultuous demonstrations, the voice of reason was scarcely heard.

On 6th December a petition was drawn up by the Bristol West India group and sent up to Parliament in the following February. The signatories complained bitterly of the vindictive manner in which they had been attacked and maligned by the champions of the negroes. They were now denounced, they said, because of the ownership of property which had been acquired by their ancestors with the cognizance and consent of the Mother Country. They felt themselves entitled to claim the protection of the laws of England. They denied that they had done nothing to improve the lot of their slaves, nor had they opposed every prudent measure designed for that purpose. As proof of this they pointed to the laws that had been passed since 1823 by various colonial legislatures. Notwithstanding the undertaking of Parliament that when Emancipation took place, it would be carried through by slow and successive stages, there were now many petitions which prayed for immediate and complete liberation. If carried through, this would constitute an alarming inroad on the rights of private property. It would be dangerous to the safety of the colonies and destructive of the rights of the planters. As some of the Abolitionists were now vigorously denouncing any proposed compensation to be made to the slave owners, this petition must be regarded as very moderate in tone.

[1] *Felix Farley's Bristol Journal,* 27th February, 1830.

Throughout 1831 the journalistic war went on, and great things were expected to follow on the passing of the Reform Bill, but *Felix Farley* now definitely came out in favour of planter rights. It rejoiced to think that the long-suffering West Indians were at last to receive justice, in spite of the numberless falsehoods and misrepresentations from which they had so long suffered. The House of Lords, in response to the repeated requests of the West India interests to look into their grievances, at length decided to appoint a committee, and *Felix Farley* was sure that justice would prevail. News of the destruction of property arising from slave insurrections, encouraged by false news of immediate Emancipation, strengthened the hands of the planters. Finally, at the end of 1831, the West India Society again protested to the King against an Order-in-Council relating to the slave question which had been transmitted to all colonies, although it was to apply only to the new colonies acquired in the last war. They denounced this measure as unnecessary, illegal, unconstitutional, vexatious and unjust. It was a direct and arbitrary interference with the rights of private property.

The end, however, was near, and finally, after many alarms and excursions in both camps, the Emancipation Bill passed through Parliament and became law. Though the planters were furious over the paltry sum voted as compensation, and with the manner in which it was administered, and although the extremists on the other side considered that the sum was far too large, men of moderate opinion felt that substantial justice had been done, and that Great Britain at last, to some extent, had atoned for her past crimes against the Africans, and so closed a long chapter in the history of Bristol and the Empire.

CHAPTER XVII

RETROGRESSION AND RECOVERY

"*Two Navigable Rivers flow thro' Bristol—the* Avon, *and the Froom. The Avon is the principal, and is capable of floating a Seventy Four Gun Ship at the Quay. This River, to which Bristol is indebted for its Origin, and support, has at low Water, a very unpleasing appearance Being filled with a disagreeable Slimy Mud—A stranger upon viewing the Avon at Ebb Tide is generally struck with astonishment and can scarcely conceive it possible for Ships of any Burden to approach the City, by so insignificant a Gut (it being at no part a Furlong in Width—and in the Summer it is almost dry at low Water). But the improbability ceases when he is informed that at Spring tide the Water rises at Pill 40 Feet—and sometimes overflows Bristol Key and even runs into the Neighbouring Houses. . . .*"

DONNE SENR. *MS. City of Bristol* (before 1831).

THOUGH no one at the time recognized it, the trade of Bristol at the close of the eighteenth century had become dangerously specialized. Her commerce with the former continental colonies never recovered from the blow of the American Revolution. The enormous risks of the slave trade and its growing unpopularity among merchants and sailors alike, coupled with the keen competition of Liverpool, rendered that branch of commerce less and less attractive. Though some merchants were still engaged in the Newfoundland fish trade, while others were beginning to develop commercial connections with Canada and the Maritimes, the West Indian trade alone was worth twice as much to Bristol as all her other oversea commerce combined. The sugar refining industry, a variety of provisioning and other trades and the greater part of her shipping, as well as the subsidiary crafts whose existence depended on it, all alike drew their main support from the commerce with the Caribbean.

Even when the violent fluctuations between periods of boom and depression, which were characteristic of the sugar trade at that time, are allowed for, it was a prosperous business. Thus Bristol felt no necessity to follow the example of her northern competitors in the establishment of new industries and new branches of commerce. Her merchants were prosperous, her craftsmen were fully employed, and there was no dearth of ships for her sailors to man. In spite of the Anti-Slave Trade campaign, it was impossible in 1800 to foresee that utter ruin of the sugar islands which was to occur during the next fifty years. Bristol continued to identify her fortunes with those of the Islands, and her prosperity waned with theirs. The West Indies depended not only upon the use of slave labour; their well-being was also conditional upon the continuance of the Old Colonial System, with all the special devices of Protection which it enshrined. Thus, in the first half of the nineteenth century, Bristol, the great champion of the West Indies, fought and lost many battles in defence of the old order. She fought for the

358

slave trade and lost; she defended bounties, drawbacks and all the outworn economic devices that Adam Smith denounced, and was beaten. Despite overwhelming evidence to the contrary, she asserted that the planters were doing their utmost to ameliorate the lot of their slaves. She opposed Emancipation, but in vain; she was dissatisfied with the sum voted for compensation and with the manner of its distribution, and she opposed the shortening of the period of apprenticeship.

Bristol also fought the Free Trade movement and denounced the repeal of the Navigation Acts. On 2nd March, 1849, it was resolved by the Merchant Venturers that a petition be sent up to Parliament opposing the Bill for the repeal of these laws. About the same time, a general petition on the subject was prepared by the shipping interests, and signatures were invited :

" MERCHANTS! SHIP-OWNERS! SHIP-BUILDERS!
ARTISANS! AND CITIZENS!
of Every Class

Who have a spark of Patriotic Feeling, and do not wish to see the best interests of your Country sacrificed at the shrine of a mistaken Policy, hasten to

SIGN THE PETITION

against the

PROPOSED

REPEAL

of the

NAVIGATION
LAWS:

A Measure which, if carried, will speedily bring down our beloved Country from the proud position she has so long maintained, cripple her Naval and Maritime resources, and be, doubtless, the cause of her ultimate ruin.

THE QUESTION IS A NATIONAL ONE—
'England expects every
Man to Do his Duty.'

———

The PETITION now lies for Signature at the *Commercial Rooms; The Exchange;* the Ship Yards of Mr. PATTERSON, Wapping, and Mr. Hill, Limekiln-Lane; and the Office of Mr. M. Whitwill, Middle-Avenue, Queen-Square."

This did not mean that her citizens were stupid or hopeless reactionaries; it simply meant that under the Old Colonial System Bristol had prospered. Her merchants were still progressive and active, but within the four walls of the old order. It was their misfortune that a system, which former generations had hailed as the quintessence of economic wisdom, was denounced by their own as the embodiment of all that was economically unscientific, unsound and obscurantist. So old Bristol was vanquished by the spirit of the new age, but she went down to defeat still fighting and with no word of surrender.

There followed after that about half a century of quiescence, in the course of which England forgot that the old city on the Avon had at one time been the second in the kingdom. But though quiescent, she was not in decay, even though, in comparison with the great cities of the north, whose progress was prodigious, she seemed to stand still and even to retrogress. The triumph of cotton in Lancashïre, the enormous expansion of the Yorkshire cloth industry, the rise of heavy industries in the midland and northern towns all played their part. Glasgow, Liverpool, Newcastle, Hull and many more forged ahead. Even before 1833, it was said that owing to a lack of shipping, some of the colonial produce consumed in Bristol found its way thither via Liverpool. Also, Bristol merchants who had colonial connections for the same reason were often obliged to send their goods north to the Mersey for exportation to the West Indies. As will be seen later, the unenlightened and penurious policy pursued by the Bristol Dock Company for so many years contributed materially to this semi-paralysis.

But as the nineteenth century drew to its close Bristol's old industries expanded, new ones were established and, after years of criminal neglect, her port was modernized and enormously extended. In the twentieth century, while her great nineteenth-century trade rivals, who had repeated her mistake of over-specialization, were paralysed by declining trade and vast problems of unemployment, Bristol, unconsciously perhaps, had learned her lesson, for by the variety of her industries and economic interests, she was able to maintain a mild prosperity, even through periods of severest economic depression, and very slowly she began to advance once more toward her former place among the great ports of England.

In addition to the general reasons for the comparative stagnation of Bristol in the middle of the nineteenth century, the ineptitude of the Dock Company must also be taken into account. Harbour works in Bristol started as early as 1239, when a quayed trench about half a mile long was constructed at the cost of £5,000, but no serious effort was made to expand its capacity to any great extent until the nineteenth century, when parts of the Avon and Frome were impounded between 1803 and 1809. This involved the diversion of the Avon to a new channel. It also involved substantial increases in port dues, which, as will be seen later, led to a riotous election in 1807. Bristol shippers expostulated and entreated in vain. Dock charges remained inordinately high, and they became intolerable when, in spite of the ever-increasing requirements of shipping, little or nothing was done in the first half of the nineteenth century to modernize the port. So her rivals advanced to greatness, and such obscure places as Cardiff sprang from most humble origins to a first place among British ports. The Bristol Dock Company was not only hide-bound and unprogressive, it also lacked financial resources. When the *Great Western* was winning new laurels for Bristol a vigorous forward policy should have been adopted, in order that the Avon might anticipate the growing requirements of steam, but that was not done, and Bristol acquired an evil name among shippers. At length, in 1848, to the great satisfaction of the mercantile community, the docks were taken over by the city, but for many years thereafter, although the exorbitant dues and irritating restrictions of former days ceased to hamper shippers, there were few other signs of improvement. When, at the time of the transfer, the Lords of the Admiralty held an enquiry into the scheme, William Bald, the engineer in charge, was mystified by the manner in which Bristol had already fallen out of the race. To him it appeared obvious that, from her geographical position, Bristol should have continued to be the second city in the kingdom. She was so well placed for a wide commerce, approached as she was by a deep bed of water which opened to the Atlantic, and having such a channel of communication surrounded by an extensive, fertile and populous country.

"Looking at all these things, it does certainly seem strange to me that Bristol has not risen in as great a proportion as other cities and places of less geographical importance have done. . . . The Bristol Channel, we find, is deep and open; the approach is safe and easy of navigation, and it is . . . unsurpassed by any port. I think, therefore, that under this and every other point of view, if the difficulties under which the port has been labouring can be removed in any way satisfactory to the citizens, and in a fair, just and equitable manner, it will be very desirable, in order that the trade of the place may be restored and extended in a way proportioned to its important geographical position."[1]

In the 'sixties a group of citizens agitated for a more forward policy, and finally, two new companies were organized which began the construction of docks at Avonmouth and Portishead. In spite of all the improvements that have taken place in the Bristol City Docks in the last century, the facts of geography have put a definite limit to development. Thus, in 1938 no ship with a greater length than 325 feet between perpendiculars came up the river Avon. The largest vessel which at that time entered these docks was the *Montreal City*, with a gross displacement of 3,666 tons. It was to overcome this difficulty that the extensive harbour works were undertaken in the 'seventies at the mouth of the Avon. The Avonmouth Dock, with a lock 454 feet long and 70 feet wide, was opened, which at the time was large enough to accommodate the greatest vessel afloat. In 1879 the Portishead Dock, on the other side of the river, was opened, and finally, in 1884 the Port of Bristol Authority acquired the Avonmouth and Portishead Docks from the Dock Companies. Since then improvements have been fairly continuous, and to-day the principal entrance lock is 875 feet long and 100 feet wide, and can accommodate all but the very largest passenger vessels. Unfortunately, however, these improvements came late, and Bristol had lost for a time her chance

---

[1] *Bristol as a Depot and Port of Departure for Emigrants*, 1854, pp. 25–6.

of maintaining her position as a popular port, but in the days to come, if a mere historian may for once assume the mantle of the prophet, there is good reason for believing that by vigorous and concentrated propaganda, plus a forward policy of improvement, the possibilities for development are unlimited. It was clear that by the end of the nineteenth century the period of quiescence was over, and although the old trades in negroes, fish and sugar were gone, Bristol merchants knew that the Empire was wide and that it produced many other things besides these.

In the course of the nineteenth century the Merchant Venturers, as a corporate body, ceased to have any direct concern with trade. They continued to discharge various important civic functions, but more and more their energies were devoted to the administration of the various educational and other funds that had been entrusted to them. The work which they had previously done was inherited by several other bodies. Reference has already been made to the New West India Society which came into existence in the early 'eighties of the eighteenth century. For many years the agitation against the Anti-Slavery movement centred in the Commercial Rooms, but from 1822, the Bristol Chamber of Commerce became the chief champion of the city's business interests, more particularly in petitions to Parliament and negotiations with the various public departments.

In the first half of the nineteenth century Bristol was so deeply concerned in the West Indies that one of her two Members in Parliament was always a man specially chosen for his intimate knowledge of the plantations. Evan Baillie, Edward Protheroe, Senr., Henry Bright, James Evan Baillie, Philip J. Miles, P. W. S. Miles, were all either planters themselves, West Indian merchants or closely connected in some way with that part of the Empire. Their constituents required that in Parliament these men should champion the interests of the planters and work in the closest co-operation with the various colonial agents. Through these representatives, the Bristol West Indian group maintained a vigilant lookout on the promotion of any new policy calculated to increase their own charges or to lessen those of their competitors. Thus, in the 'eighties and 'nineties of the eighteenth century, they were fully alive to the dangerous potentialities of the East Indies as a new and rival producer of sugar.

"The West Indians," declared John Pinney, ". . . are alarmed at the late importation of a few casks and Boxes of Sugar from Bengal. . . . In our opinion Those Sugars have been brought from the East Indies in order, purposely, to furnish the advocates for the abolition bill with a new argument, or at least positive evidence that Europe may be supplied with Sugar (from the East Indies) without the labour of Slaves." [1]

In 1806 a great storm arose over a Bill which proposed to enable neutral ships in time of war to trade in certain commodities with the British West Indies and South America. The Merchant Venturers vigorously protested against this measure on the ground that it would enable foreigners to make serious incursions into a trade which Bristol considered her particular preserve. About the same time the West Indians were threatened in another quarter, to the unspeakable disgust of "the poor planters," as Pinney described the group to which he himself belonged. The Dock Company, through Mr. Bathurst applied to Parliament for powers to increase its scale of charges. As already on many occasions and with good reasons, merchants, shippers and planters had all protested against the exactions of the Dock Company, this demand appeared to be wholly unreasonable. Frequently in the past it had been declared that many ships which would otherwise have come to Bristol, because of the Company's policy had proceeded to London, Liverpool and other more enlightened ports. The Dock Company was justly unpopular in Bristol, and in the elections which took place in the following year, the people made it plain to Mr. Bathurst what they thought of him and the part he had played in forwarding the evil intentions of the Company.

"During his Election there was a manifest dislike shewn to him by all ranks. . . . Soon after he got into his Chair the

---

[1] *Pinney Papers, Business Letter-book*, 1789–92, fol. 271.

Mob began to pelt him with stones and Clubs so very determined they seemed to be to destroy him—His friends immediately were obliged to unseat him and carry him off—
if he had proceeded he most certainly would have been
killed." [1]

In the tumult all the windows of the "Red Lion," the tavern
in which the meeting was held, were broken. The Riot Act
was read, and the Volunteers were called out to quell the
mob.

"Every Person who exhibited a blue cockade was obliged
to hide it, or they were insulted—even Ladies who wore
blue Ribbon had it thrown in their faces." [1]

In spite of the short comings of the Dock Company and the
abolition of the slave trade, the West Indians, on the whole,
continued to prosper during the first three decades of the nineteenth century. Throughout these years, however, they suffered
from one real grievance which became acute in the early
'twenties. Prior to the American Revolution, the sugar islands
received the greater part of their foodstuffs, their barrel-staves,
lumber and other necessities from the continental colonies in
exchange for their sugar, molasses and rum. A long period of
economic hostility followed in the years after the peace. It
became the avowed policy of Great Britain to prohibit all intercourse between the sugar plantations and the United States.
This very unwise course benefited no one. It injured the Americans, it injured the sugar planters and the traders of Bristol as
well. At last, in 1822, the West Indian group petitioned Parliament against the continued prohibition of trade between the
Islands and the United States. They contended that because
of this policy they were compelled to dispose of their rum in
England where the market was overstocked, and the money
realized on its sale was barely sufficient to cover the costs of
distillation. In response to their request that the old trade
between the Islands and the mainland of America should once

---

[1] *Pinney Papers, Business Letter-book*, 1806, fol. 89.

more be permitted, a Bill was passed through Parliament which helped to remove part, at least, of this long standing cause of irritation.

From 1823 onwards, the difficulties which confronted the planters increased on all sides. Nevertheless, during these years the West India Society in Bristol, despite all its worries, had its moments of relaxation. Thus, on 8th March, 1826, it was

> "Resolved unanimously that on any Member entering into the state of Matrimony he have the pleasure of presenting a dozen of claret to the Club, that his Health, Happiness and Prosperity, may be drunk in a bumper by the Society." [1]

In furtherance of this occurs an entry in 1831, that Charles Pinney, having "entered the state of matrimony," paid the fine. Again, on 9th August, 1827,

> "Mr. Pinney betted Mr. Payne that in the formation of a new Administration, consequent upon the death of Mr. Canning, the Whig members would preponderate. . . . Mr. Pinney lost—paid." [1]

It seems that these jovial West India merchants were, like the people of the present generation, interested in questions of weight, but it does not appear from the context whether decreases or increases were considered desirable. In August, 1826,

> "Mr. Anstice betted Mr. Daniel the Six Gentleman on the Chairman's right side of the Table, weighed heavier than the Six Gentleman on his left side.
> "Mr. Daniel lost by 17 lbs—the weights being 994 to 977. 1 doz. claret p^d." [1]

Even in the critical year 1831, when according to their own petitions, they were ruined and lost men,

> "Mr. Bernard betted with Mr. Sheriff Claxton, that his, Mr. C's, Side of the Table did not weigh as much as his,

[1] *Merchant Venturers, West India New Society*, 1822–38.

Mr. Bernard's, seven members and friends were weighed on each Side, and Mr. Claxton was declared the loser by 33 lb— 1 doz. claret, paid." [1]

Again, as it has already been seen, it was customary for the owner of the first sugar ship to arrive home in the new season to pay £4 10s. to the Society to defray the cost of claret to be drunk in honour of the occasion. In 1829, 1830, 1831 and 1832, Messrs. Pinney and Case duly paid their fine.

The unrest among the negroes of Demerara, which became serious in 1823, was hailed by the West Indians as a proof that the Government should hasten slowly in the furtherance of any contemplated reform. In that year, however, they were more perturbed by the Government scheme for reducing the duties on East India sugar to the West Indian level. A long letter on this subject was sent up to Parliament, which enumerated the injuries which such changes in the tariff would bring upon Bristol, but though the movement for the equalization of sugar duties might be arrested, it could not be permanently stayed. Thus, in spite of strenuous opposition from the West Indian group, in which all the old arguments were elaborated, the Imperial Government, in 1828, admitted Mauritius sugars at West Indian rates, and greatly reduced the charges on those from India.

In the same year, another set of grievances was referred to in a petition to Parliament. The extra duties imposed upon sugar in the late war had been retained, though the price of sugar, as well as the quantity imported from the British islands, had greatly decreased. This was due both to the retention of extra duties, and also to the fact that foreign plantations, which contained the finest sugar land in the world, were still able to plant by slave labour imported from Africa. The Government proposal to decrease the duties on foreign and East Indian sugar was, in effect, an encouragement to those who, in spite of international agreements, still persisted in the slave trade. A long list of the special disabilities from which they suffered was then enumerated, and the petition wound up by pointing out that a

---

[1] *Merchant Venturers, West India New Society*, 1822-38.

vast amount of British capital was sunk in the sugar industry, and that if foreign and East Indian producers were placed on a footing of equality with the West Indies, they would, by the special advantages they already enjoyed, ruin the old colonies, and strike a serious blow at the prosperity of the Mother Country.

These petitions made much of the high cost of sugar which, by that time, the signatories declared, had become a necessity of life to all classes, but owing to the existing duties on West Indian sugar was beyond their means. The cure for this evil was not, according to them, to open up the market to East Indian and foreign slave-produced sugar, which would seem to the impartial historian the obvious course to follow, but to lower the duty on their own product and revise it on that of their competitors. In obedience to the wishes of the Mother Country, they went on to say, they had accepted the abolition of the slave trade and done their best to ameliorate the lot of their slaves.

On 17th January, 1829, *Felix Farley* published a letter which denounced the West Indian Committee in London for gross mismanagement of the West Indian case. Two-thirds of its members were retired planters who had forgotten their business, and one-third was made up of London merchants and other gentlemen who had never visited the Islands. Many members of the Committee were too old, ignorant and indolent to be active, and this incompetent body was helpless before the vigorous and well-led onslaught of the anti-colonial party. The result was that both in Parliament and in the Press, the worse appeared the better course. A more competent body should be set up to furnish the British Government with reliable, up-to-date information and advice on the West Indies. In this same year, and again in 1830, petitions along similar lines were sent up to Parliament, and pressure was brought to bear on various important ministers by personal approaches. These petitions speak of decay and approaching insolvency. The cure which the petitioners still demanded was the continuance in force of the special protection for their rum and sugar and, indeed, the lowering of the existing duties. The wickedness of the foreigner was stressed at length. Since 1815, in violation of international agreements, he had imported 600,000 negroes from Africa, by which he had been enabled to extend his cultivation and enormously to increase his output. Again, Mauritius was now importing sugar into England greatly in excess of the amount agreed upon by the British Ministry. The net result of all this was that West Indian sugar was now placed at a hopeless disadvantage in foreign markets, and as the market in England was over-stocked, it was unsaleable at home. Fortunately, it is not the task of the writer to justify the arguments of the planters nor even to imply that they were consistent. At one time they attacked duties because they were too low, and at another they attacked them because they were too high, while always, for some obscure reason, the consumers' interests were presumed to be served best by low duties on West Indian sugars and prohibitive rates on the same commodity when it emanated from the East or foreign plantations. With more reason, they deplored the unrelenting misrepresentations of which they were the victims at the hands of the anti-colonial party, a faction that appeared to overawe the Government and which, unless checked by the voice of Parliament, would at no distant time cause the British colonies to be a scene of desolation and horror, inferior only to that of San Domingo.

As Emancipation became certain, other groups concerned with the West Indian commerce were stimulated to activity. Thus, in 1831, the sailors engaged in the West India trade passed certain resolutions in Bristol, first on their ships and then on the quayside, in which they deplored the state of that part of the Empire, and they prayed that

"His Majesty's paternal regards be at this period particularly directed to his suffering subjects on the other side of the Atlantic." [1]

In the following year, *Felix Farley* published a slashing article which denounced the Government's mishandling of the colonies.

[1] *Felix Farley's Bristol Journal*, 22nd October, 1831.

Either the Imperial Government must change its policy or the colonies would throw off their allegiance. The repeated protests of the colonies had been disregarded, and it was well known that they were devising means of escape from so ignorant and ruinous a domination. No one could doubt the reason why West Indian emissaries were now visiting the United States.

"That ambitious state cannot be an inattentive observer of the fair prey which is thus held out to it." [1]

Even after 1833, petitions and expostulations continued to flow up to London, but it is surprising how slight was the effect of all of this on the Government. Slowly but surely the sugar trade was destroyed, and when all is taken into account, whatever the individual losses may have been, it was right that an industry built upon slave labour should be destroyed. Unfortunately for Bristol, she had reared her prosperity on the insecure foundations of slave labour and Protection.

Although from time to time during the first quarter of the nineteenth century it was stated that, even in the West Indian trade, Bristol was being ousted by Liverpool, that branch of commerce retained its pride of place for a long time. According to Charles Pinney in 1830, five-eighths of the trade of the city was with the West Indies. Three years later, another leading Bristol merchant declared that without the West Indian trade Bristol would be a fishing port. James Evan Baillie exhorted his fellow citizens not to lay the axe at the root of their own prosperity and commercial greatness by risking the desolation of the British West Indian colonies, to which they owed in so great a degree the employment of their artificers and general population.

Within a few years it was plain that permanent decline had begun. In 1840 14 ships cleared from Bristol for Newfoundland, 9 for Canada, 5 for New Brunswick, and 1 for Prince Edward Island. Fourteen set sail for the West Coast of Africa, 3 to the East Indies and China, 7 to Australia and 45 to the West

---

[1] *Felix Farley's Bristol Journal*, 24th March, 1832.

Indies, Guiana and Demerara. In that same year, 12 returned from the West Coast, 12 from Mauritius, India and Canton, 1 from Australia, 18 from Newfoundland, 106 from Canada, New Brunswick and Prince Edward Island, and 38 from the British West Indies, Trinidad and Demerara. In tonnage in that year, about 29 per cent. outward went to the West Indies and about 40 per cent. returned from that part of the Empire.

In 1847 the total tonnage outward was 35,940, of which over 14,000 tons was bound for the West Indies. Ships returning from the Islands aggregated 12,000 tons out of a grand total of 104,546 tons. After that, decline was rapid. In 1861 the total tonnage which cleared for the Islands and South America from Bristol amounted to about 7,000 out of a total of 64,111 tons, while out of a total inward tonnage of 233,681, less than 10,000 tons came from the sugar colonies of the Caribbean. Ten years later, less than 6,000 tons cleared for the Islands out of a total of 51,343 tons, and it is significant that in this year, no ship cleared from Bristol for Jamaica, while less than 6,000 tons returned from the Islands out of a total inward tonnage of 314,264. By 1890 practical extinction was reached. One ship cleared for the West Indies that year and only 9 small trading vessels, representing 2,730 tons, cleared for British Guiana. Four sailing ships and one steamer returned, with a combined tonnage of just over 2,000, while the total inward shipping for that year, including both steam and sail, amounted to 221,180 tons. Ten years later, the total inward tonnage from the West Indies and British Guiana was 1,843 out of a total of 401,483 tons under sail, while the number of ships is not recorded.

With the new century there was a revival, but not in sugar, for already the West Indies were turning over to fruit. In 1910 no sailing ships cleared for the West Indies, but there were 29 steamers, which aggregated 86,231 tons, and the returns were approximately equal. In that year the total outward tonnage from Bristol had grown to 752,153, and the inward tonnage to 1,317,811. Thus, before the close of the nineteenth century, the once flourishing sugar trade of Bristol had disappeared.

The sugar refining industry also declined and disappeared, just as the tall and stately ships that had carried home their cargoes of sugar, rum and molasses had vanished from the scene. The banana replaced sugar, just as the unromantic steamer replaced the brigs, barques and full-rigged vessels of former days. In time Bristol wrote off her losses, adjusted herself to the conditions of the new age, and set about the development of new trades and new industries more varied and more secure than the old.

Indeed, she began to develop new branches of British imperial commerce before the eclipse of the West Indies. Her long-established interest in the Newfoundland fisheries continued down to the close of the nineteenth century and, indeed, almost to the outbreak of the Great War, but it was a mere shadow. In 1840 14 ships cleared for Newfoundland and 18 entered the port of Bristol from that colony, representing a gross tonnage of 1,462 and 1,827 tons respectively. Nine ships went to the old colony in 1847 and 8 returned. In 1860 11 British ships and 1 foreign vessel cleared for Newfoundland, representing about 2,000 tons gross, while 10 British and 2 foreign ships returned, 1,782 tons gross. Ten years later, 18 cleared for the island, while 23 sail returned, whose total tonnage was under 3,000 tons. By 1890 this trade had definitely declined, though 10 ships cleared for Newfoundland and 9 returned.

In 1900 4 sailing ships went out and 2 steamers, but the vessels were still very small, as the former totalled 1,765 tons, while the two steamers aggregated 4,793 tons. No steamers returned from Newfoundland that year, and the 7 sailing vessels aggregated only 845 tons. On 3rd June, 1910, the *Mayflower*, 138 register tons, set sail from Bristol for Newfoundland with a cargo of iron, pitch and tar, hardware and other goods. It was right and proper that she should be a windjammer. Two sailing vessels returned, with a combined tonnage of 231, of which the last reached port on 8th December. She was the *Martha Edmonds*, 153 register tons, with a cargo of 32 tons of fish, 165 tons of fish oil and 2 tons of other goods; but she did not belong to a Bristol firm, so by this time it can be said that this ancient trade, with all its associated traditions of exploration, colonization and privateering, had followed the slave trade and sugar into the limbo of vanished things. On 9th November, 1914, the *M. Lloyd Morris*, 144 register tons, with a cargo of fish, fish oil and other goods, dropped anchor in Bristol, but she was merely a wartime incident. In 1912 the *Elizabeth Pritchard*, 99 register tons, left Bristol, and she appears to have been the last sailing vessel to carry on this historic trade. In 1921 one steamer of 1,742 tons left for Newfoundland, and no ships returned. Fish had disappeared from the imports which come from Newfoundland to Bristol, and the trade now consisted of zinc ores for the Smelting Company at Avonmouth. In 1938 6 vessels of 13,340 register tonnage arrived from the old colony.

After the American Revolution, as has already been seen, it was hoped that the remaining British provinces in the Far North would be able to supply the sugar islands with the foodstuffs, timber and commodities which formerly had been imported from the old colonies. This policy failed, but gradually the North American provinces won a place in British commerce, mainly through their exports of timber and forest products, and later of ships. This trade grew slowly at first, but by the close of the Napoleonic wars British North American imports were well known in England. In the post-war period the British North American timber trade had to fight hard for the retention of wartime duties imposed on foreign products. The Baltic timber interest was strong and active, while among British builders and wood workers there was a pronounced preference for Scandinavian and Russian woods. The rivalry between the two sections of the trade was acute, and when, in 1839, it was rumoured that Poulett Thompson, later Lord Sydenham, was to be appointed Governor General of Canada, an attempt was made by those concerned with the British North American timber trade to oppose his appointment. For years Sydenham had been identified with the Baltic, and it was felt that such a man was not a suitable person for such an appointment. The Bristol Chamber of Commerce was invited by the London Merchants to co-operate in their protest against this, but, on the ground that it was not the concern of that body to mix itself up in politics, this request was refused.

When Peel's Government began its attack on Protection the Bristol Chamber of Commerce made its protests against alterations in duty. These, however, were unavailing, for the current of public opinion was beginning to flow strongly in the direction of Free Trade. At that time, the colonies were considered to be of little economic value to the Mother Country, and England, confident of her permanent supremacy in industry, and convinced that it was her mission to teach the world economic and political commonsense, looked beyond the frontier of the Empire to all lands as her natural market. Colonies were costly to maintain, they were sources of continued irritation, and in that Free Trade future, in which England was to be the workshop of the world, whose manufactures all less fortunate peoples would be glad to take in return for their own raw products, colonies would be anachronisms.

While this was becoming the general view, those connected with the colonial timber and other trades held other opinions. Though the trade with the West Indies was still more valuable than that with the northern colonies, the latter was increasing. In 1840 9 ships set sail from Bristol for Canada, 5 for New Brunswick and 1 for Prince Edward Island, but it was the inward movement of ships which was significant. The nineteenth century witnessed in British North America the rise and fall of a great industry. Dozens of little ports around the whole coast from the mouth of the St. John to the Gulf of St. Lawrence and up that river to Lake Ontario sent out innumerable ships, barges, brigs, brigantines, schooners and vessels of almost every rig. These came to England, making the north Atlantic white with their sails, and in the various ports of Great Britain, together with their cargoes of timber, many of them were sold to British owners. In that last great age of sail, some of the most beautiful ships that have ever appeared upon the sea were the products of these British colonial shipyards, and many were sold in Bristol. One such was the *Argo*, and a bill advertising her sale is still in the possession of one of the leading Bristol shipping firms.

"FOR SALE BY
PUBLIC AUCTION
at the
COMMERCIAL ROOMS,
BRISTOL,
ON TUESDAY, JAN. 30, 1849,
at Twelve o'clock precisely,
THE FINE NEW BRIGANTINE
A R G O ,

195$\frac{9}{94}$ TONS, O.M. | 177$\frac{3455}{8500}$ TONS, N.M.
Length, 78 Feet 8–10ths—Breadth, 20 Feet 3–10ths—Depth,
13 Feet 1–10th.

This Vessel was Built at Prince Edward Island, principally of
Hackmatac, and Launched in November last; will carry about 300
Tons dead weight at a light draught of Water; is a good model, and
a strong faithfully built Vessel.

NOW LYING IN THE FLOATING HARBOUR.

For further Particulars, apply to Messrs. CANNON, MILLER,
& Co., Liverpool; or to
MARK WHITWILL,
SHIP BROKER, BRISTOL.
Bristol, January 20, 1849."

In the year 1840 79 vessels from Canada dropped anchor in
Bristol, 25 from New Brunswick and 2 from Prince Edward Island.
In the 'forties railroad construction throughout the country and
a boom in building speculation caused a great demand for timber.
Thus, in the three years 1845, 1846 and 1847 the port of Bristol
received large quantities of Canadian forest products. In
1847 though only 25 vessels set sail from that port for British
North America, Canada alone sent 38 to Bristol, of 25,677 tons,
followed closely by New Brunswick with 30, whose gross tonnage was 12,815; Prince Edward Island sent 4 of 1,320 tons and
Nova Scotia 3 of 1,294 tons. In 1860 ships outward numbered

21 and showed a slight fall in tonnage as compared with 1848, but 89 sail arrived from the North American provinces with a combined tonnage of over 46,000. Ten years later, only 25 ships sailed for the northern mainland colonies with the combined tonnage of over 5,000 tons. When steam and iron began to triumph over sail and wood there was a marked drop in the number of ships sent to Bristol. Eighty-two in all in 1870, with a combined tonnage of nearly 40,000 came in, but the sailing ship was not yet beaten, and in the 'seventies some of the most splendid vessels built in colonial ports were sent to Great Britain from the shipyards of Nova Scotia, New Brunswick, Prince Edward Island and Quebec. During this decade the export trade from Bristol to Canada also expanded. In 1880 60 sailing vessels representing 41,152 tons, and 9 steamers of 11,854 tons sailed for Canada, while 73 sail of 49,039 tons, and 18 steamers of 21,617 tons returned.

But the great days of sail were now over, and from the 'eighties onward wood gave place to iron and steel, while steam drove the sailing ship from the sea. By the end of the 'eighties the revolution was clearly discernible, and in 1890 18 sailing ships cleared from the port of Bristol to the Dominion of Canada, of 8,606 tons, but the 16 steamers that also cleared for the same destination represented 33,730 tons. This transition is even more marked in the movement inward, for there were 31 sail of 20,119 tons, and 19 steamers of 38,023 tons. In 1900 the tonnage that cleared for Canada under sail was less than 7,000 tons, while that under steam was 66,328 tons. Fifteen sailing vessels arrived from Canada and 31 steamers, of 13,066 tons as compared with 72,313 tons. Before another decade was over, sail had disappeared and the trade with Canada was carried on by steamers and had continued to expand. After the Great War trade with Canadian Pacific ports had increased. In 1938 75 steamers arrived from Canada.

In the course of the nineteenth century Bristol showed a certain appreciation of the possibilities of the Canadian market, which is illustrated by various petitions sent up from the Chamber of Commerce to Parliament on the subject of Canadian tariff policy. It was appropriate that in 1897, when Canada celebrated the tercentenary of Cabot's voyages, Bristol representatives should be present at the unveiling of the tablet in Halifax, Nova Scotia. At the same time, in Bristol itself Lord Dufferin and Ava, a former Governor General of the Dominion, laid the foundation stone of the Cabot Tower. By that time the import of ships had ceased and the timber trade had declined in relative importance, but 1897 was memorable for the arrival at Avonmouth of the *Montcalm* with 6,728 tons of grain aboard, the largest cargo of its kind hitherto brought to that port. This marked the fact that the new trade in corn was replacing the lost one in ships. Shortly before this, the Dominion Line had established a weekly steamer service between Canada and Bristol, and thereafter the importation of grain expanded enormously. With the new century there was a very much keener appreciation of the possibilities of this trade to be seen on both sides of the Atlantic. Canadian representatives, official and mercantile, came fairly frequently to Bristol, and always with the same intention of emphasizing the importance of developing closer relations between the Dominion and the Avon. Officials of the Dock Authority, followed in later years by delegations of Bristol merchants, visited Canada to study its market possibilities, and to establish personal contacts with its important traders.

All of this was helped by the policy of the Canadian Government. In 1887 it was decided to establish a special Department of Trade and Commerce, and in 1892 this came into existence. One of the chief concerns of this Department was to develop Canadian overseas trade, and at first there was maintained in Bristol a Canadian representative or commercial agent, whose function was to provide information about Canada and generally to keep the Department informed about the situation in Bristol. Usually, a Bristol business man performed this service in return for a small honorarium and the use of the title "Canadian Commercial Agent." Before the close of the century, however, it was felt that Bristol's commercial connections with the Dominion were sufficiently important to justify a more permanent arrangement. It was in these years that Joseph Chamberlain was spending his matchless energy in the cause of closer imperial relations.

He asked for, and received from the Bristol Chamber of Commerce a great deal of information and advice, and no one was more anxious than he to assist in the furtherance of any request made to him whose object was the strengthening of inter-imperial economic bonds. Canadian trade was developing rapidly, but a great many difficulties constantly arose over the Canadian tariff system and her policy of rebates. Bristol traders felt that a resident Canadian trade expert could help in these and many other ways, and generally promote a good understanding between Canadian and British traders. In 1899, therefore, the Council of the Chamber of Commerce wrote to Lord Strathcona, the Canadian High Commissioner, on this subject, but nothing was done for several years. It reported to the Council that the attempt had failed, as the Canadian Agent in Cardiff had succeeded in impressing Lord Strathcona with the greater claims of that port for the concentration of Canadian trade. Another communication was, therefore, sent to the High Commissioner, which set out the many advantages which Bristol could offer and emphasized the need for a permanent resident Trade Commissioner in that place. On this occasion the Bristol request was supported by a number of leading trade journals in the Dominion, and finally, in 1904, to the great satisfaction of all concerned, the Bristol office of the Canadian Trade Commissioner was opened.

Before the War, then, by means of unofficial visits of Bristol traders, special trade delegations and the participation of Bristol in various exhibitions throughout the Dominion, assisted by assiduous press propaganda and the counsel and advice of the Trade Commissioner, the old city showed that she had not lost that ancient spirit of enterprise which had made her name famous throughout the world. Canadian Ministers and distinguished visitors were welcomed by the city, while the Port Authority was zealous to do everything possible to render the port attractive to Canadian and other oversea shippers.

In 1918 a special trade commission visited Great Britain from Canada, and in its report it expressed satisfaction at the various encouragements offered by the Mother Country to Canadian trades.

"This applies perhaps with special reference to Bristol, where the Dock authorities have made special provision for handling Canadian produce, and welcome every indication of increased trade with Canada. Cold storage plants of the most modern type and grain warehouses have been erected, and the Commission was assured that every possible encouragement would be given to merchandise coming from the Dominion." [1]

In the past another product which formerly came from the old Empire to Bristol began to figure once more as a British North American import. The Imperial Tobacco Company imported a sample shipment of Canadian Burley tobacco of the 1919 crop, and after the methods of growing and curing had been greatly improved, increased quantities were imported. The improvement was so marked by 1925, that the Company decided to build its own handling plant in Ontario, so that tobacco might be bought direct from the growers and be graded and packed by the Company's experts. This plant was completed in 1926, and since that time Canadian tobacco has been regularly shipped to various British ports, including Bristol. The policy of Imperial Preference encouraged this development, and by 1936, in addition to Burley tobacco, Bristol was also importing a certain amount of Canadian flue-cured tobacco. In 1939, however, Canada's chief imports into Bristol were grain, flour, feeding stuffs, provisions, timber, metals and fruit. Thus, although old trades had declined or completely disappeared, and in spite of many vicissitudes, the city of Jay, Cabot and the Thornes still received great quantities of vital supplies from that part of the New World with which its history had been closely linked for more than four hundred years. In return, it sent out its own commodities as well as those of the neighbouring counties, and still greater expansion was expected.

[1] *Bristol Incorporated Chamber of Commerce, Annual Meeting*, 7th June, 1918, p. 27.

CHAPTER XVIII

AFRICA, INDIA AND THE ANTIPODES

"... *as to the seat of the city and its environs, it surpasses all that I ever saw. A great commercial city in the midst of cornfields, meadows and woods, and the ships coming into the centre of it, miles from anything like sea, up a narrow river, and passing between two clefts of a rock probably a hundred feet high; so that from the top of these clifts you* look down *upon the main-top gallant masts of lofty ships, that are gliding along!"*

WILLIAM COBBETT, *Rural Rides* (1830).

IT has been seen that in the years immediately after the American Revolution Bristol began to develop a direct trade with the West Coast of Africa wholly unconnected with the slave trade. In the early decades of the nineteenth century this commerce developed slowly, and by 1840, it was still inconsiderable. In that year 14 ships cleared from Bristol for the British stations on the West African coast and 12 returned. Seven years later, 14 ships went out and 13 arrived in Bristol. In the 'fifties the Board of Trade became seriously perturbed about the state of the African trade in general and the illicit slave trade in particular. Enquiries were sent out to various Chambers of Commerce throughout the country for opinions on the need, or otherwise, of developing the West African commerce as a means of arresting the slave trade. The Bristol Chamber was unable, however, to give any coherent reply, as those who knew most about the subject expressed so many contradictory opinions. In the course of this investigation, it was said that a large soap manufactory in Bristol was compelled to use water in lieu of palm oil, which seems to suggest that the African trade of the city at that time was very sluggish. Nevertheless, 23 vessels cleared for the African coast from Bristol in 1860, while 22 English and 1 foreign ship returned, 5,446 tons and 5,550 tons respectively. A decade later, 21 sail, of a gross tonnage of 5,206, cleared from Bristol, while 16 sail, of 4,084 tons, came home.

Though this traffic was now beginning to decline, Bristol merchants were still aware of its economic potentialities, even though they did little to develop them. When, therefore, in 1870, it was rumoured that Great Britain was about to cede Gambia to France, the Chamber of Commerce, together with other bodies interested in the African trade, became active in opposition. A memorial was presented to the Colonial Secretary, in which it was stated that there was abundant evidence to show that this cession should not take place before the whole subject was more fully discussed by Parliament and the country.

It was reported to the Chamber that because of this and similar protests from other places, the Colonial Secretary had given written assurance that the negotiations for the cession of Gambia to the French Government had been suspended.

By 1890 the direct trade between Bristol and the West African coast was dead, as no ship cleared from or returned to that port, and though for the next thirty years the city continued to increase its consumption of West African products, it had no direct shipping connections with that part of the Empire. At the same time, it would be wrong to attribute this wholly to lack of enterprise. In the later nineteenth century a great revolution took place in the shipping industry, and one steamer could easily carry as much cargo as a dozen sailing vessels fifty or seventy-five years before. It took the products of many ports to make up one cargo, and in that way the steamer made for concentration at a few great home ports. Thus, if Bristol did not happen to be the headquarters of a particular shipping line, it tended to obtain its products by rail or coasting vessels from other ports of the kingdom. It was not until after 1918 that direct trading between the Avon and the West Coast was resumed, but in the interval, great quantities of products from that region reached the city indirectly from other ports, and several West African merchants continued to have their headquarters in Bristol.

Although direct connections ceased for a time, Bristol was still deeply interested in West Coast politics. In 1885 the Chamber of Commerce requested Mr. Lewis Fry, one of the Members for Bristol, to use his influence in order that the proposed treaty between Great Britain and Portugal relative to the Congo should not be ratified. It pointed out that, if carried through, this agreement would have entailed the extension of the Portuguese tariff to a section of the African coast. This would adversely affect British interests and ultimately mean the total abandonment by British traders of the important commerce on that part of the West Coast. Portugal was one of the most backward countries of Europe, the corruption of whose officials was proverbial. The transfer of territories to her sovereignty would be detrimental to the moral interest of their peoples, as well as to the development of commerce.

Further, the Chamber alleged that Portugal was not above suspicion in its attitude to the slave trade, and the conclusion of this treaty would nullify all the rights and privileges granted to the chiefs of that region by Great Britain in eleven separate treaties.

> "Your petitioners . . . pray that . . . your Honorable House will be pleased not to sanction the ratification of the treaty." [1]

The Annual Report for that year stated that the efforts of the Chamber had been successful since the treaty had been dropped.

About the same time the Chamber was also active in opposing the annexation of the Cameroons and Batanga by Germany. For many years past a flourishing trade had been carried on there in which three important Bristol firms were deeply concerned. Bristol co-operated with Manchester and Liverpool in placing the point of view of British traders before the Imperial Government. Through the local members of Parliament, a petition was sent to Lord Granville which expressed the fear that if Germany secured her control of these districts, English traders would be excluded. It was, therefore, suggested that in any final settlement it must be laid down that English traders should continue to enjoy, as formerly, equal trading rights with Germans and others, and that for the future, Germany should guarantee not to impose any oppressive differential tariff on British traders. At that time, however, the Imperial Government was more concerned to reach a settlement with Germany than to defend British commerce, so the Cameroons passed into German hands and British trade at once declined.

In 1890 Bristol, with other cities, drew the attention of the Government to alleged misdemeanours of the French at Cape Lahou. Without warning France had imposed a prohibitive tariff on imported merchandise. Although this memorial was supplemented by several letters directly addressed by the merchants concerned to the Imperial Government, the Foreign Office replied that it was powerless, as there was no treaty in

[1] *Bristol Incorporated Chamber of Commerce, Annual Meeting*, 15th April, 1885, p. 10.

existence which gave it the right to object to French possession of Cape Lahou. Four years later, French policy once more aroused the opposition of Bristol. The Chamber of Commerce requested Lord Salisbury to direct his attention to the monopolies then being granted by the French authorities on the West Coast of Africa to their own citizens in the settlements between Ashanti and Liberia. The Government, however, did nothing, and so for the next four years there was a protracted correspondence between the Bristol Chamber of Commerce and the Prime Minister on this subject. In the meantime, the French continued their exclusive policy, and so brought renewed losses upon English traders.

Finally, in 1898, a memorial was sent up to Lord Salisbury which recapitulated the history of this dispute from the beginning, and stressed the unsatisfactory conditions which then existed. The Bristol Chamber spoke, it declared in this memorial, for merchants who had carried on trade with the French Ivory Coast for the past century. The Prime Minister was reminded that because of the long and well-established connection between their city and that part of Africa, it was generally known as, and described on maps as, the Bristol Coast. When, in 1844, the French annexed that part between Assinee and Half Jack, their Government gave most positive assurances to the British Ambassador that France did not intend to impose any restrictions on trade because of the new French establishment, and that France, in her fiscal policy, was content to follow that of Great Britain in the territories over which she exercised authority. Later, a small export duty was imposed, but during the Franco-Prussian War, French officials were withdrawn, and the pre-1844 Free Trade conditions once more prevailed until 1889. Then French officials suddenly appeared, and at once began to impose enormous duties which varied from 10 per cent. to 300 per cent. on all goods landed in the colony. As, however, this tariff was to apply to all traders impartially, it was considered that the English could hold their own, but subsequently some doubt arose as to the accuracy of this assumption. Naturally, English traders were anxious to know precisely what their position was, and whether differential duties in favour of the French were to be imposed on imports. The memorial reminded Lord Salisbury of the long correspondence that had ensued between the Bristol Chamber and himself. Then the French objected to the practice which had hitherto prevailed of carrying on traffic with the natives in trading ships. This again had given rise to further correspondence with his Lordship, and at last, on 23rd January, 1890, Lord Salisbury categorically stated:

"no tariff can be imposed in Assinee which would be differential against English trade." [1]

Partly because of this statement, thousands of pounds of British capital had been sunk in this commerce. Factories had been erected in various places; but now Great Britain was suddenly confronted with an absolute breach of the Convention of 1889. The memorialists prayed that this subject might be brought before the commission, then sitting in Paris, for settlement, and that the Foreign Secretary would receive a deputation from all the Chambers of Commerce in the country interested in it. It was further suggested that, as the matter was pressing, action should be taken forthwith. At the annual meeting of the Chamber of Commerce held in 1899, it was announced that in consequence of this pressure on the authorities, the initial steps which had been taken by the Government

"have resulted in a manner satisfactory to merchants engaged in the West African Trade." [2]

Down to the time when England and France composed all their bickerings in the face of a greater threat from across the Rhine, similar difficulties continued to arise, and similar protests were made against differential duties and unfair obstacles placed by the French on English trade on the West Coast.

With the beginning of the new century, Bristol's interest in this branch of commerce developed rapidly. Her expanding chocolate industry required West Coast products, and other manufacturers depended to some extent on ground nuts and

[1] *Bristol Incorporated Chamber of Commerce, Annual Meeting*, 1898, p. 107.
[2] *Ibid.*, 1899, p. 18.

West Coast commodities. In 1907 the Chamber of Commerce was exhorted to initiate a campaign in Bristol to win back for that port her lost West African trade, as with every year the trade connections between the Avon and that region were growing. On historical grounds, as well as on many others, it was felt that Bristol had a peculiar right to participate in the economic expansion of the West Coast. Though the Chamber expressed its sympathy with the aim in view, its Council felt that it was debarred by its rules from such activities, so nothing was done. Indeed, to the impartial historian it seems that too often in the last century of Bristol history the excuse of rules, or genuine timidity and lack of vision, did much to cripple the city. In this port, as in others throughout the country, too many unconnected or partially connected bodies are engaged in work which overlaps, and because no one feels that it is his special responsibility, nothing is done. The Port of Bristol Authority, the Commercial Rooms, the Chamber of Commerce and the Development Board all had distinctive and important work to do, but there was a point where their united and organized effort would be of service to the city as a whole without infringing on their separate specialized functions.

Bristol still had the necessary initiative, however, as was shown when a successful effort was made to bring direct shipments of cocoa from West Africa to the Avonmouth Docks, and this business has become a prominent feature. In 1938 13 steamers of 36,038 register tons arrived from Gambia, the Gold Coast and Nigeria, and it may be expected that in time to come this trade will be substantially increased.

Although as early as 1847 the Cape was listed among the countries with which the city traded, Bristol was not for many years greatly interested in South Africa. In that year, in fact, no ship sailed from the Avon for the Cape or returned, and in 1860 it was no longer listed, while for forty years thereafter, except for occasional accidental arrivals, there was no regular commerce. It is evident, nevertheless, that ships outward bound to India, the Far East and Australasia, as well as those homeward bound around the Cape, carried freight to that colony from Bristol or brought it home. In its annual report for 1882, for example, the Bristol Chamber of Commerce mentions the wholesale clothing trade in relation to the Cape, and the effect produced upon it by the First Boer War. At that time, also, Bristol traders were beginning to be perturbed by German competition. The shipments of exports from Bristol direct to South Africa began in 1902, and continued for about a quarter of a century. By 1906 Bristol's connection with the Cape had become substantial and important enough to induce the Council of the Chamber of Commerce to protest to the Agent General of the Cape against certain new import duties that were about to be imposed by that colony.

A year later, Natal was the offending party. The fees in that province for commercial travellers' licences were to be increased, and the Chamber considered the matter to be urgent. Its President, therefore, wrote to the Premier of Natal. According to him, some members of the Chamber who were trying to develop closer trade relations between the Colony and the port of Bristol would be seriously hindered if these proposed changes became law. Therefore, while fully aware of the necessity of raising revenue in the colony, and while not wishing to interfere in its internal affairs, the President went on to say,

"I should like to suggest in our mutual interests that some other means, if possible, should be devised to meet the requirements of the case, and which would not tend to hinder or prevent the development of trade." [1]

On this occasion the protest appears to have been successful, for it was reported that in reply, the Premier of Natal had announced that the Bill had been most carefully scrutinized by a Select Committee, and he hoped all serious objections had been removed. Later, the Colonial Secretary intimated that the objectionable measure had been withdrawn.

By 1923 ships from the Cape were calling regularly at Bristol, and in consequence of the growing importance of this trade, a South African section of the Chamber had been established. In 1931 the Chamber of Commerce, together with the Port of

---

[1] *Bristol Incorporated Chamber of Commerce, Annual Meeting,* 1908, pp. 78-9.

Bristol Authority, invited the chairman of the British Trade Commission to South Africa to address a representative meeting of those interested. In its annual report, the Chamber quoted from a speech delivered by the Chairman of the Docks Committee. From this it appeared that South African grain, meal, sugar, tanning extracts and other products came to Bristol, and an extension of this trade was expected. This hope was well founded.

In 1925, in pursuance of the policy of developing empire tobaccos, the Imperial Tobacco Company despatched a representative to South Africa to examine and report upon tobacco produced there. As a result of this visit, the Company purchased 100,000 pounds of Southern Rhodesian flue-cured tobacco at the end of that year for trial manufacture. At first the packing was done by a local firm, but in 1927–8, the Company erected its own handling and packing plant near Salisbury. Later, this plant was developed, and after that large quantities of Southern Rhodesian tobacco were sent to England, a substantial proportion of which came to Bristol.

Bristol has had a long, though spasmodic, connection with Mauritius and East Africa. For years the import of sugar from the old French colony was bitterly opposed by the city whose fortunes were so closely entwined with those of the West Indies. But when it became clear that the Government was inclined to encourage sugar production in the East, Bristol traders began to take a direct share in the new commerce. In 1840 1 ship cleared for the sugar island in the Indian Ocean, and 4 came up the Avon with cargoes from that place. In 1847, although no ships cleared for Mauritius, 8 returned from thence, and 1 foreign and 9 British ships in 1860. But by that time, the export trade from Bristol had entirely disappeared. Ten years later, there were no outward shipments, but 12 British and 3 foreign vessels brought cargoes to the Avon from Mauritius. Then, in the 'seventies, this promising trade died out entirely, and half a century elapsed before Bristol had any appreciable traffic with the island. At last, her long established sugar refining industry collapsed and disappeared, and trade with Mauritius was confined to a very occasional cargo of sugar.

For many years of the nineteenth century, Bristol had no commerce with the East Coast of Africa. The Imperial Tobacco Company, however, began to concern itself with Nyasaland tobacco in 1906. In that year it took a small trial shipment from the British Central Africa Company. This had been grown from American seed supplied by the Company, one of whose experts had supervised its planting, growth and preparation for shipment. Later, as this first consignment was considered to be satisfactory, a handling plant was built at Limbe, near Blantyre. In 1907 the Nyasaland shipment amounted to 7 tons, and in 1937 it had grown to the neighbourhood of 7,600 tons, of which the port of Bristol received its share. Trade in other commodities with East Africa began after the Great War and has shown signs of healthy development. The principal commodities which were shipped to Bristol were cotton-seed, sugar, sisal, hemp and tobacco. The trade was well established and still greater expansion was experienced.

In an earlier chapter it has been seen that Bristol and the other Outports, including Liverpool, together with many London merchants, resented the monopoly enjoyed by the East India Company. The attempt made in the eighteenth century to break through into the charmed circle of Indian trade was a failure. But with the successive re-issues of the Company's charter from 1773 onwards, the enemies of that body grew in strength. In 1793 its champions were compelled to fight a hard parliamentary battle before sanction was given, and when the time approached for the next consideration of the charter, 1813, the forces of opposition once more gathered for the fray. On 28th March, 1812, a meeting was held at the Commercial Rooms in Bristol, at which it was resolved to seek the co-operation of the Merchant Venturers in petitioning both Houses of Parliament against the exclusive commercial privileges of the East India Company. This meeting also requested the financial aid of the Merchant Venturers towards the costs of any parliamentary action which might ensue. The Merchant Venturers considered these recommendations at a full meeting of the Hall held on 14th April, and the terms of a petition to be presented to Parliament were settled. In this, the Society prayed that the trade with the East Indies should be thrown open to all His Majesty's subjects, and it also voted £100 to be added to the sum then being raised to conduct this agitation in and out of Parliament. In June the Corporation voted £200 for the same purpose, and on 4th February, 1813, it was resolved by the Merchant Venturers to send another petition up to both Houses of Parliament similar in tone to that of the previous year. Bristol was strongly opposed to the renewal of the Company's charter on the old terms. On this occasion, as on other previous ones, the Duke of Beaufort was requested to present the petition in the House of Lords, while the city's representatives were to lay it before the Commons.

This agitation, which had the general support of the country, was completely successful, and at long last the glittering East India trade was thrown open to all subjects. Bristol at once availed herself of the new opportunity, and in April, 1814, two vessels set sail for India, but she did not profit to any considerable extent by the new commerce. In anticipation of the development of a rich trade in tea after 1813, a warehouse was erected in Prince Street, but the hoped-for commerce never came to the Avon. In 1818 a ship dropped anchor in Cumberland Basin, bringing the first cargo of East Indian goods ever sent direct to Bristol. At the time it was hoped that this marked the beginning of a new phase in the city's commercial history, so the ship was welcomed by five thousand spectators, while the bells rang with joy. The rejoicings, however, were premature, and the innumerable great ships laden with Indian and Chinese products which were expected to follow in her wake never appeared. Indeed, throughout the latter part of the nineteenth century, in so far as Bristol used East Indian products, she received them from other more fortunate and more energetic British ports.

In the 'twenties there was much wrangling in the Press about the respective claims of the East and West Indies, and it has been seen how to West Indians the expansion of the East Indian trade became a nightmare. By every possible means they opposed any concessions to their rivals which might enable them to expand their sugar estates. Even in those years, however, there was a group of merchants in Bristol, whose number and influence steadily grew, which championed the East Indies. They did this partly because the sugars from the East were not produced by slave labour and partly because in Bristol, as throughout the country, there was a growing irritation against the privileges and greed of the West Indians. Further, England was beginning to awaken to the potentialities of India as a market for British products by comparison with which the old sugar plantations were poor and contemptible. Several letters appeared on the subject in the Press during 1826, and in the following year, a petition was sent up to Parliament which was supported by a number of merchants and others. This demanded that the differential duties then imposed on the East India commerce should be removed, and it went on to state that one of the most obvious methods of relieving contemporary economic distress was the extension of the Indian market for British products. The petitioners were confident that in the British dominions in the East were to be found unlimited possibilities for trade expansion. Between 1815 and 1825 this trade, in spite of unfair discriminatory legislation, had almost doubled. If these restrictions were removed, they believed that there would be an enormous expansion of Indian trade which would take off great quantities of British products. The well-worn mercantilist argument that a distant and extensive commerce, such as that with India, was vital to the shipping interest of the country, was also elaborated at length. In view of all of this, the petitioners felt sure that when Parliament reflected upon the obvious advantages which would arise from this reform, they would immediately recognize its expediency, and remove all harmful restrictions on the commerce of Great Britain with the most important of her dependencies.

In response to such pressure from all parts of the country, the duties on East Indian products were substantially reduced. According to the report of the Chamber of Commerce for 1828, the reason why Bristol had not, up to that time, participated in this commerce as much as was expected, was that owing to the high duties imposed on the products of that country, there had not been any considerable demand for them in the city or the area which it served. Unless there was a greater demand for Indian cotton, shippers to Bristol would labour under a disadvantage, as that commodity was invariably one of the chief parts of a cargo from India. Indeed, the Chamber believed that until manufactured cotton goods formed part of Bristol's exports, no great expansion of Indian commerce was to be expected. The decreases in the Indian duties were not sufficient to meet the wishes of the reformers, and, therefore, in 1829, a general meeting of citizens was held which passed several resolutions in favour of further reductions. This meeting also appointed delegates to a representative meeting in London which was convened to organize an agitation for more substantial concessions.

In February, 1830, a writer in *Felix Farley* deplored the lack of interest evinced by his fellow citizens in the effort to curtail the monopoly of the East India Company. According to this writer, Bristol was the centre and store house, as well as the market, for more than one hundred smaller towns, in which about half the British manufactures exported to India were produced. Its citizens, therefore, should be more concerned in the opening up of the Indian and China trades than any city in the kingdom. The writer exhorted the Bristolians not to be deluded into abstention from sending a petition to Parliament by misleading assurances given in both Houses.

"The absence of the expected Deputation from Bristol will not alone be a defect; it will operate favourably for the enemy," [1]

as it would be taken as a proof that Bristol did not wish this trade to be thrown open. Whether the East India group in Parliament still stood at 26 votes in the House of Commons, at which figure it was estimated to stand in 1812, or more, undoubtedly it was still of great consequence to the ministry. Bristol, therefore, should not only send an energetic delegation to London to work against the Company, it should also despatch a strongly worded petition to Parliament on this subject. It was not, the

[1] *Felix Farley's Bristol Journal*, 27th February, 1830.

writer declared, the business of British merchants to make
sovereigns nor to decide on the best method of governing India,
but on every ground they had a right to demand that the
directors of the Company should be debarred from trade. This
letter winds up with the somewhat trite aphorism,

"Sovereigns can never be good merchants—Merchants
can never be good Sovereigns." [1]

Again, in this same year, the Merchant Venturers petitioned
the Lords and Commons for the abolition of all restrictions
imposed upon British subjects in the Indian and China trades.
By the 1833 charter, all the rights which the merchants of Bristol
had asked for were granted, but again the result did not justify
the high expectations of the preceding years. In 1835 a cargo
of tea was brought direct from Canton to the Avon, but the
attempt to establish a Bristol Tea Company was a failure, and
many years were to elapse before the city took any substantial
interest in the expansion of British trade in the Far East. In
1840 only one ship sailed for Calcutta and one for Canton,
while 7 reached the Avon from the former place and one from
the latter. In 1847 the city's trade with the East and the
Antipodes had become so slight that the East Indies and Australasia were grouped together. Only 5 vessels, aggregating 1,652
tons, cleared for these places, and 6, of 2,318 tons, arrived at
the port.

When the East India Company's Charter came up again
for reconsideration in 1853, Bristol was one of several towns
that pressed for a more progressive policy in relation to the
agricultural and economic development of India. Greater
encouragement, it was urged, should be given to merchants and
industrialists in England to concern themselves more directly
in the Indian trade. In spite of all the limitations imposed upon
the Company in the last forty years the old hostility to that body
continued, and, in particular, Bristol demanded that the Imperial
Government should be vigilant for the well-being of the Indian
masses. Further, she drew attention to the Company's salt
monopoly. Because of this, the price of that necessary com-

[1] *Felix Farley's Bristol Journal*, 27th February, 1830.

modity had risen from 40s. to £21 per ton, with the result that Indians consumed only about half as much as they should. Indirectly, this harmful monopoly, by pressing upon the Indian peoples, adversely affected British trade, shipping and industry. It was the contention of Bristol that it should be done away with at once, a conclusion which was strengthened by the consideration that it existed in contravention of the Company's charter, which specifically forbade that body to engage in trade. In spite of this activity, however, direct trade between the Avon and the East languished during the 'fifties, and in 1860 was still very slight. One ship cleared for the East from Bristol and none came home. Indeed, when, two years later, a vessel arrived from Calcutta, the local newspapers declared that there had been no direct importation into this port from India for a quarter of a century, and although this statement is not wholly borne out by the records, it gives a clear indication of the insignificance of this branch of commerce at that time.

The American Civil War gave direct stimulus to the Indian trade. Locked in a life and death struggle with the north, the south had little time to think of crops, so the mills of Lancashire stood idle while the factory hands were brought to the verge of starvation. Before the war was over, it was generally acknowledged in England that complete dependence on one foreign source of so important a raw material of British industry was dangerous. Investigations were, therefore, set on foot to explore the possibilities of developing cotton production in the West Indies and increasing that of India, as well as of improving the quality of the Indian product. Though little appears to have resulted from these efforts, the city's interest in India still continued. In 1869 the House of Commons was petitioned by the Chamber of Commerce on the subject of the *Government of India Acts Amendment Bill*, of whose general principles it approved. In particular, the Chamber was gratified by the clause in the Bill which provided for the appointment of the members of the Council of India. It was convinced that the efficiency and value of that body, both to India and the Mother Country, would be increased by the inclusion among its members of representatives of the commercial interests, and they prayed that the House would agree to the insertion of such specific provisions in the Bill as would ensure this. Much good, the Council felt, would result from the appointment of a committee or department of agriculture by the Council of India, whose special care would be the improvement of commercial relations and the promotion of the general interests of both countries.

At the end of the next decade the export trade to India scarcely existed. One ship of 1,572 tons burden cleared for that destination but none returned. Ten years later no ships cleared and 2 of 2,730 tons returned. In 1900 one sailing ship and one steamer, 3,126 combined tonnage, cleared from the Avon for Bengal, and two sailing vessels brought cargoes from that place. In 1910 no ships sailed from Bristol to India, but 19 steamers of 43,998 tons arrived from Bombay, and two steamers of 5,933 tons from Bengal. One steamer cleared for Bombay in 1920, and one for Bengal, while one returned from the former place and one from the latter. By 1921 liners from Rangoon and Colombo were regularly making calls at Avonmouth, and this service was extended to include ships from Penang, Singapore, Hong Kong and other ports of the Far East. In 1935 and 1936 83 ships called at Avonmouth and landed 175,000 tons of feeding stuffs, lead, rice, tea, oilseeds and fruit from India, Burma, Ceylon and the Malay Straits, while in 1937 and 1938 the number of vessels was 35 of 152,500 tons and 51 of 231,500 tons respectively. Though in this period trade with the East expanded it was inward only. Unfortunately, by then the bulk of Bristol exports were sent through other English ports.

The Australian trade was slow in developing, though by 1840, it was well established. Seven ships cleared from Bristol for Sydney and Van Dieman's Land in that year, of 2,150 tons burden, and one small vessel of 278 tons returned from New South Wales and Tasmania. The unwise policy of the Dock Company, however, proved a serious handicap to the development of this commerce. Thus, in 1845, a Bristol firm complained that the dock dues on Australian wool were seven times those charged at Liverpool and London. Later, the concentration of wool imports in London for the auction sales deprived Bristol of any opportunity of further expansion in that direction. It has already been seen that in 1848 the East Indian and Australasian trades had become so insignificant that they were grouped together. By 1860 a small outward trade to Australia had developed, but in that year there were no imports direct to Bristol from any of the antipodean ports, and by 1870 the trade had died out entirely. Ten years later, however, Australia was once more listed, but again no ship cleared for that destination, and only one vessel of 636 tons burden arrived from Australian ports. At the annual meeting of the Chamber of Commerce held on 27th April, 1881, it was stated that Bristol had fallen behind the leading ports of the kingdom in this trade, and that she no longer received consignments from British India or grain from Australia. Though, at the end of the 'eighties, South Australia, Victoria, New South Wales and New Zealand were all listed, the combined tonnage engaged was still very small. After that, announcements of the visits of special Trade Commissioners or politicians from the Australian colonies, who had addressed meetings in Bristol, and discussed ways and means of increasing trade between Bristol and the Antipodes, recur with increasing frequency in the records.

By the beginning of the new century Bristol had emerged from her fifty years of comparative quiescence, and led by her Docks Committee, a more vigorous policy was initiated. Her exports to Australia had previously been shipped chiefly from other ports, but had now become sufficiently large to warrant liners calling at Avonmouth. In 1901 Messrs. Bethell, Gwyn and Company inaugurated a new line of steamers to ply between Bristol and the Antipodes. This marked the beginning of a new era. Large shipments of galvanized iron manufactured in Bristol were shipped from the Avonmouth Docks, which also became the gathering point for the export of tin-plate and iron from South Wales and the manufactures of the Midlands. An Australian section of the Chamber of Commerce was established in that year, and thereafter visits from the Commonwealth's statesmen became fairly common. The records of the Chamber show that this body, in common with many others of its kind in the country, was already much disturbed by the alarming upward tendency of Australian tariffs. When, on investigation, it was found that these would injure certain trades and manufactures, the information collected was sent to the Colonial Office, with the request that it should be forwarded to the Australian Government.

In 1910 the President of the Chamber of Commerce followed the example of his predecessor in making a determined attempt to develop a greater volume of trade between Bristol and Canada, Australia and New Zealand. In furtherance of this, he approached every Chamber of Commerce in these three Dominions with a view to the establishment of close personal contacts between colonial producers and shippers, and suitable brokers, agents or importers in Bristol. At that time it was the opinion of shippers that insufficiency of outward cargo prevented the development of a large trade, while Bristol merchants retorted that, because of the lack of direct and regular steamer communications with Australia and New Zealand, they were prevented from importing into Bristol up to the full measure of their distributing power. In the years before the War Bristol was active in all the Dominions, and according to contemporary reports, her efforts were well received. Outward traffic steadily expanded, and for some time the shipments to Australia and New Zealand were the brightest spots in Bristol's export trade. For a number of years there were sailings almost every week to the former Dominion, and about every three weeks or a month to the latter. However, in the course of time the export trade fell off. The galvanized iron manufacturers opened works in Australia, steamers began to call at South Wales ports for the exports of that area, and, finally, the large iron-works in Bristol were transferred to Newport in 1931. Galvanized iron was the basic cargo, and thus Bristol's direct export trade with the Antipodes came abruptly to an end.

The first decade of the present century saw important developments in the import trade from Australia and New Zealand. Frozen meat began to arrive, and cold storage accommodation was provided by the Port Authority at the quayside. After the Great War further developments took place. Large new cold stores were constructed and equipped, and these provided special facilities for handling meat and dairy produce.

The imports of butter and cheese from New Zealand had been for many years concentrated on London, but under the enlightened policy of the New Zealand Dairy Board, decentralization took place. More of the imports were shipped to provincial ports, and Bristol was able to obtain a good share. There was also a large, although somewhat fluctuating, trade in grain with Australia which brought a number of steamers to the docks, and, occasionally, one of the rapidly disappearing windjammers. The trade with Australia also received a further impetus in 1925, when the National Smelting Company started to import zinc ores for their works at Avonmouth. In 1938 43 steamers brought 177,000 tons of Australian produce to the port, whilst New Zealand was represented by 33 steamers and 32,000 tons of cargo. The growth of the imports had, therefore, to some extent consoled Bristol for her disappointment in the loss of the export trade.

Thus, in the last century Bristol extended her trade to include most of the countries of the Empire. In addition to the places already enumerated, at one time or another the city had carried on commerce with the Channel Isles, Gibraltar, Malta, Cyprus, Egypt, Palestine, Ceylon, Aden, the Malay Straits, Hong Kong and other scattered outports of Empire. She was no longer predominantly concerned with one particular part of the Commonwealth, and although her commerce with foreign countries far exceeded that with British possessions overseas, Empire trade was vital to her prosperity and showed signs of expanding. In 1938 354 ships landed 1,046,000 tons of Empire produce in the docks of Bristol, and in the following year 282 vessels landed 882,000 tons. In 1937 40 per cent of all the ships that arrived in the port were from the overseas Empire, and they carried 30 per cent of the goods landed. With a few exceptions, Bristol had some share, large or small, in almost all the principal products of the Empire.

CHAPTER XIX

LINKS OF EMPIRE

"Ships come right into Bristol town . . . and the men of Bristol think nothing of it! They have been accustomed to this disturbing sight for over nine centuries. It must occur to a man looking at Bristol for the first time that a city which welcomes ships to her bosom in this manner could not help carving a great future on the seas."

H. V. Morton, *In Search of England* (Methuen)—
by permission of the author and the publishers.

THOUGH slow to improve her docks, Bristol was a pioneer in the use of the steamship. It is said that on the suggestion of the great engineer, Brunel, the idea of connecting Bristol with New York was first taken up by Mr. Guppy and a number of his fellow Directors of the Great Western Railway Company. This led to the floating of the Great Western Steamship Company with a capital of a quarter of a million pounds, and to notable developments in the use of steam for ocean transport. The *Great Western*, which was launched in 1837, was one of the first steamers to be constructed specifically for the Atlantic service. She was built for this Company on the design of Brunel at Wapping Wharf, and the *Great Britain*, also built in Bristol, was another pioneer of steam on the north Atlantic.

In 1838 the *Great Western* began to ply regularly between Bristol and New York. Experimental trials were made in the carriage of mails, and these were so successful that by 1839, the Government was satisfied of the superiority of the steamer to the sailing vessel for this purpose. At once, therefore, a keen competition arose between a number of competing ports for the Government contract. At this time strong hopes were entertained that Bristol would be chosen as one of the favoured ports from which the royal mails would be carried by steam. She held the contract for a short time, and in 1841 she competed for the West Indian service as well. In that year a Royal Commission was appointed to investigate and report on this subject. Mr. Philip Miles, one of Bristol's representatives in Parliament, was a member of this committee, and vigorously advocated the claims of his constituents. Evidence was given in favour of Bristol, Dartmouth, Devonport, Falmouth, Plymouth, Portsmouth and Southampton. The commander of the *Great Western* and the Bristol Harbour Master appeared on behalf of Bristol. The Bristol Channel, they urged, was safe for navigation at all seasons of the year, ample anchorage was always available at Kingroad, and though Bristol was not the nearest port to Barbados, it afforded greater facilities for the quick transmission of mails to London, the Midlands and the North than her competitors. The committee, however, was not impressed, and so from the 'forties, Bristol ceased to be a mail port for almost sixty years.

In 1864 a memorial was sent up to the Postmaster-General, which was later supported by a deputation from Bristol. This attempted to impress him by arguments in favour of his appointment of that city as a port of departure for West Indian mails. Though the Master of the Merchant Venturers was optimistic about the result of these efforts, nothing transpired, and the Government remained unconvinced. Twenty years later, the subject again came up, and on this occasion the Chamber of Commerce took a lead. The Government asked for tenders for the carriage of mails, and intimated that the contractors would be allowed to name their own port, so the claims of Bristol were once more urged. It had been stated by the Government on a previous occasion that if Bristol would provide suitable accommodation, she would not be omitted next time. The Chamber, however, communicated with several of the leading shipping lines, but it was discovered that this effort was too late, and so her claims were passed over once more.

As a result of the personal influence of Mr. Joseph Chamberlain, then Secretary of State for the Colonies, Bristol, in 1901, was granted the coveted privilege of being made the West Indian mail port. In that year direct steamship communications with the West Indies, subsidized by the Government, were opened up, and ships especially built for this trade, carrying passengers, mails and freight, were commissioned to the service. The first ship, R.M.S. *Port Morant*, 1,322 tons net register, sailed from Avonmouth on 16th February, 1901. The city made great preparations for the resuscitation of her old West Indian connection, but by that time sugar had yielded in pride of place to other West Indian products, mainly bananas. In 1911 the Government subsidy came to an end, and Messrs. Elder Dempster and Company, who had run a line of steamers between Avonmouth and Jamaica, gave up this business. The

carriage of mails and passengers, however, was taken over by
Messrs. Elders and Fyffes who, since 1906, had been carrying
bananas to Avonmouth.

It was not until the 'eighties that regular direct steam communication was established between the Avon and the St.
Lawrence. In a previous chapter it has been seen that prior to
this a close connection was maintained by sailing ships. Before
1885, also, there was an irregular steam service, but at last, in
response to the repeated demands of various groups of merchants, a regular fortnightly service was arranged in that year.
In the early 'nineties the records of the Chamber of Commerce
testify to the growing interest of Bristol in the promotion of
more and faster communication with the Dominion of Canada.
In 1898, after almost sixty years of intermittent complaint,
expostulation and exhortation from Bristol, arrangements were
made for the carriage of private ship mails from Avonmouth to
Montreal by a fortnightly steamer service. In the following year
the Canadian Government concluded an agreement with the
Elder Dempster Line, by which their ships were to carry mails
from Avonmouth to Canada. This news was greeted with great
jubilation in Bristol, whose claims were at last recognized, but
the service was very soon discontinued. In 1902 the Council of
the Chamber pressed on Lord Strathcona the claims of Bristol
to be considered by the Canadian Government as a port of
departure for fast mail steamers between the Mother Country
and the Dominion. Before 1939, the tendency on the part of
big shipping lines to concentrate their activities on one or two
great ports had become all too common. Frequently this was
done at serious inconvenience to the travelling public, shippers
and consumers alike. Indeed, it is doubtful if in the national
interest this concentration was desirable, and except for the
largest ships, there was no reason why the port of Bristol should
not be served by a fast line of steamers between England and
Canada. By her geographical position she was well placed to
serve the South Midlands and a great part of the south of
England, and by train she was almost as close to London as
Southampton.

It has already been seen that in the 'fifties Bristol became deeply concerned in the Australian colonies. Here again, she was constantly agitating for the provision of better and more regular shipping services with those distant parts of the Empire. Together with London, she brought this subject before the Government, and the Chamber of Commerce memorialized the Postmaster-General on the desirability of sending Australian mails by the quick route over the Suez peninsula. It was estimated that this would enable letters to be landed in England in sixty days from Melbourne, as against seventy-six, which was the usual time by other routes. A great public meeting was held at Merchants' Hall, attended by representatives of nearly all the leading firms in the city, at which resolutions on this subject were passed. But though pressure came from every considerable city in the kingdom, the Government was slow to act. In 1906, for the first time, direct steamship communication was established between Bristol and New Zealand, though here again this service was discontinued shortly afterwards. The Chamber of Commerce, supported by the provision merchants, in 1923 pressed upon the Ministry of Food the need for more regular and suitable shipping connections between the two Australasian Dominions and Avonmouth. Fourteen years later vessels of several lines berthed at Bristol, and were regularly engaged in carrying Australian and New Zealand products to England.

As soon as steamship development had definitely passed the experimental stage, Bristol supported various schemes for faster communications with India. In 1839 and 1840 there was much discussion about the proposal to use steamers on the Mediterranean route. Ships were to go from England to Suez, where cargoes would be carried by camels across the Isthmus, and placed aboard steamers on the Red Sea for carriage to India. Indeed, before the advent of steam the possibilities of this route had long been appreciated and, to some extent, developed. One of the arguments in favour of this way to India was that it would serve to develop new markets for British goods, particularly in the Red Sea region. In 1840 the Merchant Venturers considered a letter which they had received from the secretary of the Great Western Railway Company, together with a resolution passed by that body. This expressed the Company's wish that the Society of Merchant Venturers, the Chamber of Commerce and the Dock Company should combine with it in an attempt to promote steam intercourse with India via the Red Sea, and it was an essential part of this scheme that the steamers should sail from Bristol. After discussion, the Society appointed the Master and two members as representatives on the committee which was to consider this subject in detail.

As far as Bristol was concerned this proposal never materialized, and in 1840 the Chamber of Commerce was requested by the promoters of all their undertakings to support their separate prospectuses. One of these was a scheme similar to that suggested three years earlier, though on this occasion the undertaking was to be assisted by annual grants from the Government and from the East India Company. The alternative scheme was for the establishment of a line of large size steamers which would carry mails to India via the Cape of Good Hope. As the city was apparently to have no direct share in the advantages accruing from either of these undertakings, the Chamber felt that the investors of Bristol were at that time sufficiently occupied in the support they were giving to various local improvement schemes, and so it was decided to take no action. Four years later the same subject came up again. This time the Chamber of Commerce pressed upon the East India Company the need for better and quicker communications with India overland. By that time a number of competing proposals were put forward by rival organizations. While the Chamber specifically refrained from supporting any of these, it expressed the hope that the Company would take the steps necessary to ensure the best means of expediting communications between India and England.

None of these proved acceptable, however, and though the overland route via Suez entailed a substantial saving in time, it was awkward, expensive, and never satisfactory to the mercantile community. Both the Imperial and the Indian Governments were concerned from time to time with this problem of developing a better system of communications. Finally, at a meeting presided over by the Master of the Merchant Venturers, which was held in the Commercial Rooms in June, 1857, resolutions were passed in favour of the proposals laid before it by Monsieur Lesseps for the construction of the Suez canal. Two resolutions were passed, in the first of which the meeting expressed its approval of Lesseps's proposals for the construction of a ship canal across the Isthmus of Suez, being of the opinion that it was of the greatest importance to the commerce of the whole world, and that it would afford facilities which no railway could provide. In the second resolution the meeting declared its approval of a memorial to be sent up to the Bristol representatives in the House of Commons for immediate presentation to the Government. They requested that the latter would make every exertion to overcome all opposition to the scheme which might stand in the way of its immediate execution. Lord Palmerston, however, was much opposed to the idea, and refused, therefore, to support it, for reasons apparently clear to him, but obscure to-day, if, indeed, they ever existed. He believed that the project was not in English interests, so for the time being, as far as Great Britain was concerned, no action was taken.

It was possibly because of this shortsightedness that when the canal was completed, Great Britain had so small a share in it. This error was corrected a few years later, however, by the far-seeing Beaconsfield. Already the absurdity of Palmerston's opposition was recognized by all parties, for the canal proved to be of immediate and enormous importance to the trade of the country, and by the middle of the 'seventies, the Government was alive to its supreme imperial significance. A great amount of British shipping passed through it annually, and by the 'eighties some people were beginning to think that more facilities were required. An agitation arose for the construction of a new canal in which, from the beginning, Great Britain should have the control. Three resolutions on this subject were laid before the annual meeting of the Association of Chambers of Commerce at Derby in 1883. One of these, which was from Bristol, declared that on account of Great Britain's enormous commitments in the East, it was desirable that a second canal should be provided between the Mediterranean and the Red Sea. This should be undertaken with the full agreement and permission of the Khedive, and British interests should be adequately represented. Though this resolution was passed, no further action was taken either by the Chambers of Commerce or by the Government.

At various times during the century, the Bristol Chamber of Commerce interested itself in the establishment of better connections with the East coast of Africa. This it did, not only in the interest of British trade in that region, but also because it was hoped that such developments would assist in the long and arduous campaign against the slave trade, which still flourished along the African coast from Zanzibar to the Red Sea. Direct communications with the Cape frequently gave rise to dissatisfaction during the nineteenth century, but at length, at the close of the Boer War, efforts were made to draw the attention of Joseph Chamberlain to the unsatisfactory state of the export trade to the Cape. He was informed that improved facilities had recently been provided for great commercial development by the establishment of steamship connections between Avonmouth and South Africa, and his attention was also drawn to the unwise policy which, according to the Bristol Chamber of Commerce, was then pursued by the South African Conference. According to the letter which accompanied this petition, the Avonmouth line was compelled to compete with Conference lines, which, although subsidized by the British Government, were pursuing a policy calculated to drive British freight to foreign flags. Owing to their privileged position, the Conference lines were able to penalize any trader who used non-member ships, and if their competition were allowed, it would soon attract trade. This was now impossible because of the rebate system of the Conference lines, a group which had attempted to extinguish all competition by threatening traders, both in England and in South Africa, with dire results if they patronized competitors, and ". . . we respectfully ask you to give this question your careful consideration."

Though Chamberlain replied that he had the subject under consideration, another letter was sent to him in the following year, which proved that up to that time his consideration did not result in action. In this the writers deplored the weak attitude of the Government to the Conference lines. In their view it amounted to an encouragement of them in their wrong-doing. They hinted that it seemed as if the Government itself feared some sort of reprisals, and the Chamber of Commerce begged that this misapprehension should be removed. In reply, Chamberlain announced that tenders would shortly be invited for Government freight to South Africa. Two years later, however, the position was still unsatisfactory, as was shown by a resolution passed by the Association of British Chambers of Commerce. On the initiation of Bristol, that body declared its belief that the rates charged by shipping lines to South Africa and New Zealand were so high as to cause diversion of trade to the Continent and America, where much more reasonable charges were obtainable. A committee was, therefore, appointed to interview the authorities responsible for the direction of the various lines concerned, and to induce them, if possible, in the interest of British trade, to reduce their freight rates, or the committee was to take such necessary steps for the achievement of that end as it might think desirable. In their final form, the resolutions which were passed included the word Australia, as well as South Africa and New Zealand. A resolution similar to this was passed at about the same time by the Bristol Boot Manufacturers' Society.

In the nineteenth century Bristol continued to manifest some interest in the internal affairs of the overseas Empire. Reference has already been made to her deep concern for the well-being of the West Indies. She also bestirred herself from time to time to promote and develop better internal communications in various parts of the Empire. Thus, in the early 'sixties her support was given to the British North American provinces in their agitation for the construction of a railway which was to connect Halifax, Nova Scotia, with Quebec. In 1861 a deputation from the colonies explained the scheme to the Chamber of Commerce, and on the strength of what it heard, that body petitioned the Government to support the undertaking. Such a railway, the memorial stated, would save thirty-six hours in the delivery of Canadian mails. Moreover, these would be carried through British territory and not, as at present, through the

United States. The railway company merely required a guarantee from the British Government, and the Chamber believed that this would be more than made up to it in the saving effected in the carriage of mails and military stores. This subject acquired a new significance in the following year when strained relations developed between Great Britain and the United States on account of the Trent affair, and certain injudicious speeches made by Gladstone and other public men. The Chamber, therefore, invited a group of distinguished politicians from the North American provinces, who had come to England to press the Halifax-Quebec railway scheme on the Imperial Government, to come to Bristol, and explain their proposals to a public meeting specially convened to hear them. Among others, Joseph Howe, the famous Nova Scotian statesman, and S. S. Tilley, of New Brunswick, both spoke, but there is no record of what either of them said on that occasion. The upshot of this meeting was two further memorials. One of these was sent from the meeting itself and another from the Chamber of Commerce. They were both directed to the city's representatives in the House of Commons, with the request that they should be laid before the Prime Minister, Lord Palmerston. The meeting was convinced of the wisdom of the proposed undertaking.

> "Thus will be accomplished a work which will be more effectual in securing the permanent attachment of the North American Colonies to this Country than probably any other means that could be devised, whilst it will increase incalculably the mutual prosperity of both countries."[1]

It was reported at the annual meeting in 1863, that the scheme was going forward in a satisfactory manner, and in due course this railway was completed.

It has already been seen how deeply interested Bristol became in the commerce and general conditions of India, and this applied to Indian internal transport as well. In 1884 the Chamber of Commerce stated in a resolution which it forwarded to Lord Kimberley, then Secretary of State for India, that further railway developments there would be of immense

---

[1] *Bristol Incorporated Chamber of Commerce, Annual Report,* 1862, p. 9.

economic importance to that country and to Great Britain, and the Government was, therefore, requested, at the earliest possible time, to embark upon a vigorous forward railway policy in India.

For many years of the nineteenth century Bristol had no commerce with the East Coast of Africa, though one solitary ship of 760 tons burden sailed for Aden in 1870. In the early 'nineties the Chamber of Commerce busied itself in supporting the railway policy of the British East Africa Company. It was generally believed that a substantial trade would result from the construction of a line from Mombasa to the north-east shore of Lake Victoria Nyanza. In a memorial to the Foreign Secretary, the Chamber stated that the opening up of trade with the interior of Africa would prove lucrative to Bristol merchants. It would also be an effective preventative of the slave trade which still flourished there. Owing to the fact that all goods carried in or out of the country had to be borne by carriers, the expansion of the existing commerce was impossible. The Minister was assured that the land was well suited to the pro-duction of many valuable tropical crops, but nothing of any importance could be done without improved transport facilities. A railway would not only make commerce possible, it would remove the need for slaves as porters, and would put an end to the infamous practices of slave hunting and kidnapping in the interior.

In 1896 the Chamber congratulated Joseph Chamberlain on the opinion he had recently expressed to a deputation from the Chambers of Commerce of London, Liverpool and Manchester, which had approached him in connection with railway con-struction in West Africa. Bristol had long been closely associated with the West African trade, and the Council expressed its hope that the favourable attitude of the Colonial Secretary would be reflected in due course in the public opinion of the country. It trusted that at long last the people of Great Britain would come to understand that their greatest opportunities for develop-ing the trade and commerce of the Mother Country lay in the direction of assisting her sons beyond the seas.

From time to time, various groups of individual citizens have taken a leading part in the campaign for lower postal rates throughout the Empire. In 1852 this subject was considered by the Merchant Venturers, and a sub-committee was appointed to look into the matter and to report to the Society. In the following year, among many others, Bristol was represented in a deputation to the Prime Minister. The intention was to impress upon the Government the desirability of substantial reductions in colonial postage rates. These should be uniform, threepence for letters of one and a half ounces. But the Prime Minister refused to consider the proposals. He contended that the Postmaster-General already had arranged to establish a six-penny postage rate to the colonies, and that no further demands for still lower rates could be entertained. He pointed out that the various mail companies were already highly subsidized by the Government, and to ask for more concessions was, in his opinion, unreasonable. Nevertheless, in spite of this un-favourable reception, the business community throughout the country, year after year, continued to press for reform until it was granted. In due course still further reductions were de-manded. Thus, for example, in 1896, the Chamber of Com-merce in a memorial sent up to the Postmaster-General, the Duke of Norfolk, stated that for many years past it had enthusias-tically supported the proposal for an Imperial Penny Post. Such a system would not only strengthen the bonds between Great Britain and the overseas Empire, and stimulate trade, but would greatly promote the strength of the Empire. It was with great satisfaction that, in 1905, the Chamber heard that henceforward there was to be a penny post on letters sent from England to Australia, though those going in the opposite direction were to cost twopence. In the post-war period Bristol was foremost in advocating the restoration of the Imperial Penny Post. After repeated efforts in the 'twenties, the Chamber resolved, in 1928, to support the Associated Chambers of Commerce who were about to send a deputation to Westminster. The Bristol Chamber believed that imperial trade would materially benefit from restoration of the penny post, and it felt that representations to that effect should immediately be made to His Majesty's Government.

During the Great War, she became once more a leading imperial port. All of her shipping lines took their full share in the splendid effort of the British Mercantile Marine, and many of their ships were lost. As Avonmouth was a relatively safe port, thousands of troops from the Dominions landed there, and so Bristol welcomed home many of the descendants of those men and women whom she had formerly sent forth. There were so many connected with Bristol in one Canadian battalion that before leaving for the Front, its colours were left in the custody of the Dean and Chapter of Bristol Cathedral. Again, a distinguished member of an ancient Bristol family, Mr. R. E. Bush, who had spent much of his life in Western Australia, maintained a hospital at his own expense for wounded Australian and New Zealand soldiers. Great stores of supplies from the Empire and the world at large poured into Avonmouth, and from February, 1917, to July, 1918, 13,000 Canadian, Australian, New Zealand and South African soldiers went aboard hospital ships at Avonmouth to be returned to their respective countries. Thus, in spite of the march of science and the superior opportunities of other ports, it was shown that in time of need the geographical position and facilities of Bristol still conspired to make her one of the most vital centres of inter-imperial communication.

Just as Bristol in the nineteenth century was a pioneer in the use of steam on the Atlantic crossing, so in the twentieth she has been foremost in the development of aerial transport. The manufacture of aeroplanes began in a small way in 1910 at Filton, on the outskirts of the city. The founder of this industry, Sir George White, a pioneer of electric traction in this country, was also one of the first to grasp the possibilities of aerial transport in the defence and commerce of the future. In 1910 the "Bristol" box-kite type of machines appeared in the army manœuvres at Salisbury Plain, and were the first aeroplanes ever to be used by the British Army for this purpose. By 1914 "Bristol" planes were already known throughout the Empire, and, indeed, throughout the world. In the meantime, "Bristol" flying-schools had been established; and when the War broke out, it has been estimated that 80 per cent. of the British pilots were "Bristol" trained. During the period of hostilities her aeroplanes won new laurels for the ancient city and the eternal gratitude of the troops in the field. In their time, the "Bristol" *Bullet* and the "Bristol" *Fighter* played a notable part in imperial defence and in bringing about final victory.

When peace returned, the industry was so well established that not even the depressing chaos of post-war finance could prevent its further progress. In spite of all difficulties, this period has seen "Bristol" planes and "Bristol" aero-engines going on from triumph to triumph, and the mere enumeration of their names is in itself almost the story of British aerial development up to 1939. The "Bristol" *Racer* was the first cantilever monoplane to be constructed with a retractable under-carriage, monocoque fuselage and cowled-in engine. The "Bristol" *Bulldog* was for long adopted as the standard single-seat fighter of the Royal Air Force. The *Britain First*, which was the first British all-metal cantilever-type monoplane, was in its time the fastest commercial aeroplane in the world. The "Bristol" *Blenheim* was the fastest standard medium bomber, and was selected by the British Air Ministry for quantity manufacture under the Shadow Industry scheme. Each of these machines in turn have thus marked new and important developments which alone is a singular record of achievement for any one firm. But this is not the whole story. The Bristol Aeroplane Company did not confine itself to the construction of superb aeroplanes. It was responsible for the appearance of engines whose achievements were as notable. *Jupiter*, *Pegasus*, *Mercury* revealed new triumphs in engine design. A veritable revolution in aero-engine construction was inaugurated at Filton by the substitution of the simpler and more efficient sleeve-valve for the poppet-valve ,a departure in which Bristol led the whole world. The "Bristol" *Perseus*, *Aquila*, *Hercules* and *Taurus* represented a sustained record of astounding improvement.

With the aeroplane, as with the steamer and the locomotive in an earlier age, the engineer has been confronted with the problem of increasing efficiency while diminishing fuel consumption, so as to provide for greater carrying capacity. Here, again, the achievements of the Bristol products were remarkable. Thus, after 1918, the power output of the engines was increased by more than 150 per cent for the same cylinder size, while, at the same time, the proportion of weight to engine power was reduced by nearly 50 per cent, and this in spite of the fact that with the onward march of invention, new devices were added. Again, in this same period the speed of revolution rose by nearly 100 per cent., while the specific fuel consumption decreased by 25 per cent. Indeed, it may almost be said that, in all these respects, as many improvements were crammed into these twenty years of air transport development as occurred in the long period which separates the *Queen Mary* from the *Great Western*. Perhaps the best way to illustrate this amazing succession of engineering triumphs over air and material is the story of actual achievement. Bristol engines acquired such a reputation for reliability and efficiency that they were widely used in Britain, in the Empire and in foreign countries.

As early as 1926, the *Jupiter* was chosen by Imperial Airways for their new fast passenger and mail liners, and by 1938 a great fleet of "Bristol" engined flying-boats carried mails and passengers to the most distant parts of the Empire, and each week covered more than 113,000 miles. The new transatlantic service, which began in 1939, consisted of four "Bristol" *Perseus* engined flying-boats, of which the first was appropriately named Cabot. Again, from this famous Empire aircraft plant went out the engine which, in 1936–7 won a new world altitude record for heavier-than-air craft, when the *Pegasus* climbed to over 50,000 feet. In 1938 three Royal Air Force planes, using this same remarkable type of engine, set up a new non-stop flight record when they flew in two days from Egypt to Australia, a distance of 7,162 miles. Bristol engines were selected for exclusive manufacture in the Shadow industry, and by the beginning of 1939, they were exported regularly to Canada for use in British-type aeroplanes manufactured there. As decentralization must, in the conditions of the modern world, be an important feature of imperial defence, it seemed certain that this system would later be extended to other Dominions. Thus the

old city on the Avon still took a full share both in the defence
and in the consolidation of the Empire with which her fortunes
have been linked for the past four centuries, and it seemed clear
that her importance in imperial relations would increase in the
future. While the Filton works were thus making their full
contribution to imperial defence and the greater facilities of
increased aerial commerce, the city, by opening her airport,
made ready to take full advantage of the activities which those
contributions had done so much to create. So, in addition to the
many lines of steamers which bound her to the Empire, Bristol
was in as good a position as any other British port to strengthen
those connections still further by the, as yet almost undeveloped,
means of aerial transport.

CHAPTER XX

EMPIRE BUILDERS

"I talk of the Empire movement to Bristol's citizens with the greatest pleasure and also with the greatest humility, because I really feel that I have no right to talk about the Empire to people of a city which has perhaps done more for our Empire than any other."

EARL OF MEATH.

EVER since the American Revolution Bristol has taken her full share in peopling the United States and the Empire. Perhaps some indication of the enormous diffusion of her children is to be seen in the number of places on the map that bear her name. Continental hotels called "Bristol" may commemorate the high standard of creature comforts exacted by a peripatetic and not particularly worthy earl, but isolated settlements and remote capes and islands marked "Bristol" testify to hardy settlers and daring explorers who came from the banks of the Avon.

In the building up of the Second Empire Bristol was concerned with emigration from the beginning. The loss of the old colonies dammed up the stream of convicts which, prior to the outbreak of hostilities, had flowed into the southern plantations. So it came about that, as in other towns in the country, the magistrates of Bristol were perplexed about the problem of providing accommodation for their surplus criminals. The prisons were insufficient and overcrowded. In 1786, therefore, the Mayor and Aldermen resolved to petition the Crown to pardon two women who had been condemned to transportation, but who had lain in Newgate for the past three years. There was, apparently, no thought of transporting convicts to the remaining provinces in the north, and by that time the West Indies had ceased to receive them. In the third quarter of the eighteenth century transportees had almost all been sent to the southern provinces on the mainland, where slavery flourished.

In 1787 a plan which had been proposed several years earlier to transport convicts to some part of that antipodean continent which the great Captain Cook had explored twenty years before, entered practical politics. Among the band of wrong-doers who sailed with Captain Philip to found Australia, Bristol was represented by at least one criminal of outstanding achievement in law breaking. After that, prisoners were regularly sentenced to transportation and dispatched to Botany Bay and other penal settlements at the Antipodes. The ages of these convicts ranged from thirteen to fifty. They were drawn from both sexes, and their most usual offence was stealing in some form or other, though more serious crimes also appear in the records. The usual period of penal servitude to which they were sentenced was seven years, but there were some who were transported for fourteen.

It soon became clear that the new land to which these un-desirables were sent deserved a more worthy destiny than to become a human cess-pit for the unwanted filth of England. Within a few years of Philip's landing in Australia, news reached home of good agricultural land, healthy and pleasant climate, and later, of unsurpassed pastures for sheep. Samples of Australian wool began to arrive in England, and McArthur started to produce wine in New South Wales. In spite of the poor human material which that colony received, and in spite of its unpropitious early history, which culminated in the Gilbertian performances of that versatile mariner, Captain Bligh, New South Wales prospered. Free settlers began to sail for the Antipodes, attracted by what they had heard of its great agri-cultural possibilities and the abundance of free labour. By 1822 Bristol was interested in the new settlement, and a contributor to *Felix Farley* defended New South Wales and expressed his surprise that while there were American societies which directed the flow of emigrants to the United States, none existed to perform a similar service for New South Wales. Emigrants who settled in the former country were lost to the Empire, but those who went to the latter remained British subjects, and in time would supply the Mother Country with many com-modities which at present she was compelled to purchase from foreign countries. The writer stressed the advantages which would result from the establishment in Bristol of a New South Wales Emigration Society. Such a body would provide emi-grants with information and advice. He also recommended group settlement, a system which has been advocated both before his time and since. In their new country, the writer considered, the settlers would naturally draw their imports from the part of England in which they were born, and this would greatly benefit Bristol's trade. Moreover, they would send their products to the Avon, greatly to the profit of Bristol merchants. This Emigration Society could make all necessary arrangements about passages, always a problem which confronts intending emigrants, many of whom have never left their native parishes before. It would have connections with New South Wales, where it would be sufficiently powerful to ensure that each settler would receive a grant of land and all assistance necessary to enable him to establish himself.

Such advocacy, however, did not prove very effective, and for many years Bristol sent to Australia mainly its criminals and some of its superfluous paupers. Organization was frequently defective. Thus, for example, in 1833, after £1,309 had been expended on dispatching a party, the scheme broke down, and the Guardians found themselves with their unwanted poor still on their hands. On this occasion, for some reason, the vessel in which they were to have sailed was prevented from doing so, and so the emigrants, having gone to Liverpool, came back to Bristol. Nevertheless, in 1834, the Guardians unanimously resolved that it would be highly beneficial to the city and to the individuals concerned to encourage the emigration of the pauper population to the British colonies. The Committee was, therefore, instructed to carry these resolutions into effect, but always to bear in mind the comfort and future well-being of the emigrants, and to take care that no one was urged to go against his will. The quality of these settlers, however, was not always above suspicion. An instance of this is to be found in the passengers of the *Vestal*, which, in 1834, sailed for Van Diemen's Land with a number of emigrants. Apparently they were not up to requirements.

"It is incumbent upon me to express my conviction of the impolicy of a measure of expatriation *conducted as this has been*. The immigrants themselves do not appear to be persons qualified from their previous habits, to become a very useful class of colonists, and it is probable that the establishment here of at least some of them will be rather a change of place than of condition." [1]

[1] Madgwick, R. B., *Immigration into Eastern Australia*, 1788–1851, p. 98.

This somewhat discouraging view of Bristol's apostles of Empire was supplemented and reinforced by the chief police magistrate of Hobart, who stated,

"It is evident that some of the females if not actually common prostitutes were of very easy virtue before they embarked." [1]

In the 'fifties Australia became very popular among those who emigrated from Bristol. By that time its agricultural possibilities were more generally known, and its unsurpassed wool had made it famous throughout the world. In addition to this came the news of gold, and Australia seemed to beckon all who were anxious to make their fortunes or find adventure. A brisk emigrant trade grew up which centred on the Avon, and for fifteen or twenty years the papers abound in references to the departure of emigrant ships. Stimulated by this movement, great efforts were repeatedly made to induce the Imperial Government to classify Bristol as a recognized emigrant port, in order that her ships might be able to carry out assisted as well as free colonists, but, as will be seen later, although the reasons produced in favour of this seem unanswerable, no action was taken. It has been seen that by the 'fifties Bristol had earned a bad name in shipping circles and among those, both official and private, who were concerned with overseas development, so she was ignored, while Liverpool and other ports basked in the sunshine of public approval. As, with the exception of the paupers whose emigration was financed by the Guardians, the majority of the emigrants from Bristol were unassisted, they were often in a better position to exact more commodious conditions afloat than were to be found on many of the ordinary emigration ships of the time.

In 1852 the *Mirror and Advertiser* rejoiced that Bristol had now become a first-class emigration port from which emigrants sailed, not only to America, but to the Australian colonies. The *Deborah*, which belonged to Mr. Dobbin, was the second that year to sail direct from the Avon to Port Philip and Sydney. She

---

[1] Madgwick, *op. cit.*, p. 98.

carried out a large cargo and 194 passengers. This vessel was followed a few days later by the *Lady Fitzherbert*, the *Australian* and the *Kyle*, in which many berths were reserved long before the day of sailing.

While some Bristol ships provided suitable entertainment for the jovial and cheerful passengers on the long voyage to Australia, others studied the needs of the sober and serious. Thus, the owners of the *Clara Symes*, after enumerating the qualities of the captain, officers, surgeon, cooks, stewards and one stewardess announced:

> "To render the voyage pleasant and agreeable to all, a party of musical gentlemen, professional and amateur, have arranged to provide a piano and instrumental band, to have glee singing, and to assist in the religious service on Sundays." [1]

When this ship arrived in Australia its passengers were to have the privilege of sleeping aboard for seven nights after arrival, and to be provided with food at reasonable prices. The owners of the *Mary Ann* catered for the needs of the more serious minded type of passenger.

> "This fine ship having been taken by a Company—Members of Christian Churches—will be conducted on Religious and Total Abstinence Principles; Sunday and Day School, Library, will be established on Board." [1]

On the *Elizabeth*, it was declared:

> "It is the Owners' intention to ship materials to enable Passengers to employ themselves at their different callings . . . for which they will be paid accordingly." [1]

When it is remembered that at that time seventy-five days was considered to be a quick passage from Bristol to Melbourne, and when even the best of these ships were small, long journeys by sea, even under the most favourable conditions, tended to be monotonous. In the 'fifties and early 'sixties there are constant

---

[1] *The Bristol Mirror and General Advertiser*, 18th September, 1852.

references to the departure of emigrant ships for Australia and their return to the Avon with cargoes of Australian products. In consequence of this expanding commerce, it was hoped that Bristol would become one of the chief British ports concerned with the reception of wool and other commodities. In 1852 13 emigrant ships sailed for Australia, 1 for Prince Edward Island and 1 for Quebec, while 14 went to New York. This trade developed so rapidly that during three or four months 15 new vessels were purchased to meet the increasing need, which represented the addition of 9,000 tons to the tonnage of the port. It was said that this was a larger increase than had ever previously been made in a similar period. Some of these ships were, for the time, large and well-founded. Of them all, the *William Miles III* was the largest sailing vessel that had ever belonged to, or entered, the port of Bristol. Like so many of her great contemporaries, this vessel was colonial built, and was one of the finest products of the ship-yards of Quebec. Of all the vessels engaged at this time in trade with the Empire by far the most illustrious was the *Charlotte Jane*, built in 1848 in Bristol. She was one of the eight vessels which, between September, 1850, and January, 1851, carried the Canterbury settlers to New Zealand. The *Charlotte Jane* was actually one of the four which sailed from Plymouth on 7th September, of that year. Of these four ships three, on 16th December, reached Port Lyttleton, and the *Charlotte Jane* was the first to drop anchor. Some of these mid-nineteenth century passenger vessels seem diminutive when the enormous distances which they covered are borne in mind, and the lot of the passengers must indeed have been deplorable in that time before refrigeration, electric fans and all the other mechanical devices that make travelling in the tropics to-day not only endurable, but pleasant. Nowadays, the traveller thinks himself an adventurer of a high order when he crosses the ocean in a vessel of under 2,000 tons, but those aboard the schooner *Commodore*, which left Bristol on 17th May, 1853, sailed in a ship of 75 tons.

It was because of this brisk passenger trade to the Antipodes that Bristol felt that she was entitled to be classified as a regular emigrant port, and for many years her citizens endeavoured to convince the Government of the city's claim to enjoy that privilege. In 1849 the Merchant Venturers decided to memorialize the Government on this subject, but as no action resulted, and as the number of emigrants which left the port continued to increase, a determined effort was made in 1854 to induce the Government to bestow on Bristol this coveted status. The Chamber of Commerce began by memorializing the Duke of Newcastle, who was then Colonial Secretary. This document stated that two conditions were essential. The port should be chosen with a view to the greatest possible convenience of the intending emigrants, and, at the same time, it should be so situated as to provide for the most economical expenditure of the funds advanced by the Government to assist them. By her geographical position, Bristol was naturally the port of departure for a large section of the country. She was, in fact, more centrally situated than either Liverpool or London, as she was so easily accessible from South Wales, the Midlands and the West country. Thus, it was cheaper for emigrants from these districts to sail from Bristol than from any other port. If, later, steamers were used in this trade, Bristol, by her close proximity to the South Wales coal districts, would be more suited for the emigration trade than any other port in the kingdom. Within recent years port dues had been substantially reduced. Already, in fact, Bristol had become very popular among intending emigrants because of the quality of her ships. In the year ending 31st December, 1852, 16 ships, representing 8,336 tons, had carried 1,574 passengers to North America. Thirteen ships, of 6,286 tons burden, had carried 2,197 passengers from the port of Bristol to Australia. The memorialists complained that, as a result of the Government's policy, the natural stream of emigration which tended to flow through Bristol had been diverted to other ports, which suffered from the triple disadvantage of being distant, inconvenient and expensive. Moveover, they declared it was well-known that Liverpool received more emigrants than it could handle, and that many of the ships which sailed from the Mersey were disgracefully overcrowded. The records of this period prove conclusively that the passenger ships which sailed from the Mersey, the Thames and elsewhere were frequently over-crowded, often unseaworthy and always insanitary. Probably there were few, if any, which sailed from the port of Bristol which could begin to compare with the floating infernos which, in the later 'forties and early 'fifties, carried starving Irish from the ports of Ireland and from Liverpool.

In proof of the popularity of Bristol, the memorialists drew the attention of the Duke to the evidence, accumulated some years before, by a committee of the Bristol Free Port Association. In response to enquiries directed to the Unions in the adjacent districts, thirty-five of them, which comprised 745 parishes, declared that they were in favour of Bristol as the most suitable port through which to send their emigrants. In view of all this, the memorialists prayed that the Government would appoint the port of Bristol as

"a Depot and Port of Departure for Emigrants under the regulation of the Government." [1]

In reply, the Duke of Newcastle began by pointing out that Australian assisted emigration was carried on by means of funds supplied by various Australian governments, and the sole points to be borne in mind were to furnish all colonies, in the most efficient manner possible, with the labour they required. The Government believed that these objects were being met by a concentration of this outward movement of people at Birkenhead, Plymouth, Southampton and London. The addition of another port would serve no useful purpose. The Duke brushed aside the argument that these ports were inaccessible and costly to reach. He pointed out that there were excellent railway services which rendered them easily accessible to any intending emigrants in the country. Moreover, as these people were already given a free passage to Australia, such complaints were unreasonable and deserved no consideration. This *non possumus* attitude of the Government was considered in Bristol to be both absurd and erroneous. It was not a question of establishing an entirely new emigration port, since there was already, in fact, a brisk outward movement of people from the Avon.

[1] *Bristol as a Depot and Port of Departure for Emigrants*, 1854, p. 24ff.

This subject was again considered in 1854, at a meeting of shipowners-and shipbrokers. Much irritation had been caused by the unfavourable opinions of Bristol expressed by the Colonial Land and Emigration Commissioners. According to them, there were not enough ships there to meet the requirements of the emigrant trade and, moreover, the rates charged at that port were unreasonably high. In reply to this, the meeting agreed to the terms of a statement which the Chamber of Commerce was requested to forward to the Colonial Secretary and Colonial Land and Emigration Commissioners. In this it was pointed out that the port could offer a very extensive choice of shipping and an unlimited supply of suitable cargoes. There were, in fact, no port charges whatever on outward ships, passages or goods. The district which the port served was populated with the very best quality potential emigrants. The Bristol Channel was safe and the port itself convenient. Further, in spite of what had been said to the contrary by those ill-acquainted with the facts, the shipowners expressed their readiness to provide suitably equipped ships at terms which would be found to be as good, if not, indeed, better, than any to be obtained in other ports of the kingdom. The one condition which the statement required was that Bristol would be named by the Government as an emigrant port. This document was signed by 54 Bristol shipowners. Later, at the request of the Chamber of Commerce, Mr. John Edwards gave evidence before a Select Committee of the House of Commons on emigration ships. Forty-five questions were put to him, and in reply, he elaborated at some length the opinions expressed in the last petition. Finally, on 7th June, the chairman of the Chamber received another communication from Downing Street, which merely repeated what had already been said. The Duke of Newcastle did not feel justified, from the knowledge he had, in naming the port of Bristol as a depot for Australian emigration, and so the official door was not only closed, but bolted and barred.

It was now clear that direct approaches to the imperial authorities were useless, but at the same time, the end in view was still considered to be a subject of first rate importance. So the Chamber of Commerce decided to proceed with its campaign, but indirectly. With this purpose in mind, approaches were made to the various Chambers of Commerce in Australia, including those of Adelaide and Melbourne. It was hoped that if their efforts were successful, the Australians themselves might prevail upon the Imperial Government to classify Bristol as an emigration port. Though in the following year, 1855, satisfaction was expressed with the progress so far made, no material consequences issued from these negotiations. In 1857 the Master of the Merchant Venturers reported that he had accompanied a delegation from the Town Council and from the Chamber of Commerce, which had once more elaborated Bristol's opinions at great length, but with no result. The importance attached to participation in this trade is shown by the tenacity with which Bristol continued its campaign with the Government. Indeed, there was every reason for this interest. The counties adjacent to Bristol made substantial contributions to the annual exodus from the Mother Country. The emigrants required outfits, equipment and stores, as well as berths on the vessels which were to carry them to their new homes. In fact, they brought a new and increased trade to the port of their departure, and Bristol saw no reason why these benefits should be tamely surrendered to Liverpool, Plymouth, Southampton or London. Therefore, in 1861, an association was founded whose object was to furnish intending emigrants with reliable information about British colonies throughout the world, and to facilitate their settlement. Two years later, another body was formed in Bristol, as the city had not yet given up all hope of becoming an official emigration centre. Its purpose was to obtain information and to make such arrangements as might be deemed necessary to meet the requirements of the navigation commissioners.

So long as the sailing ship held its own, Bristol, in spite of the doubts of the colonial and imperial authorities, maintained her position without their official support. The triumph of the steamer in the later 'sixties and early 'seventies ended this prosperous commerce, as no one was prepared to suffer the miseries of a long voyage in the sailing ship when he could travel more quickly and in comparative comfort in a steamer. So the stately ships which Tennyson, from the high ground above

Clevedon Church, had watched as they went onward to their haven under the hill, were no more to carry emigrants from that haven to the New World, to the Cape and to the Antipodes. The backward policy of the Dock authorities enabled Bristol's progressive rivals to forge far ahead. When improvements came the city had lost the tide, and so, in the present century those who have supported a forward policy have been compelled to pull against the stream. Dock improvements in abundance came, but it has already been seen that they were begun about thirty years too late.

The outward movement of people to British North America began in earnest after the close of the Napoleonic Wars, though even before that time it seems certain that some people from Bristol settled in those provinces. Throughout the greater part of the nineteenth century, however, it was the United States and not the British colonies that received the lion's share of British migrants to the other side of the Atlantic. At first, indeed, there was a marked inclination to discourage all emigration. This was in accordance with the established policy of the past century and a half, a policy which public opinion had fully endorsed. *Felix Farley*, for example, agreed whole-heartedly with Cobbett's detestation of migration. Even in those depressing years which followed the battle of Waterloo, this journal declared that it was madness for anyone to emigrate, as England was now very happy and free. Gradually, public opinion changed, and terrified by the dreadful spectres conjured up by Malthus and his school, emigration was encouraged. This encouragement was designed more for the relief of England than for any benefit which the emigrants might confer upon the countries in which they settled. So by the 'thirties, a great outward movement of people had begun, and each year ship after ship laden with passengers passed down the Avon to the Channel. William Lyon Mackenzie, the leader of the Rebellion of 1837, describes the arrival of such immigrant vessels in Quebec. He speaks of people from Bristol and Frome, and describes the songs of the Somerset peasants, who, in spite of their dreary voyage and terrible conditions, contrived still to be cheerful and hopeful. Such vessels were expected to make two voyages a year. They sailed in March and again in August, and usually carried the full complement of emigrants, though, as in the Australian trade, it does not seem that these vessels from Bristol were so badly overcrowded as were those of Liverpool. One barque, in 1832, carried out 250 passengers whose passages were provided by various Somerset parishes. At this time, in fact, the bulk of the emigrants were paupers or people verging on that state, and among other things, it was this which aroused the bitter criticism of Gibbon Wakefield and his friends. They did not believe that an Empire built on the unwanted, and possibly inferior, human material, shovelled out of the country in a haphazard and reckless fashion, would endure.

The Bristol Corporation of the Poor, however, was only concerned with its own immediate problem. It had more poor than it knew what to do with, and the wider ramifications of migration in relation to the future of the Empire had no meaning for it. Thus, on 31st July, 1832, the Corporation decided that provided they were willing to emigrate to Canada and were over the age of fourteen, it was prepared to assist a number of boys, not exceeding twelve in all, by a grant of £8 apiece. This sum was to cover the cost of their clothing and to assist in the price of their passages. Apparently the Guardians were satisfied that private charity would make up any deficiencies. The Act of 1834 empowered parishes to assist financially in the emigration of their poor, but for many years Bristol wholly ignored this clause. In 1857, when application was made to the Guardians for a grant of money to assist a particular individual to emigrate, the response was that they were not, at that time,

"prepared to entertain the question of the Emigration of the Poor at the expense of the Poor's Rate." [1]

A dozen years later the Guardians were again approached for help. It was urged that by the timely outlay of a small sum of money, the city would rid herself of people who otherwise would

[1] *Board of Guardians Minute Book*, 17th April, 1857 to 5th February, 1858, fol. 57.

become permanently chargeable on the rates. On this occasion they wrote to the Poor Law Board for information, and finally decided unanimously to make a small grant of £10 to supplement that already raised by private charity to be used for the emigration of a particular family. By then, the Board was beginning to realize the advantages arising from timely grants of assistance, but it was still very disinclined to spend money outside the city of Bristol. It seems that up to that time, the Bristol Guardians had not complied with regulations of the Poor Law Board, but by 1870 it had come into line. Thereafter, with the full approval of the authorities in London, various batches of orphan girls and boys were assisted to emigrate. The Guardians also made advances up to the sum of £8 for each migrant, and provided the girls with complete outfits. In the course of the next two or three years several parties of juveniles were sent oversea and a number of adults were also assisted to emigrate. All of these went to Canada, where, according to the letters received by the Guardians, abundant work at good wages was at once found them.

The emigration of pauper boys and girls, however, had scarcely got well established before it aroused a storm of opposition. The critics declared that this system imposed unnecessary suffering on these young people, since there was more than enough work for them in their native city and its neighbourhood. They were under age, and it could not legally be said that they went of their own free will. Such people should not be allowed to leave the country until they had reached the age of maturity, when they would be in a position legally to declare their wishes. The policy of the Guardians was bitterly attacked in several letters which appeared in the Press. They were denounced as heartless men, whose main interest was not the good of the children, but the relief of the rates. In the view of some correspondents these unhappy children virtually became slaves in Canada. There was no one in those distant provinces to watch over them and to ensure that they received justice from their colonial employers. As these critics found that the majority of the Guardians supported the chairman, who was at that time an enthusiastic champion of emigration, they intensified their activities in the Press, and appealed in particular to the rate-payers, whose money, they contended, was being squandered. In order to arouse the somnolent citizens, these letters drew attention to the fact that in the previous three years the Board had sent oversea 151 children and 16 adults, at an average expenditure of £12 a head. Such a policy was improvident in view of the fact that in the neighbouring villages these children could easily have been found places, and during these same years only 27 had been boarded out. In order to encourage this emigration mania, one correspondent went on to say, the Guardians placed every possible obstacle in the way of those who were anxious to take children out of the workhouse as servants. He ridiculed the chairman, who had recently stated in defence of his policy that emigration was the only possible course, as they were so bad that no one would have them here.

"But he would have us believe that they are models of propriety in Canada. . . . This, I venture to think, is proving rather too much, unless the sea produces moral effects with which I am not acquainted." [1]

According to this same writer, there were many employers in the neighbourhood who were ready to provide work for these children. If the Board of Guardians intended to expend £700 per annum in emigrating children, the families of the hard-working ratepayers, as well as those who were supported out of the rates, had a right to benefit.

A week later "The Father of Nine Children" supported this attack. Pauper children who had been maintained, clothed and fed by the Guardians, when the time came could easily be placed out with benevolent employers in the neighbourhood, who would not work them to death as white slaves.

"We are very busy just now endeavouring to put down black slavery. I look upon this system as bartering away, at all events, the liberties of these children. Let them live in England in the way suggested until they are old enough to emigrate of their own free will, and not be shipped off by the

---

[1] *The Daily Bristol Times and Mirror*, 17th April, 1873.

payment of an outfit and passage money to Canada with the
money of the poor struggling ratepayers, who have more than
they can do at times to meet the demands of the rate collector." [1]

These letters reveal an attitude compounded of genuine humanity, desire for cheap labour and opposition to increasing rates.
The insinuations as to the character of the colonial employers
had little or no justification, and it is undeniable that children
who were sent from a Bristol workhouse to find a new life as
members of families on farms in Nova Scotia, New Brunswick
or Ontario, had much better prospects than if they had been
placed in the employ of English factory owners. Nevertheless,
after prolonged correspondence, ignorance, prejudice and avar-
ice flavoured by humanity won the day, and the emigration of
children was stopped. Ten years later, therefore, when application was made to the Board of Guardians to assist certain paupers
to emigrate, they unanimously declared their opinion that it was
not desirable to promote the exodus of paupers generally.

In the meantime, steam had replaced sail, and emigrants
from Bristol were now compelled to take ship from other ports.
But by the close of the century, with the establishment of regular sailings between Bristol and Montreal, direct outward
movement from the Avon began again. The *Arawa*, the third boat
to carry mails to Canada, also conveyed 400 emigrants. In the
early years of the new century migration to Canada was intensified. During this period the prairie lands were opened up by
improved railway facilities, and there was a rush to these unsurpassed farms. At various times in the past colonial representatives had come to Bristol to advocate migration, and at one
time there was a Queensland office in the city. In the years preceding the War Canadian farmers, in order to encourage people
to migrate, came to Bristol to provide advice and counsel to
intending colonists. Shortly after the establishment of the
Canadian Trade Commissioner's office, the Canadian Pacific
Railway also appointed a representative in the city, and the
Government of Manitoba opened an emigration office. Later,

---

[1] *The Daily Bristol Times and Mirror*, 24th April, 1873.

this was taken over by the Dominion, and for over twenty years thereafter the Canadian Emigration Office was retained.

It is quite impossible to say how many people from Bristol settled in the Empire during the past century. Thousands went direct from the Avon, but an indefinite and probably larger number sailed from other ports. In the aggregate, it is quite clear that the volume of migration was very large. Thus, in its latest phase, Bristol's interest in emigration extends back to the Napoleonic Wars. At some periods it amounted merely to the isolated efforts of a few benevolent individuals, while at others a definite organization of some kind existed. Much of the criticism levelled at the system by the opponents of child migration in the 'seventies and 'eighties, was justified. There was no after-care and no supervision, but with experience, a better technique was developed, with the result that such opposition was deprived of any meaning. Before 1914 such organizations as Doctor Barnardo's Homes, the Salvation Army, the Church Army and the Y.M.C.A. had entered the field. These bodies had wide ramifications throughout the Empire, and by long experience understood the need for adequate supervision. Where these organizations did not exist, the various state and provincial Governments, now fully alive to the proper care of immigrants, developed their own systems. Thus, most of the evils associated with the migration movement in the nineteenth century were removed. The ships were carefully inspected, emigrants were given every attention aboard, and they were met at the port of landing and kept under some form of surveillance until they were able to stand by themselves. Child migration was robbed of its terrors and, indeed, this form had come to be regarded as the most desirable of all. The young migrant is young enough to bear the break with the past with comparative ease, and still sufficiently pliant to establish himself comfortably in his new surroundings.

Bristol was still much concerned with the problem of emigration. This period witnessed the establishment of one of the most successful and promising of all its emigration bodies, the Bristol and West of England Migration Committee. It was founded in 1927, under the patronage of the Lord Mayor.

It devoted its attention mainly to the migration of boys, ranging in age from fourteen to nineteen, the type of immigrant for whom there was at that time a steady demand both in Canada and Australia. As most of these young persons were to come from great urban areas, the Committee wisely decided to give them some preliminary training in agriculture before they proceeded overseas. This would serve the dual purpose of weeding out those for whom the open-air life was unsuited, and it would give the others practice in farm work, and some rudimentary ideas about agriculture. In 1928 the Corporation of Bristol granted a free site on its Ham Green Farm Estate, about five miles from the city, and there the Committee built a hostel to accommodate forty boys. The Overseas Settlement Department co-operated fully in the scheme, and the Hostel was formally opened in 1929 by H.R.H. Prince Arthur of Connaught, in the presence of Dominion Office and other Government representatives.

Abundance of practical instruction was available on the municipal and neighbouring farms, and the boys were given courses of nine to twelve weeks' duration. When working to its full capacity, the new hostel could accomodate 160 to 200 boys per annum. By the end of 1929, 74 boys had been trained, of whom 50 went overseas that year and 20 early in 1930. Eleven of these went to Queensland and the others to Ontario. They were fed, clothed, housed and trained free of charge, and were provided with an outfit when they left the hostel and given a free passage. In order to make sure that the old criticism of dumping unhealthy and unwanted paupers in the colonies should not arise, these migrants, before their departure, were required to be approved provisionally by the representative of the Dominion to which they were going, and passed as fit by the medical officer. With the slump of the early 'thirties all emigration ceased, and, indeed, an inward movement of people to the Mother Country began. This very promising scheme, therefore, was held up almost as soon as it was well established, but with the improved conditions of the later 'thirties, especially in Australia, it was hoped that work at Ham Green would be resumed. Thus, although Bristol sent few of her products to the Empire overseas, she was in the forefront of the migration movement, and was probably better equipped than any city in the kingdom to send the Dominions the kind of people they required.

This chapter has been concerned with the mass of people who have migrated, and not with the individuals who have won distinction, yet not a few of Bristol's sons have distinguished themselves in the lands of their adoption. Such, for example, is Ernest Giles, the explorer of Western Australia, and there have been many such as he. Lord Durham, the Lawrences, Sir Bartle Frere, Lord Roberts and many others, were all connected with the city at some time, by birth, education or residence. Tablets and monuments in the churches of the city and its vicinity bear witness to the distinguished succession of admirals, generals, governors and administrators whom the home of the Thornes and Aldworths has sent forth to serve the Empire. To-day, in her schools and in her University, she is training men and women who later as doctors, missionaries, merchants, soldiers, sailors, civil servants and teachers will still further the fame of the city and maintain her imperial tradition. She was still the gateway of that Empire in the foundations of which her sons played so conspicuous and honourable a part. Though that forest of masts in the midst of the city streets, which for centuries amazed all visitors, and which kindled a momentary flicker of enthusiasm even in the cold heart of Pope, has now vanished, ships may still be seen lying at anchor at the very heart of the city, for now, as always, Bristol is a city of ships. From her seven hills she looks down the river, past the line of vessels moving slowly up the Avon Gorge to the City Docks, past the great ships lying at anchor at Avonmouth, past the famous anchorages of Hungroad and Kingroad, and out to sea, to welcome the shipping of the world and, most of all, the shipping of the Empire. Her old men, when they remember all these things, dream dreams of their city's great past, but her young men see visions of a yet more ample future.

BIBLIOGRAPHY OF WORKS CONSULTED

I. SOURCES.

(a) Unpublished.

Bristol Archives Office:
Apprentice Books.
Board of Guardians' Minute Books.
Gaol Deliveries, 1741–71.
William Penn, Indenture, 27th September, between William Penn and Arnold
Browne, &c.
—— Lease for a Yeare, 6th October, 1708.
—— Mr. Thomas Cade, Declaration of Trust as within, 1713.
Servants to Foreign Plantations, 1654–63, 1664–86.

Ship Insurances.

Bristol Library: All books of South Africa.
Jefferies Collection of MSS.

British Museum:
Add. MSS. 9764, fol. 116.
—— 29680.
—— 34956, fol. 334.
The Case of the *Merchants*, and *Others*, of the *City of* Bristol, Trading to the
British Colonies in America (1731?).
The Humble Petition of the Merchants and others of the Cities of London
and Bristoll. 1650.

Central Reference Library, Bristol:
Braikenbridge Collection, MSS.
Donne Senr., Map of City of Bristol, 1831.
Jefferies Collection of MSS,. newspaper and magazine extracts, public notices,
etc., relating to the History of Bristol.

House of Lords:
30th May, 1739. Petition of the Merchants and Traders of Bristol against the
Sugar Colonies Bill.
5th March, 1766. Petition of the Merchant Venturers with regard to 6 Geo. III
to repeal the Sugar Act.

Public Record Office:
C.O. 101: 2 (Grenada), B.20.
C.O. 102: 1 (Grenada).
C.O. 194: 4.
C.O. 388: 45.
C.O. 388: 48.
H. C. A., Letters of Marque, Bonds, &c.
T.47: 11.

Racedown, Dorset:
Pinney Family Letter-books.
Pinney Papers: Boxes.
The Private Account Book of Nathaniel Pinney.
The Private Letter and Account Book of Nathaniel Pinney.

437

Society of Friends, Bristol:
  Minutes of the Men's Meeting.

Society of Merchant Venturers, Bristol:
  Book of Petitions.
  Book of Trade.
  Index to Book of Proceedings.
  Letters, 1754– .
  Papers Read at the Hall.
  Book of Proceedings.
  West India New Society, 1782, 1822–38.

17th-century Commonplace Book in the Williamscote Library (Dr. T. Loveday's).
Society for the Propagation of the Gospel:
  Annual Reports.
  Papers.

Trinity House:
  Transactions, 1609–25.

University of Bristol Library:
  MS. Collection No. 41.
  Pinney Family Business Ledgers, 1764–1816.
  Pinney Family Business Letter-books, 1761–1831.

(b) Published

Butcher, E. E., Bristol Corporation of the Poor, Select Records, 1696–1832. Printed
    for the Bristol Record Society. Bristol, J. W. Arrowsmith Ltd., 1935.
Calendar of State Papers, Colonial (America and West Indies).
Calendar of State Papers, Domestic.
Carus-Wilson, E. M. (selected and ed. by), The Overseas Trade of Bristol in the
    Later Middle Ages. Printed for the Bristol Record Society. Bristol, J. W.
    Arrowsmith Ltd., 1937.
Colonial Papers, 1759–74. Committee of Correspondence. (Virginia State Library.)
Donnan, E., Documents Illustrative of the History of the Slave Trade to America.
    4 vols. Washington, The Carnegie Institution of Washington, 1930 ff.
Guttridge, G. H., The American Correspondence of a Bristol Merchant, 1766–76,
    University of California Publications, 22 Berkeley, California, University of
    California Press, 1934.
Journal of the Commissioners for Trade and the Plantations preserved in the Public
    Record Office, 1704–41. 7 vols. London, H.M.S.O., 1920 ff.
Kingsbury, S. M. (ed. by), The Records of the Virginia Company of London.
    4 vols. Washinton, Government Printing office, 1906 ff.
Hansard's Parliamentary Debates, 1811 ff. London.
Nott, H. E. (ed. by), The Deposition Books of Bristol, vol. I, 1643–7. With an
    Introduction by Josiah 'Green, Town Clerk. Printed for the Bristol Record
    Society, Bristol, J. W. Arrowsmith, Ltd., 1935.
Report and Proceedings of the Bristol Chamber of Commerce, at the Annual Meeting
    of the Members, 1822 ff.
Report of the Lords of the Committee of Council appointed for the Consideration of
    all Matters relating to Trade and Foreign Plantations . . . 1789.
Stock, L. F. (ed. by), Proceedings and Debates of the British Parliament respecting
    North America. 4 vols. Washington, D.C., The Carnegie Institution of
    Washington, 1924–37.

(c) Books and Pamphlets

Barlow, R., A Brief Summe of Geographie. Edited with an Introduction and Notes
    by E. G. R. Taylor. London, for the Hakluyt Society, 1932.
[Besse, J.], An Abstract of the Sufferings of the People call'd Quakers. 3 vols.
    London, J. Sowle, 1733–8.
Best, T., The Voyage of Thomas Best to the East Indies, 1612–4. Edited by Sir
    William Foster. London, printed for the Hakluyt Society, 1934.

Bristol as a Depot and Port of Departure for Emigrants. Bristol, J. Taylor, 1854.
Bristol Auxiliary Anti-Slavery Society. Report of Proceedings from the Formation of the Institution to the 31st December, 1830. Bristol, T. D. Clark, [1831?].
Bristol Imports and Exports; 1773–80 *and* 1801–21, 16 vols.
Camden, W., *Britain, or a Chorographicall Description of the Most flourishing Kingdomes, England, Scotland, and Ireland.* Translated Newly into the English by Philemon Holland. London, Inprensis Georgii Bishop & Joannis Norton, 1610.
Camden, W., *Britannia.* Translated from the edition published by the author in MDCVII. Enlarged by the latest discoveries. By R. Gough. 2nd ed. 4 vols. London, J. Nichols & Son, 1806.
Clarkson, T., *History of the Rise, Progress, and Accomplishment of the Abolition of the African Slave Trade by the British Parliament.* London, John Parker, 1839.
Cobbett, W., *Rural Rides during the Years* 1821 *to* 1832.
Collinson, J., *The History and Antiquities of the County of Somerset,* 3 vols. Bath, R. Cruttwell, 1791.
Cox, T., and Hall, A., *Magna Britannia et Hibernia, a new Survey of Great Britain,* 1720–31. 6 vols.
Dallaway, J., *Antiquities of Bristow in the Middle Centuries, including the Topography by William Wycestre and the Life of William Canynges.* Bristol, Mirror Office, 1834.
Drake, F., *The World Encompassed by Sir Francis Drake, Being his next voyage to that to Nombre de Dios.* With Appendices illustrative of the same voyage and Introduction by W. S. W. Vaux. London, Printed for the Hakluyt Society, 1854.
Foxe, L., and James, T., *The Voyages of Captain Luke Foxe of Hull, and Captain Thomas James of Bristol in search of a North-West Passage in* 1631–2. Ed. by Miller Christy. 2 vols. London, Printed for the Hakluyt Society, 1893.
Frobisher, M., *The Three Voyages of Martin Frobisher, in search of a Passage to Cathaia and India by the North-West,* A.D. 1576–8. London, Printed for the Hakluyt Society, 1867.
Fuller, T., *The History of the Worthies of England,* 1662. 3 vols. With Notes and Indexes by R. Austin Nuttall, LL.D. London, Tegg, 1840.
Hakluyt, R., *The Original Writings and Correspondence of the two Richard Hakluyts.* With an Introduction and Notes by E. G. R. Taylor. 2 vols. London, Printed for the Hakluyt Society, 1935.
—— *The Principal Navigations, Voyages, Traffiques and Discoveries of the English Nation.* 12 vols. Glasgow, James MacLehose and Sons, 1903–5.
Hotten, J. C., *Original Lists of Emigrants . . . who went to America,* 1600–1700. London, Chatto and Windus, 1874.
Jessop, A. (ed. by), *The Lives of the Rt. Hon. Francis North, Baron Guildford; the Hon. Sir Dudley North, and the Hon. and Rev. Dr. John North.* By the Hon. Roger North. 3 vols. London, George Bell and Sons, 1890.
Letters received by the East India Company from its Servants in the East, 1602–17 6 vols. Oxford University Press, 1896–1902.
A List of the Society, instituted in 1787, *for the Purpose of effecting the Abolition. of the Slave Trade.* London, 1787.
Mather, C., *Antiquities.* London, Thomas Parkhurst, 1702.
Penn, W., *The Select Works of William Penn.* 4th ed. 1925. 3 vols.
Penzer, E. N. (ed. by), *The World Encompassed and Analogous Contemporary Documents concerning Sir Francis Drake's Circumnavigation of the World.* With an Appreciation of the Achievement by Sir R. C. Temple. London, The Argonaut Press, 1926.
Proceedings of the Anti-Slavery Meeting held at the Guildhall, Bristol, on Thursday 2nd February, 1826.
Purchas, S., *Hayklutus Posthumus or Purchas His Piligrimes, Contayning a History of the World in Sea Voyages and Land Travells by Englishmen and Others.* 20 vols. Glasgow, James MacLehose and Sons, 1905.
Roe, Sir T., *Embassy to the Court of the Great Mogul,* 1615–9, *as narrated in his Journal and Correspondence.* Edited by W. Foster. 2 vols. London, Printed for the Hakluyt Society, 1899.
Rogers, Woodes, *A Cruising Voyage Round the World.* Introduction and Notes by G. E. Mainwaring. London, Cassell and Co. Ltd., 1928.

Royal African Company. A Collection of 24 *Broadsheets relating to the Affairs of the Royal African Company. Early eighteenth century.*

Smith, L. T. (ed. by), *The Itinerary of John Leland in or about the years* 1535–43. London, G. Bell and Sons Ltd., 1910.

Speed, J., *The Theatre of the Empire of Great Britain.* London, 1611.

Wright, I. A. (ed. by), *Documents concerning English Voyages to the Spanish Main* 1569–80. London, Printed for the Hakluyt Society, 1932.

(d) Periodicals

Butler, J. D., "British Convicts Shipped to American Colonies," in *American Historical Review*, II, 1897, pp. 12–33.

Christy, Miller, "Attempts toward Colonization: the Council for New England and the Merchant Venturers of Bristol, 1621–3," in *American Historical Review*, IV, 1899, pp. 678–702.

Dunaway, W. F., "The English Settlers in Colonial Pennsylvania," in *Pennslyvania Magazine of History and Biography*, LII, 1928, pp. 317–41.

Dyer, F. E., "Captain Christopher Myngs in the West Indies," in *Mariner's Mirror*, XVIII, 1932, pp. 168–187.

Harrison, W. E. C., "An Early Voyage of Discovery," in *Mariner's Mirror*, XVI, 1930, pp. 198–9.

Hay, D., "The Manuscript of Polydore Vergil's 'Anglica Historia,' " in *English Historical Review*, LIV, 1937, pp. 240–51.

M. R. C., "William Canynges' Ships," in *Mariner's·Mirror*, III, 1913, p. 57.

Powell, J. W. Damer, "The *Charlotte Jane*, A *Mayflower* of New Zealand," in *United Empire*, XXIII (new series), 1932, pp. 607–8.

—— "The Explorations of John Guy in Newfoundland," in *Geographical Journal*, LXXXVI, 1935, pp. 512–8.

—— "John Guy: Founder of Newfoundland," in *United Empire*, XXIV, (new series), 1933, pp. 323–7.

—— "John Guy's Voyage in the *Endeavour*," in *United Empire*, XXVIII, (new series), 1937, pp. 16–7.

—— "Richard Steel: A Forgotten Envoy to Persia," in *United Empire*, XXIII, (new series), 1932, pp. 503–6.

—— "Sir James Russell: Defender of Nevis," in *United Empire*, XXII, (new series), 1931, pp. 557–9.

—— "Thomas Aldworth: Founder of British India," in *United Empire*, XXII, (new series), 1931, pp. 588–91.

Poynton, F. J., "The Family of Haynes, of Westbury-on-Trym, Wick and Abton and other places in Gloucestershire," in *Transactions of the Bristol and Gloucestershire Archaeological Society*, IX, 1884–5, pp. 277–97.

Quinn, D. B., "Edward IV and Exploration," in *Mariner's Mirror*, 1935, XXI, pp. 275–84.

Skeel, C. A. J., "References to Ships, etc., in early English Wills," in *Mariner's Mirror*, 1925, XI, pp. 316–7.

Smith A. E., "Transportation of Convicts to America," in *Amercan Historicals Review*, XXXIX, 1933–4, pp. 232–49.

Taylor, E. G. R., "The Missing Draft Project of Drake's Voyage, 1577–80," in *Geographical Journal*, LXXV, 1930, pp. 46–7.

—— "More Light on Drake, 1577–80," in *Mariner's Mirror*, XVI, 1930, pp. 134–51.

The Gentleman's Magazine.

The Virginia Gazette.

(e) Newspapers

Bonner and Middleton's Bristol Journal.

The Bristol Mirror and General Advertiser.

The Daily Bristol Times and Mirror.

Felix Farley's Bristol Journal.

II. SECONDARY.

(a) Books and Pamphlets

Adam's Chronicle of Bristol. Bristol, J. W. Arrowsmith, 1910.

Andrews, C. M., *The Colonial Period of American History.* 2 vols. New Haven, Yale University Press: London, Oxford University Press, 1934.

Anspach, L. A., *A History of the Island of Newfoundland.* London, Sherwood, Gilbert and Piper, 1832.

Arrowsmith's Dictionary of Bristol. 2nd edition. Bristol, J. W. Arrowsmith, Ltd. 1906.

Barker, E., *Burke and Bristol.* Bristol, J. W. Arrowsmith Ltd., 1931.

Bowman, W. Dodgson, *Bristol and America.* London, Geoffrey Bles (1928?).

Bruce, P. A., *Economic History of Virginia in the Seventeenth Century.* 4 vols. New York, Macmillan & Co., 1896.

Burrage, H. S., *The Beginnings of Colonial Maine,* 1602–58. Portland, Me., Marks Printing House, 1914.

Clark, D. M., *British Opinion and the American Revolution.* New Haven, Yale University Press, 1930.

Clarkson, T., *Memoirs of the Life of William Penn.* 2 vols. 1813.

Crundall, F., *The Governors of Jamaica in the Seventeenth Century.* London, The West India Committee, 1936.

Dixon, W. H., *History of William Penn, Founder of Pennsylvania.* London, Hurst and Blackett, 1872.

Dobrée, B., *William Penn, Quaker and Pioneer.* London, Constable and Co., 1932.

Doyle, J. A., *The English in America, Virginia, Maryland and the Carolinas.* London, Longmans, Green and Co., 1882.

Duff, C., *The Truth About Columbus and the Discovery of America.* London, Grayson, 1936.

Edwards, B., *The History, Civil and Commercial, of the British Colonies in the West Indies.* 2 vols. London, 1793.

Gosling, W. G., *Labrador, Its Discovery, Exploration and Development.* London, Alston Rivers Ltd., 1910.

Guillemard, *Life of Ferdinand Magellan,* 1890.

Harvey, A., *Bristol. A Historical and Topographical Account of the City.* London, Methuen and Co., 1906.

Hudleston, C. R., *The Bristol Cathedral Register,* 1669–1837. Bristol, St. Stephen's Press, 1933.

Hunt, W., *Bristol.* London, Longmans, Green and Co., 1887.

Hutton, S., *Bath and Bristol.* London, A. and C. Black Ltd., 1915.

—— *Bristol and its Famous Associations.* Bristol, J. W. Arrowsmith, 1907.

Langdon, W. C., *Everyday Things in American Life,* 1607–1776. New York and London, Charles Scribner's Sons, 1937.

Latimer, J., *Annals of Bristol in the Seventeenth, Eighteenth and Nineteenth Centuries.* 4 vols. Bristol, J. W. Arrowsmith, 1887–1902.

—— *The History of the Society of Merchant Venturers of the City of Bristol. With some Account of the Anterior Merchants' Guilds.* Bristol, J. W. Arrowsmith, 1903.

—— *Sixteenth-Century Bristol.* Bristol, J. W. Arrowsmith, 1908.

Lounsbury, R. G., *The British Fishery at Newfoundland,* 1634–1763. New York, Yale University Press, 1934.

Lowes, J. L., *The Road to Xanadu—a Study in the Ways of the Imagination.* London, Constable, 1927.

MacInnes, C. M., *An Introduction to the Economic History of the British Empire.* London, Rivingtons, 1935.

—— *England and Slavery.* Bristol, J. W. Arrowsmith Ltd., 1934.

Madgwick, R. B., *Immigration with Eastern Australia,* 1788–1851. London, Longman, Green and Co., 1937.

Newton, A. P. (ed. by), *The Great Age of Discovery.* University of London Press Ltd., 1932.

Nichols, J. F., and Taylor, J., *Bristol Past and Present.* 4 vols. Bristol, J. W. Arrowsmith, 1881.

Powell, J. W. Damer, *Bristol Privateers and Ships of War.* Bristol, J. W. Arrowsmith, 1930.

Power, E., and Postan, M. M. (ed. by), *Studies in English Trade in the Fifteenth Century*. London, Geogre Routledge and Sons, 1933.
Prowse, D. W., *History of Newfoundland, from the English, Colonial and Foreign Records*, London, 1895.
Pryce, G., *Memorials of the Canynges' Family and their Times*. Bristol, John Wright and Sons Ltd., 1854.
Sharpless, I., *Political Leaders of Provincial Pennsylvania*. New York, The Macmillan Co., 1919.
Smith, G. C. Moore, *The Family of Withypoll*. Walthamstow Antiquarian Society. Official Publications, No. 34. 1936.
Stone, G. F., and Wells, C. (ed. by), *Bristol and the Great War*, 1914–9. Bristol, J. W. Arrowsmith, Ltd., 1920.
Taylor, E. G. R., *Tudor Geography*, 1485–1583. London, Methuen and Co., Ltd., 1930.
Tombs, R. C., *The Bristol Royal Mail, Post, Telegraph and Telephone*. Bristol J. W. Arrowsmith, 1899.
Weare, G. E., *Edmund Burke's Connection with Bristol, from 1774 till 1780: with a Prefatory Memoir of Burke*. Bristol, William Bennett, 1894.
Wells, C., *Short History of the Port of Bristol*. Bristol, J. W. Arrowsmith. 1909.
Wilkins, H. J., *Edward Colston (1636–1721)—a Chronological Account of his Life and Work with an Account of the Colston Societies and Membership in Bristol*. Bristol, J. W. Arrowsmith Ltd., 1920.
Williamson, J. A., *Maritime Enterprise*, 1485–1558. Oxford, Clarendon Press, 1913.
—— *A Short History of British Expansion*. London, Macmillan and Co., 1922.
—— *The Voyages of the Cabots and the English Discovery of North America under Henry VII and Henry VIII*. London, The Argonaut Press, 1929.

INDEX

INDEX